## Alpha Development Team

**Publisher**
*Kathy Nebenhaus*

**Editorial Director**
*Gary M. Krebs*

**Managing Editor**
*Bob Shuman*

**Marketing Brand Manager**
*Felice Primeau*

**Acquisitions Editor**
*Jessica Faust*

**Development Editors**
*Phil Kitchel*
*Amy Zavatto*

**Assistant Editor**
*Georgette Blau*

## Production Team

**Development Editor**
*Amy Zavatto*

**Production Editor**
*Michael Thomas*

**Copy Editor**
*Amy Borelli*

**Cover Designer**
*Mike Freeland*

**Photo Editor**
*Richard H. Fox*

**Illustrator**
*John Bergdahl*

**Book Designers**
*Scott Cook and Amy Adams of DesignLab*

**Indexer**
*Greg Pearson*

**Layout/Proofreading**
*Angela Calvert*
*Laura Goetz*
*Mary Hunt*
*Jeanette McKay*
*Julie Trippetti*

# Contents at a Glance

**Part 1: What Does "Financial Security" Mean to You?**   **1**

  1 Put Your Money to Work for You   3
*Putting your money to work for you is the essence of investing.*

  2 How Do You Really Feel About Risk?   15
*Evaluate your risk tolerance before you invest.*

  3 Are You a Grasshopper or an Ant: Selecting Your Investment Objectives   29
*Sorting out your financial objectives.*

  4 What Have You Got Right Now—And What Are You Going to Need?   39
*Take a snapshot of your current financial picture.*

**Part 2: Shore Up Your Foundation**   **57**

  5 A Closer Look at Employment Benefits   59
*Squeezing the max from employer-sponsored investment plans.*

  6 Cutting Expenses *Is* Investing!   71
*Getting a grip on your spending.*

  7 Solving Debt and Credit Problems   89
*Managing debt so it doesn't manage you.*

  8 Trim Your Taxes   99
*Deduction strategies for your income and investments*

**Part 3: Investing 101**   **111**

  9 What Are They Up to on Wall Street, Anyway?   113
*How the financial markets work—the stock market from the ground up.*

  10 So You Want to Play with Stocks   127
*How to choose and trade individual stocks.*

  11 Slow and Steady Wins the Race: Fixed Income Securities   141
*The balancing role bonds play in your portfolio.*

  12 Why Mutual Funds Have Ruled the '90s   153
*Giving the small investor diversification and choice.*

**Part 4: Rolling with Life's Changes**   **167**

  13 Work Smart, Not Just Hard: Getting the Max from Your Job   169
*Clear answers to complex questions about retirement, health, and incentive plans.*

14  The Ramifications of Romance                         179
    *Surviving marriage...and divorce!*

15  Home Ownership: What You Need to Know                185
    *Where to get the down payment, how to qualify for a*
    *mortgage, and more.*

16  Educating the Little Rascals                         195
    *Using investments to save for college.*

17  Covering Your Assets                                 207
    *Making sure you have adequate medical, home, auto,*
    *and life insurance.*

18  Keeping Uncle Sam's Greedy Mitts Off Your Estate     215
    *Estate planning is not just for the wealthy.*

**Part 5: Investing Online                              227**

19  Getting Started with Online Investing                229
    *Gearing up to bank, research investments, track your*
    *portfolio, and trade online.*

20  Online Trading and Tracking                          245
    *How to trade and manage your portfolio online.*

**Part 6: Advanced Investment Plays                     259**

21  Hedging Your Options                                 261
    *Using options to protect and enhance your investments.*

22  Fancy Futures                                        273
    *How futures contracts are used to offset the great un-*
    *known.*

23  Realizing Real Estate Dreams                         283
    *Investing in real estate and real estate investment trusts*
    *(REITs).*

24  Alternative Investments                              293
    *Hedge, venture capital, and LBO funds—plus SPDRs,*
    *UITs, and other critters.*

**Appendices**

A   Useful Investing Info                                301

B   Glossary                                             307

    Index                                                315

# Contents

## Part 1: What Does "Financial Security" Mean to You?    1

### 1 Put Your Money to Work for You    3

Become an Educated Investor, Not Just
a Consumer .................................................................. 4
The Miracle of Compounding ..................................... 4
An Easy Way to Figure Compound Interest ............... 6
The "Blow-Your-Mind-by-Adding-Time" Chart ......... 7
The 10-Percent Habit .................................................. 8
Time, Risk, and Your Sanity ...................................... 9
The Fed's Balancing Act: Dampening Inflation Without
Dumping on Us ......................................................... 10
   *The Problem with Inflation* ..................................... *11*
   *What Do Interest Rates Have to Do with Stocks and*
   *Bonds? Glad You Asked!* ....................................... *12*
Your Personal Time Frame ........................................ 13

### 2 How Do You Really Feel About Risk?    15

What Is Return? ........................................................ 16
What You Made, What You Paid ............................... 16
Fear of Heights: The Higher the Return, the Greater
the Risk ..................................................................... 17
The Tools of the Trade ............................................. 18
   *Standard Deviation and a Podunk Potato* ............. *18*
   *Deviant Behavior* ................................................... *19*
The Three Broad Investment Classes ....................... 20
Variety Is the Spice of Life ...................................... 21
Quiz Thyself to Know Thyself: Risk Tolerance Quiz .......... 22
Got the Time? Take the Time Horizon Quiz ............. 25

### 3 Are You a Grasshopper or an Ant? Selecting Your Investment Objectives    29

Just-in-Case Cash ..................................................... 30
   *Mattresses Are for Sleeping, Not Stashing* ............. *30*
   *Treasury Bills* ......................................................... *31*
   *Certificates of Deposit* ............................................ *32*
   *Savings Accounts* ................................................... *33*
   *Money Market Funds* ............................................. *33*
   *Eenie, Meenie, Minie, Mo* ..................................... *34*

How Can I Bring Home the Bacon, Fry It Up in a Pan,
and Have Some Left Over? ...................................................... 35
*And Baby Makes How Much?* ............................................. 35
*Oh, Give Me a Roof* ............................................................. 36
*Who's the Boss? You!* .......................................................... 36
How Gold Do You Want Your Golden Years to Be? ........... 37

**4  What Have You Got Right Now—And What
Are You Going to Need?                                    39**

So What Will Social Security Do for Me, Anyway? ............. 40
*Figuring Out Your FICA* ....................................................... 40
Getting a Handle on Your Retirement Benefits by
Pestering Human Resources ............................................... 41
Help, I'm Self-Employed! ....................................................... 42
A Super-Easy Way to Figure Out How Much You
Need to Save ......................................................................... 43
Use the Plan, Stan ................................................................... 46
Trust Us, You Really Don't Want to Wait ............................ 47
But My Circumstances Will Change... Won't They? ......... 47
Stagger Your Debt .................................................................... 48
Your Personal Balance Sheet: A Snapshot of
Your Finances ....................................................................... 49
Get a Grip with a Personal Income Statement .................... 50
A Happy Couple on the Right Track ..................................... 52
Your Typical Young Guy Living Hand to Mouth ............... 54

**Part 2:  Shore Up Your Foundation                       57**

**5  A Closer Look at Employment Benefits               59**

Retirement Plans 101 ............................................................. 60
*Defined Contribution Plans at a Glance* ............................ 60
*Defined Benefit Plans at a Glance* ..................................... 60
Defined Benefit Plans ............................................................. 61
*How the Amount of Your Monthly Pension Is Determined* ..... 61
*A Whole Lotta Lumps or Just One: The Lump-Sum Option* ... 63
*If Your Employer Drops the Ball* ....................................... 64
Defined Contribution Plans .................................................. 64
*You Can Contribute After-Tax Dollars, Too* ...................... 65
If Your Employer Matches, Invest the Max ......................... 65
*Can I Borrow from My 401(k)?* ........................................... 66
*What if I Change Employers?* .............................................. 67
Should You Put All Your Eggs in the Company Basket? ..... 67

What About Stock Options? ................................................ 68
No Company Plan? Create a Pension with an IRA ............ 69
When Is a Roth IRA the Right Choice? ............................. 70
    *Wiggle Room* ................................................................. 70
    *No Taxes on Asset Growth—Whoopee!* ........................... 70
    *Passing Along the Wealth* ............................................. 71
Converting a Traditional IRA to a Roth IRA ...................... 71
The Two Best Investments for Your IRA: Stocks
  and STRIPs ..................................................................... 72
    *Stocking Up* ................................................................. 73
    *STRIP Tease* ................................................................. 73
What to Do When You're Small and Solo ......................... 74
    *Adding a Money Purchase Pension to the Mix* .................... 75

**6 Cutting Expenses *Is* Investing!**                **77**

Become a Hunter/Gatherer .............................................. 77
Your Tax Bracket Is Higher Than You Think ...................... 78
Figuring Your Marginal Tax Rate ..................................... 79
Risk-Free Saving Where You Least Expect It ...................... 79
Buying Bulk Is a Great Investment ................................... 80
Your Car: Leasing vs. Ownership ...................................... 81
    *Advantages of Leasing* ................................................. 81
    *Disadvantages of Leasing* ............................................. 82
    *The Bottom Line on Leasing* ......................................... 82
    *If You Buy a Car* ......................................................... 83
Car Insurance—Shop Around! ......................................... 84
Choosing a Bank ............................................................. 84
Life Insurance ................................................................. 85
Knocking Down Real Estate Taxes ................................... 85
Credit Cards .................................................................... 86
Little Things That Add Up ............................................... 87

**7 Solving Debt and Credit Problems**               **89**

What Does Your Credit Report Say About You? ................. 90
CRA Horror Stories ......................................................... 90
How to Check Your Credit Reports ................................... 91
    *Your Credit Reporting Rights* ....................................... 91
    *No Credit Is Not Good Credit* ...................................... 92
Credit Cards: You Only Need One .................................... 93
How to Really Get Your Act Together ............................... 94
A Checking Account? Who Needs It! ................................. 94

Debit Cards—A Better Choice? ............................................ 95
How Much of Your Income Should Go Toward
  Reducing Debt? ...................................................................... 95
Good Debt vs. Bad Debt ........................................................ 96
  *How Much to Set Aside for Peace of Mind* ........................ 96
  *If You Spend It, Replenish It* ............................................ 97

**8  Trim Your Taxes**                                                 **99**

What Are All Those Different "Incomes" Anyway? ........... 99
Uncle Sammie and Your Marginal Income Tax Rate ........ 101
Employer-Based Health and Childcare Funds.................. 103
Medical Savings Accounts: Are They a Good Deal? ......... 103
  *How the Medical Savings Account Works* ........................ 103
  *Buying Your Own Health Insurance May Be a Better Deal* ... 104
Gains and Losses on Securities Transactions ................... 104
  *Save Big Bucks by Holding Out for Capital Gains* .............. 105
  *Using a Loss to Offset a Gain* ............................................ 105
Did You Say Tax-Free Interest Income? ............................ 106
  *Types of Muni Bonds* ...................................................... 106
  *Why Not Load Up on Munis?* ............................................ 107
Home Equity Loans Are Deductible ................................. 108
  *Home Equity Loan vs. Second Mortgage* .......................... 109
Timing Can Make a Big Difference ................................... 109

**Part 3:  Investing 101**                                           **111**

**9  What Are They Up to on Wall Street, Anyway?**      **113**

A Little Background Music, Please ................................... 114
What's with All the Animal References? .......................... 115
But What Do All Those Numbers Mean? ......................... 116
The Key to Your Stock Knowledge: Price-Earnings Ratios .. 117
Look into My P/E Crystal Ball ............................................ 118
Should You Play with the Big Kids or Just Get a
  Piggyback Ride? ................................................................... 119
  *Take the Easy Route* ........................................................ 119
  *Creating Your Own Stock Index Fund* .............................. 120
  *Just Buy Large-Cap Stocks* .............................................. 120
  *How to Manage Your Index Fund: Leave It Alone!* ............. 123
  *The Best Ways to React to Blips* ...................................... 123
Asset Allocation/Rebalancing ............................................ 123

How Much Stock Should Be in Your Portfolio? ................ 124
    *If You're over 55* ........................................................ 125
Dollar Cost Averaging, or "How to Own Stocks and
    Stay Happy" ............................................................... 126

**10 So, You Want to Play with Stocks**           **127**

Tips for Trading Like a Pro .................................................. 128
If You Buy It, You'd Better Love It ..................................... 128
The Biggest "Do" of All ....................................................... 129
Researching Individual Stocks ............................................ 131
    *The Priceless Value of Value Line* ................................. 131
    *S&P Stock Guides: Another Great Tool* ........................... 132
    *The Best Newspapers for Stock Info* ............................... 132
All the News That's Fit to Print: Company
    Annual Reports .......................................................... 132
    *Analyzing a Company's Annual Report* .......................... 133
    *Analyzing the Balance Sheet* ........................................ 134
How to Use a Broker to Place a Trade ................................ 135
    *Placing an Order with Your Broker* ............................... 136
    *Discount Brokers* .......................................................... 137
When Should You Buy Stock? ............................................. 137
    *Rebalancing Your Stock Holdings* .................................. 138
Diversifying Your Stock Portfolio: How Many
    Holdings Are Enough? ............................................... 138

**11 Slow and Steady Wins the Race: Fixed-Income
Securities**           **141**

What Are Fixed-Income Securities for? .............................. 141
When Do You Get That Groovy Interest Income? ........... 142
    *Beware the Call Feature* ................................................ 142
    *Sinkers* ......................................................................... 143
    *The Wonderful World of Bond (No, Not James)* ............. 144
    *How Inflation Erodes Bonds* ........................................ 145
    *When Do You Want Bonds in Your Portfolio?* ................ 146
    *How to Read a Bond Table* ........................................... 147
Corporate Debt—An Unwise Choice for Small Investors ... 147
Okay, Corporate Debt Is Out—What Should I Buy? ........ 149
    *How to Buy Treasuries* ................................................. 150
    *Buying Outstanding Treasuries* ..................................... 150
    *Savings Bonds* .............................................................. 150
    *Agency-O-Rama* ........................................................... 151
CDs: A Viable Alternative to Government Debt ............... 152

**12  Why Mutual Funds Have Ruled the '90s                 153**

What Exactly Are Mutual Funds? ...................................... 154
Open-End and Closed-End Funds ..................................... 154
Avoid Load Funds .............................................................. 155
 *Back-End Loads and 12b-1 Fees* .............................. 156
 *Index and Tax-Advantaged Funds* ......................... 156
What's Out There in the Fund Universe? ....................... 157
Why Funds Are a Great Investment Option .................... 157
How to Pick a Winning Fund ............................................ 159
Check Out These Funds ..................................................... 160
Money Market Funds ........................................................ 162
Variable Annuity: A Mutual Fund Wrapped Around
 an Insurance Contract .................................................. 163
Lifestyle and Tax-Efficient Funds .................................. 164
Pick a Date to Rebalance Your Mutual Fund
 Holdings Annually ........................................................ 164
 *Rebalancing Taxable Accounts* ............................... 165

**Part 4:  Rolling with Life's Changes                     167**

**13  Work Smart, Not Just Hard: Getting the Max
      from Your Job                                        169**

What to Ask a New Employer ........................................... 169
Transferring Retirement Accounts ................................... 171
So You're Your Own Boss .................................................. 171
 *Setting Up Your Own Retirement Plan* .................. 172
Retirement...At Last! ......................................................... 173
How the Retirement Age You Choose Affects
 Social Security ............................................................... 173
Pay Tax on Social Security Benefits? Sad, but True .......... 174
Can You Work and Still Collect Social Security? ............. 175
Advantages to Delaying Retirement ............................... 175
When and How to Apply for Your SS Benefits ................ 175
How Does Medicare Work? ............................................... 176
 *Part A and a Hospital Stay* ..................................... 176
 *How to Pay for the Expenses Medicare Doesn't Cover* ........ 176
 *Medicare Is in Flux* ................................................. 176
What About Lump-Sum Retirement Benefits? ................. 177
 *Taking Your Home As a "Lump Sum"* .................... 177

**14  The Ramifications of Romance                                    179**

When You Need a Pre-Nup ................................................ 179
  *What Can Happen If You Don't Have a Pre-Nup* .............. 180
The Marriage Tax ............................................................. 180
Joint Bank Accounts ........................................................ 181
Should You Keep Separate Investment Portfolios? ........... 181
Untangling Your Assets During Divorce ........................... 182
  *Handling the House* .......................................................... 183
  *Divvying Up Other Assets* ................................................. 183
Negotiate with Your Head, Not Your Spleen ................... 183
Other Divorce Options .................................................... 184

**15  Home Ownership: What You Need to Know            185**

The Down Payment ......................................................... 185
Timing Is Everything ....................................................... 186
Evaluate Your Mortgage-Worthiness Before a
  Banker Does ................................................................ 187
Compare Renting to Owning ........................................... 187
Over Time, Owning Should Save You Money .................. 188
Renting Pluses ................................................................ 189
How Much of Your Income Should You Spend
  on Housing? ................................................................ 189
Fixed Rate vs. Adjustable Rate Mortgage ........................ 189
The Costs of Closing ...................................................... 190
Second Mortgages—Pros and Pitfalls ............................. 191
Pluses to Paying Off Your Mortgage ............................... 191
Should You Shorten Your Mortgage? .............................. 191
The Relocation Package .................................................. 192
Renting Out Your Home When You Move ...................... 193
Real Estate Agents .......................................................... 194
Closing the Deal ............................................................. 194

**16  Educating the Little Rascals                                      195**

Put Your Financial Security First .................................... 196
Setting Up Educational Funds ......................................... 196
  *Using a Traditional IRA to Save for College* ..................... 197
  *Advantages of the Roth IRA* ............................................ 198
  *New in '98: The Education IRA* ........................................ 198
  *EE Savings Bonds* ............................................................ 199
Qualified Tuition Programs .............................................. 200

New Income Tax Credits for Education Expenses ............ 202
  *The Hope Scholarship Credit* ............................................. 202
  *Lifetime Learning Credits* .................................................. 202
  *The Education-Loan Interest Deduction* ............................ 202
Other Options .................................................................... 202
Sorting Out All the Options ................................................ 203
Sorting Out the AGI Level Morass ..................................... 204
In Whose Name? ................................................................ 204

**17  Covering Your Assets                                          207**

Don't Insure What You Can Afford to Replace ................. 207
Life Insurance Simplified ................................................... 208
Determining Your Insurance Needs .................................. 208
  *The Five Basic Types of Life Insurance* ............................ 209
Annuities ........................................................................... 211
Your Kids Don't Need Life Insurance ................................ 212
  *Disability Insurance Is a Must* .......................................... 212
Insuring Your Home and Other Assets ............................. 212

**18  Keeping Uncle Sam's Greedy Mitts Off Your Estate   215**

Why You Don't Want to Die Without a Will ..................... 216
Probate: The Process of Administering Your Will ............ 217
  *Living Trust* ....................................................................... 217
  *Joint Ownership* ................................................................ 217
How to Take the Bite Out of Estate Taxes ....................... 218
  *They Can Tax That?!* .......................................................... 219
  *Cons of Passing Everything onto Your Spouse* .................... 220
  *Watch That Generation Gap* .............................................. 220
Tax-Saving Alternatives ..................................................... 220
  *Gimme Shelter* ................................................................... 220
  *QTIP: No, Not the Kind You Stick in Your Ear* .................. 221
  *Charitable Trusts* ............................................................... 221
Other Ways to Reduce Estate Taxes ................................. 222
  *Life (Saver!) Insurance* ...................................................... 222
  *The Gift That Keeps on Giving* .......................................... 222
  *Just a Little Token—Gifts to Minors' Trusts* ...................... 222
  *Personal Residence Trust* ................................................... 223
What If You Inherit Money? .............................................. 223
  *What to Do When Your Ship Comes In* ............................. 224
  *Beyond Cash: Property, Businesses, and Valuables* ............ 224
  *What to Do with the Dough* .............................................. 225

## Part 5: Investing Online      227

### 19   Getting Started with Online Investing      229

Once Upon a Time There Was a Big Fat Computer .......... 229
    *The World Wide Web* .................................................. 230
    *Take a Test Drive* ..................................................... 230
Online Shopping ........................................................ 232
Hey, How Do I Turn This Thing On? ............................. 232
Choosing an ISP ........................................................ 233
You Need a Surfboard…We Mean, a Browser ................. 234
    *Secret Agent Man* ..................................................... 235
Banking Online ......................................................... 235
    *Sign Me Up!* ............................................................ 235
    *No More Waiting in Line When You're Online* ................ 236
The Best Financial Software ........................................ 237
Now Can I Trade? Selecting an Internet Broker .............. 237
Evaluating Your Online Trading Needs ......................... 239
The Online Commission Picture ................................... 241
If You Are a Frequent Trader… .................................... 241
Investment Research .................................................. 242
The Comfort Factor .................................................... 242
Ancillary Services ...................................................... 243

### 20   Online Trading and Tracking      245

Speed and System Backups .......................................... 245
How to Use an Online Broker ...................................... 246
    *The Typical Broker's Home Page* .................................. 246
How an Online Broker Works ...................................... 247
Researching Investments Online .................................. 248
    *Avoiding Investment Research Overload* ......................... 249
    *Search Engine Fun* ................................................... 249
    *Using a Search Engine* .............................................. 250
    *Portals Just for Investors* ........................................... 250
Tracking Your Portfolio .............................................. 251
    *Portfolio Management Programs* ................................... 251
Three Isn't Necessarily a Crowd ................................... 252
    *Financial Markets* .................................................... 252
    *Quotes* ................................................................... 252
    *Financial News* ....................................................... 253
    *Investment Research* ................................................. 253
    *Investment Message Boards and Chat Rooms* .................. 254
    *Investment Clubs* ..................................................... 254

*Mutual Funds* ............................................................ 254
*Financial Magazines* .................................................. 254
*Technology Magazines* ............................................... 255
*Insurance Sites* ........................................................ 255
*Government Agencies* ................................................. 255
*Investor Services* ..................................................... 255
*Media and Other Resources Available Online* ................... 256

## Part 6: Advanced Investment Plays                    259

### 21   Hedging Your Options                            261

Puts and Calls ............................................................ 262
*Hedge Your Bet with a Call* ........................................ 262
*Prevent Portfolio Wipeout with a Put* ........................... 263
How Did This Get Started? ............................................ 263
Risk-Loving Speculator Seeks Cautious Hedgehog ............. 264
In the Money ............................................................. 264
Reading an Option Table .............................................. 265
*Options Galore* ........................................................ 266
*Most Active Contracts* ............................................... 266
Selling Short vs. Trading Options .................................. 266
Risky Business ........................................................... 267
Option Strategies That Protect Your Stock Positions ........ 267
*Using Puts for Downside Protection* ............................. 268
Stock Index Options .................................................... 268
*S&P Index Options* .................................................... 269
*Hedge Strategies for Index Options* ............................. 269
The Braveheart of Wall Street ....................................... 270
LEAPS ...................................................................... 270

### 22   Fancy Futures                                   273

What Is a Commodity? .................................................. 273
It All Began with Farmers ............................................. 274
How a Future Differs from an Option .............................. 275
How Margins Work ...................................................... 275
Using Futures to Offset Uncertainty .............................. 276
Financial Futures ....................................................... 277
Options on Futures. Oy! .............................................. 278
Spread Strategies for Speculators ................................. 279
*Program Trading* ...................................................... 279
Gold Nuggets ............................................................ 279
*Precious Metal Companies and Funds* ........................... 280

**23  Realizing Real Estate Dreams**                                   **283**

   Why Own Real Estate? .................................................... 283
   The REIT Stuff .............................................................. 284
     *Types of REITs* ......................................................... 284
     *Emphasize Quality and Safety* ........................................ 285
   Types of Real Estate Ownership ....................................... 286
   So, You Want to Own Real Estate ..................................... 286
   Purchase and Rental of Homes and Apartment
     Buildings .................................................................. 287
     *Financially Prepared and Market-Wise* ............................ 287
   How Rental Income Hits Your Tax Return ...................... 288
   Location, Location, Location ......................................... 290
   Financing Real Estate Investments ................................. 290

**24  Alternative Investments**                                         **293**

   How Regular Folk Discovered Alternative Investments .... 293
   Hedge Funds ............................................................... 294
   Venture Capital and LBO Funds ..................................... 294
   The Private Equity Fund of Funds .................................. 295
     *What You Need to Qualify for a Fund of Funds* ................. 295
     *How Limited Partnership Works* .................................... 296
   Pros and Cons of LP Investments .................................. 297
   Unit Investment Trusts ................................................. 298
   Along Came a SPDR ..................................................... 298

**A  Useful Investing Info**                                            **301**

   *Government and Regulatory Contacts* .............................. 301
   *Financial Exchanges* ..................................................... 301
   *Credit Reporting Agencies* ............................................ 302
   *Consumer Info* ........................................................... 302
   *Investment Research* ..................................................... 302
   *Amazing Online Research Sites* ...................................... 303
   *Mutual Funds* ............................................................ 303
   *Money Market Funds* ................................................... 305
   *College Contacts* ........................................................ 306
   *Internet Connections* ................................................... 306
   *Internet Brokers* ......................................................... 306
   *Mortgages* ................................................................ 306

**B  Glossary**                                                         **307**

   **Index**                                                    **315**

# Foreword

This week my daughter wanted to lease a car. How to do it? *The Complete Idiot's Guide®
to Investing Like a Pro*. My wife and I are revising our estate planning and our wills. How
to do it? *The Complete Idiot's Guide® to Investing Like a Pro*. Taxes, household budgeting,
when to buy muni bonds, stock picking, pre-nuptial agreements, refinancing mortgages, life insurance, and online shopping are all included—plus, of course, advice on
how to invest like a pro. This book has it all. And it's not just for idiots—unless of
course a Ph.D.'ed Economics Professor who chairs a money management firm is an
idiot. Come to think of it, some people think I probably am...

The book is a dream come true when you need the information. And, rest assured, you
*will* need the information sometime. In fact, at one time or another you'll need most
of this book's contents and you probably could use several sections of this book right
now. It's all here. In my case the manuscript has already saved me a bundle within a
week of reading it. How's *that* for the best investment tip of the year?

In all my years as a professor, advisor to presidents, businessman, father (of six),
money manager, and just plain old inhabitant of planet Earth, I've never seen anything as down-to-earth, practical, and comprehensive as Ed Koch and Debra DeSalvo's
*The Complete Idiot's Guide® to Investing Like a Pro*.

Dr. Arthur Laffer

*Dr. Arthur B. Laffer's academic specialty on tax issues and his close involvement in the tax-
cutting movement around the world have earned him the distinction in many publications as
"The Father of Supply-Side Economics." He was a member of President Reagan's Economic
Policy Advisory Board for both of his two terms (1981–1989), as well as a member of the
Executive Committee of the Reagan/Bush Finance Committee in 1984, and a founding
member of the Reagan Executive Advisory Committee for the Presidential race of 1980. He
also served as the first-ever Chief Economist at the Office of Management and Budget (OMB)
under former Secretary of State George Shultz. He is the founder and Chairman of Laffer
Associates, an economic research and consulting firm, which provides investment research
services to institutional asset managers.*

# Introduction

Even though this book is called *The Complete Idiot's Guide® to Investing Like a Pro*, we wrote it for smart people—people with the common sense to know that investing can't be all that difficult. After all, lots of people do it very successfully (even some real dimwits!). You may even have a sneaking suspicion that investing is the key to making dreams come true. Guess what? You're 100 percent correct!

You may have tried to tackle investing before and had a bad experience with a blowhard financial advisor or a tedious, confusing book. If you threw up your hands in frustration and said "Forget it!" but can't get rid of the nagging feeling that you're missing out on something very important, well, we wrote this book for you.

This book assumes you know less than nothing about investing, but doesn't patronize you by telling you what to do. Instead, we offer you a step-by-step guide so that you can figure out exactly what investment strategies will work for your situation:

➤ How much you need to save to put the kids through college *and* retire happily

➤ How much risk you can take on and still sleep at night

➤ How to create a balanced portfolio of investments tailored to your financial goals

➤ How to manage your investments from year to year and still roll with life's changes

Questionnaires, worksheets, dreadful jokes—they're all in here. It's best to start at the beginning and work through to the end, but feel free to skip around until you get comfortable. Just remember that you'll find everything you need to know in this book to become someone who can make savvy investment decisions with calm confidence. Here's the gist....

**Part 1, What Does "Financial Security" Mean to You?** helps you figure out exactly that, because there's no point in investing without specific goals. You'll also take a risk tolerance questionnaire and create your own income statement and balance sheet.

**Part 2, Shore Up Your Foundation**, is based on the premise that you have to know what you've got before you can get any more. Here, you'll take a close look at your job benefits and find out how to trim your taxes to the bone (so you can keep more of what you make). You'll also learn some neat tricks to keep spending down and get a grip on any debt.

**Part 3, Investing 101**, is a primer in investment basics. Everything you ever wanted to know but felt too stupid to ask, from what they're really up to on Wall Street to why everyone's gaga over mutual funds.

**Part 4, Rolling with Life's Changes**, confronts the inevitable upheavals that many investment books ignore. Sure, you can steadily sock away dollars on your investment plan when life is smooth, but what about when you get married, get divorced, have kids, buy a house, change jobs? This section contains event–specific advice so that no matter what life throws at you, your investments keep growing.

**Part 5, Investing Online**, gets you up and running on the Internet and shows you how to bank, trade, and track your portfolio online. You'll learn it all, from the best ways to research investments online to the best brokers on the Web—this is fun stuff!

**Part 6, Advanced Investment Plays**, is for readers who want to explore more complicated, alternative investments. It's also a source of answers for questions you may have when you hear words like "option" or "futures contract" bandied about.

In addition, you get a comprehensive glossary with clear, straightforward definitions of investment terms and an appendix with some recommendations for further reading and financial exploration.

One caveat: Although we have made every effort to confirm our data, accidents do happen. Equally important to keep in mind is that tax laws are under constant revision, reinterpretation, etc. So, please double-check with the sources listed in the back of the book before proceeding with any financial endeavor.

# Extras

If you're more a scanner than a reader, you'll appreciate our sidebars. These explain confusing jargon, help you avoid expensive mistakes, and offer super inside strategies. Look for the following boxes:

### Investor's Idiom

Yes, investing has its own language, but it's not hard to learn. Peek in this box for clear, succinct explanations of any italicized terms.

### Crash Alert

When dealing with money, mistakes can be costly. This box alerts you to tax issues, legal snarls, and scams so you can steer clear.

## Super Strategy

These boxes outline super-smart investing strategies you can apply right away to improve your finances. Hint: Some of these strategies appear only in the box, not in the text, so don't pass 'em up!

## Fiscal Facts

These little boxes contain just-for-fun facts about the financial world. Great for cocktail party chatter.

# Acknowledgments

This book may have been written by us, but an awful lot of it was typed first by Ed's tireless assistant at Fleet Financial Group, Chris Ziegler, who not only prepared the first draft but graciously fielded Debra's countless requests for faxes. Without Chris's efforts, this book could not have been written. Ed would also like to acknowledge his employer, Fleet Financial Group, without whose permission this project could not have moved forward.

This book hit a snag when we realized we didn't know all that much about online investing. Much thanks to consultant and Internet trader Michael Meer for bringing us up to speed, as well as to Jeff Epstein of High Grade Beverage; thanks also to Gary Katz of Lincoln Financial Services for his insights into insurance-related issues.

We'd also like to thank acquisitions editor Gary Krebs and his brother-in-law, Steve Moscovitz, Ed's associate at Fleet Investment Advisors, for rescuing Ed's original manuscript from the slush pile and bringing this project to fruition. Development editor Amy Zavatto deserves special mention for her hands-on guidance, as well as her ability to maintain an upbeat-yet-determined attitude even when deadlines were being trounced on and checks mysteriously vanished. Debra would like to thank her agent, Jeffrey Herman, for the same sterling qualities.

Debra would also like to acknowledge her friend and coauthor on several books about entrepreneurship for kids, Steve Mariotti, president of the National Foundation for Teaching Entrepreneurship, Inc. (NFTE). This organization has had a tremendous positive impact on at-risk youth and urban communities. She'd also like to thank her parents, Joe and Sandra DeSalvo, for their never-ending support and encouragement.

Finally, Ed would like to thank his wife, Joan, whose continuing support during this long process was greatly appreciated, and his daughter, Emily, and son, John, for their assistance and support. They do a father proud.

## Special Thanks to the Technical Reviewer

*The Complete Idiot's Guide to Investing Like a Pro* was reviewed by an expert who not only checked the technical accuracy of the information in this book but also provided valuable insight to help ensure that it tells you everything you need to know to invest with ease.

Our special thanks are extended to Laura Castañeda. Laura Castañeda is a Philadelphia-based freelance writer. A graduate of the University of Southern California and Columbia University, she has worked as a staff writer for the *Associated Press*, the *Dallas Morning News*, and the *San Francisco Chronicle*. Her first book, *The Latino Guide to Personal Money Management*, will be published in May by Bloomberg Press.

# Part 1

# What Does "Financial Security" Mean to You?

I don't know what the Seven Wonders of the World are, but I know what the Eighth Wonder is: compound interest.

—*Baron Rothschild*

*Investing is really very simple—it's about putting your money to work for you over time. The longer your money is parked in an investment, the more time it has to grow...and grow...and grow!*

*But what are you growing it for? Before you choose investments, you need to choose investment objectives. Are you saving to buy a home? To put kids through school? For retirement? Or all three? How much time do you have to reach those objectives?*

*Next, you need to figure out how much risk you're willing to take with your hard-earned cash to try to meet those objectives. Finally, you need to take a look at what you've already got—and what you owe.*

*There's no point in putting yourself into some cookie-cutter investment plan. To invest really well, you've got to know yourself really well. In this section, we're going exploring in the dark cave that is your financial psyche.*

# Chapter 1

# Put Your Money to Work for You

## In This Chapter

➤ How investing will put your money to work for you

➤ How compounding interest can build your wealth

➤ Using time as a money-making asset

➤ Forming the 10-percent habit

➤ The relationship between time, risk, and your sanity

➤ How interest rates affect your investment choices

When John D. Rockefeller was a teen—back in the mid-1800s—he lent $50 to a neighboring farmer. A year later the farmer paid him back the $50 plus $3.50 interest on the loan. The week before, Rockefeller had earned a measly $1.12 after 30 hours of backbreaking work hoeing potatoes for another neighbor. "From that time on," Rockefeller said in his autobiography, *Random Reminiscences*, "I was determined to make money work for me."

Putting your money to work for you is the essence of investing—and this is precisely what you will learn in this book. But first, think for a moment about what you envision a successful investor to look like. Maybe you picture someone in a power suit, up at the crack of dawn reading stock quotes in *The Wall Street Journal* before he or she has even had coffee. A real mover and shaker. Well, toss that picture right out of your head and take a walk over to the closest mirror. See that good-lookin' person looking back at you? *That's* what a successful investor looks like. It's anybody. It certainly could be you. You just need a few tools to get you up to a savvy speed.

"But where am I going to get the money I need to start investing?" you may be thinking. That's simple: Any money you aren't actually using to pay bills is money you can invest. Luckily, you have a lot more investment options than young Rockefeller did. On the other hand, separating the wheat from the chaff is going to be a little more complicated for you than it was for our boy on the farm. Before you start threshing your investment opportunities, you'll need to lay a little groundwork.

# Become an Educated Investor, Not Just a Consumer

At this point in the history of the stock market, there are a lot of educated consumers, but not many educated investors. The stock market's unusually strong performance over the last decade was splashed across the covers of all the new financial magazines, convincing individual investors to "come on in, the water's fine!" All the raving about how fabulously the stock market performed created a new class of investment consumers who jumped into the stock market feet first.

Given a lengthy time frame, the stock market *is* a great investment, but you have to educate yourself about the risks involved—especially over shorter time frames. This book will help you protect yourself emotionally and financially from periods of reversal. In the next few chapters, you will transform yourself from an educated consumer to an educated investor. We're going to demystify the world of investing by helping you develop an understanding of the relationships that drive the financial markets. Let's begin with a concept that will soon be near and dear to your wallet: compounding interest.

### Investor's Idiom

*Interest* is payment you receive for lending someone your money. Interest is also the fee you pay when you borrow money.

## The Miracle of Compounding

If the first miracle is life, the second would have to be compounding interest. Simply put, compounding interest is the interest you earn on your interest. Instead of spending the interest you are earning on money you lend to corporations, banks, or neighborhood farmers, reinvest it. This is a simple but very effective way to build wealth.

To see how compounding works its magic, compare these three examples:

1.  Fred earns 5 percent per year on his investment of $100,000. He spends that 5 percent on meals at gourmet restaurants. What does Fred have after 10 years? Love handles, some nice memories, and $100,000.

2.  Mary earns 5 percent per year on her investment of $100,000 and puts her interest income in a shoe box. What does Mary have after 10 years? Well, first, here's a quick lesson on percentages for those of us who spaced out during math class!

*Percent* means *out of a hundred.* Five percent, therefore, means five out of a hundred. A dollar comprises 100 pennies, so 5 percent of a dollar is five pennies. Five out of a hundred is written as 5 percent.

When you divide five by 100, you get .05. This is another way to express any percentage—simply move the decimal point two places to the left.

➤  5% is also .05

➤  10% is also .10

➤  39.6% is also .396

Expressing 5 percent as a decimal makes it super easy to figure out what Mary earned on her $100,000 in one year. Just whip out your handy calculator and multiply $100,000 by .05.

$100,000 × .05 = $5,000

Mary earned $5,000 per year on her investment for 10 years, so she earned $50,000 total in interest. Add that to her initial $100,000 investment, and Mary ended up with $150,000 in 10 years.

### Super Strategy

You can save yourself a math step when calculating compound interest. Simply multiply the investment amount by one plus the interest percentage. If the interest on an investment is 10 percent, for example, first convert the percentage to a decimal. Ten percent becomes .10. Then add one to .10, which gives you 1.10. Now, multiply your investment by 1.10. If your investment is $50,000, for example:

$50,000 5×1.10 = $55,000

You'll have a total investment of $55,000 after the first year of compounding.

3.  Helen also earned 5 percent per year on an initial investment of $100,000, but she had the good sense to reinvest the interest that she earned each year. The first year, Helen's investment earned $5,000, so she started the second year with $105,000. The second year she earned $5,250 ($105,000 × .05 = $5,250). She started the third year with $105,000 + $5,250, or $110,250. After 10 years of earning interest on her interest (i.e., compound interest), Helen has a whopping $162,890!

## Investor's Idiom

*Compound interest* is the money you earn on interest you earned in a previous period. Compound interest enables your money to grow exponentially (okay, a lot!).

# An Easy Way to Figure Compound Interest

I'll bet you're already thinking, "Well, that Helen was smart, but I really don't want to do ten tedious calculations to figure out how much my money will earn in ten years of compounding." This, my friend, is why the Almighty invented charts.

The Future Value Chart below shows you how much one dollar will be worth over a certain time period if it is compounded at a given interest rate. In Helen's case, she let $100,000 compound at 5 percent over 10 years. Run your finger down the left side of the chart under "Years" until you find "10." Okay, now move your finger across that row until you're under "5%." There's your answer. Every dollar Helen invests will become $1.6209 dollars in 10 years compounded at 5 percent. If she invests $100,000 dollars, she'll earn $162,090. Use this chart to stoke your financial fantasies.

## The Future Value of Money

*(Amount of $1 at Compound Interest)*

| Years | Rate 1% | 2% | 3% | 4% | 5% | 6% | 7% | 8% | 9% | 10% | 11% | 12% |
|---|---|---|---|---|---|---|---|---|---|---|---|---|
| 1 | 1.0100 | 1.0200 | 1.0300 | 1.0400 | 1.0500 | 1.0600 | 1.0700 | 1.0800 | 1.0900 | 1.1000 | 1.1100 | 1.1200 |
| 2 | 1.0201 | 1.0404 | 1.0609 | 1.0816 | 1.1025 | 1.1236 | 1.1449 | 1.1664 | 1.1881 | 1.2100 | 1.2321 | 1.2544 |
| 3 | 1.0303 | 1.0612 | 1.0927 | 1.1249 | 1.1576 | 1.1910 | 1.2250 | 1.2597 | 1.2950 | 1.3310 | 1.3676 | 1.4049 |
| 4 | 1.0406 | 1.0824 | 1.1255 | 1.1699 | 1.2155 | 1.2625 | 1.3108 | 1.3605 | 1.4116 | 1.4641 | 1.5181 | 1.5735 |
| 5 | 1.0510 | 1.1041 | 1.1593 | 1.2167 | 1.2763[1] | 1.3382 | 1.4026 | 1.4693 | 1.5386 | 1.6105 | 1.6851 | 1.7623 |
| 6 | 1.0615 | 1.1262 | 1.1941 | 1.2653 | 1.3401 | 1.4185 | 1.5007 | 1.5869 | 1.6771 | 1.7716 | 1.8704 | 1.9738 |
| 7 | 1.0721 | 1.1487 | 1.2299[2] | 1.3159 | 1.4071 | 1.5036 | 1.6058 | 1.7138 | 1.8280 | 1.9487 | 2.0762 | 2.2107 |
| 8 | 1.0829 | 1.1717 | 1.2668 | 1.3686 | 1.4775 | 1.5938 | 1.7182 | 1.8509 | 1.9926 | 2.1436 | 2.3045 | 2.4760 |
| 9 | 1.0937 | 1.1951 | 1.3048 | 1.4233 | 1.5513 | 1.6895 | 1.8385 | 1.9990 | 2.1719 | 2.3579 | 2.5580 | 2.7731 |
| 10 | 1.1046 | 1.2190 | 1.3439 | 1.4802 | 1.6289 | 1.7908 | 1.9671 | 2.1589 | 2.3674 | 2.5937 | 2.8394 | 3.1058 |
| 11 | 1.1157 | 1.2434 | 1.3842 | 1.5395 | 1.7103 | 1.8983 | 2.1048 | 2.3316 | 2.5804 | 2.8531 | 3.1518 | 3.4785 |
| 12 | 1.1268 | 1.2682 | 1.4258 | 1.6010 | 1.7959 | 2.0122 | 2.2522 | 2.5182 | 2.8127 | 3.1384 | 3.4984 | 3.8960 |
| 13 | 1.1381 | 1.2936 | 1.4685 | 1.6651 | 1.8856 | 2.1329 | 2.4098 | 2.7196 | 3.0658 | 3.4523 | 3.8833 | 4.3635 |
| 14 | 1.1495 | 1.3195 | 1.5126 | 1.7317 | 1.9799 | 2.2609 | 2.5785 | 2.9372 | 3.3417 | 3.7975 | 4.3104 | 4.8871 |
| 15 | 1.1610 | 1.3459 | 1.5580 | 1.8009 | 2.0789 | 2.3965 | 2.7590 | 3.1722 | 3.6425 | 4.1772 | 4.7846 | 5.4736 |
| 16 | 1.1726 | 1.3728 | 1.6047 | 1.8730 | 2.1829 | 2.5403 | 2.9522 | 3.4259 | 3.9703 | 4.5950 | 5.3109 | 6.1304 |
| 17 | 1.1843 | 1.4002 | 1.6528 | 1.9479 | 2.2920 | 2.6928 | 3.1588 | 3.7000 | 4.3276 | 5.0545 | 5.8951 | 6.8660 |

| Years | Rate 1% | 2% | 3% | 4% | 5% | 6% | 7% | 8% | 9% | 10% | 11% | 12% |
|---|---|---|---|---|---|---|---|---|---|---|---|---|
| 18 | 1.1961 | 1.4282 | 1.7024 | 2.0258 | 2.4066 | 2.8543 | 3.3799 | 3.9960 | 4.7171 | 5.5599 | 6.5435 | 7.6900 |
| 19 | 1.2081 | 1.4568 | 1.7535 | 2.1068 | 2.5269 | 3.0256 | 3.6165 | 4.3157 | 5.1416 | 6.1159 | 7.2633 | 8.6127 |
| 20 | 1.2202 | 1.4859 | 1.8061 | 2.1911 | 2.6533 | 3.2071 | 3.8697 | 4.6609 | 5.6044 | 6.7275 | 8.0623 | 9.6463 |
| 21 | 1.2324 | 1.5157 | 1.8603 | 2.2788 | 2.7860 | 3.3995 | 4.1405 | 5.0338 | 6.1088 | 7.4002 | 8.9491 | 10.8038 |
| 22 | 1.2447 | 1.5460 | 1.9161 | 2.3699 | 2.9252 | 3.6035 | 4.4304 | 5.4365 | 6.6586 | 8.1403 | 9.9335 | 12.1002 |
| 23 | 1.2572 | 1.5769 | 1.9736 | 2.4647 | 3.0715 | 3.8197 | 4.7405 | 5.8714 | 7.2579 | 8.9543 | 11.0262 | 13.5523 |
| 24 | 1.2697 | 1.6084 | 2.0328 | 2.5633 | 3.2251 | 4.0489 | 5.0723 | 6.3412 | 7.9111 | 9.8497 | 12.2391 | 15.1785 |
| 25 | 1.2824 | 1.6406 | 2.0938 | 2.6658 | 3.3863 | 4.2918 | 5.4274 | 6.8484 | 8.6231 | 10.8346 | 13.5854 | 16.9999 |
| 26 | 1.2952 | 1.6734 | 2.1566 | 2.7725 | 3.5557 | 4.5494 | 5.8073 | 7.3963 | 9.3991 | 11.9181 | 15.0798 | 19.0399 |
| 27 | 1.3082 | 1.7069 | 2.2213 | 2.8834 | 3.7334 | 4.8223 | 6.2138 | 7.9880 | 10.2450 | 13.1099 | 16.7385 | 21.3247 |
| 28 | 1.3213 | 1.7410 | 2.2879 | 2.9987 | 3.9201 | 5.1117 | 6.6488 | 8.6271 | 11.1670 | 14.4209 | 18.5798 | 23.8837 |
| 29 | 1.3345 | 1.7758 | 2.3565 | 3.1186 | 4.1161 | 5.4184 | 7.1142 | 9.3172 | 12.1721 | 15.8630 | 20.6235 | 26.7497 |
| 30 | 1.3478 | 1.8113 | 2.4272 | 3.2434 | 4.3219 | 5.7435 | 7.6122 | 10.0626 | 13.2676 | 17.4493 | 22.8921 | 29.9597 |
| 31 | 1.3613 | 1.8476 | 2.5001 | 3.3731 | 4.5380 | 6.0881 | 8.1451 | 10.8676 | 14.4616 | 19.1942 | 25.4103 | 33.5549 |
| 32 | 1.3749 | 1.8845 | 2.5751 | 3.5080 | 4.7649 | 6.4533 | 8.7152 | 11.7370 | 15.7632 | 21.1136 | 28.2054 | 37.5815 |
| 33 | 1.3887 | 1.9222 | 2.6523 | 3.6484 | 5.0032 | 6.8405 | 9.3253 | 12.6759 | 17.1819 | 23.2250 | 31.3080 | 42.0912 |
| 34 | 1.4026 | 1.9607 | 2.7319 | 3.7943 | 5.2533 | 7.2510 | 9.9781 | 13.6900 | 18.7283 | 25.5475 | 34.7519 | 47.1422 |
| 35 | 1.4166 | 1.9999 | 2.8138 | 3.9461 | 5.5160 | 7.6860 | 10.6765 | 14.7852 | 20.4138 | 28.1022 | 38.5746 | 52.7993 |
| 36 | 1.4308 | 2.0399 | 2.8983 | 4.1039 | 5.7918 | 8.1472 | 11.4238 | 15.9680 | 22.2510 | 30.9125 | 42.8178 | 59.1352 |
| 37 | 1.4451 | 2.0807 | 2.9852 | 4.2681 | 6.0814 | 8.6360 | 12.2235 | 17.2454 | 24.2536 | 34.0037 | 47.5277 | 66.2314 |
| 38 | 1.4595 | 2.1223 | 3.0748 | 4.4388 | 6.3854 | 9.1542 | 13.0791 | 18.6251 | 26.4365 | 37.4041 | 52.7558 | 74.1792 |
| 39 | 1.4741 | 2.1647 | 3.1670 | 4.6163 | 6.7047 | 9.7034 | 13.9947 | 20.1151 | 28.8157 | 41.1445 | 58.5589 | 83.0807 |
| 40 | 1.4888 | 2.2080 | 3.2620 | 4.8010 | 7.0399 | 10.2856 | 14.9743 | 21.7243 | 31.4092 | 45.2589 | 65.0004 | 93.0503 |

*(1) To find the future value, take a given rate, go down column to correct year; multiply this by your actual number; e.g., $28,000 growing at 5% for 5 years:  $28,000 x 1.2763 = $35,736.40.*

*(2)  Can also be used for inflation impact; e.g., what does $5,000 have to grow to in 7 years to offset 3% inflation?  $5,000 x 1.2299 = $6,149.37*

# The "Blow-Your-Mind-by-Adding-Time" Chart

I'll bet you've already guessed that the longer your money compounds, the more deliciously rich you'll get. Letting time work for you is the key to growing your green. The earlier you start investing, the better off you'll be. In fact, the difference between someone who starts investing at age 22 and someone who waits until age 28 is really dramatic, as illustrated here:

➤ Person A invests $2,000 a year for six years at 12 percent, starting at age 22. Person A's total investment is $12,000.

➤ Person B spends her first six years out of college blowing her salary on facials and designer suits. But then she settles down and invests $2,000 a year for the next 35 years at 12 percent. Her total investment is $70,000.

Now, here's the "blow-your-mind-by-adding-time" moment. If you read standing up, you might want to sit down. Get this—at age 62, Person A, who only invested $12,000, has earned $959,793. Person B, who invested $70,000, has earned $966,926. Person A earned nearly as much as Person B even though she invested $58,000 less! Ah, but Person A started early....

What's the moral of the story? All together now, kids: Start early. Let time work for you!

**Fiscal Facts**

An easy way to figure out how long it will take an investment to double is to use the "Rule of 72." Take any fixed annual interest rate, and divide it into 72 (the average life span nowadays). The result will be the number of years it will take your investment to double. If you expect to earn 6%, for example, divide 6 into 72. Your investment will double in 12 years!

Bear in mind that this formula is based on the assumption that the interest rate never changes.

# The 10-Percent Habit

In the likelihood that you're over the age of 22, don't despair. (Between you and me, how many 22-year-olds do you know who are investing in anything but having fun?) If you are in your early 20s, though, I hope you're feeling fired up enough to start investing—if only so you can spend your 30s feeling smug. There's a great psychological advantage to starting early. It's easier to get into the investing habit when you're unencumbered by kids. You may be sharing an apartment and making a fairly low income, but you don't have to send anyone to college and you're certainly not staring down the barrel of retirement.

No matter what your age, the sooner you get in the habit of investing 10 percent of every paycheck, the more time your investment plan will have to work. Why 10 percent? It's not a big chunk, but it's not insignificant either. Most people can find ways to cut their spending by 10 percent pretty easily (we'll get into cutting expenses in Chapter 6).

Now, back to time. When talking about investing, time is simply how long you can let your investment program work. Time affects your investment decisions in two ways:

1. The more time you have, the longer your investment has to compound.

2. The more time you have, the more risk you can handle.

# Time, Risk, and Your Sanity

One definition of risk is the chance that you'll lose money. Here's a real, extreme example from the stock market of the interrelationship between time, risk, and your sanity.

A *stock* is simply a share of ownership in a corporation. A stockholder literally owns a piece of a company. When you buy AT&T stock, for example, you become one of many owners of AT&T. This, in turn, entitles you to a share of AT&T's profits (or losses!). That share is paid to stockholders as a dividend. Just like an interest payment, you can reinvest a dividend or spend it.

Corporations issue stock to raise money to finance everything from the building of factories to the creation of new divisions or products. This is called *equity* financing, because equity means ownership, and a corporation that sells stock to raise money is selling ownership. Money raised for business purposes is called *capital*.

Assume it is the end of October 1987 and you are heavily invested in stocks. You've witnessed the following sickening drops in the stock market:

➤ In one day, October 19, 1987, the *Dow Jones*, an average of a group of stock prices used to monitor the stock market, dropped 20 percent.

➤ Within 10 days, the market had dropped 34 percent.

➤ By the end of October, the market was down 21.5 percent.

If one month was your time frame, you were one unhappy camper. Putting your family's Christmas money into the stock market in September would have been a lousy idea, because you didn't have time to recover from the crash.

But what if you were in the stock market for the long haul? Let's expand the time frame. Including

**Crash Alert**

The single most important thing you can do for yourself as an investor is to develop a long-term perspective. This will inoculate you against persuasive pitches to buy the latest hot investment and prevent you from selling based on bits of news and rumors.

**Investor's Idiom**

When you own *stock*, you own a piece of the company that issued it. Like any owner, you are entitled to a share of the company's profits. The share is paid to stockholders as a *dividend*. You are also vulnerable to the company's losses. Corporations issue stock to raise *capital*, which is a fancy word for money used for business purposes. Raising capital this way is called *equity* financing. *Equity* means ownership.

### Investor's Idiom

Stocks are bought and sold on the *stock market*. The stock market doesn't exist as a physical place—stocks are traded at various stock exchanges, such as the New York Stock Exchange or the American Stock Exchange. The *Dow Jones Average* (DJIA) is an average of 30 well-known companies, such as AT&T or McDonald's, chosen by the editors of *The Wall Street Journal* to represent trends in the stock market.

### Investor's Idiom

The *S&P 500* is a group of 500 stocks that the Wall Street rating company Standard & Poor's tracks to get a picture of the stock market.

the crash of Black October, let's see how well you would have done over the last 10 years. Take a look at the following chart to see how investing 10 years in the stock market stacks up against investing 10 years in treasury bonds and treasury bills. FYI: The *S&P 500* is a group of 500 stocks that a Wall Street rating company called Standard & Poor's tracks to get a picture of the stock market. Treasury bonds (T-bonds) and Treasury bills (T-bills) are very safe (i.e., low-risk) investments that are backed by the U.S. Government (we'll talk more about these later in Chapter 3).

| Thru 10/31/87 | S&P 500 Stocks | 20-Yr. Treasury Bonds | Treasury Bills |
|---|---|---|---|
| 1 year | +6.7% | –4.6% | +4.7% |
| 5 years | +131.0% | +86.1% | +45.0% |
| 10 years | +232.6% | +148.0% | +101.8% |

Wow! Even including the crash, stocks were a superior investment for investors who had the time to ride out the ups and downs.

# The Fed's Balancing Act: Dampening Inflation Without Dumping on Us

Probably the most fundamental relationship you'll need to learn about is the one between interest rates and the markets. Maybe at times you've wondered how interest rates are determined.

You've probably heard of the Federal Reserve. That's our country's central bank, and it monitors the activity of all banks in the nation. The Fed is charged with only one task, but it's a doozy. The Full Employment Act of 1946 and the Humphrey-Hawkins Act demand that the Fed keep the economy stoked so people can find jobs, yet also control inflation. This is an almost impossible task—like squeezing a balloon at one end without the other end blowing up with air.

*Inflation*, as you probably know, is an overall increase in prices. Inflation tends to occur when, as economists love to say, "too much money is chasing too few goods." If everyone in the country has a job and is earning plenty of money to spend, a situation may arise where companies are not able to make enough products to satisfy the demand for them.

If you own a factory that makes stereos and your stereos are flying off the shelves, you will want to make more to satisfy the demand. Only problem is, with full employment, you can't find any workers to hire. So you can't make more stereos. "Well," you think, "all those flush consumers really want to buy my stereos, so I could definitely make some money here. I can't find anyone to help me make more stereos, but I'll bet if I raise the price, people will pay it." This is how full employment can fan the fires of inflation.

## The Problem with Inflation

The problem with inflation is that once it takes off, it can outpace wages and lower living standards. If you can buy a bag of groceries in August for $60 and by December the same groceries cost you $75 but your salary hasn't budged, well, you're going to have to start eating less or going to fewer movies or playing fewer rounds of miniature golf on the weekend. Now that's no fun!

When the Fed sees evidence of inflation building up, it takes the one action it can, which is to raise interest rates. If you're one of those folks rushing out to throw a new stereo on your credit card and your credit card company informs you that your rate has gone up from 12.5 percent to 14.5 percent, you may give that purchase a second thought. When the Fed raises interest rates, spending calms down a bit and inflation is dampened.

**Investor's Idiom**

The Fed manipulates the interest rates we pay for auto loans, mortgages, and like in two main ways. It raises or lowers the *discount rate*, which smaller banks must pay when they borrow from the Fed. If the banks have to pay more, they'll turn around and charge you more. The Fed can also indirectly affect the *funds rate* that banks charge each other by adding or draining cash from the banking system.

How does the Fed raise rates? Well, every bank in the country is required to keep at least 20 percent of its customers' deposits in its vault overnight. But sometimes a bank runs short at the end of the day and has to borrow money from another bank. The rate that banks charge each other for these short-term loans is called the *federal funds rate*.

Okay, stay with me now. The Fed doesn't set the funds rate directly but can affect it by adding or draining the cash reserves to or from the bank system.

In the same way that too much money chasing too few goods causes inflation, if the Fed drains reserves from the system, banks have fewer dollars on hand to lend each other overnight. Since they have less to lend, there will be pressure on the funds rate to rise.

The Fed can also directly control interest rates by raising and lowering the *discount rate*. This is the rate at which smaller banks borrow from the Fed.

**Investor's Idiom**

A *bond* is an I.O.U. that a corporation or government issues when it wants to borrow money for more than 10 years. The issuer agrees to pay back the bond holder at a specified *maturity* date, with interest.

Now, the one thing you can count on is that when it costs a bank more money to borrow money, it'll turn around and charge you more money to borrow. So when the funds rate or the discount rate rises, every other interest rate in the country starts to climb. Suddenly, it costs you more money to buy that stereo or a new house. You slow down your spending. Factories slow down their hiring. The economy begins to contract.

Conversely, when interest rates fall, it encourages borrowing, expansion, spending, and hiring. When the Fed thinks inflation is under control but jobs are scarce, it encourages the economy to grow by adding reserves to the banking system. This increases the cash available for banks to lend each other, and the funds rate comes down. Interest rates start to decline—people start buying again and companies start expanding and hiring. The economy begins to expand.

## What Do Interest Rates Have to Do with Stocks and Bonds? Glad You Asked!

What does all this have to do with stocks and bonds? Plenty! You've already learned that stocks are a form of equity financing—corporations sell ownership in the form of stock to raise capital. Well, bonds are simply a different instrument corporations use to raise capital. A *bond* is a form of debt financing.

When you buy a bond, you are *lending* money to a corporation for a specified length of time, not buying ownership. In return, the company promises to pay back the value of the bond at *maturity* with interest. We'll get into this in more detail later, but for now all you need to know is that if you buy a $100 bond today, when the bond matures in, for example, five years, you will get that $100 back, plus interest. Nothing more, nothing less.

But what if inflation has risen so much during those five years that your $100 only buys $80 worth of groceries? Bonds don't protect investors from inflation at all. That's why when investors hear economic news that makes them worry about inflation, they tend to become more interested in stocks. Inflation can really degrade the value of a bond. Stock prices, on the other hand—just like all other prices in the economy— tend to rise over time, so if you are worried about inflation, you'll find stocks more attractive than bonds because they offer some protection from the corrosive effect of inflation.

Both the stock and bond markets react to changes in interest rates, which in turn affects expectations about inflation—which in turn affects investors' decisions. If you understand that, you're on your way to becoming an educated investor.

# Your Personal Time Frame

You could hold one stock forever and:

➤ make a lot of money

➤ lose a lot of money, or

➤ break even.

Add another stock and, statistically, you will make less or lose less. Keep adding stocks until you own the S&P 500 and you will earn close to the market return. Over periods of 20 years or more, investors have always made money from a market-like portfolio. The average return over that time is around 10 to 12 percent. During a shorter time period, however, the likelihood increases that you will make a lot less or a lot more than 10 to 12 percent. On one day, October 19, 1987, the stock market declined 20 percent. But for the year, it was up 5 percent, and for that decade it was up nearly 18 percent. Go figure!

What does this all mean? Simply, that the risk you assume decreases the longer your time frame is. Risk is reduced as time is added. Here is the relationship between time, risk, and return.

In other words, the later you start investing, the less risk you can afford to take. If you're 60 and hope to retire at 65, and you do some calculations on the back of an envelope and realize you'll be $50,000 short of income when you retire, you shouldn't turn to the stock market because you aren't giving yourself enough time to ride out its risk. If you start to invest for retirement at a young age, on the other hand, you can put a high percentage of your savings in the stock market because you have time to ride out the highs and lows. A good rule of thumb is to give your investments at least 10 years to ride out stock market volatility.

Given a decent time frame, though, stocks have historically performed quite well. Here's the data going back to 1926, when the forerunner to the Standard & Poor's 500, the Standard & Poor's 90, was first tabulated:

## Compound Annual Return 1926–1997

| | |
|---|---|
| Standard & Poor's 500 Stock Index | +11.0% |
| Long-Term Government Bonds Index | +5.3% |
| U.S. Treasury Bills Index | +3.8% |
| Inflation (Consumer Price Index) | +3.1% |

*(Source: Ibbotson Associates, 1998 Yearbook)*

As you can see, the total return for stocks was 2 times that for risk-free government bonds and 3.5 times the inflation rate for the last 72 years. Looks like stocks are worth the risk, if you can hold them for at least 10 years.

Every investment goal will have a different time frame, though. It depends on what your personal short- and long-term goals are. You might want to buy your first house in five years, for example. Your savings for that goal would have to be in investments that won't fluctuate too much during that short time period. Perhaps you just got married, and, although there might not be a child on the scene for a couple of years, you want to begin a 20-year savings plan for his or her college education. In this case, you have a lot more freedom in how to invest.

In general, what you invest in depends on your investment time frame. The less time you have to achieve your goal, the less you should invest in riskier investments like stocks. If you have a longer time frame, your chances of success on the market will increase. We'll go into your personal time frames in much greater depth in Chapter 2. But first, let's figure out how you *really* feel about risk.

---

### The Least You Need to Know

➤ Instead of spending any money you earn on an investment, reinvest it and let compounding interest build your wealth.

➤ Start to invest as early in life as you can by making a habit of saving and investing 10 percent of your salary.

➤ Riskier investments, like the stock market, can make you a lot of money, but only if you have time to ride out the ups and downs.

➤ Expectations about inflation affect the financial markets and investors' decisions.

➤ The later you start investing, the less risk you can afford to take.

# Chapter 2

# How Do You Really Feel About Risk?

---

## In This Chapter

➤ How much risk is too much for you?

➤ How to figure out your return on any investment

➤ Understanding the relationship between risk and return

➤ Getting a grip on your own risk tolerance

➤ Evaluating your unique time frame

---

Jumped out of any airplanes lately? Or are you the type who white-knuckled it and sucked down three drinks during your last commercial flight?

Whether we perceive a given situation as exciting or terrifying has to do with our tolerance for risk. Many of us like to kid ourselves about how much risk we're willing to accept. We dream of jumping out of a plane or skiing top-speed down a sheer slope—but when we find ourselves at the door of that plane or the top of that slope, we wish we had our feet firmly planted on terra firma.

You can chicken out of skydiving or skiing with only your pride to salvage, but if you make investments that require more risk tolerance than you have, you'll be a miserable, sleep-deprived wreck. So the first step before you invest in anything is to analyze and get comfortable with your risk tolerance. The investment world is no place for false bravado.

# What Is Return?

In investing, risk doesn't mean credit risk or the risk of bankruptcy, but rather the risk that an investment's return will disappoint or surprise you. When you invest in something, you decide to do so because you expect to get more money out than you put in. The difference between the amount you put in and the total amount you receive at the end of the investment period is your *return*.

*Return on investment* (ROI) is also called rate of return. It's typically expressed as a percentage of the original investment. Let's say your little brother asks to borrow $500 to buy an old car that he intends to fix up and resell. When he sells the car for $1,000, he gives you back your $500 and splits the $500 profit with you. You get $500 plus $250, or $750. Since $250 is half of $500, for every dollar you invested, you earned 50¢. Your ROI is 50 percent.

# What You Made, What You Paid

Here's a formula you can use to calculate the return on any investment:

1. The total you receive at the end of the investment period is your end-of-period wealth (A).

2. Your original investment is called your beginning-of-period wealth (B).

3. If you subtract your beginning-of-period wealth (B) from your end-of-period wealth, you'll get your return: A − B.

**Investor's Idiom**

*Risk* is the chance that your investment's return will either disappoint or pleasantly surprise you.

*Return* is the amount you earn from an investment over a given period of time. Generally, higher returns require the investor to assume greater risk.

*Return on investment* (ROI) is also called rate of return, and is expressed as a percentage of your original investment.

Now that you've figured out your return, you can easily calculate your ROI. Use the formula below to figure out your return as a percentage of your original investment (B).

$$\frac{[A - B]}{B} \times 100 = ROI$$

Applying the formula to the above example, you get:

$$\frac{[\$750 - \$500]}{\$500} \times \$100 = \frac{\$250}{\$500} \times 100 = .50 \times 100 = 50\%$$

Hopefully, this doesn't look too hard to you. But if it does, an easy way to remember this formula is the following:

What you made (e.g., $250) over what you paid (e.g., $500), divided by what you paid, times one hundred.

# Fear of Heights: The Higher the Return, the Greater the Risk

When you lent your brother the money to buy that car, you took on the risk that a number of things could have gone wrong:

➤ He might not have been able to sell the car.

➤ The car might have been stolen or vandalized before he sold it.

➤ He could have sold it for a disappointing return.

Before lending him the money, you calculated your ROI in your head—even if you didn't know that's what you were doing!—and found it acceptable payback for the risk you were accepting. If your brother lives in a neighborhood where cars are stolen every night, maybe you would have decided not to risk your $500. Then again, if he swore to you that he could resell the car for $1,500, making your return $500 instead of $250, maybe you'd have gone for it anyway. After all, a 100 percent return on investment is nothing to sneeze at.

In this case: $\frac{[\$1,000 - \$500]}{\$500} = \frac{\$500}{\$500} = 1 \times 100 = 100\%$

You've just uncovered an unimpeachable rule of investment: the higher the return, the greater the risk. If you ever had a coach whose mantra was "No pain, no gain," you've already digested this concept. No matter what someone tries to tell you, the higher the return you are offered on an investment, the greater the risk.

The rate of return from investing in a small business, for example, can be very high. But roughly one out of every seven small businesses fails, so the risk of losing your investment is very high as well. In contrast, the return banks offer on savings accounts is typically very low—3 or 4 percent. But the risk that you will lose your money if you put it in a savings account is also very low.

**Fiscal Facts**

When the word *on* shows up in a business term, it means "divided by." So return *on* investment really means return *divided by* investment. Looking at the formula for ROI, this becomes clear. Return is A – B, which is then divided by B, giving you the investment amount. We just multiply by 100 to express the result as a percentage.

**Crash Alert**

Now that you understand the relationship between risk and return, you'll never be fooled by investments that promise a high return with little or no risk of losing your money. Remember, if someone is offering you a high return on your investment, it's because the investment is high risk. There's no such thing as a low-risk investment that generates high returns.

In addition, you learned in Chapter 1 that risk is reduced as time is added because over time ups and downs in your investment have a chance to even out. In other words, risk falls as time passes—and this increases your chances of superior returns. The relationship between risk, return, and time looks like this:

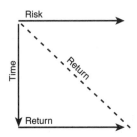

# The Tools of the Trade

To control risk, investment professionals use several tactics, which you can apply yourself to your own portfolio of investments.

Before we discuss these tactics, let's look at a basic tenet of investment theory: *standard deviation*. Don't panic. No need to fear scary flashbacks of the math section of the SAT. It's just a mathematical term that helps to frame the likelihood (or, in math terms, probability) of a given number recurring.

**Investor's Idiom**

Your *portfolio* is the mix of assets in which you have invested. A portfolio contains investment instruments that you've selected to achieve your financial goals, such as common stocks, bonds, Treasury bills, etc.

An *asset* is any item of value—from baseball cards to stocks—that you own.

A *liability* is a debt you owe, while an asset is something you own.

## Standard Deviation and a Podunk Potato

Freddie has played third base for the Podunk Potatoes for the past 12 years. His batting average each year has been:

| | | | | | |
|---|---|---|---|---|---|
| 1) | .290 | 5) | .390 | 9) | .330 |
| 2) | .380 | 6) | .320 | 10) | .340 |
| 3) | .300 | 7) | .270 | 11) | .350 |
| 4) | .310 | 8) | .370 | 12) | .370 |

What will he bat in his thirteenth year? Let's look at his average. To calculate the average of any group of figures, simply add them together and divide by the number of figures—12, in this case.

Freddie's average is .335. But maybe in years two and five, Freddie got lucky and his batting average was boosted by a stew of easy pitches.

And, let's say he was bothered by injuries in years one and seven, when he did particularly badly. These aren't normal situations, so why don't we just throw out those four years? This is similar to what figure skating and gymnastics judges do when scoring a routine—they throw out the highest and lowest scores. This is also what financial analysts do when they are trying to find a pattern in a bunch of numbers. They disregard the very highest and the very lowest numbers. Analysts usually dump about a third of the numbers they are given, which is what we're doing in this case by getting rid of four out of 12 of Freddie's batting averages.

If we get rid of years one, two, five, and seven, Freddie's lowest score turns out to be the .300 he batted in year three. His highest score becomes the .370 he batted in year 12. The difference between those two years, or the spread, is:

$$.370 - .300 = .70$$

So we could think of Freddie as someone who tends to bat between .300 and .370. If we divide that .70 difference in half, we could say that Freddie bats his average of .335 plus or minus .35. That "plus or minus .35" is called the *first level standard deviation*. It gives you a pretty clear picture of Freddie's potential future performance: His batting average in a given year can *deviate* up or down from the overall average by .35.

## Deviant Behavior

We can follow the same procedure with the stock market by looking at the annual returns for the market as far back as we want to go. Let's assume that for a single year, the stock market returned 12 percent with a standard deviation of plus or minus 15. This would mean that stocks returned between +27 percent (12 + 15) and –3 percent (12 – 15) that year.

That same year, bonds returned 5 percent and money market instruments returned 3 percent. Well, if the stock you were holding was at the low end of the stock market return, you would've actually lost –3 percent and probably would've been happier with your money parked in bonds or even in a savings account.

What's interesting, though, is that when we look at stock market returns over a 20-year period, the standard deviation really comes down from +/–15 to closer to +/–3. This means stock investors who stay in the market for 20 years could expect returns of 12 percent +/–3. The low would be 12 percent – 3, or 9 percent. The high would be 12 percent + 3,

**Fiscal Facts**

A huge amount of wealth is invested in the stock market. The estimated value of American stocks is $11.3 trillion, according to Herbert Barchoff, who's been around long enough to see the confidence Americans have in the stock market go from zero to today's somewhat unrealistic level. Barchoff was a member of the President's Council of Economic Advisor's during the Truman Administration. (Source: *The New York Times,* June 19, 1998.)

or 15 percent. This means that, for investors with a 20-year time horizon, stocks have historically performed very well. Also, for each and every 20-year period, stocks have returned more than bonds. Over time the returns from stocks smooth out and the deviation drops.

Basically, the longer you hold a high-risk investment like stock, the smaller the standard deviation will become. Over time all the fluctuations matter less and less. What matters is how the investment performs over the long run, not the short term. Historically, stocks have been very volatile over short periods, but have performed very well over 10–20 year horizons. The more time you have, therefore, the more risk you can handle.

Therefore, we can say that the standard deviation (risk) of the highest risk/highest return investment declines as the time frame increases. This is a key concept in investment theory and, for your purposes, asset allocation.

How does this all apply to you? Well, once you understand how time, risk, and return interact, you can begin to think about how to allocate your investment assets. Simply put, if your time frame is short, you shouldn't own much common stock. If you have a long time frame, you should have a substantial portion of your assets allocated to stock, because over time the ups and downs in the stock market—as represented by the standard deviation—tend to cancel each other out.

# The Three Broad Investment Classes

There are basically three broad classes of investments from which you can choose when you build your portfolio:

1. Common Stocks
2. Bonds
3. Money Market Instruments

As you learned in Chapter 1, common stocks represent shares of ownership in a company. Corporations sell ownership in the form of stock to raise capital. This is called equity financing.

As an owner, you are entitled to the fruits of the company's success: higher cash dividends and, ultimately (and hopefully), a higher stock price. On the other hand, you are vulnerable to the costs of failure: a reduction in (or even elimination of) the cash dividend and a lower (perhaps substantially lower) stock price.

**Investor's Idiom**

When a corporation issues stock, it is essentially selling pieces of ownership (called "equity") in the company. When you buy a share of GM common stock, you become an owner of General Motors. You are now entitled to a share of the company's profits, which are paid to stockholders *as dividends*. Most stock is simply *common stock*, but some is preferred. The owners of *preferred stock* get their dividends first.

Bonds, you'll recall from Chapter 1, are a form of debt financing. When you buy a bond you are lending money for a specified length of time.

Money market instruments pay rates that vary from day to day, week to week, or month to month. They are very liquid. This means they can be converted to cash easily and quickly. A savings account or a money market fund can be cashed in any day for the same price you paid. Treasury bills can be sold within 24 hours. To liquidate a bond (or stock), on the other hand, might take some time because you have to find someone to buy it. The purpose of money market instruments is to provide instant (or close-to-instant) liquidity in your portfolio.

Stocks are riskier investments than money market instruments or bonds, but because they are riskier, they generate higher returns.

### Investor's Idiom

An investment is considered *liquid* if it can be converted into cash quickly and easily. Money market instruments offer liquidity, because they can be converted to cash right away or within 24 hours.

## Variety Is the Spice of Life

What's life without a little diversity? Well, in the world of investing, diversity can mean the difference between taking off or crashing and burning. *Diversification* is another method investment pros use to increase your portfolio's ability to handle greater risk—and thereby earn greater returns.

In Chapter 1 we discussed how if you keep adding stocks to your portfolio until you own the 500 stocks in the S&P 500, you will earn close to the average market return. The reason for increasing your number of stock holdings is to help minimize *event risk*. This is the risk that one event could really damage the value of a stock you own.

In 1997, while the S&P 500 Stock Index was up 33 percent, McDonald's stock rose only 6 percent. Why? Well, the Arch Deluxe didn't exactly fly off the grill, if you recall. There was also some media flap about the quality of your average McDonald's meal. So, if you had all your money in McDonald's stock, you were probably too queasy to eat a dozen Arch Deluxes for the sake of saving your investment.

On the other hand, in the first six months of 1998, the S&P was up close to 18 percent, but McDonald's stock price skyrocketed 50 percent. Why? McDonald's went on a campaign to solve its problems—dumping the loser burger and running some

### Investor's Idiom

*Diversification* is a method of decreasing risk by increasing the variety of assets in a portfolio. If you own lots of different stocks, for example, your whole portfolio won't tank if one company goes bankrupt.

popular specials, like its Beanie Baby™ giveaway. Now here's what's really interesting—over that year and half, the returns for the S&P 500 and for McDonald's stock are very close. The S&P 500 didn't perform as spectacularly as McDonald's did in the first six months of 1998, but neither did it drop as dizzyingly in 1997. This is the value of diversification—over time it may dampen the highs, but it cushions the lows.

# Quiz Thyself to Know Thyself: Risk Tolerance Quiz

The key to successful investing is to determine how much risk you can handle, taking into consideration:

➤ Your future obligations, such as children, a mortgage, or a business.

➤ Your liquidity constraints, for example, if you don't have health insurance and you break your leg, you'll need cash to cover the medical bills.

➤ Your growth requirements, such as the standard of living you want to maintain when you retire. Social Security probably won't do it for you, so you'll need some investments that really grow, like stocks.

➤ Your investment objectives—such as keeping your investments safe—growth, and income.

➤ Your investment philosophy, i.e., how willing are you to take risk? How much time do you have?

**Investor's Idiom**

*Risk tolerance* is how much risk an investor is willing to assume in order to increase the level of potential reward.

But how do you know whether you can ride out the bumps and take the lumps that long-term investors in high-risk, high-return investments like stocks have to tolerate? How do you know what your risk tolerance level is? To complete the quiz, simply make a check mark next to the statement that best describes your feelings. To score the quiz, simply add up the numbers next to your check marks. Then look up your score on our handy Risk Chart.

A. ____ 1) I'd be willing to do without some of the potential to earn more money on my investments in order to receive some minimal assured rate of return.

____ 2) I'm much more concerned with getting solid, consistent results on my investments than superior investment returns.

____ 3) Hey, you've got to be in it to win it! I can accept fluctuating year-by-year returns in order to achieve higher total returns in the long run.

B. ____ 1) Although I may not get as much income right now on my investment, I'm interested in preserving what capital I have and don't want to see the market value of my securities decrease. When it comes to my future, I like to play it safe.

_____ 2) When it comes to my investments, show me the money: Current income is more important than capital preservation.

_____ 3) Sure, I'm interested in preserving my capital, but I can take some decrease of market value to increase the income I'm earning on my investments right now.

C. _____ 1) Even looking at dice gives me the willies! I am definitely not much of a gambler. I'm more concerned in preserving the value of my current assets than in investing in riskier securities that have the potential to increase in value later on.

_____ 2) Growth of my assets in the future is as important to me as preserving the value of my current assets.

_____ 3) I am more concerned with providing greater future growth than playing it safe now and preserving my current assets.

D. _____ 1) Keeping risk very low is more important for me than taking a chance in order to achieve superior investment returns.

_____ 2) Hey, there's chance in everything. Some market risk is inevitable in order to get the growth I deem necessary from my investments.

_____ 3) The final result is more important than how I got there. If I have to risk a bad year to meet my goal, that's okay.

E. _____ 1) I feel I can make a fairly accurate prediction of what my future liabilities will be.

_____ 2) Well, I may not have a crystal ball, but I think I can accurately predict some of my future liabilities. Other possible liabilities are subject to rough estimates.

_____ 3) Do I look like a fortune teller? I am relatively uncertain about what my future liabilities will be.

F. _____ 1) I don't like to put my eggs in one (or two) baskets. I believe in keeping my investment portfolio well diversified.

_____ 2) I don't like complications. I think it's best to keep the investment process simple. I use one or two types of investments with which I am comfortable. That's all I need.

_____ 3) You don't get to be a billionaire by playing it safe. The final result is more important than how it was derived. Diversification is not a major issue for me.

G. _____ 1) The Blue Chip (high quality) stocks of solid, mature companies give me the perfect combination of income and stability. I don't need to have superlative growth on my investments to be satisfied.

**Fiscal Facts**

Interestingly enough, the term *blue chip* was coined in nineteenth century poker games. The blue chip is the one with the highest value.

____ 2) Blue chip companies are great, but I don't necessarily need to be that conservative with my investments. The stocks of solid companies in growing businesses will give very good results with a level of risk I can tolerate.

____ 3) Entrepreneurship is where it's at. Small companies' stocks may be more volatile, but I prefer them because they reward me with the highest long-term rates of return.

H. Given the choice of the following three investments identical in every other respect, I would choose:

____ 1) Investment 1: 100 percent chance of a 5 percent rate of return per year over the next five years.

____ 2) Investment 2: 75 percent chance of a 10 percent rate of return per year, 25 percent chance of a 4 percent rate of return per year over the next five years.

____ 3) Investment 3: 50 percent chance of a 20 percent rate of return per year, 50 percent chance of a 0 percent rate of return per year over the next five years.

I. Use the graph below to answer the following question.

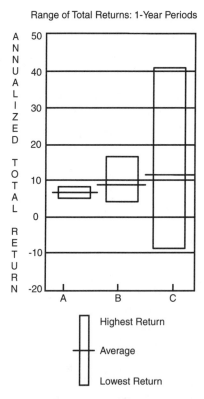

Range of Total Returns: 1-Year Periods

Assuming the expected rate of inflation over the next year is 4 percent, which investment option would you choose for a one-year time horizon?

_____ 1) Investment A would be the most appropriate of the three alternatives for my needs.

_____ 2) Investment B would be the most appropriate of the three alternatives for my needs.

_____ 3) Investment C would be the most appropriate of the three alternatives for my needs.

Calculate Your Score:

## Your Risk Tolerance Rating

| POINT TOTAL | | RISK LEVEL | |
| --- | --- | --- | --- |
| | Low | Medium | High |
| 9–14 | X | | |
| 15–21 | | X | |
| 22–27 | | | X |

# Got the Time? Take the Time Horizon Quiz

Are we done? Can you go to sleep now? Not quite. We haven't addressed time frame.

Each of us has our own attitude toward time, and before you invest a dime, you need to determine yours. Believe it or not, though, almost everybody is a short-term, medium-term, and long-term investor simultaneously. How so? You might be saving for retirement, investing to send your kids to college, *and* saving for a vacation all at once. Each of these savings plans has its own time horizon; that is, each has a limit as to how much time is needed to reach the intended goal. How do you figure out what this time horizon is? Well, sometimes you may find that your investment priorities conflict. The manner in which you most consistently opt to resolve those conflicts indicates your true investment time horizon. Take the following quiz and check your results on the scale. Again, simply add up the numbers next to each question and find where you fall on the Time Frame Chart:

A. Considering time to be the most important factor distinguishing the three investments shown on the following page:

_____ 1) Investment A would be most appropriate for my needs.

_____ 2) Investment B would be most appropriate for my needs.

_____ 3) Investment C would be most appropriate for my needs.

**B.** ____ 1) It is most important to grow assets in an investment fund in the next one to two years.

____ 2) It is most important to grow assets in an investment fund in the next five years.

____ 3) It is most important to grow assets in an investment fund in the next 10 years or longer.

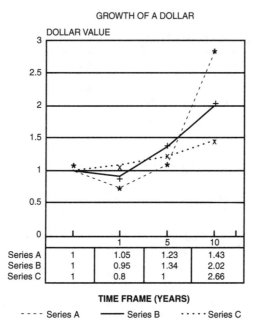

GROWTH OF A DOLLAR

DOLLAR VALUE

| | | 1 | 5 | 10 |
|---|---|---|---|---|
| Series A | 1 | 1.05 | 1.23 | 1.43 |
| Series B | 1 | 0.95 | 1.34 | 2.02 |
| Series C | 1 | 0.8 | 1 | 2.66 |

TIME FRAME (YEARS)

- - - - Series A ──── Series B · · · · Series C

**C.** ____ 1) I'm not one to jump to conclusions. I don't feel it's necessary to make decisions based on individual quarterly rates of return. However, four consecutive disappointing quarters may cause me to rethink my investment strategy.

____ 2) I do not make decisions based on one year of investment returns. However, two consecutive disappointing years or a disappointing five-year period may weaken my confidence in my current investment strategy.

____ 3) I know that good things are worth waiting for. Ten years is my preferred barometer for measuring investment results.

**D.** ____ 1) My concerns lie in the here and now. I am most interested in maintaining my current financial position.

____ 2) I've done fairly well over the past five years. Why not continue in that progress over the next five years?

____ 3) Time is on my side. My financial position has barely started to reach its potential. I look forward to rapid growth.

E. \_\_\_\_ 1) Safety first, I always say. If I can get high yields from bonds, I will forgo the future potential for gains in stocks.

\_\_\_\_ 2) I don't need to totally play it safe, but I would be willing to accept lower levels of growth over a period of five years in order to hold on to consistent year-to-year returns.

\_\_\_\_ 3) You've got to take the bad with the good. I'm willing to accept one year with a negative rate of return (for example, between –5 percent and –10 percent) in order to provide greater total returns over a period between five and ten years.

F. Given a choice between receiving $100,000 this year or $300,000 10 years from today:

\_\_\_\_ 1) I would accept $100,000 this year.

\_\_\_\_ 2) I consider both offers to be equally attractive.

\_\_\_\_ 3) I would accept $300,000 10 years from today.

> **Investor's Idiom**
>
> In the investment world, the year is divided into three-month *quarters*. Companies are required to report their financial performance to stockholders every quarter. the *quarterly rate of return* is the return on investment for one quarter, as opposed to *annual return,* which is an investment's return over one year. Companies and mutual funds report results both quarterly and annually.

Check Your Score:

## Your Time Horizon Score

| POINT TOTAL | TIME FRAME | | |
| --- | --- | --- | --- |
| | Short (0–2 yrs.) | Intermediate (2–10 yrs.) | Long (over 10 yrs.) |
| 6–9 | X | | |
| 10–13 | | X | |
| 14–18 | | | X |

If you had any difficulty getting through these quizzes, don't panic. You're just going with your gut reaction right now. In fact, for those who are intimidated, we recommend that you return to them after you've read a few more chapters and feel a little more confident. Once you've completed these quizzes and found yourself on the tables, you should have a much clearer picture of your time frame and how you really feel about risk. Now your personal investment philosophy is shaping up.

### The Least You Need to Know

➤ Return is the amount you expect to earn from an investment.

➤ The higher the promised return on an investment, the greater the risk that you will be disappointed in the investment's performance.

➤ To reduce risk, you can increase both the time you give your investments to perform and the diversification of your portfolio.

➤ There are three broad investment classes: stocks, bonds, and money market instruments.

➤ Money market instruments, unlike stocks and bonds, offer liquidity; that is, they can be easily and quickly changed into cash.

# Chapter 3

# Are You a Grasshopper or an Ant? Selecting Your Investment Objectives

## In This Chapter

➤ Getting you investment objectives straight right now

➤ How to build your emergency fund

➤ Where to keep your rainy day cash

➤ How best to juggle your present and future investment objectives—without dropping any balls

➤ What does comfortable retirement mean?

➤ Pros and cons of retiring early

Remember Aesop's fable of the Ant and the Grasshopper? In a nutshell, the Grasshopper mocks the hard-working Ant for wasting a beautiful summer afternoon toiling away storing food for the winter. Of course, the warm summer rays give way to colder northern winds. As the Grasshopper gets stuck out in the cold with nothing, nada, zip to eat, the Ant is happily feeding his face in his warm anthill.

The moral of the story is, of course, if you don't prepare now, you're going to be one sorry grasshopper later. But does this mean you can't have any more fun? Of course not. It just means that if you want to have *any* fun in the future, you'd better get your investment objectives straight now. For instance, most people don't think about retirement planning for the simple reason that they've got plenty of other really important things to think about and plan for right now. And then there are the other near-future goals looming ahead, like getting married, buying a house, or sending the kids (whether you have them now or are planning to soon) to college. How do you juggle your multiple financial goals and pressures and still save for a comfortable retirement? Read on!

# Just-in-Case Cash

Most investors either never get around to establishing a plan for retirement, or if they do they deviate from it. Think of your financial plan as a stroll down a beautiful trail in the woods. If you stay on the path, you'll eventually reach your destination, but if you chase every butterfly or every storm sends you running for shelter, you'll get lost and may never find your way back to your path.

Hospitalizations, funerals, weddings, auto or home repairs, gifts, taxes, etc., don't show up programmed on a calendar. They occur with little or no advance warning, and you either have funds set aside to cover them or you go into debt. And going into debt, both financially and psychologically, can take the fun out of a happy event or make a sad one even sadder.

Your umbrella for those times when life drenches you with unexpected expenses is your emergency fund. This should be roughly 10 percent of your annual income or $10,000, whichever is greater. Some experts recommend keeping half your annual salary in an emergency fund, but that's a bit extreme. If you're making $50,000 a year or less, it's awfully hard to save $25,000. These days—what with low down payments available on homes and easy car financing—few emergencies require $25,000, as long as you have health insurance. Ten percent or $10,000 should cover you for most of life's financial emergencies. This is the single most important thing you can do to secure your financial future; an emergency fund ensures that you never have to touch your investments.

## Super Strategy

Don't forget the 10 percent rule: Put aside 10 percent of every paycheck and you'll be able to painlessly create your emergency fund.

# *Mattresses Are for Sleeping, Not Stashing*

It's important to save money for emergencies—but it's equally vital that you have immediate access to that money when a serious situation does arise. (And, no, keeping your cash under the mattress is *not* the best place, even if it is immediately accessible!) So, what investments are available that combine liquidity and safety for amounts under $100,000? (We assume you are not John D. Rockefeller.) You basically have four options:

1. Treasury Bills
2. Certificates of Deposit
3. Savings Accounts
4. Money Market Funds

All these investments are called cash equivalents, because they can be quickly and easily turned into cash.

## Treasury Bills

You can park your emergency fund in Treasury bills (or T-bills) and earn a nice return on your money while you enjoy the security of knowing that your funds are now a direct obligation of the U.S. Government. This means that, if necessary, the Treasury will turn on the printing press to make sure you receive your principal. Treasury bills are sold at a discount that reflects their yield, or interest. A $10,000 six-month T-bill, for example, might be sold for $9,750. You buy the bill for $9,750 and six months later you get $10,000.

To figure out the yield, simply apply our old pal, the ROI (return on investment) formula:

$$\$10,000 - \$9,750 \div \$9,750 \times 100 = 2.564\%$$

That's the return for six months; the annual return would be 2.564 percent times two, or 5.1282 percent.

Bills are sold by the Treasury at sales called "auctions." They are available in three-month, six-month, or 1-year maturities. The minimum purchase is $1,000. Auction purchases for three- and six-month T-bills are every Monday for Thursday settlement. The settlement date is the day you must actually pay for your bill purchase.

### Investor's Idiom

*Liquid investments* are those which can be turned into cash within 24 hours. Treasury bills, CDs, savings accounts, and money market funds are all *cash equivalents* that are highly liquid.

### Investor's Idiom

*Treasury bills*, or *T-bills*, are essentially I.O.U.s from the U.S. Government. They are available in three-month, six-month, and one-year maturities and are used by the U.S. Treasury Department to finance the national debt and day-to-day government cash flow crunches. They are fully guaranteed by the government and can be sold within 24 hours.

### Crash Alert

Although you can always cash Treasury Bills within 24 hours, if you sell before the maturity, you will be penalized.

**31**

One-year T-bills are auctioned the third Thursday of each month. Sales proceeds are available on a next-day basis.

You may purchase bills directly from the U.S. Government via the Treasury Direct Program or via banks or brokers, usually for a service fee. If you buy directly from the Treasury, you can do so in person, by mail, by phone (1-800-943-6864), or via the Internet at www.publicdebt.treas.gov. To utilize the latter two alternatives, you will need to provide a signature to open your account.

### Investor's Idiom

The *yield* on a Treasury bill is its return on investment; it's a way of expressing as a percentage the difference between the discount price and the value at maturity of the bill. You place an order to buy Treasury securities at auctions and actually pay for them on the settlement date.

### Crash Alert

If you cash in a CD early, you will be penalized. For example, the typical six-month $1,000 CD might incur a penalty of around $12 if you cashed it at three months. If the CD was paying 4 percent interest, you would have expected a return of $40 for a year or $20 for six months, so that $12 penalty sucks up more than half of what you'd hoped to have earned.

## Certificates of Deposit

"CDs" are issued by banks or thrifts (another term for savings and loans), with the first $100,000 insured by the federal government. Terms typically are for a fixed maturity ranging from 3 months to 10 years. If you need your funds before maturity, you will pay a penalty that may run as high as three months of interest for CDs maturing within one year, and six months of interest for CDs maturing after a year. The minimum purchase required is $1,000, but any dollar sum above $1,000 is acceptable ($1,100.21, for example).

When using CDs you have to stay on top of your maturity dates or the bank will automatically roll it over for another period. Prior to maturity, the financial institution will usually inform you in writing of the upcoming maturity date and give you three options:

1. Collect the proceeds
2. Roll over the sum due, or
3. Change the amount or the maturity.

Usually the CD is rolled over into a new CD of like maturity if you do nothing. If you invest in CDs, just be aware that banks love to automatically roll them over when they mature. If you don't tell your bank prior to maturity that you want to collect the proceeds of your six-month CD, for example, the bank will automatically lock you into another six months and you won't be able to withdraw your money before then without paying a penalty. And the penalties for early withdrawal can be pretty stiff.

## Savings Accounts

Savings accounts offer one advantage over T-bills and CDs—same day deposit and withdrawal. With T-bills and CDs it takes 24 hours to get at your emergency fund. Like CDs, saving accounts are insured by the federal government up to $100,000. Rates typically run 1–2 percent below other money market fund rates. Interest checking accounts pay even less (e.g., 1–2 percent) but are very convenient.

## Money Market Funds

Money market funds (MMFs) are mutual funds that invest only in safe, short-term money market instruments, such as Treasury securities, CDs, or short-term debt (called commercial paper) issued by creditworthy corporations.

Shares in a money market fund are bought and sold on a daily basis and are priced at $1 each. Although these funds are not insured or guaranteed, no money market fund wants to "break the buck" or admit to being unable to pay your $1 per share price if you want to cash in your shares. In those few instances where an asset was in question, the fund stepped in to insure the $1 price.

If you want greater assurance, limit your choice to money market funds that only buy Treasury or other government securities, without *repos*. Repos are securities the fund lends to broker-dealers who pledge assets to cover the loan equal to typically 102 percent of the sum borrowed. Much as a bank earns interest by lending out your deposits as loans, the MMF earns interest on these repos.

The other catch with repos is that you can't deduct all the interest on your state tax return. The interest earned by the repos is taxable.

*The Wall Street Journal* lists approximately 630 taxable money market funds and approximately

### Fiscal Facts

The Federal Deposit Insurance Corporation (FDIC) was created in 1933 to furnish insurance protection for depositors in the event that their bank fails. Savings and checking accounts, and certificates of deposit are all protected up to $100,000 by the FDIC.

### Investor's Idiom

*Money market funds* are mutual funds that invest in safe, short-term investments like Treasury securities or CDs. Some also invest in commercial paper, which is short-term debt issued by corporations to raise cash. Some MMFs lend the securities in their funds to broker-dealers in order to earn more interest. These securities are called repos.

**Crash Alert**

If you have mutual funds, don't use them for emergencies. Many folks get so excited about investing that they run out and purchase mutual funds before setting up emergency funds. But if your adventurous significant other wrenches his or her back while skydiving in Zimbabwe and you suddenly need a $2,000 airplane ticket and don't have an emergency fund, you'll have to sell your mutual fund. That's a taxable act, bud, so not only will you trash your investment program, you'll pay the Feds for the privilege.

370 tax-free funds. The *Journal* also lists the average maturity of the assets in each fund. Look in *The Wall Street Journal* on Thursdays under Money Market Mutual Funds in the Money & Investing Section. Your local newspaper also probably lists MMFs.

For a minimum balance, your money market fund may provide you with a free checking account. Checks usually have to be for at least $250. If you have a brokerage account, your broker may offer you a limited choice of MMFs. You may also open an account directly with some money market funds, such as Vanguard, for example. Some people really like the convenience of opening a brokerage account with their local bank and transferring funds between the brokerage account and their checking account. Before you take this route, investigate the fees, if any, your bank will charge for transfers and other services.

## Eenie, Meenie, Minie, Mo

Let's take a moment to evaluate these four options, as they pertain to your emergency fund:

|  | Pros | Cons |
|---|---|---|
| Savings Account | insured, liquid | low rates |
| CD | insured, competitive | fixed rates and maturity, penalty if redeemed before maturity |
| Money Market Account | liquid, competitive rates | not insured |
| Treasury Bills | liquid, competitive rates | can lose some principal if sold before maturity, min. purchase required |

Before deciding where to keep your emergency fund, think, above all, about what's most convenient for you:

➤ How easy or inconvenient is it for you to get to your bank?

➤ Does it offer all the services you desire, such as Treasury securities, savings bonds, CDs, automatic teller machines (ATMs), brokerage services, etc.?

➤ How do the interest-earning rates on liquid accounts at your bank compare to others? Can you earn more somewhere else? Is it convenient?

➤ Would you prefer to let a bank reinvest (roll over) your CDs rather than have to call or see your broker when T-bills mature?

# How Can I Bring Home the Bacon, Fry It Up in a Pan, and Have Some Left Over?

You want cash for a rainy day. You want to chill out on a warm beach when you hit 65 because, hell, you deserve it. But what about all the in-between stuff? You want a nice house. You want smart, well-educated kids. Maybe you even have dreams of becoming your own boss one of these days. These aren't such lofty goals—but achieving them will require some careful planning. We're going to go into greater detail about these topics later on, but for now, let's take a quick look at these near-future investment objectives.

## And Baby Makes How Much?

New parents dote on their kids, live and breathe for their kids, usually; at least until the little darlings hit surly adolescence and start applying Goth makeup. That's perfectly fine and how it should be, but be careful that your children don't become butterflies that delight you but who lure you off your financial path into dark and spooky woods.

### Super Strategy

A good habit to establish early in your family's beginnings is to dump all cash gifts for the children from relatives and friends into their educational funds.

When you have children, it's natural to want to plan to send them to the finest schools in the land and to save for their education first and foremost. At the risk of heresy, though, let's agree that your retirement needs must take precedence over your children's education. Remember, first, that their admission to the college of their (or your) choice is driven as much by their secondary school achievements as by the size of your checkbook. In addition, there are many more options available to fund a college education—such as loans, grants, gifts from relatives, scholarships, work/study programs, and summer jobs—than there are for retirement. And if you *really* want to secure a happy future for your children, don't saddle them with destitute elderly parents. Risking your financial security to ensure your child's college education does not make sense. (The same advice applies to grandparents who are involved in financing their grandchildren's educations.)

Also remember that you will have devoted much love and support to bringing them to the point where they are eligible for college. Let them help you share the next step by contributing money from summer or part-time jobs to their college funds. Their own contributions might make their college experience more meaningful to them, grumble as they may.

**Crash Alert**

The biggest financial planning error new parents make is to put saving for their children's education ahead of saving for their own retirement. It's much wiser to put your own financial security first. A great rule of thumb is to divide the 10 percent of your salary you should be saving for the future so that 2 percent of it goes to college funds and 8 percent goes toward your retirement.

Having said all that, of course you should save for your children's education. But first establish your emergency fund. By the time you've done this, you should have established a pretty steady habit of saving 10 percent of your salary for investment purposes. From this sum, target 20 percent for educational purposes from the time of the birth of your first child until the graduation from college of your last child. So, for every $10 of your salary you save, invest $2 in education and put $8 toward retirement.

This time frame means that if you're going to work for 40 years, for about half of those years you can save 10 percent exclusively for retirement. The remaining 20 years you will probably be splitting the 10 percent 20/80 between education and retirement. We'll take a close look at the best places to put your education dollars in Chapter 16.

## Oh, Give Me a Roof

Another big expenditure you may face, besides retirement and college, might be the down payment on a home. But if you think of this expense properly, it needn't throw you off your path to retirement savings.

First off, think of a home as shelter, not as investment—no matter how many ex-baseball pitchers you've heard extolling second mortgages on TV. A home down payment, ideally, would come from the $10,000-plus in emergency savings you've already set aside. We'll get into home ownership in greater detail in Chapter 15.

## Who's the Boss? You!

Are entrepreneurial dreams occupying your unconscious nocturnal activity? You may think you need to use every ounce of capital you have to start your own small business. Before you go cracking open the piggy bank, though, remember this: it is akin to buying shares in a business, and you might be tempted to rationalize the use of equity dollars from your retirement plan for this purpose. Bear in mind our discussion in Chapter 2 about diversification, though. Do you really want to sink your retirement dollars into one business—even if it is your own? Would you feel comfortable buying only Sears & Roebuck stock for your portfolio? Undiversified equities are high risk and you would be mortgaging your retirement by resorting to this approach—not to mention the unpleasant fact that many business start-ups fail. In fact, most successful entrepreneurs have had several failed businesses under their belts before hitting one out of the park. As Henry Ford said, "Failure is a chance to begin again more intelligently."

# How Gold Do You Want Your Golden Years to Be?

If planning for retirement is the farthest thing from your mind, you're not alone. According to the *1998 Retirement Confidence Survey* conducted by The Employee Benefit Research Institute, only 45 percent of all workers have figured out how much they'll need to retire—up from 32 percent the prior year. What's more:

➤ Half of all baby boomers born between 1946 and 1953 haven't given it a thought, reports The Institute's Paul Yakoboski (Source: *Pensions & Investments Magazine*, Arleen Jacobius, June 29, 1998).

➤ Among boomers born between 1954 and 1964, 47 percent are investigating their retirement savings needs this year, up from 32 percent last year.

➤ Only 33 percent of Generation X-ers have looked into retirement, up a mere 3 percent since 1997.

And for some weird reason, the percentage of smug individuals who say they are "very confident about retirement" has remained flat at 20 to 25 percent for the last six years. (Who are those people, anyway?) This means that three quarters of us have either blocked the entire disconcerting business out of our minds or toss and turn enough at night to wrinkle our wrinkle-free sheets.

Unless you want to spend your twilight years pushing a shopping cart around town looking for recyclables, you must add retirement into your overall investment-objective picture. Your logical next step in planning your financial future is to figure out how much money you need to put aside so you can not only retire, but retire comfortably.

What does this mean, exactly? Just this: A comfortable retirement is the manner in which you will maintain your present standard of living without heading off to the salt mines 40 plus hours a week. Presently, you probably don't often have to do without or scrimp; you have the means to eat well and entertain when you wish. When you retire, you'll have roughly the same expenses, with four possible exceptions.

The good news is there are four categories of expenses in which you will probably save money once you retire:

1. Car expense. If you have two cars now and one is primarily used for commuting, you might be able to get by with one after retirement. This'll mean significant savings on car payments, insurance, gas, and maintenance.

2. Home expense. If you have a four-bedroom colonial, you might consider moving to a smaller house or condo when the kids leave the nest. This would free up capital and reduce monthly payments and taxes.

3. Clothing expense. Not going to work means not having to wear a different snazzy suit or dress everyday; Bermuda shorts and Converse hi-tops are a lot cheaper.

4. Taxes. Income tax will come down as your income declines; property taxes can be reduced if you sell a large home.

Because these expenses are likely to be reduced once you retire, and because the dollars you're saving now for retirement will become dollars you can consume, a good rule of thumb is to expect that you'll require an annual retirement income of 50 to 70 percent of your present salary. The range accounts for a mortgaged home versus one owned free and clear. So, for example, if you live comfortably now on $60,000 a year and you expect to pay off your home by the time you retire, you need to save a pool of money that will generate 50 percent of $60,000, or $30,000, per year for your retirement.

Now the question is do you spend down that pool of money you have accumulated by age 65, or do you leave it to your heirs? It's probably wiser to assume that you'll spend it to zero by, say, age 85. If you include your savings as part of your retirement support (and face the gruesome fact of your own actuarial mortality!), you'll have to save far less to reach your goal. It's very important when planning your financial security to set realistic, reachable goals. If you establish a goal that requires too much scrimping and saving, you'll eventually shrug your shoulders and say, "Well, whatever happens, happens." Better to set a goal you recognize as doable. Start now, save consistently, get reasonable rates of return, and you'll have that pool of money when you retire.

In Chapter 4 we'll figure out exactly how much you will need to save in order to retire comfortably.

---

### The Least You Need to Know

➤ Before you invest in anything, set up an emergency fund, so you never have to dip into your investments to cover unexpected expenses.

➤ Keep your emergency fund in a liquid account or investment you can cash within 24 hours.

➤ The amount of income you'll need to retire is about 50 to 70 percent of what you need now to live comfortably.

➤ For every 10 percent of your salary you save to invest, put 2 percent toward your children's education and 8 percent toward retirement.

# Chapter 4

# What Have You Got Right Now— And What Are You Going to Need?

## In This Chapter

➤ Determining your Social Security benefits

➤ Figuring out your employment retirement benefits

➤ Saving the right amount for retirement

➤ Creating a personal balance sheet

➤ Creating a personal income statement

➤ Real-life examples of personal financial statements

Believe it or not, over 80 percent of baby boomers think they're going to keep working at least part-time after age 65, according to a survey published in the July/August 1998 *AARP Bulletin*. Of these boomers who intend to stay in the harness, 52 percent claim they're going to do it for fun, while 13 percent cop to fearing that they'll need to work into their dotage just to keep up payments on the Beamer.

When you consider that only 12 percent of people over 65 hold jobs today, you have to wonder whether the boomers who say they intend to work as seniors are deluding themselves out of fear that they won't be able to fund decent retirements. In fact, as long as you start reasonably early, it's not that difficult to fund retirement. In the same issue of the *AARP Bulletin*, William M. Mercer Inc. calculated that, assuming an 8 percent return, the following savings are required to accumulate $100,000 by age 65.

➤ At age 25: $7.14/week

➤ At age 35: $16.32/week

➤ At age 45: $40.40/week

➤ At age 55: $127.61/week

As you can see, the person who waits until age 55 to start saving for retirement will have to save almost eight times as much per week as the person who starts at 35. So if your head has been in the sand, pull it out and let's take a look at what you have—right now—and what it'll take to make your dreams of a great retirement come true.

# So What Will Social Security Do for Me, Anyway?

Half of the baby boomers surveyed by AARP said they had no faith that Social Security would be there for them when they retire. But the fact is, Social Security is one of our most revered social programs, and no young congressional firebrand is going to be able to dismantle it anytime soon. At least not with fearsome senior groups like the Gray Panthers ready to storm the Capitol with Uzis in hand. No politician wants to have anything to do with abolishing Social Security.

There are some campaigns under way to modify it, however. There are discussions in Congress that range from allowing you to invest a portion of your Social Security benefits yourself to allowing the government to invest some of the Social Security pool in stocks, which it can't at the moment. For now, include Social Security payments as a portion of your retirement income. Just don't plan to live on Social Security alone, unless you have a fondness for cat-food casserole.

**Investor's Idiom**

*Social Security* is a system managed by the federal government that provides money to people who are retired or are not able to work due to disability.

*FICA* stands for the Federal Insurance Contributions Act.

*Medicare* is included under Social Security. This is a national health program that pays certain medical and hospital expenses for elderly and disabled people. The Social Security system is funded by employees, employers, and the government.

## Figuring Out Your FICA

Look at your paycheck. See the section marked FICA? That's how much you pay each week into the Social Security system, which pays out Social Security and Medicare benefits. If you are employed, your employer pays an amount equal to 7.65 percent of your income to Social Security. The other 7.65 percent comes out of your paycheck, for a total of 15.3 percent of your income each year, up to a salary of approximately $65,000. After that, only Medicare is deducted, which is about 1.5 percent of your salary.

The Social Security Administration can tell you what your Social Security benefits will be based on when you retire. Call them at 1-800-772 (SSA)-1213 or visit their Web site at http://www.ssa.gov to obtain Form SSA-7004, the Request for Personal Earnings and Benefit Estimate Statement. You will receive, by mail, your Personal Earnings and Benefit Estimate Statement. The left page shows how much you have contributed to Social Security and to Medicare for every single year you've been employed. On the right page are your estimated Social Security benefits. This shows how much you can expect to receive each year from Social Security:

➤ If you retire at age 62 (reduced benefit)

➤ If you retire at full-retirement age, 65

➤ If you work until age 70

**Fiscal Facts**

To estimate what Social Security will pay you during your leisurely retirement years, call 1-800-772-1213 or visit the Social Security website at http://www.ssa.gov. You'll need to fill out Form SSA-7004. Social Security will send you your very own Personal Earnings and Benefit Estimate Statement. Check it carefully for bureaucratic boo-boos.

Check to see if there are any mistakes. If, for example, you know you earned about $30,000 in 1989 and your Personal Earnings and Benefit Estimate Statement shows $0 for that year, call the Social Security Administration and go through your statement carefully with someone. It's a good idea to get this statement updated every five years.

# Getting a Handle on Your Retirement Benefits by Pestering Human Resources

Now let's figure out what, if anything, you've built up in retirement benefits at your job. Stop by your employer's personnel or human resources department and ask them to calculate your retirement benefits for you. (They probably won't be thrilled, but hey, this is your future we're talking about here.)

Do this only if your employer offers a defined benefit or pension plan, or *DB*. A DB is simply an employer-financed retirement plan that promises to pay you a certain sum annually at retirement, with the sum dependent upon when you retire, how long you worked, and how much you received in salary. (If your employer doesn't have a DB, you can skip the rest of this section.)

Ask your HR representative two questions:

1. "What would my annual benefits be (if any) at age 65 if I left the firm tomorrow?" If you haven't put in the minimum time (e.g., five years), tell them to assume that you have. Having put in the minimum time is called *vesting,* or *being vested.*

### Investor's Idiom

A *pension* is simply a regular payment made to you (or your family, if you've passed away) by your employer that reflects how much you earned and how many years you worked at your job.

A *defined benefit plan,* or *DB,* is an employer-financed retirement plan that will pay you an annual sum upon retirement. Pensions typically require you to have worked for the employer at least five years before you are considered *vested,* or eligible, for the pension.

A *defined contribution plan* is a retirement plan that allows *you* to define how much is contributed to it. You tell the company how much to take from your check and put into your retirement plan.

### Fiscal Facts

According to the American Association for Retired People (AARP), the average annual benefit for retired workers is $9,180. The maximum benefit available from Social Security for someone retiring at age 65 is $16,104. So if you want to have fun when you're retired, better start your own plan!

2. "What would my annual benefits be at 65 if I continued to work here until 65?" Have human resources either use your present salary or assume a 3 percent annual raise.

Generally, the second number is going to be bigger than the first number. For our purposes in this chapter, use the smaller number. If you've had several jobs where you've earned retirement benefits, go back to each of the human resources departments and repeat the above procedure. You may get snarled at, but that's a small price to pay to get a grip on your finances.

# Help, I'm Self-Employed!

If you are self-employed, you make (or should be making!) quarterly estimated tax payments. Included in these tax payments is a federal self-employment tax that covers Social Security and Medicare.

When you work for an employer, it is required to contribute a sum equal to 7.65 percent of your income into the Social Security system. The other half is deducted from your paycheck. Self-employed people pay the whole amount, which is presently 15.3 percent of income, themselves. On the plus side, self-employed people get to deduct half of this self-employment tax from their income tax. If you're running your own business, you must pay self-employment tax if you earn more than $400 per year after expenses, even if you have another job.

If you are fully or partially self-employed, check in with Social Security to find out how your retirement benefits are looking.

Whether you work for yourself part-time or full-time, you are entitled to create a pension for yourself, since an employer isn't creating one for you. Or, if you own a small business, you can create pensions for yourself and your employees. This is also a great way to reduce your income tax, as contributions to self-employment retirement plans are deductible up to a point. We'll get into this in more detail in Chapter 5, but you have three options:

➤ SEP. This is a Simplified Employee Pension, which is very easy to set up with most banks, mutual funds, brokers, or insurance companies. All you have to do is complete Form 5305-SEP, which your financial institution can supply. Currently, the most you can deduct each year to contribute to a SEP-IRA is the smaller of either 13.04 percent of your net earnings from self-employment up to $150,000, or $19,565.

➤ Keogh Plan. It takes a lot of paperwork to set up one of these, so you'll probably need professional help. They are primarily for small-business owners who need to set up retirement plans for themselves and employees.

➤ SIMPLE. SIMPLE stands for Savings Incentive Match Plan for Employees. This is new and seems to be taking the place of the SEP-IRAs. An employer can match up to 3 percent of your compensation.

# A Super-Easy Way to Figure Out How Much You Need to Save

Now that you know how much will be coming in from Social Security and any retirement plans, you're ready to figure out how much you need to save and invest each year to retire, using the worksheet below. This worksheet gives you two options. One assumes that you'll own your house by retirement, so you'll only need 50 percent of your current annual income. The other assumes that you may still be paying a mortgage and will need 70 percent of your current annual income.

1. Present Annual Salary $_____ $_____

2. Times Percent at Age 65 _____.50_____.70

3. Gross Amount Required _____

4. Less: Social Security[1] _____

5. Less: Pension (if any)[2] _____

6. Less: Existing Savings & Investment Income[3] _____

7. Equals: Add'tl Income Required _____

[1] *Get this number from the Personal and Benefit Estimate Statement sent to you by Social Security.*

[2] *Get this number from your employer's personnel office. If you have worked there fewer than five years, request that they use five years in the calculation. Do the same with all previous employers. Enter the total on Line 5.*

[3] *Do not use your savings account balances here; what you want is the current annual income that savings and all other investments are generating annually. An easy way out is to simply multiply your total balances by .06 and use that sum for Line 6.*

Your total in Line 7 is how much additional income you will need each year of retirement to supplement what you will be receiving from Social Security and any existing pension. Your goal now is to save and invest a pool of money that will generate that additional income.

Let's say, for example, that you are a 35-year-old making $30,000, and your worksheet looks like this:

| | | |
|---|---|---|
| 1. Present Annual Salary | $30,000 | $30,000 |
| 2. Times Percent at Age 65 | .50 | .70 |
| 3. Gross Amount Required | $15,000 | $21,000 |
| 4. Less: Social Security[1] | $7,000 | $7,000 |
| 5. Less: Pension (if any)[2] | $5,000 | $5,000 |
| 6. Less: Existing Savings & Investment Income[3] | $0 | $0 |
| 7. Equals: Add'tl Income Required | $3,000 | $9,000 |

You need at least $15,000 per year of retirement income, and your Social Security ($7,000) and pension benefits ($5,000) add up to $12,000. That means when you retire, you'll be $3,000 short per year. Uh-oh.

Let's say you had $37,500 in investments that generated 8 percent income. You would get an extra $3,000 per year from those investments. That's exactly what you need. But you don't have $37,500 in investments, do you? So you have to grow it by saving over the next 30 years.

Let's say you invest these savings at 8 percent, and assume inflation is going to eat 4 percent per year. How much should you invest each year? Well, we can multiply $37,500 by 1.04 (4% = .04; $100 that earns 4% = $104, or $100 × 1.04) each year for 30 years or just sneak a peak at our old friend the Future Value of Money Chart back in Chapter 1. Either way, we'll find out that $37,500 today will have to grow to $121,627 by age 65 for you to avoid having your savings eroded by inflation. Remember, a dollar tomorrow won't buy as much as a dollar does today, but you want to be able to maintain your standard of living. You need to include inflation, therefore, when you calculate how much money you'll need to retire happily. If $37,500 a year would be enough for you today, you'll need $121,627 in 30 years to buy the same stuff.

So how much will you have to invest each year, assuming it will grow at 8 percent per year, in order to reach $121,627 by age 65? Well, we can do a whole bunch of calculations or we can look on the "Annual Savings Required" Table below. (Note: This table assumes you are earning 8 percent per year on your investments.) Look down the "Residual Needs" column until you get to $3,000, which is the annual amount you're looking to cover during retirement. Now, if you're 35, you have 30 years until retirement, so look under the "30" column across from $3,000 and there's your answer: You'll need to save $1,074 a year to create a pool that will generate $3,000 a year once you retire.

## Annual Savings Required

| Residual Needs[6] | Years to Retirement | | | | | | | |
|---|---|---|---|---|---|---|---|---|
| | 40 | 35 | 30 | 25 | 20 | 15 | 10 | 5 |
| $ 2,000 | 463 | 573 | 716 | 912 | 1,197 | 1,658 | 2,555 | 5,185 |
| 3,000 | 659 | 859 | 1,074 | 1,367 | 1,796 | 2,487 | 3,832 | 7,777 |
| 4,000 | 927 | 1,145 | 1,431 | 1,823 | 2,394 | 3,316 | 5,109 | 10,369 |
| 5,000 | 1,158 | 1,431 | 1,789 | 2,279 | 2,993 | 4,145 | 6,386 | 12,962 |
| 6,000 | 1,391 | 1,717 | 2,148 | 2,732 | 3,593 | 4,974 | 7,663 | 15,553 |
| 7,000 | 1,623 | 2,003 | 2,506 | 3,187 | 4,192 | 5,803 | 8,940 | 18,145 |
| 8,000 | 1,855 | 2,289 | 2,864 | 3,642 | 4,791 | 6,632 | 10,217 | 20,737 |
| 9,000 | 2,087 | 2,575 | 3,222 | 4,097 | 5,390 | 7,461 | 11,494 | 23,329 |
| 10,000 | 2,319 | 2,861 | 3,580 | 4,552 | 5,989 | 8,290 | 12,771 | 25,921 |
| 11,000 | 2,551 | 3,147 | 3,938 | 5,007 | 6,588 | 9,119 | 14,048 | 28,513 |
| 12,000 | 2,783 | 3,433 | 4,296 | 5,462 | 7,187 | 9,948 | 15,325 | 31,105 |
| 13,000 | 3,015 | 3,719 | 4,654 | 5,917 | 7,786 | 10,777 | 16,602 | 33,697 |
| 14,000 | 3,247 | 4,005 | 5,012 | 6,372 | 8,385 | 11,606 | 17,879 | 36,289 |
| 15,000 | 3,479 | 4,291 | 5,370 | 6,827 | 8,984 | 12,435 | 19,156 | 38,881 |
| 16,000 | 3,711 | 4,577 | 5,728 | 7,282 | 9,583 | 13,264 | 20,433 | 41,473 |
| 17,000 | 3,943 | 4,863 | 6,086 | 7,737 | 10,182 | 14,093 | 21,710 | 44,065 |
| 18,000 | 4,175 | 5,149 | 6,444 | 8,192 | 10,871 | 14,922 | 22,987 | 46,657 |
| 19,000 | 4,407 | 5,435 | 6,802 | 8,647 | 11,380 | 15,751 | 24,264 | 49,249 |
| 20,000 | 4,639 | 5,721 | 7,160 | 9,102 | 11,979 | 16,580 | 25,541 | 51,841 |
| 21,000 | 4,871 | 6,007 | 7,518 | 9,557 | 12,578 | 17,409 | 26,818 | 54,433 |
| 22,000 | 5,103 | 6,293 | 7,876 | 10,012 | 13,177 | 18,238 | 28,095 | 57,025 |
| 23,000 | 5,335 | 6,579 | 8,234 | 10,467 | 13,776 | 19,067 | 29,372 | 59,617 |
| 24,000 | 5,567 | 6,865 | 8,592 | 10,922 | 14,375 | 19,896 | 30,649 | 62,209 |
| 25,000 | 5,799 | 7,151 | 8,950 | 11,377 | 14,974 | 20,725 | 31,926 | 64,801 |
| 26,000 | 6,031 | 7,437 | 9,308 | 11,832 | 15,573 | 21,554 | 33,203 | 67,393 |
| 27,000 | 6,263 | 7,723 | 9,666 | 12,287 | 16,172 | 22,383 | 34,480 | 69,985 |
| 28,000 | 6,495 | 8,009 | 10,024 | 12,742 | 16,771 | 23,212 | 35,757 | 72,577 |
| 29,000 | 6,727 | 8,295 | 10,382 | 13,197 | 17,370 | 24,041 | 37,034 | 75,169 |
| 30,000 | 6,959 | 8,581 | 10,740 | 13,652 | 17,969 | 24,870 | 38,311 | 77,761 |
| 31,000 | 7,191 | 8,867 | 11,098 | 14,107 | 18,568 | 25,699 | 39,588 | 80,353 |
| 32,000 | 7,423 | 9,153 | 11,456 | 14,562 | 19,167 | 26,528 | 40,865 | 82,945 |
| 33,000 | 7,655 | 9,439 | 11,814 | 15,017 | 19,766 | 27,357 | 42,142 | 85,537 |

[6] *From line 7 on Annual Savings Required Form.*

*continues*

*continued*

| Residual Needs[6] | Years to Retirement | | | | | | | |
|---|---|---|---|---|---|---|---|---|
| | 40 | 35 | 30 | 25 | 20 | 15 | 10 | 5 |
| 34,000 | 7,887 | 9,725 | 12,172 | 15,472 | 20,365 | 28,186 | 43,419 | 88,129 |
| 35,000 | 8,119 | 10,011 | 12,530 | 15,927 | 20,964 | 29,015 | 44,696 | 90,721 |
| 36,000 | 8,351 | 10,297 | 12,888 | 16,382 | 21,563 | 29,844 | 45,973 | 93,313 |
| 37,000 | 8,583 | 10,583 | 13,246 | 16,837 | 22,162 | 30,673 | 47,250 | 95,905 |
| 38,000 | 8,815 | 10,869 | 13,604 | 17,292 | 22,761 | 31,502 | 48,527 | 98,497 |
| 39,000 | 9,047 | 11,155 | 13,962 | 17,747 | 23,360 | 32,331 | 49,804 | 101,089 |
| 40,000 | 9,279 | 11,441 | 14,320 | 18,202 | 23,959 | 33,160 | 51,081 | 103,681 |
| 42,000 | 9,743 | 12,013 | 15,036 | 19,112 | 25,157 | 34,818 | 53,635 | 108,865 |
| 44,000 | 10,207 | 12,585 | 15,752 | 20,022 | 26,355 | 36,476 | 56,189 | 114,049 |
| 46,000 | 10,671 | 13,157 | 16,468 | 20,932 | 27,553 | 38,134 | 58,743 | 119,233 |
| 48,000 | 11,135 | 13,729 | 17,481 | 21,842 | 28,751 | 39,792 | 61,297 | 124,417 |
| 50,000 | 11,599 | 14,301 | 17,900 | 22,752 | 29,949 | 41,450 | 63,851 | 129,601 |
| 52,000 | 12,063 | 14,873 | 18,616 | 23,662 | 31,147 | 43,108 | 66,405 | 134,785 |
| 54,000 | 12,527 | 15,445 | 19,332 | 24,572 | 32,345 | 44,766 | 68,959 | 139,969 |
| 56,000 | 12,991 | 16,017 | 20,048 | 25,482 | 33,543 | 46,424 | 71,513 | 145,153 |
| 58,000 | 13,445 | 16,589 | 20,764 | 26,392 | 34,741 | 48,082 | 74,067 | 150,337 |
| 60,000 | 13,919 | 17,161 | 21,480 | 27,302 | 35,939 | 49,740 | 76,621 | 155,521 |
| 62,000 | 14,383 | 17,733 | 22,196 | 28,212 | 37,137 | 51,398 | 79,175 | 160,705 |
| 64,000 | 14,847 | 18,305 | 22,912 | 29,122 | 38,335 | 53,056 | 81,729 | 165,889 |

This works out to about $83 per month. That's not a whole lot, when you think about it. Of course, this is what you'll need to meet your *minimum* requirements for retirement. If you want to really be secure and comfortable, you may want to save enough to generate the $9,000 in additional income you'll need if you follow the far right side of your worksheet. If you look on the table under $9,000 and 30 years, it says you'll have to save $3,222 per year.

# Use the Plan, Stan

So how do you save this much? Well, if your employer offers a groovy matching 401(k) or 403(b) pension plan, it's a great start. Many companies offer plans where for every $1 you contribute, the company will put in 50¢ (or 25¢ or 75¢, depending on the company—companies aren't *required* to contribute anything). That's free moolah for you. If you are lucky enough to be in this situation, contribute the maximum of pre-tax earnings—usually around 6 percent of your annual gross income. Now, if your employer contributes half of that, or 3 percent, that's 9 percent (which is really close to the 10 percent we recommend you invest, anyway). Just increase your deductions to

7 percent by continuing to have that 6 percent taken out of your pre-tax earnings and ask the personnel department if it can arrange for you to invest another 1 percent of your after-tax earnings in your company's plan. Voilà! You're painlessly on your way to establishing the 10-percent habit—and you don't even have to contribute all of it yourself. Just remember that the 10-percent rule applies as your salary increases, giving you a growing pool of assets that benefit from the magic of compounding interest each and every year.

Use your employer's plan first, if offered. There are tax advantages in that you may be able to shelter up to 15 percent of pre-tax earnings in an employer's plan depending on your salary and other restrictions. That's pretty cool—it means some of your hard-earned money escapes the clutches of the IRS by going straight into your tax-sheltered retirement plan. In addition, there are usually partial company matching dollar contributions.

### Investor's Idiom

Many corporations offer *401(k)* plans to their employees. Under this type of retirement savings plan, employees who are eligible are allowed to choose how much of their pay is to be deducted for investment purposes. They also decide how the dollars are to be invested. The *403(b)* is a version of the 401(k) used by public employers, such as schools, hospitals, and governmental bodies.

## Trust Us, You Really Don't Want to Wait

Now let's look at an annual savings worksheet for someone age 50 earning $50,000. She'll need 50–70 percent of her annual salary for retirement, or $25,000–$35,000. Social Security and retirement benefits will be greater than those for our 35-year-old, but not dollar-for-dollar, because there is a cap on annual Social Security benefits.

Let's assume that her combined benefits are $18,000. She needs to self-fund at least $7,000 per year. Assuming a return on investment of 8 percent, she'll need a pool of $87,500 to generate $7,000 per year in retirement income. Assuming 4 percent inflation, she'll actually need $157,583 ($87,500 × 1.04 for 15 years).

So, how much does she need to invest at an 8 percent return per year to reach $157,583 in 15 years? More than $5,000 per year, or $417 per month. Argh! That's a hefty chunk—five times the annual investment needs of our 35-year-old. Plus, age 50 is a time when you are usually deep into college expenses for the kiddies and can least afford to put aside retirement dollars. Yet put them aside she must.

## But My Circumstances Will Change... Won't They?

Of course, we all pray for raises, promotions, lottery winnings, and the like to lift us out of our present standard of living. How do you account for higher income over time when figuring out your retirement savings needs? By using a *fixed percent*, not a fixed dollar sum, of salary for retirement planning.

Back to our example of using you as a 35-year-old putting aside 3 percent of $30,000. If you get a 3.5 percent raise every year, by age 50, your salary will be about $50,000. You wouldn't need to change a thing about your investment strategy. In fact, if you get a 3.5 percent raise every year and continue to invest a steady 3 percent per year of your salary (and earn 8 percent on it per year), you'll have accumulated $34,792 by age 50 and $154,354 by age 65. Trust us, we did the math! That's pretty close to what we calculated as the pool you'll need to generate as additional required retirement income.

You still need to redo your annual savings worksheet periodically, though, to see if a higher or lower percent is warranted. The best time to do this is every year on your birthday. This is also the time to have Social Security and pension benefits recalculated. You may need to start saving more, but never set aside less than the percent of salary with which you started.

## Stagger Your Debt

In *Hamlet*, Shakespeare wrote: "Neither a borrower nor a lender be." These are wise words to heed these days, as we are strongly encouraged by advertising and tempting credit card offers to live debt-heavy lives. But if you're earning 8 percent on your investments and paying 18 percent in credit card and other debt, you're never going to get ahead.

The two biggest debts you are likely to take on are the following:

1. College loans for you or your children
2. Your home mortgage

Try to avoid incurring both at the same time. A great rule of thumb is this: Pay off your student loans before assuming a mortgage, and pay off your mortgage before incurring children's educational loans. The good thing about both education and home mortgage loans is they are used to finance assets that will probably increase in value over time. An education will ideally increase earning capacity and a home should appreciate over the years. Try timing your indebtedness something like this:

**Crash Alert**

Whatever you do, don't wait to start investing for retirement. Every 10 years the amount you'll have to put aside goes up drastically. A 50-year-old will have to invest roughly *seven times* the amount a 35-year-old will invest to get the same results. Plus, remember that the older you get, the less risk you can afford to take by holding stocks. This means you have to turn to investments that don't earn as much as stocks usually do—slowing down the growth of your retirement pool further.

**Fiscal Facts**

Many early American homes have a knob on the top of the banister that leads to the second floor, which signifies that the home was owned free and clear. Some early Americans even hollowed out the banister and inserted the paid-off mortgage!

| Age 21 | Take out student loans |
|---|---|
| Age 30 | Pay off student loans |
| Age 30 | Buy a home |
| Age 45 | Pay off mortgage |
| Age 45 | Take out loans for first child's college education |

Of course, this is idealistic for most people, but it's a good idea to at least start thinking this way!

We'll get more into how to dig yourself out of debt in Chapter 7, "Solving Debt and Credit Problems."

# Your Personal Balance Sheet: A Snapshot of Your Finances

Some people spend less than they earn, but most do not. How do you enter into the category of the frugal former? Make it your goal to spend 10 percent less than you earn.

Your first reaction is probably: "Are you kidding? I can hardly make ends meet now." Well, you can find that 10 percent, but only if you know where your money is coming from and going to right now. The best way to do that is to use simple versions of the same financial statements corporations use: a balance sheet and an income statement.

Let's do the balance sheet first. A balance sheet shows your assets, liabilities, and net worth. Your *net worth* is the difference between your *assets* (what you own) and your *liabilities* (what you owe). It's sort of a snapshot of your finances.

To create a personal balance sheet for you or your family, fill out the worksheet on the following page. Make a habit of doing this every year on your birthday.

**Crash Alert**

Avoid taking on loans to finance assets that lose value over time, such as home furnishings, clothing, and cars.

**Investor's Idiom**

A *balance sheet* is like a photograph of your finances at a given moment in time. It shows what you own (your *assets*) and what you owe (your *liabilities*).

Your *net worth* is the difference between assets and liabilities. Net worth can be positive (if assets are greater than liabilities) or negative (if liabilities are greater than assets). Each side of the balance sheet should "balance," or have the same total.

An *income statement*, in contrast, shows the flow of money through your life. It allows you to compare your income with your expenses.

## John Q. (and Suzie Q.) Personal Balance Sheet as of 00/00/99 (Your Birthday)

| Assets | Liabilities |
|---|---|
| Cash _____ | Credit Card Debt _____ |
| Checking Account Balance _____ | Student Loans _____ |
| Savings Account Balance _____ | Other Personal Loans _____ |
| Individual Investments _____ | Home Mortgage _____ |
| Profit Sharing (401k, 403b, etc.) _____ | Car Loan _____ |
| Home (best-guess value) _____ | |
| Car (best-guess value) _____ | |
| Collectibles (antiques, stamps, etc.) _____ | |
| Furnishings (best-guess value) _____ | |
| **Total** _____ | **Total** _____ |

Your first goal is to get your assets to exceed your liabilities. Your ongoing goal is to continually widen that spread so that you maximize your net worth.

On the asset side, we have left out two potential retirement benefits that some financial advisors would include: Social Security and earned pension benefits. You may add them in if you are close (e.g., five years or less) to retirement, but otherwise exclude them because:

1. They cannot be converted to cash if necessary.

2. They don't technically belong to you right now. In some cases, a former employer may offer to meet your earned pension sum by offering a lump-sum payment. In that case, you would transfer the sum to an IRA rollover and include it under the profit-sharing line.

# Get a Grip with a Personal Income Statement

So much of financial planning is just getting a clear view of your situation. Before you can get a handle on your spending, you'll need to tally up your expenses and compare them to your income. If your expenses are 90 percent of your income, great! If they are equal to or are greater than your income, well, now you know what you're dealing with.

Creating a personal income statement which clearly sets out your income and expenses will help you bring your expenses in line. While a balance sheet is a snapshot of your finances that is typically prepared once a year, income statements track your finances over time. If you prepare an income statement once a month, you can really get a grip on how much money is coming in and how it's being spent. Before you fill out the worksheet below, you might want to make 20 or so copies of it. Fill out one using yearly figures and use the others to create an income statement each month.

## John Q. (and Suzie Q.) Personal Income Statement Twelve Months Ending 00/00/99 (Your Birthday)

| Income | Expenses |
|---|---|
| Salary _____ | FICA, etc. _____ |
| Gifts to you/yours _____ | Federal Taxes _____ |
| Income from Savings[1] _____ | State Taxes _____ |
| Alimony Received _____ | Life Ins. Premiums _____ |
| | Rental/Mortgage Payments _____ |
| | Real Estate Tax[2] _____ |
| | Food _____ |
| | Clothing _____ |
| | Alimony Paid _____ |
| | Medical/Dental _____ |
| | Entertainment _____ |
| | Gifts Given _____ |
| | Auto Payments _____ |
| | Student Loan Payments _____ |
| | Credit Card Payments[3] _____ |
| | Other Loan Payments _____ |
| | Auto Related (gas, service, etc.) _____ |
| | Home Repairs _____ |
| | Furnishings _____ |
| | Vacation _____ |
| | Utilities (gas, electric, phone) _____ |
| | Education Related _____ |
| | Other _____ |
| **Total** _____ | **Total** _____ |

[1] *Limited to savings for car, etc.*

[2] *If not included in mortgage payment*

[3] *Deduct sums covered elsewhere (e.g., clothing, etc.)*

Now that you have your expenses broken down and on paper, you'll be prepared to tackle reducing them when you reach Chapter 6, "Cutting Expenses *Is* Investing."

On the income side, there are a few things you can do right away:

➤ Divert any raises you get at work toward your 10-percent goal.

➤ Make sure your savings are with the bank that offers the highest savings interest rate in your area.

➤ If you have a five-year target for a home down payment, find the safest investment that will earn you the most interest. For instance, if Treasury notes yield 1–2 percent more than Treasury bills or money market funds, go for it. Or maybe your bank has a "teaser" rate on CDs that is significantly higher than money market funds or Treasury bills. However you do it, be sure to keep your emergency savings fund in the most liquid and marketable investments available, which means money market funds or Treasury bills. It's not likely that you'll be able to postpone surgery to match up with a Treasury note to mature so you can get your principal back!

➤ Be sure to put any cash gifts into your savings/investing accounts. This is "found" money for you. And you might hint to family members that you would prefer cash to gifts going forward. It all counts toward that 10-percent goal.

# A Happy Couple on the Right Track

If you've had a little trouble filling out your balance sheet, here's an example from real life. Let's call this couple "Bill and Mary." They are both 33 years old, with one 3-year-old child. They own their condo. Bill is a private school teacher and Mary works part-time at a retail firm. Credit cards are paid off in full each month.

## Balance Sheet—Bill and Mary   July 15, 1998

| Assets | | | Liabilities | |
| --- | --- | --- | --- | --- |
| Savings | | $20,000 | Student Loans | 0 |
| Investments | | | Other Personal Loans | 0 |
| Bill (403b) | $12,000 | | | |
| Pension | 5,600 | | | |
| Mary (401k) | 600 | | | |
| Child | 5,000 | | | |
| Roth IRA | 2,000 | 25,200 | | |
| Home | | 240,000 | Mortgage | $99,000 |
| Auto | | 5,400 | Auto Loans | 0 |
| Total | | $290,000 | Total | $99,000 |
| Net Worth: $191,600 | | | | |

## Income Statement—Bill and Mary   July 15, 1998

| Income | | | | Expenses | |
|---|---|---|---|---|---|
| Salary: | Bill | $37,000 | | Mortgage | $8,184 |
| | Mary | 11,000 | $48,000 | Real Estate Tax | 1,416 |
| Investment Income | | | 800 | FICA | 702 |
| (from savings) | | | | Medicare | 684 |
| Gifts (cash) | | | 1,000 | Federal Tax | 6,004 |
| | | | | State Tax | 2,950 |
| | | | | Medical Plan | 1,344 |
| | | | | Pension | 2,064 |
| | | | | Gifts | 1,000 |
| | | | | Auto Repair | 1,000 |
| | | | | Credit Cards | 200 |
| | | | | Home Insurance | 783 |
| | | | | Auto Insurance | 510 |
| | | | | Phone | 672 |
| | | | | Electric & Gas | 1,192 |
| | | | | Food | 5,200 |
| | | | | Clothing | 6,500 |
| | | | | Home Repairs | 2,000 |
| | | | | Entertainment | 2,600 |
| | | | | Vacation | 1,000 |
| | | | | Balance Savings/ | |
| | | | | Investments | 3,795 |
| **Total** | | | **$49,800** | **Total** | **$49,800** |

Incidentally, Bill and Mary are still young enough to be able to keep all their investments in stock, and therefore can take advantage of the high returns available. Their investments are structured as follows:

Bill's 401(k): All equity (TIAA-CREF Growth Fund—Teachers Insurance and Annuity Association College Retirement Fund)

Mary's 401(k): All equity (70 percent Growth, 20 percent SmallCap, 10 percent International)

Roth IRA: All equity (50 percent S&P 500 Index, 50 percent Int'l Index)

Child's Savings: All equity (US Equity Market Index)

Looking good!

# Your Typical Young Guy Living Hand to Mouth

Here is another real-life example. Fred is also a teacher, but he's 30 and single. You can see how the unpaid balance on student loans hinders his opportunities for savings and investment.

## Fred's Balance Sheet as of 7/98

| Assets | | Liabilities | |
|---|---|---|---|
| Checking | 0 | Car Loan | $ 1,000 |
| Retirement Plan | $7,088 | Student Loans | 36,400 |
| Car | 2,000 | Student Loans | 1,000 |
| | | Credit Cards | 325 |
| | $9,088 | | $38,725 |

Net Worth: ($29,634)

## Income Statement as of 7/98 (Monthly)

| Income | | Expenses | |
|---|---|---|---|
| Salary | $2,517 | Federal Tax | $ 275 |
| Other | 147 | State Tax | 170 |
| Gifts from | 90 | FICA | 165 |
| | | Medicare | 39 |
| | | Workers Comp | 2 |
| | | Union Dues | 51 |
| | | Retirement Plan | 160 |
| | | Student Loans | 164 |
| | | (8%) | 243 |
| | | Credit Cards | 15 |
| | | Rent | 615 |
| | | Gifts to | 35 |
| | | Auto Insurance | 70 |
| | | Auto Club | 5 |
| | | Gas | 50 |
| | | Telephone | 40 |
| | | Electricity | 50 |
| | | Cable | 45 |
| | | Water & Sewer | 12 |
| | | Food | 170 |
| | | Entertainment | 200 |
| | | Other | 20 |
| | | Auto Loan | 58 |
| | | To Savings | 100 |
| | $2,754 | | $2,754 |

Fred has a negative net worth, and pretty much lives hand to mouth on a month-to-month basis. The student loans are his big handicap, but the first one will be paid off in November (saving Fred $164 per month). Unfortunately, payments on the other loan increase to $318 per month, so his net savings will be $89 per month.

Fred's very first goal must be to build up an emergency savings balance. Any of life's blips would put him deeper in debt (auto repairs, etc.).

His second goal must be to work off the remaining student loan. Although the interest rate (8 percent) is reasonable, the size of the debt is going to prevent him from getting ahead. But the good thing about looking unflinchingly at your finances like this is it forces you to face your problems—and every problem has a solution. In Fred's case, for example, he might consider taking a part-time job for one or two years to knock off that loan. He could take a roommate or get into a share to lower his rent.

Fred's situation is typical of recent college graduates. They need to catch a break, get a promotion and/or raise, inherit some cash, or all of the above in order to cross over into financial security. Let's hope all three happen to Fred so he can shore up his foundation, which is the focus of our book's next section.

---

### The Least You Need to Know

➤ You can request a statement from Social Security that will show exactly how much per month you can expect to receive from Social Security upon retirement.

➤ Ask your personnel department to figure out how much you stand to receive from your company retirement plan.

➤ You can start financing your own retirement plan to make up the difference between what Social Security and your employer's plan will give you and what you will need.

➤ The sooner you start saving for retirement, the less you'll need to save.

➤ Figure out what percentage of your salary you need to save to meet your goals and stick to it.

➤ Try to stagger college loans and your home mortgage so they don't all hit you at once.

➤ Create a personal balance sheet and income statement at least once a year—on your birthday.

# Part 2
# Shore Up Your Foundation

Prosperity is the fruit of labor. It begins with saving money.

—*Abraham Lincoln*

*Um, we have a personal question: What's the interest rate on your maxed-out credit card? Eighteen percent? Youch! So what if your investments are earning a whopping 20 percent if you're paying 18 percent to those sharks at First Credit of North Dakota? Kinda defeats the purpose, wouldn't you say?*

*Well, you're in luck, because this section is about wiping out debt, trimming your taxes, cutting your spending, and maximizing your job benefits; swabbing your deck and hoisting your sails...sorry, got carried away there for a moment.*

*The point is, this section will help you get your financial ship in strong and seaworthy shape.*

# Chapter 5

# A Closer Look at Employment Benefits

## In This Chapter

➤ Determining your retirement benefits

➤ IRAs

➤ Pensions vs. 401(k) plans

➤ What if you change employers?

➤ Self-employment retirement benefits

➤ Evaluating stock options

How many of you reading this book have invested in an employer-sponsored retirement plan? Can we see a show of hands? Okay, not bad. Now for the real question: How many of you, upon leaving a job and receiving a lump-sum payment out of your retirement account, invested it in your new employer's plan? And, um, how many of you spent it?

That's what we thought. Well, if you did, you're not alone. At least a third of the people who receive lump-sum payments of their retirement savings when they change jobs fail to roll the money over into other tax-deferred accounts, according to the *AARP Bulletin* from July/August 1998. And approximately one-third of employees who qualify for 401(k) plans don't bother to contribute to them at all.

If you never have contributed, it's probably because you don't really know what employer-sponsored retirement plans are and what they can do for you. And you've been too busy to really pay attention to the whole deal anyway. Well, since you've taken the time to crack this book, let us make it easy for you. Let's take a look from the ground up at the kinds of retirement plans that employers offer and the role these plans should play in your investment strategy.

# Retirement Plans 101

Millions of people in this country contribute to retirement accounts sponsored by their employers. There are several types of plans, but they all work on the same basic principle: You don't have to pay taxes on the money you put in your retirement plan until you start taking it out to support yourself during retirement. And no tax is due while it grows. That's why these are called tax-deferred plans.

A corporation is under no legal obligation to set up a 401(k) plan for its employees—it's a perk, part of your total package of employee benefits. In the past, most retirement plans offered by employers were defined benefit plans. The employer promised you a specific pension upon retirement (in other words, the "benefit" was defined) and invested money with insurance companies or bank trusts in order to be able to provide that benefit.

## Defined Contribution Plans at a Glance

Today, most employers offer plans that allow you, the employee, to decide how and where you want to invest your tax-deferred retirement savings. You choose from a menu of investment options offered by the employer. These types of plans are called *defined contribution plans* because the employee decides ("defines") how much he or she is going to contribute. The *benefit* (your retirement income) is not defined because it depends on how much you contribute and how well your investments perform.

The most popular of these plans are 401(k) and 403(b) plans. If you recall from Chapter 4:

➤ *401(k)* plans are for employees of private companies.

➤ *403(b)* plans are for employees of public employers and nonprofits, such as public schools, governments, philanthropic foundations, or police and fire departments.

Tens of millions of employees in this country contribute to 401(k) and 403(b) plans, mainly because many employers add 25¢ or 50¢ or even more to every dollar an employee puts into his or her plan. If your employer contributes to your 401(k) plan like this, there's one simple rule for you to follow: Fund it to the max! This is FREE MONEY you're getting here—and how rare is that?

## Defined Benefit Plans at a Glance

The other main family of retirement plans is *defined benefit plans*. In a defined benefit plan the employer guarantees the sum and is liable if the actual assets are less than the required sum.

➤ In a defined benefit plan, the amount of the employee's pension is established but the employer's contribution is not.

➤ In a defined contribution plan, the employer's contributions are fixed, but the amount of the employee's pension is not.

Now let's get into the various types of plans available in more depth.

# Defined Benefit Plans

As we mentioned in Chapter 4, defined benefit plans are employer-financed plans that promise to pay you a certain sum annually upon retirement. This is the traditional corporate pension plan that many of our parents probably retired on. Employees with pension plans don't contribute to them or help decide how to invest the money in them.

**Investor's Idiom**

In a *defined contribution plan,* the employee decides ("defines") how much he or she is going to contribute. The most popular defined contribution plans are 401(k) and 403(b) plans.

In a *defined benefit plan,* an employer guarantees the sum, or pension, and is liable if the actual assets are less than the required sum.

Most defined benefit plans have four characteristics:

1. A vesting schedule requiring that you work a minimum number of hours per year—a thousand, for example. This eliminates part-timers.

2. A minimum number of years must be vested before qualifying for the pension— five years is common. This is to discourage job-hoppers. The total of vested years you've accumulated is called "credited service."

3. The value of the pension increases as you put more years in at the company.

4. The value of the pension is weighted so that if you work at the company until you retire, the last five years or so before you retire earn you a big chunk of your pension. This is to encourage you to stay at this company until you retire. You maximize your pension by staying put.

## How the Amount of Your Monthly Pension Is Determined

The amount of your pension is based, in the end, on a formula that takes all these factors into consideration. For example, Ralph's Dog Biscuit Company figures out its employees' monthly retirement benefit based on the following convoluted formula:

➤ Take 2 percent of final average monthly pay.

➤ Multiply it by number of vested years (credited service) up to a maximum of 35 years.

**Fiscal Facts**

Just in case some of you have forgotten how to convert a mixed fraction to a decimal, here's the trick: Multiply the denominator (the bottom number of the fraction) by the whole number. Add the resulting number to the numerator (the top number of the fraction). Now, divide the denominator by the new numerator. For example, for the mixed fraction $1^2/_3$:

3 (the denominator) × 1 (the whole number) = 3;

3 + 2 (the numerator) = 5, giving you a new fraction of $^5/_3$;

5 ÷ 3 = 1.66

➤ Subtract $1^2/_3$ percent of Social Security benefit and then multiply the resulting number by credited service up to a maximum of 30 years.

➤ Finally, subtract the latter from the former.

➤ This equals the monthly benefit at age 65.

Whew!

Let's look at an example. Assume loyal Ralph's Dog Biscuit Company employee Scooter Snodgrass will be 65 on January 1, 1999, and will have 20 years of fully vested, credited service at that time. Let's say his Social Security benefit in 1999 is $1,007 a month. Let's also assume that his final average pay is $2,500 a month ($30,000 a year). Now we can apply the formula from hell.

Figure out 2 percent of $2,500 (final average monthly pay), and multiply it by 20 (total vested years of slaving away).

$$2\% = .02$$

$$
\begin{array}{r}
2,500 \\
\times\,.02 \\
\hline
50.00 \\
\times\,20 \\
\hline
\$1,000
\end{array}
$$

Then, subtract $1^2/_3$ percent of $1,007 (the S.S. benefit), and multiply that by 20 (those hard-earned years again)$1^2/_3$ percent expressed as a decimal is 1.66.

$$
\begin{array}{r}
1,007 \\
\times\,1.66 \\
\hline
\$16.72
\end{array}
$$

$$
\begin{array}{r}
16.72 \\
\times\,20 \\
\hline
\$334.40
\end{array}
$$

$$
\begin{array}{r}
1,000 \\
-334.40 \\
\hline
\$665.60
\end{array}
$$

Monthly Benefit = $665.60

Mr. Snodgrass will receive a monthly pension of $665.60, as well as $1,007 per month from Social Security. His total monthly retirement income, unless he has other investments, will be $1,672.60.

# A Whole Lotta Lumps or Just One: The Lump-Sum Option

Pensions are a promise or guarantee from your employer to you to pay a certain sum at a certain age until death. A regular payment over time like this is called an *annuity*. In some cases, you may be given a choice between either the monthly pension payment or receiving the entire pension upon retirement as a lump sum.

How can you tell if the lump sum is better than the monthly payment? Well, first it depends on how involved you want to be. Some people are simply intimidated by large sums of money and are grateful to get a monthly check from their former employer. But you could shop the lump sum to several reputable insurers for their annuity rates and then compare. Many insurers "write" annuities and may offer you a better deal (i.e., higher monthly payment) for your lump sum than your employer's plan does. You can also use your broker or friendly banker to help in the process. However, you will not be given all the time in the world to decide which plan is best for you, so be aware that you need to give this some thought before the day of your retirement party.

If you choose the lump-sum option, you will want to invest it in something that will generate regular interest payments so that you have income to live on. Basically, there are two ways to go:

1. Buy an annuity from an insurance company. You can call up any insurance company and ask about its annuity plans. Ask friends and neighbors to recommend a good insurance agent. Insurance company annuities can be expensive, though. Check out the no-load annuities available from companies like Vanguard, Schwab, or T. Rowe Price.

2. Buy a long U.S. Government Treasury bond. By "long," we mean a bond that takes 20 to 30 years to mature. Long bonds make interest payments twice a year. So if you want monthly interest-payments, you could buy six bonds with different semi-annual interest-payment dates. Bond #1 would pay interest in January and again six months later in July; Bond #2 would pay in February and August; Bond #3 would pay in March and September, etc. Kinda neat, huh? How can you tell when a bond pays interest? Check the maturity date. That tells you one of the two interest dates. The second interest date is six months

**Investor's Idiom**

An *annuity* is an investment that yields fixed payments during the investment holder's lifetime or for a stated number of years. Payments are typically made monthly. A *lump sum*, in contrast, is the entire value of the investment taken in cash at once.

later. For example, if you buy a bond with a maturity date of January 31, 2005, the two interest-payment dates are January 31 and July 31. This way, you will have income coming in every month.

### Investor's Idiom

There are three basic types of securities issued by the U.S. Treasury: *bills*, *notes*, and *bonds*. Bills are short-term investments; that is, they mature in under a year. Notes have longer maturities—from one year to 10 years. Bonds are maturities over ten years. Historically, the Treasury has issued 20- or 30-year bonds. The longest auctioned today are 30 years, which are referred to as the long bond.

### Fiscal Facts

Safeguards to prevent pension plans from defaulting on paying retirement benefits to employees were an important reason for the passage of the Employee Retirement Income Security Act of 1974 (ERISA). ERISA also codified 401(k) and 403(b) plans and prohibited employers from conducting certain transactions with retirement plan dollars.

## If Your Employer Drops the Ball

Note that a defined benefit plan like a pension is a promise to pay on the part of the employer. The employer, or plan sponsor, is totally responsible for providing pension payments to retired employees. Traditional profit-sharing plans only tie the employer's contribution to the plan to the level of profitability of the corporation: no profit, no contribution.

The employer is supposed to be making annual contributions to the company's retirement fund and investing this money wisely. If the CEO embezzles the fund and splits for Rio or the company goes bankrupt—or anything else happens to the employer's ability to pay—the obligation to provide pensions for retirees of the company is turned over to a federal agency called the Pension Benefit Guaranty Corp. (PBGC). Probably not who you expected to be handling your future, but at least it's a back-up plan.

## Defined Contribution Plans

Defined contribution plans, unlike defined benefit plans, limit the employer's role and responsibility. With a 401(k) plan, for example, the employee, if eligible, determines how much of his or her pay is to be deducted for investment purposes, and decides how the dollars are to be invested.

Your employer may offer matching contributions equal to a percentage of how much you contribute to your 401(k) or 403(b). Some employers put in 25 or 50¢ for every dollar you contribute. Others might match, for example, up to 100 percent of the first 6 percent of salary contributed by the employee.

Defined contribution 401(k) plans limit the maximum amount that an employee can contribute on a pre-tax basis, with the current figure around $10,000. Nonprofit employees can typically contribute up to the lesser of 20 percent or $9,500 of their salaries to a 403(b). If you are investing in a 403(b), you will be offered basically a menu of tax-sheltered annuities provided by insurance companies.

This is to prevent the very highest-salaried employees from being able to shelter a much higher share of their income than lower-salaried employees can. It also encourages companies to offer a higher level of matching funds. If the fat cats at the top of your company could shelter huge chunks of their salaries in retirement accounts and the company had to pay them, say, 50¢ on every dollar they saved in their 401(k) plans, pretty soon the company might decide it can only afford to pay 25¢ on the dollar, thus lowering the retirement benefit for everyone.

**Investor's Idiom**

The money that is deducted from your pay before taxes are applied is called *pre-tax dollars*. These enable you to avoid paying taxes on whatever you contribute to your 401(k) or 403(b).

## You Can Contribute After-Tax Dollars, Too

You can also contribute an additional sum in after-tax dollars, typically up to a total of 12 percent. This sum is taxed *before* you put it into the account; however, once it's in the 401(k), it gets to grow tax-deferred until withdrawal. Confusing? Let's look at an example.

Jack earns $30,000 a year. He contributes a total of 12 percent to his 401(k), and his employer matches 50 percent on the first 6 percent of pre-tax dollars. Let's figure out what Jack's total addition to his 401(k) plan is.

Well, 12 percent of Jack's pre-tax salary of $30,000 is $3,600. (Just multiply $30,000 by .12). His employer matches 50 percent on the first 6 percent of pre-tax dollars an employee contributes, which in Jack's case is $1,800. His employer matches 50 percent, or half, of that $1,800, and that means his employer kicks in an additional $900. Cool!

So the total contributed to Jack's 401(k) is the $3,600 he puts in, plus $900 from his employer. That's $4,500.

Jack's W-2 form at the end of the year will reflect the fact that he's contributed some of his salary before taxes. What's the sum that will appear on his W-2 form? W-2 salary $30,000 less 6 percent (in this case, $1,800) = $28,200. The first 6 percent is a deduction from his salary, so the government sees Jack's salary as $28,200.

## If Your Employer Matches, Invest the Max

Why wouldn't everybody do what Jack does? This is "found" money! If your employer offers a 401(k) with any matching percent contribution, contribute to get the full benefit. Don't hesitate, don't quibble, just do it.

To be perfectly clear, talk to your personnel or HR representative and confirm the maximum employer contribution and the maximum amount you can contribute and still have the sum deducted before taxes from your salary.

### Investor's Idiom

An *IRA* is an Individual Retirement Account. Basically, it's a shell that protects money you put in it from taxation until you start to take money out. A *Rollover IRA* is used to shelter money that was in a 401(k) at your job when you change jobs and find you have nowhere else to put it.

### Fiscal Facts

If your employer puts money in your 401(k) account when you do, definitely invest the maximum you are entitled to invest each year. Your employer is simply giving you money when it matches your investment—how often does that happen? Even if your employer doesn't match, investing as much as you can afford in a 401(k) is wise, because the investment options offered are usually really solid.

If your employer does not offer a matching contribution but does offer a 401(k), it's still a good idea to make it part of your retirement plan. Your best bet will probably be some combination of a traditional IRA, Roth IRA, and the 401(k) (don't worry, we're going to get into this more later). For now, all you need to know is that IRA stands for Individual Retirement Account. It's an account you set up for yourself, as opposed to something arranged by an employer. IRAs also offer some really nice tax deductions.

So, you may want to put most of your yearly contributions into an IRA and contribute to your 401(k) any additional sum you can afford. Why not just by-pass the 401(k)? Because even if your employer's not offering matching funds, that menu of investment options it offers has been carefully chosen and is probably quite solid. Managers of mutual funds and other investments compete quite intensely to convince corporations to offer their funds as 401(k) plan options.

## Can I Borrow from My 401(k)?

Can Jack take or borrow any of this money? Yes, but only under certain conditions enforced by the employer (and dictated by the federal government). If he borrows it, he will have to pay competitive interest rates established by the employer. It is strongly recommended that this option be utilized only for a dire emergency, and that any sum borrowed be repaid ASAP!

You can borrow from your 401(k) for any reason. You can borrow up to $1/2$ of your total vested amount (typically in increments of $100). There's usually a minimum amount (e.g., $1,000) and a maximum (usually the lesser of 50% of what's vested or $50,000). The interest rate you are charged when you borrow from your 401(k) is competitive and you can choose a repayment period of anywhere from 3 to 54 months. If you don't pay back the loan according to its terms, the amount of the loan will be considered a taxable distribution to you and you will owe taxes!

## *What If I Change Employers?*

What if Jack leaves his employer? What happens to his 401(k)?

➤ Jack could leave his 401(k) with his old employer. Some employers allow you to maintain your account in their 401(k).

➤ If Jack's old employer won't allow him to do that, or he doesn't want to, he could transfer his 401(k) assets into his new employer's 401(k) plan. No tax will be generated by this transfer.

➤ Jack could establish a separate IRA account and transfer his assets to this account. He has 60 days to do this before the assets will be taxed and subject to a 10 percent penalty. Because he is *rolling over* his assets into another account, this is called a Rollover IRA.

Once you create a Rollover IRA, you can't move those funds in the future to a traditional IRA or a 401(k) plan.

# Should You Put All Your Eggs in the Company Basket?

Often, a company will offer its employees an opportunity to buy its stock as part of the menu for its 401(k) plan. At first glance, this might seem like a pretty good idea. Why not have your company act as a stockbroker for you? You give them all your blood, sweat, and tears, why not let them work for you? Well, because on closer examination this may not be such a great idea. Even if the stock is being offered to you at a discount, you'll be putting all of your eggs in the company basket. Your future is already heavily invested in the success of your company—you work there! To invest your savings with it, too, goes against the principle of diversification we talked about earlier.

**Crash Alert**

Bear in mind that when you leave a job you have only 60 days to shelter your 401(k) from that job before the IRS swoops down on it. Even though changing jobs is hectic, make sure you either arrange to keep that money in the 401(k) plan at your old job or transfer it to your new employer's 401(k) or to a Rollover IRA.

**Crash Alert**

We've seen several instances where employees had all their 401(k) or profit-sharing money in company stock and the company went bankrupt, leaving them with nothing. We're not trying to scare you, and you may work for one of the biggest and sturdiest companies in the world, but dire consequences can affect any company.

If you do want to own some company stock in your 401(k), you should limit it to what you would invest in if you were creating your own equity portfolio. A good rule of thumb is to invest no more than 4 percent of your portfolio in the stock of any individual company, so apply that rule to your company's stock. And don't worry, your employer can't punish you for taking minimal or no participation in the company stock option. There are laws against that. One advantage of share ownership, though, is that it entitles you to receive annual reports and other information that goes to stockholders, so you can keep current on your company and its fiscal healthiness (or lack thereof), if you so desire.

# What About Stock Options?

If your company offers you *stock options*, as opposed to stock, go for it. These can be very profitable. You'd be amazed how many top executives in corporate America own little or no stock in their companies, but have large stock option grants.

Because there is no risk—you don't exercise your option unless the exercise price is less than the current price and you can make a profit—stock options are really a form of compensation.

If you are eligible for stock options, there are two things you can do with them:

**Investor's Idiom**

A *stock option* is the right, but not the obligation, to buy a stock at a fixed price after a specified period of time (usually 12 months) for a fixed period of time (10 years). Prices and time periods are all specified in the option contract.

**Investor's Idiom**

A *capital gain* is any money you intake from an investment. If you've held the investment longer than one year, the capital gain is not subject to income tax; instead, it's subject to capital gains tax, which is typically lower.

1. *Buy and sell on the same day.* You immediately exercise your option because the strike price is less than the current price and you can make a profit. You purchase the shares and sell the shares on the same day. This saves you the trouble of having to raise the money to buy the stock. You simply go to your human resources person and say you want to exercise your stock option. Your profit is taxed at ordinary income tax rates (which can be as high as 39.6 percent, depending on your tax bracket). You pay tax on the amount resulting from the difference between the exercise price (sometimes called the "strike" price) and the sales price.

2. *Hold onto the stock now, sell later.* You can buy the stock and hold it, hoping that its price will go up and you can sell at a profit. First, you'll need the money to buy the stock. It can come either from your own savings or by borrowing from your friendly banker. Then you exercise your option,

or buy the stock. If you hold the stock for at least one year, you are taxed at capital gains rates (maximum of 20 percent), which is probably lower than your income tax rate. You just have to keep your fingers crossed that the stock's price will go up and stay up.

What would we do? Well, we prefer the bird in the hand rather than trying to search through those damn bushes, so we'd probably choose the same-day transaction and deal with the ugly income tax. But, hey, this is your decision: You know your inclination, you know the company's prospects, and you know your personal financial situation. Take all of these factors into consideration before you make your decision.

# No Company Plan? Create a Pension with an IRA

What's an IRA? Nope, it's not the Irish Republican Army, although it can pack the same punch. IRA stands for Individual Retirement Account. This is a retirement account that you set up for yourself, as opposed to a 401(k) or 403(b), which would be set up by your employer.

The IRA itself is not an investment, it's a tax-sheltered account into which you put money that you can then invest as you choose. You don't have to pay taxes on the money that accumulates until you start taking it out after retirement. Whether you choose a traditional IRA or a Roth IRA, a working spouse can contribute $2,000 per year for him- or herself and $2,000 per year for a nonworking spouse to an IRA set up in the nonworking spouse's name.

There are several different kinds of IRAs, each with its own quirks and purpose:

➤ *Traditional IRA*—developed in 1975 to help people who were not covered by an employer-sponsored retirement plan to save for retirement.

➤ *Rollover IRA*—used to shelter retirement savings that have been taken out of a 401(k) due to job change.

➤ *Roth IRA*—these were created in 1998 to give people a little more flexibility when saving for retirement, buying a house, or financing children's education. For example, if you've invested in a Roth IRA for at least five years, you can take up to $10,000 out to make a down payment on a first home.

➤ *SEP-IRA*—a Simplified Employee Pension; essentially an IRA for someone who is self-employed. A SEP is like a 401(k), but contributions are limited to 15 percent or $30,000, whichever is less.

➤ *SIMPLE-IRA*—the Savings Incentive Match Plan for Employees is a new option for self-employed people that's growing in popularity because they are very easy to use.

Whatever IRA best suits your purpose, you can set it up with a bank, broker, or a mutual fund company.

# When Is a Roth IRA the Right Choice?

In general, the younger you are and the less money you make, the more attractive the Roth IRA option is. Your adjustable gross income (AGI) must be less than $100,000 (or less than $150,000 combined for married working couples) for you to be eligible for a Roth IRA. So if you earn more than that, guess what? You can skip this section!

### Investor's Idiom

Your *gross income* is the income reported on your W-2 form, plus interest income, rents, royalties, alimony, etc. To calculate your *adjusted gross income* (AGI), the IRS makes a few minor adjustments, such as medical account deductions. Gross income and AGI are usually pretty similar.

Traditional IRAs have no income limit, so if your income fluctuates, you may want to set up both a Roth and a traditional IRA. That way you can contribute to the Roth IRA in the years your income is low enough for you to qualify and contribute to the traditional IRA when your income is higher.

The Roth IRA offers three huge advantages:

1. flexibility
2. no taxes on earnings/asset growth
3. an opportunity to pass money onto your children tax free

Let's look at each advantage in more depth.

## Wiggle Room

Traditional IRAs allow you to start taking money out of them as early as age $59^1/_2$ and require you to begin distributions by age $70^1/_2$. In addition, if you take money out of a traditional IRA before age $59^1/_2$, you'll be hit with taxes and a substantial penalty.

In contrast, there is no age at which you are required to start spending down your Roth IRA, and as long as your Roth IRA account has been open at least five years, you can take out up to $10,000, penalty-free, to buy a first home.

### Investor's Idiom

The *Roth IRA* is a new type of IRA that is more flexible than the traditional IRA but is only available to individuals earning under $100,000 or families earning under $150,000 a year. You can't take money out of a traditional IRA before age $59^1/_2$ without being penalized, but as long as your Roth IRA has been open for at least five years, you can withdraw up to $10,000 to buy a first home.

## No Taxes on Asset Growth— Whoopee!

When you start withdrawing money from a traditional IRA, you pay taxes on the earnings (not the contributions) as if it's ordinary income. With the Roth IRA, any gains that your invested dollars have earned are tax-free upon withdrawal, provided that the account has been open for at least five years and you are older than $59^1/_2$.

## Passing Along the Wealth

If you don't need the money you put into your Roth IRA to keep you in golf balls during retirement, the Roth offers an amazing tax break for your heirs. First, you don't have to start taking distributions at $70^1/_2$, like you do with the traditional IRA. So you can leave your kids quite the tax-sheltered pile.

If you name a child (or children) as beneficiary, the monthly distributions from a traditional or a Roth IRA will go to that child upon your death. With the traditional IRA, the distributions are taxable. With the Roth, they aren't. And, of course, the money passed onto them continues to grow tax-free.

# Converting a Traditional IRA to a Roth IRA

If you decide to convert your traditional IRA to a Roth IRA, be aware that you will have to pay taxes on the earnings in the traditional IRA. Remember, the government will tax that money as soon as it comes out from under the IRA tax-protection shell. In addition, you must pay these taxes from a source other than the IRA.

Be aware, though, that the amount of money coming out of the traditional IRA during conversion is added to your adjusted gross income. If it's added all at once, this can really screw things up by putting you over the $100,000 income limit required for you to be eligible to open a Roth IRA.

Converting an existing IRA to a Roth requires that taxpayers have less than $100,000 in adjusted gross income (whether single or married).

**Fiscal Facts**

Between you and us, most of these estate-planning issues favoring the Roth IRA represent forsaken dollars on the part of the federal government. How long until politicians notice this and close the loopholes? If you're interested, you'd better act soon. And if you switch by the end of 1998, you can spread out the taxes due on the switch over four years, instead of having to pay them all at once.

|  | Roth IRA | Traditional IRA |
|---|---|---|
| Maximum Annual Contribution per Person | $2,000 | $2,000 |
| Who Is Eligible | Earned income below $110,000 (single) and $160,000 (joint); $2,000 applies to any combination of Roth and Traditional. | Unlimited income; anyone under age $70^1/_2$. |

*continues*

*continued*

|  | Roth IRA | Traditional IRA |
| --- | --- | --- |
|  | $2,000 contribution allowance phases out between $95,000 to $110,000 (single) and $150,000 to $160,000 (joint). |  |
|  | Nonworking spouse can contribute up to $2,000. | Ditto. |
| Tax Advantages | Investment grows free from federal income tax. | Growth is tax-deferred; taxes paid on earnings when money is withdrawn. |
| Tax Deductibility of Contributions | Not tax deductible. | Based on adjusted gross income (for 1998 tax year) of $30–40,000 (single) and $50–60,000 joint. This range represents maximum minimum deductibility. |
| Withdrawal of Assets | Free from federal income tax if account open 5 years *and* age 59$^1/_2$ *or* purchase of first home ($10,000 lifetime cap) *or* permannent disability or death. | Penalty-free withdrawals before age 59$^1/_2$ *only* for first-time home or higher education. Taxes apply on earnings withdrawn. Other withdrawals before age 59$^1/_2$ subject to 10% penalty tax. |
| Age Limit for Contributions/ Distributions | None. | No contributions after age 70$^1/_2$. Distributions must begin at age 70$^1/_2$. |
| Rollovers and Transfers | Can rollover Traditional IRA to Roth if adjusted gross income no more than $100,000. Sum subject to taxation. | Can transfer to and from other Traditional IRAs. Can rollover from employer plans (e.g., 401[k]). |

# The Two Best Investments for Your IRA: Stocks and STRIPs

Okay, so you've set up your retirement accounts and now the question is this: What the heck should you put in them? No need to rack your brain, because we've got the answer: stock mutual funds and Treasury STRIPs. We'll explain STRIPs in the next section, but first, let's look at stocks.

## Stocking Up

If you look at consecutive 10-year periods of time going back 40 to 50 years, stocks made investors more money than Treasury bonds and T-bills 80 percent of the time.

You can use this little nugget of financial history to your advantage when investing for your IRA. First, you'll want to spread out your retirement savings among a broadly diversified list of stocks. Why? So you minimize the risk of any one company going under and taking your savings with it. To be truly diversified, you should own at least 25 stocks, ideally 50. If we assume that you're going to own 100 shares of each stock and that the average stock prices are $25–$50 a share, the minimum diversified portfolio would require $62,500–$125,000. Do you have this amount of savings to invest in common stocks?

Most of us don't. So, the best place to get stock for your IRA is from mutual funds. Stock mutual funds companies collect money from many investors, pool it, and use the pool to buy stocks. Yes, you could pick your own stocks, but do you have the time, and do you think you will beat an established mutual fund? Probably not. Mutual funds provide the small investor with far greater diversification than he or she could achieve alone. With a mutual fund, you own a share of the fund, and the fund may own hundreds of stocks. Don't forget, you're probably only eligible to contribute $2,000 a year.

### Investor's Idiom

A *mutual fund* is a company that collects money from investors and invests on their behalf, usually in diversified securities.

We'll get into mutual funds in Chapter 12, but for now just think about looking for funds with:

➤ At least $100 million in assets

➤ Low expenses—some "active" funds charge for expenses as high as 1.5 percent, and these expenses come right out of your return. Your investment could be earning 10 percent, but if the fund takes 1.5 percent, your return is only 8.5.

➤ At least a five-year or, more ideally, a ten-year history, a consistent investment approach, and a manager who has been associated with the fund for at least five years.

## STRIP Tease

Your IRA should also include some bonds (also referred to as fixed-income securities) to balance out your stock. For the fixed-income (bond) portion of your IRA, we recommend *Treasury STRIPs*.

If you recall our discussion earlier in this chapter about Treasury bonds, you'll remember that they pay interest income twice a year. Upon maturity, you'll also get your principal back.

A STRIP is one piece that has been "stripped" from a Treasury note or bond. For example, let's take a 20-year Treasury bond. It consists of 40 coupons (those two interest payments a year we mentioned earlier) and the principal payment. So that's 41 blocks of money. A STRIP is one of those 41 blocks of money. It could be the 13th coupon, it could be the 20th coupon, it could be the principal payment—it doesn't matter. What you're buying is that Treasury STRIP.

If the coupon can be redeemed at maturity 20 years from now, at, say, $100,000, it'll sell for around $20,000 to $25,000 now. That's its "discount price." You buy it today for that price knowing that you'll get $100,000 for it 20 years from now. You would buy it at a discount and redeem it at maturity for its full price.

The advantage that Treasury STRIPs have over other fixed-income options is you don't have to do anything but hold the STRIP until it matures. So whatever percentage of bonds you decide to hold in your IRA, think about Treasury STRIPs, because they're no-brainers for tax-sheltered accounts.

## What to Do When You're Small and Solo

Small businesses are defined as businesses:

➤ With fewer than 100 employees

➤ With annual revenues below $1 million

Whether you are self-employed or an employer with a limited number of employees, you are entitled (but not required) to set up a retirement plan for yourself (and your employees, if you choose). If you are a sole proprietor without employees, your best retirement-plan choice is a *SEP-IRA* or *SIMPLE-IRA*. If you have employees, however, a *Keogh* plan would be a better bet.

A Keogh is a pension plan that allows business owners to shelter more income than SEPs or SIMPLEs do and to create vesting schedules and pensions for employees.

A SEP-IRA, or Simplified Employee Pension, is essentially an IRA for someone who is self-employed. A SEP is like a 401(k), but contributions are limited to 15% or $30,000, whichever is less; a good retirement-plan choice for a sole proprietor who doesn't have employees.

A SIMPLE-IRA, or Savings Incentive Match Plan for Employees, is a new option for self-employed people that's growing in popularity because it is very easy to use.

A Keogh has two advantages over a SEP-IRA for anyone who has a few employees, but not enough to go to the hassle and expense of setting up a 401(k):

1. An entrepreneur with employees can set up vesting schedules, which require employees to remain with the company a number of years to qualify for full retirement benefits. Part-timers are typically not qualified, for example.

2. Because these are qualified plans, you (or your employee) can "roll over" the assets into another company's qualified plan.

**Investor's Idiom**

The new inflation-indexed bonds are also tempting because they represent insurance in the event that inflation flares up once again. If inflation rises dramatically, the profit from your $100,000 STRIP may not be able to purchase as much time on the golf course as you'd hoped in 20 years. How about a combination for your IRA: $3/4$ STRIPs, $1/4$ inflation-indexed Treasuries? Works for me!

Keoghs are a lot cheaper to set up than 401(k) plans, which can be too costly for a small business to handle.

But there's a lot of paperwork because a Keogh is a qualified plan, meaning it is specifically approved by the Internal Revenue Service. Because the Keogh is a qualified plan, the employer (or self-employed individual) must fill out and file specific forms each year for the IRS. Either you hire a specialist to draw up your plan, or you can use a prototype that is offered by a number of banks. The prototype will save you money.

## Adding a Money Purchase Pension to the Mix

With a Keogh, you can contribute up to 15 percent of your earned income (if you're self-employed) or 15 percent of your employees' salaries, subject to a $30,000 maximum.

Typically, you would do so by establishing a traditional profit-sharing plan. In addition, if you wish, you can also establish a *money purchase pension trust*. This allows the employee or self-employed individual to increase the percentage that can be contributed from 15 percent to 25 percent. You are still limited, however, to a total of $30,000 combined for the two plans.

The profit-sharing plan defines under what circumstances a contribution will be made for qualified employees. You could decide that qualified employees are those with at least 1,000 hours of work for two consecutive years. The employer contributes, the employee benefits, but the benefit is not defined, and the employee has no voice (unless self-employed) in how the contribution is invested.

Quick quiz: This means a profit-sharing plan is:

a. a defined contribution plan

b. a defined benefit plan

### Investor's Idiom

A *sole proprietor* is someone who owns a business and has no partners. A SEP-IRA or SIMPLE-IRA is usually a good retirement plan choice for a sole proprietor who doesn't have employees. An entrepreneur with partners or with employees should look into Keogh plans, which allow business owners to shelter more income than do SEPs or SIMPLEs and to create vesting schedules for employees.

If you answered "a," congratulations! A profit-sharing plan is indeed a defined contribution, rather than a defined benefit, plan.

A money purchase pension plan is also a defined contribution plan, in that no benefit is defined. However, it differs from a straight profit-sharing plan because a contribution must be made each year to each qualified employee. With a profit-sharing plan, the amount the business owner decides to contribute is not set in stone; with the money-purchase pension plan, it is set—unless you go through the hassle of amending the plan. Once you decide to contribute a certain percentage to a money purchase pension plan, you must do it. These plans are most popular, as a result, with clinic doctors, lawyers in small firms, or other professionals who have pretty high, relatively stable, incomes.

Whew! Aren't you glad you learned that? Dazzle 'em at your next cocktail party.

---

### The Least You Need to Know

➤ If your employer contributes to your 401(k) plan, fund it to the max.

➤ Ask human resources to help you figure out your monthly pension, if you have a defined benefit plan.

➤ If you take a lump-sum retirement payment, invest it in something that will generate income for you to live on.

➤ Don't over-invest in your company's stock.

➤ Stock options can be very profitable employment benefits.

➤ In general, the younger you are and the less money you make, the more attractive the Roth IRA option is.

➤ The best investments for your IRA are stock mutual funds and Treasury STRIPs.

➤ Keogh plans are good for small-business owners with employees and/or significant income to shelter.

# Chapter 6

# Cutting Expenses *Is* Investing!

---

### In This Chapter

➤ Getting a grip on your spending

➤ Figuring your marginal tax rate

➤ Fresh ideas on how to cut expenses

➤ Little things that add up

---

Believe it or not, it's a lot easier to spend $1 less than to earn $1 more. How so? Well, to earn more, you either have to work longer hours or take greater risks with your investments (remember the relationship between risk and return?). What's more, you pay taxes on each additional dollar you earn on your job—but saving is free!

Someone once said that the best exercise for losing weight is to push yourself away from the table. The same is true of savings: Just push yourself away from that sales counter! Spending can be addictive for many people, but learning to "just say no" is one of the best things you can do for your financial security.

## Become a Hunter/Gatherer

In Chapter 4, we provided two real-life illustrations of personal balance sheets and income statements. One set was for Fred, a young man who, if you recall, was not in great financial shape. The other was for Bill and Mary, a happy couple on the right track. One set of financial statements took about 20 minutes to compile, while it took over a day to sort out the expense side for the other set. Can you guess which set took longer to compile? (Hint: Who was in the bigger mess?)

You can't save if you don't know what you have, and the only way to figure it out is to gather information on your spending habits. So, be a gatherer! Get a notebook and create a page for each spending category (clothing, groceries, etc.), and total them up each month. Use the personal income statement we provided in Chapter 4 to make a monthly income statement for yourself. After 12 months, you'll see some patterns emerging. Was the August clothing bill higher because you took advantage of summer markdowns, or because of heavy back-to-school purchases? Did you notice your entertainment costs rising with the barometer in the summer because it was too hot to put on the stove and you ate out a lot? How about the holidays? Did your credit card bills double because you made all of your purchases in November and December?

### Super Strategy

Learn to buy off season. For instance, purchase your holiday cards in January or a winter coat in April. Because no one else is thinking about purchasing these items on the off-season, the demand is low and the price is right!

Pay close attention to these patterns. Once you start getting a grip on your spending, you will become addicted to saving because it gives you both dollars and personal satisfaction. It all begins with the monthly drill of accumulating and tabulating your expenses. It's your money, and you work hard for it. Why not work just a little harder to hold onto it?

# Your Tax Bracket Is Higher Than You Think

Saving becomes even more attractive when you realize that because income tax is graduated, you pay more tax on the last few dollars you earn than you do on the bulk of your income. For example, if you earn $35,000 a year and pay $3,500 in federal income tax, that doesn't mean you are in the 10 percent tax bracket. It means you pay an average of 10 percent in taxes on your income. But in reality, you pay no income tax on the first few thousand and probably closer to 35 percent on the last few. Now, if you were given a raise of $2,000 you'd pay nearly $500 of it in federal income tax and $153 to Social Security. That's $653 in federal tax on $2,000. That's a tax bracket of around 33 percent! So, for every additional dollar you earn, you have to pay at least *a third* in taxes. Ouch! This tax rate is called your *marginal tax rate*.

# Figuring Your Marginal Tax Rate

We love to move from the theoretical to the painfully real in this book, so dig out your 1996 tax return and let's figure out your marginal tax rate. If you look at your tax return (we know, it brings back painful memories, but bear with us), you will see a line at the bottom of the first page that is repeated at the top of the second page. This is called *adjusted gross income*, or AGI. Next, you will see a line for your deductions, either *standard* or *itemized*. The *net difference* is the amount of your income that was subject to taxes. Now you are ready to compute your tax owed. Let's assume your income subject to taxes is $80,000 and you are "married filing jointly." What is your tax, your tax rate, and your marginal tax rate?

Your tax is $17,187. How did we get this? The tax on the first $40,100 is stated as being $6,015. Reading across, though, it's clear that you are taxed at 28 percent for sums over $40,100. This is your marginal tax rate.

Now, $80,000 − $40,100 = $39,900. This is the amount of your earnings that is taxed at the marginal tax rate of 28 percent. So the amount of tax you pay on that $39,900 is $39,900 × .28 = $11,172. The total amount of tax you pay, therefore, is the $6,015 due on the first $40,100 plus the $11,172 due on the remaining $39,900, or $17,187. Your average tax rate is $17,187 ÷ $80,000 = 21.5 percent. However, every additional dollar of income over $80,000 (up to the next bracket at $96,900) is taxed at 28 percent, i.e., your marginal tax rate. (Of course, there are still state and local taxes that affect your income as well, which can drive up the taxes on those additional dollars as high as 50 percent.)

### Investor's Idiom

Our income tax is *progressive* (as opposed to flat) meaning the more money you make, the more tax you pay per dollar. You pay no tax, in fact, on the first few dollars you earn and progressively more tax as you earn more. The rate you pay on the last few dollars you earn is your *marginal tax rate.*

### Crash Alert

Federal (and state) tax withholding represents another area of potential savings. Many people over-withhold so they get a nice refund check after the tax year is over. But this lets the government, rather than you, earn interest on that money. Consider a $1,200 tax refund. If you had saved the $100 per month at 5 percent interest, instead of letting the government hold onto it, you'd be $30 ahead, because you'd get to use the money for about 6 months.

# Risk-Free Saving Where You Least Expect It

The coolest thing about saving is that it's the one investment activity that breaks the rule about high returns requiring you to take on greater risk. Let's say you have a newborn and you run through five packs of diapers a week. Buying them individually, each pack costs $5, so you spend $25 a week on diapers. Zowie, that's $100 a month on diapers. Turns out, the store sells a case of diapers, which is one month's worth, at a 20 percent discount. On $100 worth of diapers, that discount is $20. The case of diapers costs $80. Hmmm… let's figure out your return on this investment.

Before, you paid $25 a week for diapers. Now, you're putting out $80 for a month's worth. Your discount price on every pack of diapers is $4. Over a year, that will add up to a savings of $260 (i.e, $5 × 52 weeks = $260). So, for investing a measly $80 in discount diapers each month, you earn a return of $260. If we apply the ROI formula from Chapter 2, that's a return on investment of over 20 percent!

$1040 (actual annual expense) – $1300 (annual full price) ÷ $1300 × 100 = 20 percent

And the only risk is that your baby will become miraculously toilet trained before you get a chance to use up that case of diapers (you wish!). Even better, the government doesn't get its hands on that $208. It's tax-free and it's yours, all yours. If you really want to feel like a hotshot, figure that if your marginal tax rate is around 30 percent, you would have had to earn $208 plus $62.40 to cover the taxes to come up with $208. Saving money wherever you can is definitely the road to riches. The rest of this chapter should give you some fresh ideas on how to cut expenses on things like:

➤ shopping

➤ car expenses

➤ banking

➤ life insurance

➤ real estate taxes

➤ credit card fees

Let the saving begin….

# Buying Bulk Is a Great Investment

Buying in bulk, as in the example above, is a great way to save, provided that you keep it in perspective. Do you have to pile towels on the floor because the linen closet is filled with bargain toilet paper? Do you have to park your car outside because the garage is filled with discount tires? Don't laugh; we've seen it all! Just keep a couple of simple rules in mind and you'll be fine.

1. Are you taking advantage of a special sale at your local supermarket, or driving across town to a warehouse place like BJ's or Sam's? If it's the latter, is there a membership fee, and how much? Remember, you have to mentally amortize (write off) the fee against your savings. Be sure to do this. As an example, the BJ membership fee is $35 per year. Are you saving enough by making purchases there to make the $35 fee worthwhile? The fee may well be worth it for you, but be aware of it.

2. Try to limit your purchases to around a three-month supply as opposed to a year supply—unless you're planning on converting your home into a mini-supermarket, that is. And remember, prices can go down as well as up. So, if you buy a one-year supply of chocolate chip cookies after a long period of price increases, you may have bought at the "top," with little or no savings to show.

3. Factor in transportation costs. I know people in New York City who drive to Vermont and Maine to shop at factory outlet stores, only they forget to factor in the cost of the gas they spend, not to mention their time. And sometimes the prices aren't much better than they are locally.

### Investor's Idiom

To *amortize* means to write off a debt or fee over time. If you pay a fee of $240 a year to join a gym, for example, you might want to amortize that fee over the year by including $20 a month on your monthly income statement as your gym fee.

# Your Car: Leasing vs. Ownership

There are two ways to look at this issue: first, from an aesthetic point of view, and second, from a financial point of view. If you simply like to drive around in a new car every two to three years, either because it makes you feel good or because you feel it is important for your business image, then lease. If, on the other hand, you want the least-expensive alternative, then buy (or take out a loan).

## *Advantages of Leasing*

What are the advantages of leasing? Well, there's that thrill of driving a new car every two or three years. In addition, because the monthly payments are less, you are able to drive a more expensive car. Why are the payments less? Because you are not buying the car, you are simply paying for the depreciation, or the wear and tear, on the vehicle. When the lease is up, the dealer retains title to the car.

You also have a little more flexibility: at the end of the lease, you can walk away or purchase the car. Why is this important? Well, seen many Peugeot or British Sterling dealers lately? If you had purchased either car around seven years ago, you would not be a happy camper; chalk up one for leasing. On

### Investor's Idiom

*Depreciation* is the loss in value of an item over time due to wear and tear. Like amortization, the financial reflection of depreciation can be spread out over time. If you own a computer and use it in your home business, for example, the IRS allows you to deduct part of the computer's value each year as a depreciation expense.

the other hand, if you leased a Mazda Miata in 1990 for 36 months, your purchase-option price (the price you can buy the car for at the end of the lease) would have been 10–20 percent less than the then current market value. So, you could have purchased the car and immediately sold it at a profit. Finally, if you use the car in your business, you can deduct the rental payments on your business tax return.

## Disadvantages of Leasing

Leasing sounds pretty good so far, right? Let's look at the negatives and how to reduce some of them.

1. *Capitalized Cost Deduction.* This is the leasing equivalent of a down payment. The larger this figure, the lower your monthly payments. You can usually negotiate this figure lower, sometimes a lot lower. Just make sure you do so without budging on the monthly payment.

2. *Disposition Fee.* This is a fee charged if you do not buy the car. Tell the dealer you don't want to pay this fee (or have the dealer deduct this cost from some other category).

3. *Excess Wear and Tear.* This is subjective and determined by each individual dealer at his or her discretion. What about parking lot "dingers," or a broken outside mirror or antenna? Are these excess or normal? Have the dealer define excess wear and tear for you—in writing.

4. *Annual Mileage Allowance.* This usually runs 10,000–15,000 miles per year. You get no credit if you use less than the allowance and you pay a penalty (e.g., 20¢ per mile) if you run over the allowance. Be sure to determine your projected miles before making the lease decision. If you know your mileage will be greater than the allowance, you can usually "buy" additional miles (e.g., 10¢ per mile), but excess mileage can be an expensive proposition.

Here's an extreme example: Jack's contract reads 10,000 miles per year on a 36-month lease, with excess miles charged at 20¢ per mile. His actual mileage turns out to be 60,000 (20,000 per year). His charge for excess miles of 30,000 (60,000 actual – 30,000 contractual) is $6,000 (30,000 × 20¢)! Ouch! Even if he'd bought an extra 10,000 miles per year for 10¢ per mile, he's still out $3,000! Bottom line: If you are going to put a lot of miles on your car, don't lease.

## The Bottom Line on Leasing

Every situation is different, but in general:

➤ The economics favor leasing if you plan to own the car for under two years.

➤ It's a toss-up for years three and four.

➤ The economics favor buying if you plan to own your car for more than four years. Why? Because when you buy, you are financing something that will have some value when you stop making payments. All you are financing with a lease is depreciation. At the end of a lease period you have nothing. The costs of actually buying a car are simple and few in number: rate (in percent) and monthly financing charge, plus any paperwork fee. And, of course, how much you want, or have, to put down (down payment).

If you do go for the lease option, try to limit your search to cars on a lease "special." These are deals made when the manufacturer and/or dealer absorbs some of your cost and gives up some of their profit to promote a particular model. Why? Well, perhaps they have an excess inventory. For example, assume a Mazda Millenia is priced at $30,000 and the dealers are offering a "special" 36-month lease (no money down) of $325 per month. The upgraded S version, meanwhile, might be priced at $36,000, or 20 percent more. However, there is no special lease, and the best you can do is $475 per month for 36 months, or 46 percent more.

So, if you plan to put low mileage on your car and trade it in frequently, it pays for you to use a lease—but only go for cars on a special lease package. Otherwise, buy your car and bargain down everything and anything you can. It's your money! If you want additional information on leasing, check out the following websites:

1. The Federal Reserve Board's worldwide website at **www.bog.frb.fed.us/pubs/ leasing/guide.htm**

2. There is also an on-line worksheet to determine leasing pluses and minuses at **www.leasesource.com**

For more general information on car pricing and leasing, call *Consumer Reports* at 1-800-205-2445 or visit their Web site at **www.consumerreports.org**.

Other great sources of info:

➤ *Edmund's Automobile Buyer's Guide*: **www.edmund.com**

➤ *Kelley Blue Book* (indispensable if you are going to sell your current car or trade it in on a new one): **www.kbb.com**

## If You Buy a Car

If you can own your car for at least eight years, you will have maximized your investment. Before buying, don't forget to check the Internet for the lowest prices and read magazines like *Consumer Reports* for helpful tips. Above all, shop around for your financing; don't just accept the dealer's rate. Here again, the Internet can be a great source of helpful information, as can local banks.

Finally, if you live in an urban area, make sure you really need a car. If you do, don't forget to factor in the cost of parking. Good public transportation can be a great alternative, supplemented by rentals when you need a vehicle for vacations or specific trips. The savings can be substantial.

# Car Insurance—Shop Around!

Now that you've got that snazzy car in your garage, you're facing the big bite that is car insurance. Probably the easiest way to scope out auto insurance deals is via *Consumer Reports*. For a charge of $12 for the first vehicle ($8 for each additional vehicle), *Consumer Reports* will:

1. Analyze up to 175 different policies to find the company that meets your needs.

2. Provide you with a personal report listing up to 25 of the lowest-priced policies.

3. Provide a *How to Buy Auto Insurance* guide.

Call *Consumer Reports*'s auto insurance price comparison line at 1-800-807-8050. As of the date of this writing, the service is available only to residents of 15 states, so check to see if your state is included.

### Investor's Idiom

There are basically three types of insurance everyone needs to carry:

➤ Life insurance, which provides income for your family in the event of your death.

➤ Health insurance, including disability income insurance. Disability insurance should cover 50–75 percent of your salary. Make sure it's non-cancelable and guaranteed renewable.

➤ Liability insurance, which covers you if anyone sues because they are injured on your property or by your car. You'll save a bundle in premiums if you look to cover only major losses, not minor ones.

# Choosing a Bank

Banks make money by taking in deposits from customers and lending them out to other customers. That's why banks pay you less interest on your savings account than they charge you when you want a loan. The difference is the bank's profit. If a bank pays you 4 percent on your savings account and lends money to a company for 12 percent, the bank has made 8 percent. Different banks pay different savings account and CD rates, however, so shop around before you choose a bank. Many local newspapers carry various bank-account fees in table format once a week; check in the financial section of yours.

If convenience is important to you, make a short list of banks near your home or workplace. Think about the types of bank accounts you want, and then comparison shop via telephone. Before you do, estimate roughly how many checks you write per month. Different banks have different fees and requirements. Some banks will require a minimum balance, but will waive check-writing fees if you keep that balance. Others allow you, say, five free checks a month. Others charge you for each check you write, no matter what. Some banks will allow you to combine balances from savings accounts, CDs, and checking accounts to meet a minimum balance. Then there are ATM fees to contend with. Some banks won't charge you if you use their machine, but will charge you upward of $1 for using the machine at another banking institution. Some banks charge you no matter whose ATM you use. These fees may not sound like much, but they really add up.

Another option is to forego a bank checking account altogether and use one that draws from your money market fund. We discussed that option in Chapter 3.

It's a good idea to choose a bank that offers overdraft protection as well. An overdraft is a bounced check. These can easily cost you $10–$30 per pop and are usually the result of carelessness (when you don't keep your check register up-to-date) or poor communication (when you and your spouse don't update your individual entries in the joint checking account).

# Life Insurance

If you have straight or ordinary life insurance, look into term insurance. Term insurance covers you for a specific term—say, 20 years—instead of your entire life. You can obtain the same dollar amount of insurance for much lower premiums with term life insurance. Many people set the term to cover them until the year their last child is expected to graduate from college. Also check with your employer to see if you are eligible for a group insurance rate.

### Super Strategy

How much should you pay in insurance premiums? Some experts recommend 10 percent of your income, while others say whatever it takes to provide half your current income. Let a good agent help you assess your situation. How do you find a good agent? Ask friends and family for recommendations. That's your best bet.

# Knocking Down Real Estate Taxes

Real estate taxes are established by a local board of assessors or town assessor, who estimate how much your home is worth. Basically, your home is assessed a certain value, and that value is multiplied by the property tax rate, for every $1,000 of value in your home. Schools are typically the highest consumer of tax dollars (up to around 70 percent or more), followed by municipal services, such as police and fire departments.

If your home is assessed at $245,000 and your tax rate for your town is $5 per $1,000, your tax bill is $245 × $5 = $1,225. It's always possible that your house has been over-valued by the assessor. Check to see if your home has been assessed in line with your neighbors' houses, making allowance for number of bedrooms and other features, such as a deck. Also compare your house with comparable homes in other parts of town. The town office or assessor's office will make this information available to you.

If you feel your assessment is too high, check with the assessor's office for the proper procedure. Nothing ventured, nothing gained. Be careful, however, not to start the process without a good case—assessments can be raised as well as lowered.

# Credit Cards

In Chapter 7, "Solving Debt and Credit Problems," we're going to really get down to business on how to dig yourself out of debt, but let's take a moment now to think about what a drag credit cards can be on your financial plan. Credit cards are a very expensive debt if you don't pay off the balance in full each month. Annual rates of 15–20 percent are common, plus many cards charge a membership fee. Look at it this way: Let's say you're carrying around a $2,000 balance on a credit card that has an 18 percent annual interest rate. Each month you pay them the minimum amount, which we'll say is $20. The yearly interest on that $2,000 balance ($2,000 × .18) is $360. Your minimum $20 a month payment you've been making adds up to $240 for a year. *You're not even paying off the interest!* A bad investment. Very bad.

If you're doing everything "right" financially and are earning a solid return on some solid investments, what's the point if you're paying out tons of interest on your credit cards? You may be earning 15 percent on $5,000 in a great stock mutual fund, but if you're paying 18 percent on $5,000 on a maxed-out credit card, well, you're not getting ahead, are you?

**Investor's Idiom**

The difference between a *credit card* and a *charge card* is that a credit card enables you to carry a debt indefinitely, as long as you pay interest. Any debt put on a charge card, in contrast, has to be paid for within a specified period, typically 30 days. If you don't pay off your charge card account during that period, you will have to pay penalties and interest.

First, if you have more than one credit card, ditch the rest and get down to one. No one needs more than one credit card. Now, which one should you carry? If you have trouble paying off your balance in full each month, think about switching to a charge card, as opposed to a credit card, such as the American Express card. In other words, you are required to pay the balance off in full each month, so you won't be tempted to carry it (and you'll think twice about what you charge on it!).

If you do have the discipline to pay off your card every month, why not get one that works for you? If you travel frequently by air, think about a card that offers free mileage. If you drive, how about a card that earns free gas or dollars toward the purchase of a new car? Once you have your monthly balance under control, you'd be amazed at how many transactions (supermarkets, doctor/dentist bills, etc.) you can put on your card and how the bonuses pile up.

# Little Things That Add Up

Besides savings on big items like cars, taxes, and insurance, there are literally hundreds of little savings you can come up with on your own. Here are a few examples:

1. Think about alternatives: Does it cost more to pick up the paper on the way to work or have it delivered at home?

2. Make clothes last. What's the cost of a new shirt versus the cost of turning the collar and/or cuffs on an old shirt?

3. If you're a clothes horse, try to buy for next season at the end of this season, when everything's marked down.

4. To save on entertainment expenses, think about cocktails at home and just the dinner meal out. Restaurants make much of their profit from the bar. If movies are your passion, don't forget to take advantage of special weekend matinee movie prices.

5. Plan ahead on vacation trips, keeping an eye out for off-season rates on both air tickets and hotels.

6. There are great deals on phone charges right now, but be sure to read the small print. Also, have your long-distance carrier check your usage to see if there's a plan that best fits your pattern of calling. It doesn't cost anything to ask.

These are just a few tips to get those creative saving juices flowing. You may be skeptical about saving $10 here and $20 there doing you much good, but in the end those few dollars that you've saved add up to a lot more than you think!

---

### The Least You Need to Know

➤ You pay taxes on each additional dollar you earn on your job, but saving is free, so it's a lot easier to get ahead by saving than by working more.

➤ Get in the habit of preparing monthly income statements to keep track of your spending.

➤ You can earn a higher rate of return from buying in bulk than from many investments.

➤ If you plan to own a car for under two years, leasing may be a better deal than buying.

➤ Choose a bank that offers overdraft protection, as well as the convenience you need and the best rates in your area.

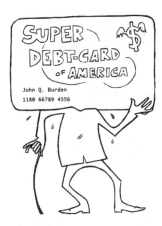

# Solving Debt and Credit Problems

---

## In This Chapter

➤ Checking and repairing your credit history

➤ Building good credit

➤ Using, not abusing, credit cards

➤ Good debt vs. bad debt

---

Credit can be either a tremendous boon to your financial life or a dangerous drain, depending on how wisely you use it. Human beings have been struggling with its temptations for centuries.

Credit preceded the coining of money by over 2,000 years. Coinage is dated from the first millennium B.C., but old Sumerian documents, circa 3000 B.C., reveal a systematic use of credit based on loans of grain by volume and loans of metal by weight. These loans often carried interest.

About 1800 B.C., Hammurabi, a king of the first dynasty of ancient Babylonia, gave his people the earliest known formal code of laws. A number of the chief provisions of this code regulated the relation of debtor to creditor. The maximum rate of interest was set at $33^1/_3$ percent per annum for loans of grain repayable in kind, and at 20 percent per annum for loans of silver by weight. All loans had to be accompanied by written contracts witnessed before officials. Land and other assets could be pledged against a debt. So could the creditor, as well as his wife, concubine, children, or slaves. Personal slavery for debt was limited to three years. And you thought you had it bad! (Source: Sidney Homer, *A History of Interest Rates,* Rutgers Univ. Press, 1967.)

Creditors may no longer be able to take your first born, but nothing can screw up your financial goals more than a bad credit report. In this chapter, we're going to show you how to avoid and fix credit mishaps—and get you into great investing shape.

# What Does Your Credit Report Say About You?

Before a credit card company issues you a card or a bank lends you money, they will check out your credit report. There are credit reporting agencies (CRAs) that do nothing but gather credit information about you from bankers and other creditors and sell that information to banks, stores, and other issuers of credit.

**Fiscal Facts**

When you apply for a credit card, a bank loan, or any other form of credit, you typically sign something that gives permission to the creditor to obtain your credit history. The creditor subscribes to credit reporting agencies, which forward your credit report. The information on the credit report is based on what other creditors have reported about you.

If you've ever defaulted on a student loan, failed to pay off a charge account at a department store, or forgotten to pay a bill because you moved, rest assured that these transgressions are on your credit report in black and white. In addition, your report carries your Social Security number, your past and present addresses, your salary, and any other details of your financial life the credit reporting agency has been able to snag. Pretty creepy, huh?

# CRA Horror Stories

Nothing can be more upsetting than to discover—the hard way—that you have a bad credit report. We've each had that experience. Ed was shocked when he was turned down for a credit card recently. He exercised his right to request a free copy of his credit report. (Whenever you are turned down for credit, you can contact the credit agency whose information was used to turn you down and get a copy of the report.)

Ed's report was clean as a whistle, except for one little detail: a state tax lien of $130, filed on 6/10/97, for the transfer tax on a home sold back in 1991. The actual tax was a measly $25; the $105 was interest.

**Investor's Idiom**

A *lien* is a legal right to take someone's property and hold it until the owner pays a debt.

Ed made a slew of phone calls. Finally someone at the state tax department explained that the state had gone after both the buyer and seller of Ed's house, but the buyer never responded and the seller (Ed) did not have a current address in their system. So, the state filed the lien! It's a good thing Ed and his wife found this out before they refinanced their mortgage several months later, because it took a month to clear up.

Another person we know was stunned when a mysterious unpaid loan for $5,000 showed up on her credit report. It took six months of persistent phone calls and letters before she figured out that her alma mater had mistakenly assigned a single college loan two identification numbers. This made it look like she had actually had two college loans—and had failed to pay off one of them.

What about you? Do you have something like this lurking in your report? Are you sure you don't?

# How to Check Your Credit Reports

We recommend that you look at your credit reports from at least the top three CRAs every year. These are:

➤ Trans Union National: 1-800-916-8800

➤ Experian (formerly TRW): 1-888-397-3742

➤ Equifax: 1-800-685-1111

If you own a business, you will want to run a credit check on it periodically, too. The three top credit reporting agencies in this field are:

➤ Dunn & Bradstreet: 1-800-234-3867

➤ NCR Corp: 1-800-262-7782

➤ Experian (formerly TRW): 1-888-397-3742

How do you get a copy of your report? Each CRA has slightly different policies, but basically they will have you send proof of your Social Security number and address. You can contact the Federal Trade Commission, Consumer Response Center-FCRA at 202-326-3761 for a specific agency's name and number. The FTC website is: **http://www.ftc.gov.**

## *Your Credit Reporting Rights*

Incidentally, FCRA stands for the Federal Fair Credit Reporting Act, which gives you specific rights regarding the privacy and accuracy of information in your credit report. Specifically:

1. If a company denies you credit based on information supplied by a CRA, it must tell you and provide you with the name, address, and phone number of the CRA.

2. You can request a free copy of your report if it has been less than 60 days since your credit request was denied. In some states (e.g., New Jersey), you are entitled to a free report the first time you request one, with or without credit denial. Otherwise, credit reports typically cost $8.

3. You can dispute inaccurate information in your credit report, and each CRA will tell you exactly how to do that. For example, if you've refused to pay for your new washing machine because it's not working and the store has reported you as a bad credit risk, you can have your side of the story reported on your credit report and have the debt designated "disputed" instead of "unpaid."

4. The CRA must remove or correct inaccurate information within 30 days of dispute.

**Crash Alert**

Credit reporting agencies can make mistakes, because they do not verify the information they receive—they just report it. So, get reports for you and your spouse regularly and check them out carefully, so you can clear up any issues pronto.

5. In most cases, a CRA may not report negative information that is more than seven years old (10 years for bankruptcies). If you have a good reason for having failed to pay a bill—maybe you failed to pay it because you moved and it was not forwarded to your new address, for example—you can pay the bill and have it erased from your report.

6. You may request that your name be removed from CRA lists for unsolicited credit and insurance offers. Incidentally, you will be surprised at how many such offers show up as "inquiries" on your credit report! Now you know how to reduce your daily junk mail overload!

**Investor's Idiom**

A *charge card* allows you to "charge" an item, or buy it without paying cash at the time of purchase. You are expected to pay the purchase off within 30 days, whereas with a *credit card* you can make monthly minimum payments indefinitely. Another way to buy without paying at the time of purchase is to use a layaway plan, which allows you to make a down payment and monthly payments. When you buy something on layaway you can't take it home until all payments have been made.

## No Credit Is Not Good Credit

Don't make the mistake of thinking that because you've never used credit, you have good credit. What you have is no credit, and if you have no credit, you won't be approved for mortgages or auto loans. Many credit card companies won't approve you, either. You need to establish a personal credit history that shows you can make regular payments on a debt over time.

Although banks and credit card companies tend not to lend to people with no credit history, department stores are usually willing to let someone with no credit history open a charge card account. A charge account lets you buy something without paying cash for it at the time of purchase. You are expected to pay the purchase off by the end of the month. Some charge accounts let you pay off only a minimum balance monthly and charge you interest on the remaining balance.

When you get your first charge account, make a few purchases each month and pay for them by the end of the month. Never miss a payment or pay late.

Another way to establish a credit history is to buy something on layaway. With a layaway plan, you make a down payment on a piece of furniture, for example, and pay it off with regular monthly payments. You can't take the item home until all the payments have been made. This is another way to prove that you can be trusted to make regular payments. But, you need to ask whether the creditor reports timely payments of items on layaway to credit reporting agencies. Not all of them do.

### Super Strategy

It's important to realize that to establish good credit you must show that you can make regular payments on a debt over time. If you take out a loan, for example, and you get an unexpected inflow of cash that enables you to pay it off all at once, that's fine—but it doesn't demonstrate your ability to make regular payments, and thus won't improve your credit history.

Finally, make sure your efforts to establish good credit are being reported to the CRAs. Check your reports six months after using a charge account or other credit regularly and if no positive information has been reported, ask the issuer of the credit you're using to send a report to the CRAs. Request a copy for yourself, also.

# Credit Cards: You Only Need One

Some people collect credit cards as if they were baseball cards. Not only is this confusing (which one do you use when, and where?), but it can get expensive. Most cards charge an annual membership fee. And credit card rates are very high compared to other lending rates: 16–18 percent, for example, versus around 8–9 percent for auto loans.

We highly recommend that you have only one credit card. Pick the card with the lowest rate and no annual fee and transfer your balances from other cards to this one. That's step one toward effectively managing credit card debt.

Step two is to pay off the balance and continue to pay in full every month.

### Fiscal Facts

How many credit cards do cardholders have? As reported on Page 11 of the Money & Business Section of the August 9, 1998 *New York Times*: "...according to the Nilson Report, which tracks the credit card industry, the average is now slightly more than four cards per cardholder, compared with slightly more than three in 1993." Good Lord!

Finally, for step three, once you pay off the outstanding balance and consolidate down to one card, rates no longer matter. Why? Because you are going to pay off the balance outstanding, in full, each month. Now you can switch, before the next annual fee (if there is one) on your current card comes due, to the card you really want. Ask yourself these questions when choosing a credit card:

➤ What card do most of the stores I frequent take? American Express? Visa? MasterCard? Discover?

➤ Do I travel by air a lot? Would a card that earns frequent flyer miles benefit me?

➤ What other benefits would I like to earn by using a card? Free gas? Shopping discounts?

# How to Really Get Your Act Together

Once you have your credit card debt under control and the best card in your wallet or pocketbook, you can take the offensive by using your card as a reporting device. Remember the advice we gave you in Chapter 4 about gathering and entering your expenses on a monthly income statement? Well, you can charge practically all your purchases—from getting your car washed to new shoes for the kids—on a credit card.

Now, here comes the cool part. Each month, you get an itemized listing of your charges for entry onto your monthly sheets. And, with some cards, you even get an annual report with all your purchases sorted into expense categories. Perfect! Your financial statements will practically write themselves.

# A Checking Account? Who Needs It!

If you go this route, you might not even need a checking account. Most money market funds (more on those coming up) allow you to write checks against the money in your money market account. These checks usually have to be for at least $250. Simply use your credit card to pay for almost every purchase you make and write one check a month, drawn from your money market account, to pay off your credit card, and a few others for rent or mortgage and car payments. No more balancing a checkbook, no more paying for checks, no more exorbitant bounced-check fees—plus you get that monthly list of exactly what you spent and on what from your credit card company. Is this smooth, or what?

Whip out your scissors and start cutting up all the credit cards you don't need. Get down to one card and you'll also be down to one easy-to-read financial statement. Now you're in control.

**Super Strategy**

Pay off your credit card every month and use it for every purchase you make. Not only will you avoid throwing away money on credit card interest, the credit card company will send you an annual list of everything you've bought, broken into categories, that you can use to create your annual balance sheet. Life doesn't get much easier than that!

## Debit Cards—A Better Choice?

Debit cards enable you to make purchases with a direct deduction from your checking account rather than a charge to a credit card account. They are often packaged together now as a combination cash card (which can be used for deposits and withdrawals at bank cash or ATM machines) and debit card.

Debit cards are very convenient, and you do avoid interest charges by using them instead of credit cards, but they can make it even more of a hassle to balance your checking account. You have to keep track of every little purchase you make with your debit card and enter it into your check register. You can quickly lose control of your balance and run into overdraft and service charges.

To avoid the risk of overdraft charges or bounced checks, open up a line of credit with your checking account. There typically is no charge unless you actually use the line, whereupon the rate is around 11–12 percent. Guess what, though? If you apply for a line of credit, your bank will check your credit report. If there are any problems, you will be turned down for overdraft protection.

**Investor's Idiom**

A *debit card* can be presented like a credit card when you make a purchase, but the cost of the purchase is deducted at the time of purchase from your checking account.

Credit card, debit card—or one of each? The choice is yours. But if you opt for the debit card, keep close tabs on your checking account balance. This includes communication and coordination with your significant other!

## How Much of Your Income Should Go Toward Reducing Debt?

"Okay," you're thinking, "this is just dandy to talk about having no credit card debt and using one credit card as my own private accountant, but I'm in debt up to my eyebrows! How do I dig myself out?" Every situation is different, but we do have a rule of thumb that should give you some guidance.

**Fiscal Facts**

After World War II, credit of all sorts proliferated (especially consumer and mortgage credit) and there were some modifications to existing credit instruments. New federal agencies used "moral obligation" notes, mostly to promote the real estate mortgage market, and these new issues often exceeded in volume the new financing of the Treasury itself. (From *A History of Interest Rates*, pp.332–334.)

Some mortgage experts recommend that your mortgage payment should be no more than 25–30 percent of your gross income. So, figure that a week's salary should cover it. Your gross income is what appears on your W-2 statement plus any other earned or unearned income (like income from a trust account). Consider earmarking an additional 5–10 percent of your gross income for reducing educational loans, auto loans, charge accounts, credit card debt, and anything else you're carrying like a load of rocks.

# Good Debt vs. Bad Debt

What's "good" debt? Debt that represents a worthwhile investment with appreciation potential is good debt. Home mortgages and education loans are good debt. Plus, mortgage interest (and taxes) are deductible on your Form 1040 Schedule A. Bad debt is loans on depreciating assets such as cars, clothing, a new pair of skis, etc. Make every effort to pay off bad debt first.

The main reason to minimize your bad debt is to increase your financial flexibility and peace of mind. Most people borrow right up to their limit and have nothing in reserve. If they face some unexpected crisis, they have to borrow more (if possible) on existing assets. This means taking out a home equity loan or refinancing their home mortgage, or tapping into their 401(k) plan. If these measures don't do the trick, they're looking at a second mortgage and, ultimately, at selling off assets (the car, the home, etc.). It gets to the point where you're trying to put a size 10 foot into a size 9 shoe.

This is why the emergency fund we discussed in Chapter 3 is so important. It provides you with the freedom to make good decisions and the flexibility to pay for them.

## *How Much to Set Aside for Peace of Mind*

We've talked before about having an emergency fund that represents 10 percent of your annual income or $10,000, whichever is greater, and we've talked before about how each individual's situation differs. But let's get into more detail. Sid Sod, for example, may participate in his employer's group health plan, short-term disability, and long-term disability plans. These are deductions from his pay slip. Nancy Nerd is self-employed; she either must try to obtain these health plans on her own (at considerably greater expense), or make sure she has enough in her emergency fund to cover broken arms and other nasty surprises. She'll need a significantly larger emergency fund than Sid Sod. In fact, she'll probably need more than she can really afford to put aside. Buying health insurance would be a wiser choice for her to make than for her to try to put aside enough to cover a medical catastrophe.

The 10-percent emergency fund is there to cover unanticipated expenses. So, if you don't have insurance, get it! Don't plan to meet the need with the emergency fund. Similarly, saving for that new car or home should be built into the emergency fund so that you don't incur "bad debt" to buy these necessities.

# If You Spend It, Replenish It

Above all, when you deplete your emergency fund, always replenish it before you invest or make any other financial allocations. And never, never use your credit card as an emergency fund. Far too many people get into terrible debt by making that mistake.

Examples of unanticipated expenses that should be covered by the emergency fund are:

➤ damage claims not covered by insurance (whether health, auto, or home)

➤ your daughter's wedding

➤ major auto or appliance repairs, etc.

➤ rent or mortgage payments if you lose your job

Whatever befalls you or any member of your immediate family, make it your goal to be able to deal with it via your emergency fund—without the need to tap your other investments or take on additional debt. Don't use the emergency fund for luxuries like a vacation in Tahiti or a sailboat.

## The Least You Need to Know

➤ Nothing can screw up your financial goals more than a bad credit report.

➤ Check your credit history once a year to catch errors.

➤ No credit is not the same as good credit; you have to use credit to build a credit history.

➤ Get down to one credit card, then pay off its balance monthly.

➤ Use your credit card to make all your purchases. This is an easy way to keep track of your expenses.

➤ Statistics show that people "spend" more when they use credit cards. Remember, a credit card is debt not money.

➤ If you want to use a debit card, get overdraft protection.

# Chapter 8

# Trim Your Taxes

## In This Chapter

➤ Figuring out your taxable income

➤ Evaluating employer-provided health and child care

➤ What you need to know about medical savings accounts

➤ Deduction strategies for your investments

This book is about putting your money to work so you can have the life you want. We've already talked about cutting expenses so you can meet your investment goals. An even more painless way to increase the amount of money you can put to work for you is to trim your taxes to the bone. We touched on this topic in Chapter 6, but here we'll explore every conceivable way you can keep more of what you earn at work with your investments.

## What Are All Those Different "Incomes" Anyway?

Most of us view tax time like a shot: We just want to get it over with as quickly as possible. Fill out those forms and stick 'em in the mail. Boom, you're done and you don't have to think about it for another year. What a relief, right? Well, it may seem less painful this way, but you're really not doing yourself any favors. When it comes to the government and your money, ignorance is not all the bliss it's cracked up to be. It's costly. So, pay attention—we're going to save you some money here.

Before we can tackle your taxes, we need to define a few terms. It can be pretty confusing to look at your tax return and see phrases like taxable income, gross income, and adjusted gross income. What are all those incomes, anyway? *Taxable income* is the number that determines how much tax you pay, but where does it come from?

We'll answer this question in a few steps. Let's start with *gross income*. Gross income includes:

➤ wages, salaries, and tips—reported on your W-2

➤ dividend and interest income—reported on Schedule B of your income tax return

➤ taxable refunds (e.g., state tax refund)

➤ alimony received

➤ business income—reported on Schedule C

➤ capital gains—reported on Schedule D

➤ taxable distributions from IRAs, pensions, and annuities

➤ rental income

➤ income from partnerships, corporations, and trusts—reported on Schedule E

➤ farm income—reported on Schedule F

➤ unemployment compensation

➤ taxable Social Security benefits

**Investor's Idiom**

A *capital gain* is any money you make from an investment—from selling a stock for a profit, for example. If you've held the investment longer than one year, the capital gain is not subject to income tax; instead, it's subject to capital gains tax, which is typically lower.

The next step is to calculate your *adjusted gross income* (AGI). Adjusted gross income is gross income less:

➤ IRA deductions

➤ medical saving account deductions (Form 8853)

➤ moving expenses (Form 3903)

➤ one-half of self-employment tax (Schedule SE)

➤ self-employed health insurance

➤ Keogh and self-employed SEP and SIMPLE plans

➤ any penalty of early withdrawal of savings (e.g., CDs)

➤ any alimony paid

Now that you have your adjusted gross income, you can take deductions and exemptions. Deductions from adjusted gross income are either itemized (meaning you list each and every one of them) or standard (meaning that you take a deduction for a specific amount allowed by the IRS). You take the standard deduction if you don't think your itemized deductions will add up to more than the standard deduction offered. Pick up a copy of *The Complete Idiot's Guide to Doing Your Income Taxes 1999* (Alpha Books) for step-by-step help in this area.

It will be worth your efforts to itemize your deductions if you have heavy expenses in the following categories:

➤ medical and dental expenses not reimbursed by insurance

➤ taxes (state, local, real estate, and personal property such as automobiles)

➤ home mortgage interest and points (Form 1098)

➤ gifts to charity

➤ unreimbursed job expenses (Form 2106)

➤ other expenses, such as safe-deposit box rental, etc.

Now, you can subtract any exemptions you may have from your AGI. Currently, the IRS says you can subtract $2,650 per household member for income up to $90,900. At higher income levels the exemptions are scaled down.

So, here's the process to get to your taxable income:

Gross income – adjustments = adjusted gross income – deductions and exemptions = taxable income

Now you've got your taxable income!

**Investor's Idiom**

A *point* is 1 percent expressed in terms of the size of your mortgage. So, 1 point on a $100,000 mortgage = $1,000; 2 points = $2,000; and so on.

## Uncle Sammie and Your Marginal Income Tax Rate

As you learned in Chapter 6, your *marginal income tax rate* is the tax rate Uncle Sam will apply to your next dollar of income. Specifically, if you look at the 1998 instruction booklet for IRS Form 1040, you will see near the back a page titled "Tax Rate Schedules." There is a schedule for each of four status categories:

1. single
2. married filing jointly
3. married filing separately
4. head of household

You will probably be in the first or second category. For each status, there is a schedule or table. There are five different taxable rates that are applied to your income. For example, the current tax rate schedule for single status is the following:

| Taxable Income | Tax Rate |
| --- | --- |
| $1–$25,350 | 15% |
| $25,351–$61,400 | 28% |
| $61,401–$128,100 | 31% |
| $128,101–$278,450 | 36% |
| $278,451+ | 39.6% |

Each status is taxed at the same five rates; the difference is the range of taxable income. For example, the above table is the current tax rate schedule for single status. If you are married and filing jointly, it looks like this:

| Taxable Income | Tax Rate |
| --- | --- |
| $1–$42,350 | 15% |
| $42,351–$102,300 | 28% |
| etc. | |

So, if you are single and your taxable income is $61,401, what is your tax and what is your marginal tax rate? Well, the first $25,350 you earn is taxed at the first tax rate for a single person, which is 15 percent. Whatever you earn between $25,350 and $61,400 is taxed at 28 percent. Your salary is $61,401 so that last dollar you earn is taxed at the next rate, which is 31 percent.

Let's figure out your total tax. Simply multiply each level of income by the tax rate.

$25,350 × .15 = $3,802.50

$36,050 × .28 = $10,094.00

$1 × .31 = $0.31

These are the taxes due on each tier of income. Adding them together, we get your total income tax due on $61,401–$13,896.81.

In this example, the marginal tax rate is .31 or 31 percent. This is the rate at which your next dollar of taxable income will be taxed. But note that your average tax rate is $13,896.81 ÷ $61,401, or 22.6 percent!

## Super Strategy

Your employer may offer group health plans (medical and/or dental) and a 401(k) plan. If you subscribe to either, a sum is deducted from your regular pay. Although this comes out of your pay envelope, it is deducted before your W-2 reportable income is determined. In other words, you do not pay taxes on that portion of your salary that goes toward health benefits and 401(k) contributions. All the more reason to maximize your 401(k) contributions and fully participate in employer group health plans. Just check to make sure your premiums do come out pre-tax.

# Employer–Based Health and Childcare Funds

Some employers offer a third type of deduction from your income: non-reimbursed health care and dependent care expenses. Examples of the former would include medical and dental deductibles and copayments, plus other expenses not normally covered (e.g., eyeglasses).

The maximum deduction is $5,000 for each, but there is a catch: The difference between legitimate expenses claimed and the total deduction is forfeited. For example, if you arrange to have $3,000 deducted from your pay at the beginning of the year but only file claims totaling $2,500, you are out the $500. In other words, use it or lose it! So, estimate carefully.

# Medical Savings Accounts: Are They a Good Deal?

In 1997, for the first time, the IRS allowed for a medical savings account deduction (Form 8853). This is still a pilot program, so changes may be made from time to time, but the basic outline is in place. If you are self-employed or work for a small business, this could be an important deduction. And, remember, all deductions reduce the amount of tax you have to pay.

The medical savings account program is designed for self-employed individuals and small companies, for whom the cost of health insurance can be prohibitively expensive. The individual (or the company) buys health insurance with a high deductible (e.g., $2,000–$3,000 for an individual, $3,000–$5,000 for a family). But how do you come up with the "scratch" to cover that high deductible, if you need to do so? This is where the medical account comes in.

## *How the Medical Savings Account Works*

You can keep up to 65 percent of the deductible for yourself alone, or up to 75 percent if you have a family, in a medical savings account. You can also deduct the full amount of your contribution to the account (it's on Line 24 of Form 1040).

Let's say Charlie Cheap has bought insurance with a $2,000 deductible. He can contribute 65 percent of $2,000, or $1,300, to his medical account every year. The sums in the account grow tax deferred to age 65. If Charlie taps into the account in the interim for medical reasons, there is no tax due. If he digs into it for non-medical reasons before age 65, there is both income tax due and a 15 percent penalty. After age 65, if he withdraws for non-medical reasons, he does not incur the 15 percent penalty.

Is this a good deal? Well, it puts a large premium on staying healthy up to the point where the account exceeds the deductible. And can you

**Investor's Idiom**

The *deductible* is the amount of expense you agree to cover before your insurance kicks in.

afford to both put aside the deductible and pay the premium? It seems like a good deal for the "healthy and wealthy." But for the rest of us, we're not so sure. Perhaps the IRS will simplify the whole process in the months to come. Keep your eyes open for any modifications announced via your local newspaper or television station. Check with local banks as well as mutual fund companies to see if they participate. They will also be up-to-date as modifications unfold.

## Buying Your Own Health Insurance May Be a Better Deal

If you are self-employed or employed by a small business, buying your health insurance may be a better deal for you than a medical savings account. Under the Taxpayer Relief Act of 1997, the deductions for health insurance expenses of self-employed individuals (and their family members) will steadily rise to 100 percent in 2007. The schedule is as follows:

| Year | % Health Insurance Deductible |
| --- | --- |
| 1997 | 40% |
| 1998–1999 | 45% |
| 2000–2001 | 50% |
| 2002 | 60% |
| 2003–2005 | 80% |
| 2006 | 90% |
| 2007+ | 100% |

That's a pretty hefty potential deduction; and the more you can deduct, the less you pay in taxes. Now let's take a look at some other deduction strategies you can apply to trim your taxes. You can also buy health insurance at group rates even if you're self-employed by joining certain professional groups or fraternal organizations.

# Gains and Losses on Securities Transactions

There are four broad deduction strategies that can help put more of your money to work for you. The first one we'll tackle concerns gains and losses on securities transactions (securities being stocks and bonds, of course).

What you paid for a security is the *cost*, and what the security is currently worth is its *current market value*.

➤ If the market value is higher than the price you paid, you have an *unrealized gain*.

➤ If it is lower, you have an *unrealized loss*.

➤ If you actually sell the security, you create a *realized gain* or *loss*.

➤ This gain or loss is called "short-term" if you held the security for up to 12 months before you sold it. If you held it for more than 12 months, you've realized a long-term gain or loss.

## Save Big Bucks by Holding Out for Capital Gains

This is a very important distinction, because short-term gains are taxed at ordinary income tax rates. Long-term gains, on the other hand, are taxed at capital gains rates, which are significantly lower.

### Tax Rates

| Ordinary | Capital Gain |
| --- | --- |
| 15% | 10% |
| 28% | 20% |
| 31% | 20% |
| 36% | 20% |
| 39.6% | 20% |

So, if you sell a security after holding it for 12 months or less and realize a gain of $5,000, and you're in the 31 percent tax bracket, you will owe $1,550 ($5,000 × .31) in tax. This realized short-term gain might also bump you up to a higher marginal tax rate, i.e., 36 percent. Ouch!

If you hold the security for 12 months and 1 day before selling it, your tax will only be $1,000 ($5,000 × .20). Clearly, you can hang on for another 24 hours to save that chunk of change, can't you? It'll be more than worth it to hold profitable securities for at least the 12 months required to qualify for a long-term capital gain and avoid Uncle Sammie getting a larger helping of your profits.

## Using a Loss to Offset a Gain

What if you have realized a gain on one security and have an unrealized loss on another security? You can realize the loss (by selling the security) and use it to offset some or all of the gain.

If the realized loss exceeds the realized gain, you can apply the difference, up to $3,000 in any given year, to reduce your ordinary income, which—yes, you guessed it—reduces your tax bill. If your loss exceeds the $3,000 limit, you can "carry" the difference over to the next year(s).

Be careful with what you do with the proceeds, however! There's a catch: If you buy the same security back within 30 days, this is referred to as a "wash sale," and you won't be allowed to take the loss. The rule refers to "substantially" the same security. You can buy a similar security (e.g., Growth Mutual Fund A vs. Growth Mutual Fund B, or ABC Drug stock vs. XYZ Drug stock). Or, just wait 31 days and buy the original stock back if you wish.

### Super Strategy

With securities, your decision should always be driven by investment merits, not tax merits. All things being equal, however, take full advantage of the tax laws. Just apply these three rules:

1. Try to hold securities longer than 12 months so you can realize long-term gains and your profit is only subject to capital gains tax, not income tax.

2. Offset gains with losses wherever possible.

3. Beware the 30-day "wash sale" rule!

All these transactions are entered on IRS Form 1040, Schedule D.

# Did You Say Tax-Free Interest Income?

Investing in bonds that generate tax-free interest is another cool tax strategy. The interest paid by municipal bonds is, with a few exceptions, not taxed by the Federal Government. A municipal bond is a bond issued by a "municipality," like your city, town, or county. A municipality is basically any self-governing region.

By the same token, interest income from direct obligations of the U.S. Government is not taxed by the individual states. The feds don't go after the interest income generated by state and local bonds and, in return, the states don't tax interest income generated by bonds issued by the federal government, like U.S. Savings Bonds or Treasuries.

Municipal bond interest income from a municipality in your state of residence is also free of state tax. Bonds like this are referred to as "double-tax free."

## Types of Muni Bonds

Municipal bonds fall within two broad categories:

1. *General obligation (GO) bonds* issued by the state or a city, town, or county within the state are backed by the tax-raising ability of the state or municipality. The issuer can't print money to get itself out of trouble like the federal government,

### Fiscal Facts

The progressive income tax created the strong demand for tax-exempt state and municipal bonds. This put pressure on bonds issued by corporations and the federal government to offer higher interest rates to attract buyers.

but it does have the power to raise taxes when it needs money.

2. *Revenue bonds* are issued by an agency of a city, county, or state for a specific purpose. Revenues from that agency pay the interest on bonds that are outstanding. Revenue bonds are issued to build toll roads, bridges and tunnels, water and sewer systems, and the like. If the agency that issues the bonds gets into financial trouble, it can raise its tolls or rates, but cannot expect to be bailed out by the local or state government.

## Why Not Load Up on Munis?

If you can avoid federal taxes by owning municipal bonds instead of U.S. Treasury securities, for example, why wouldn't everyone do this? There are two reasons:

### Investor's Idiom

If you buy a municipal bond, you won't have to pay federal income tax on the interest. There are two main kinds of municipal bonds: *general obligation bonds*, which are issued by a state or city and are backed by the taxing power of the issuer, and *revenue bonds*, which are issued by the agencies that build infrastructures for municipalities. These agencies can't tax, but do have the power to raise tolls or rates to cover debts.

1. The municipal bond is not backed by the "full faith and credit" of the federal government the way Treasury bonds are. There is a risk that you could lose your principal. You can modify this risk (but not eliminate it entirely) by limiting your holdings to municipalities with the two highest credit ratings (AAA and AA). Credit ratings are issued by Standard & Poor's and Moody's, among others.

2. Municipal bonds typically yield less than Treasury securities. The issue is how much less? To answer this question, investors translate municipal bond yields into tax-equivalent yields. This means they adjust the municipal bond yield upward to reflect the tax savings, and then compare that number to the current yield on a U.S. Treasury security.

Use the table below to calculate tax-equivalent yield: The bold numbers across the top represent the municipal bond yield percentages; the bold numbers in the left-most column represent the marginal tax rate.

## Tax-Equivalent Yields Chart

|        | 3.75% | 4.00% | 4.25% | 4.50% | 4.75% | 5.00% | 5.25% |
| ------ | ----- | ----- | ----- | ----- | ----- | ----- | ----- |
| 15%    | 4.41  | 4.71  | 5.00  | 5.29  | 5.59  | 5.88  | 6.18  |
| 28%    | 5.21  | 5.56  | 5.90  | 6.25  | 6.60  | 6.94  | 7.29  |
| 31%    | 5.43  | 5.80  | 6.16  | 6.52  | 6.88  | 7.25  | 7.61  |
| 36%    | 5.86  | 6.25  | 6.64  | 7.03  | 7.42  | 7.81  | 8.20  |
| 39.6%  | 6.21  | 6.62  | 7.04  | 7.45  | 7.86  | 8.28  | 8.69  |

How did we get these numbers? Well, if a muni bond is yielding 3.75 percent and your marginal tax rate is 15 percent, you want to know how much a non-tax-free bond would have to yield for it to be worth as much to you as the muni bond, right? So, for the taxable bond to be attractive it would have to yield at least as much as the muni, plus enough to cover the tax bill.

To figure this out, just divide 3.75 percent by .85 (1.00 minus the marginal tax rate of .15 = .85), which equals 4.41 percent tax equivalent yield.

**Investor's Idiom**

*Collateral* is something you own that can be pledged against a loan. If you fail to pay the loan, the lender can seize the collateral and sell it to pay off the loan. More people are using their homes as collateral for revolving lines of credit called home equity loans. With a line of credit, you are authorized to borrow up to a maximum amount, and you only pay interest on what you actually use.

How do we use this table? If a 20-year AAA or AA municipal bond today yields 5.00 percent, look on the table and you'll see that the tax-equivalent yield is 7.25 (at a 31 percent marginal tax rate). How does it compare to a 20-year U.S. Treasury yield?

The Treasury is yielding 5.76 percent (at the time of this writing), while the tax-equivalent yield on the muni is 7.25 percent. The muni looks like the better deal! You get a considerable pickup in yield (1.49 percent) by buying the municipal bond.

Here's another calculation investors run to decide whether or not to buy a municipal bond instead of a super-safe comparable Treasury bond. Compute the tax-free yield as a percent of the taxable yield; the closer to 100 percent, the more attractive the municipal. In the above example, 5.00 percent ÷ 5.76 percent = 87 percent, which is historically quite high. Remember that interest income is entered on IRS Form 1040 Schedule B.

## Home Equity Loans Are Deductible

For individuals, interest-expense deductions are now essentially limited to home ownership. This means that you cannot deduct interest on auto loans, credit cards, and other debts from your adjusted gross income. You can deduct interest, however, on your home mortgage and on a home equity loan.

What's a home equity loan? Essentially, it's a revolving line of credit with your home serving as *collateral*. A revolving line of credit puts an upper limit on what you can borrow. You can borrow up to that amount, and you only pay interest on what you actually use. If a bank gives you a $20,000 line of credit, for example, and you only use $10,000 of it, you'll only be charged interest on $10,000. A credit card is a revolving line of credit, essentially.

If you qualify, it may make sense to pool all your nondeductible loans and pay them off with a home equity loan. Interest payments on credit card debt, for example, are not tax deductible, but mortgage payments are. Rates are reasonable (e.g., 9 percent), especially compared to credit card debt. However, there are some qualifications you'll have to meet before a bank or mortgage company will issue you a home equity loan.

Your maximum credit will be based on the appraised value of your home times a "margin of safety" of typically 75 percent less the current mortgage outstanding. As an example:

| | |
|---|---|
| Appraised value | $100,000 |
| Percent | 0.75 |
| Base | $75,000 |
| Less mortgage outstanding | $60,000 |
| Potential credit line | $15,000 |

This borrower would be approved for a $15,000 line of credit.

**Crash Alert**

Approval of a home equity loan application will depend on how the lender views your ability to repay. You can be sure the lender will dig up your credit history and will also want to check out your income and cash flow. This is another good reason to check your credit reports for errors and problems once a year. Definitely check them months before you plan to apply for mortgages or any other important loans, to give yourself time to clear up any messes.

## Home Equity Loan vs. Second Mortgage

Home equity loans typically have variable rates, meaning the rate can change over the course of the loan. You may wish to consider a second mortgage with a fixed rate as an alternative. The differences are fairly straightforward: The home equity loan has a variable rate with a variable loan (up to the maximum approved), whereas the second mortgage has a fixed rate with a fixed loan amount. It differs from a revolving line of credit in that you pay interest on the entire loan amount.

Taking on a home equity loan or a second mortgage is not a transaction to be entered into lightly, but it may make sense if you have a lot of high-interest, nondeductible loans outstanding, such as credit card debt, and the costs are reasonable versus the amount of the credit line.

## Timing Can Make a Big Difference

All the tax strategies in this chapter are delved into in much greater depth and detail in *The Complete Idiot's Guide to Doing Your Taxes 1999*. We just want to get you thinking about these ideas.

Our final suggestion is that each year, usually around Thanksgiving, you look at your prospective tax returns for the current and following year. Did you get a big bonus this year that you don't think will be duplicated next year? Did you not get a bonus this year, but expect one next year? Try to postpone receiving any income that you can until the following year so you don't have to pay taxes on it this year.

Similarly, try to chalk up as many expenses as possible before the end of the year. If you have a big medical bill to pay, for example, pay it before December 31 and you can deduct it. Need a new computer for your business? Buy it before the end of the year, taking advantage of both Christmas sales and a tax deduction.

By reacting to actual or prospective changes in your income, you may be able to accelerate or defer certain deductible expenses to reduce your taxes. Specific areas to look at are medical and dental expenses, taxes, and mortgage payments. Moving payments from December to January or vice versa can make a difference.

---

### The Least You Need to Know

➤ "Taxable income" is the number on your tax return that determines how much income tax you owe.

➤ Taking the maximum deductions from your paycheck for group health plans and your 401(k) is a good tax strategy, but if your employer also offers pre-tax deductions for nonreimbursed health care and child care, you'll need to estimate your expenses very carefully to avoid getting burned.

➤ For many self-employed people, taking the full deduction for health-insurance expenses may be a better deal than a medical savings account.

➤ Short-term gains on investments are taxed at income tax rates; better to hold onto an investment for at least a year so that any gains are taxed at the lower capital gains rate.

➤ Offset capital gains with losses wherever possible.

➤ The interest on municipal bonds is tax free.

➤ It may make sense to pool all your nondeductible loans and pay them off with a home equity loan because the rates on a home equity loan are usually reasonable, and the interest is deductible.

---

# Part 3
# Investing 101

It is not the return on my investment that I am concerned about; it is the return of my investment.

—*Will Rogers*

*Investing is not hard to understand—really. Once you read this section, you'll understand how basic investments like stocks and bonds and mutual funds work. You'll be able to pick up the phone and order research material that'll make sense to you. You'll know how to contact and use a broker. You'll be ready to start designing an investment portfolio tailored to your investment objectives.*

*Won't it be great not to feel stupid when the talk turns to investing at your next family gathering or cocktail party? You'll be equipped to carry on an intelligent conversation about investing with just about anyone. Well, anyone except that Kruggerand-swap-options guy wolfing down the Swedish meatballs, but don't worry. No one understands him.*

# Chapter 9

# What Are They Up to on Wall Street, Anyway?

## In This Chapter

➤ How commissions on stock trades work

➤ Bull and bear baiting

➤ Making sense of a stock table

➤ Coping with market ups and downs

Fifty-odd years ago, the then-head of General Motors Corporation, "Choo Choo Charlie" Wilson, reportedly harrumphed: "What's good for General Motors is good for America."

At the time, his statement may have seemed rather arrogant and self-serving, but to those with shares in the company, his words hit home. In financial terms, the translation goes something like this: Corporate America is a key contributor to the financial well-being of this country and its citizens. And the stock market represents the ownership of corporate America. Like it or not, we live (and hope to prosper) in a capitalist society, and the capital is largely provided by the stock market.

Today, some 60 million Americans directly own common stocks listed on the New York Stock Exchange; another 130 million indirectly own shares through mutual funds. How can you get in on the action? We're glad you asked....

# A Little Background Music, Please

The stock market in this country consists of a number of exchanges, plus the NASDAQ over-the-counter market. The exchanges include:

➤ Philadelphia Stock Exchange

➤ New York Stock Exchange

➤ American Stock Exchange (recently merged with NASDAQ)

➤ Pacific Stock Exchange

➤ Boston Stock Exchange

➤ Cincinnati Stock Exchange

➤ Chicago Board Options Exchange

### Fiscal Facts

Some 40 years ago, a finance professor at Cornell University summed up the ways of Wall Street this way: "The stock market is the purest form of capitalism. What other mechanism offers the individual the opportunity to secure abundant wealth irrespective of race, color, creed, age, gender, social standing, or inheritance? All you need is a grub stake and the right combination of luck and skill."

### Investor's Idiom

The *asked price* is the price that someone who owns a stock and wants to sell it is asking for it in the market. The *bid* is the price a buyer is willing to pay for the stock. The *spread* is the difference between the asked price and the bid price. If a NASDAQ trader has a seller who is willing to sell a stock for 30 and the trader can get a buyer to bid 30$^1/_4$, the trader can keep the $^1/_4$ as his profit. That quarter point is the spread.

Philadelphia is the oldest exchange, having been organized in 1790. The New York Stock Exchange, also known as "The Big Board," is by far the largest and the best known. The organization that became the NYSE began trading stocks under a buttonwood tree at what is now 68 Wall Street on May 17, 1792. On March 8, 1817, the traders wrote a constitution and the name "New York Stock Exchange Board" was adopted. The name was changed to "New York Stock Exchange" on January 29, 1863.

Some years later, a rival exchange, the New York Curb Exchange, was founded. While NYSE members had moved indoors, "the Curb" literally traded outdoors until 1921. In 1953, the New York Curb Exchange changed its name to the American Stock Exchange. Although the short name is "the Amex," old-timers still refer to it as "the Curb." The Amex is presently in the process of merging with the NASDAQ.

The NASDAQ stands for National Association of Securities Dealers Automated Quotations. It's basically an automated information network that provides quotes (prices) on stocks for brokers registered with the National Association of Securities Dealers (NASD). Trades are done by phone or computer, with traders (members of the NASD) profiting from the spread between a stock's bid and asked prices, rather than adding a commission, as they do with exchange-listed stocks.

In rough numbers, there are about 3,200 stocks listed on the New York Stock Exchange, compared to about 900 on the Amex. The number for the NASDAQ is huge, probably approaching 40,000.

# What's with All the Animal References?

There's an old saying on Wall Street: "Bulls make money, bears make money, but pigs never do." But what's a "bull" and what's a "bear?" Bulls believe a stock or the stock market is going up in price. Bears believe the price of a stock and/or the stock market is going down.

Of course, the question still left to answer is where did these particular names come from, anyway? There are two explanations that are usually bandied about. The first is based on how each animal attacks: the bear by raking down with his large sharp claws, the bull by tossing up his large sharp horns. The second explanation comes from *The Wall Street Journal Guide to Understanding Money & Markets* and is a little fancier. According to the *Journal*, the term bear comes from sellers of bearskin who had a penchant for selling the bearskins before the bears were caught. Later on, the term morphed to represent speculators who, on a hunch that the price would drop, agreed to sell shares they didn't own. Their next move would be to quickly buy the low-priced stock and sell it for the previously agreed higher price.

Because bull and bear baiting were once popular sports, bulls came to mean the opposite of bears. Bulls were those who bought heavily expecting a stock price to go up.

Whatever explanation floats your boat, the words have carried down through the years, and people to this day describe themselves as bullish or bearish, depending on how they feel about a given stock or the market.

**Fiscal Facts**

How the broker who handles a securities trade is compensated can vary. On the New York Stock Exchange, for example, the system is "plus commission," while on the NASDAQ Over-the-Counter Market, it's "ex-commission." If you buy 100 shares of ABC stock via NYSE for $90 each, you will pay $9,000 for the shares plus a commission of $25. Your total transaction price is $9,025. If that stock were traded on the NASDAQ, the stock would be priced at $90.25, with the commission built in. You'd still pay a total transaction price of $9,025, but you wouldn't be aware that the extra $25 is commission.

**Fiscal Facts**

New York Stock Exchange volume:

December 15, 1886: First million share day (1.2 million shares)

October 29, 1929: 16.4 million shares traded as the stock market crashed.

August 18, 1982: First 100 million share day (132,681,120 shares)

October 28, 1997: First billion share day (1,202,550,000 shares)

# But What Do All Those Numbers Mean?

Have you ever ventured onto the stock pages of *The Wall Street Journal* or your local paper and been utterly overwhelmed and confused? Well, we're here to prep you so you can dive back in with total confidence. Those rows and rows of tiny numbers are called *stock tables* and are loaded with useful information, if you know how to read them.

Stock tables vary slightly from publication to publication. We have included the explanation for the daily table from *The Wall Street Journal*. The first stock listed in the August 12, 1998 edition was AAR. Reading from left to right, here's an explanation for each figure:

## 52-Week

| | Hi | Lo | Stock | Sym | Div | Yld % | PE | Vol 100s | Hi | Lo | Close | Net Chg |
|---|---|---|---|---|---|---|---|---|---|---|---|---|
| S | $32^3/_8$ | $21^3/_4$ | AAR | AIR | .34 | 1.4 | 19 | 304 | $27^7/_{16}$ | $23^1/_2$ | $23^{13}/_{16}$ | $-^{13}/_{16}$ |

1. **S. $32^3/_8$ $21^3/_4$.** The number on the left is the highest price at which this stock has traded for the last 52 weeks, excluding the last day of trading. The number on the right is the lowest price the stock has sunk to during the last 52 weeks. If there is an arrow up or an arrow down in this column, it indicates that there was a new 52-week high or low on the last day of trading.

### Investor's Idiom

If you own a share of stock priced at $100 and the company that issued it *splits* it in two, you'll own two shares of the same stock after the split worth $50 each. A stock split increases the number of shares outstanding and decreases share price of the stock. This is typically done when the share price has become very expensive, making the stock difficult to buy and sell. The stock split increases the marketability of the stock.

The S before the price range indicates that there was a stock split, or a stock dividend of at least 10 percent.

2. **AAR.** This is name of the stock. It's usually abbreviated so it can fit into these minuscule rows; e.g., AutDataProc is Automatic Data Processing.

3. **AIR.** This is the stock or "ticker" symbol. When you enter an order to buy or sell AAR, you would say, for example, "buy 100 AIR." Stock tickers were first introduced on the NYSE back on November 15, 1867.

4. **.34.** This is the annual cash dividend, based on the most recent quarterly declaration. For every share of this stock you owned, therefore, you would get 34¢ as a dividend payment every quarter (every three months).

5. **1.4.** This is the yield. Yield is derived from dividing the cash dividend of 34¢ by the closing stock price, which the table tells us farther down is $23^{13}/_{16}$.

6. **19.** This is the price/earnings ratio. It is the stock's market price divided by the company's earnings. It is a measure of the absolute and relative value of the company because it makes it easy to compare the company's performance to that of other companies with stock outstanding.

   Although the company's earnings are not listed in this table, we can derive them from the P/E ratio and the price (P) (which is down below under #10 and is $23^{13}/_{16}$). P/E ratio is a key concept to master because it tells you whether a stock is over- or undervalued. Remember, a stock that is undervalued will probably rise in price to its proper value, so when it's undervalued it could be a good buy.

7. **304.** This is the volume, or number of 100 share (round lot) trades. So, 304 means 30,400 shares traded that day.

8. **$27^7/_{16}$.** This is the high price for the last trading day.

9. **$23^1/_2$.** This is the low price for the last trading day.

10. **$23^{13}/_{16}$.** This is the closing price for the last trading day. This is the price used in the P/E ratio.

11. **$-^{13}/_{16}$.** This is the net change in price for the last trading day (net change from the previous day). $23^{13}/_{16} + {}^{13}/_{16} = 24^{10}/_{16}$ or $24^5/_8$. So the stock closed at 24 $^5/_8$ on the previous day.

Now you are ready to dazzle your friends and neighbors by whipping open the financial pages and commenting intelligently on the performance of Coca-Cola (abbreviated in the stock tables as KO) or Microsoft (MSFT) stock.

# The Key to Your Stock Knowledge: Price-Earnings Ratios

The Price-Earnings—or P/E—ratio is a key concept to master. So, let's do just that. The P/E ratio is price divided by earnings; the resulting number indicates how much or how little investors think of the earnings performance of the company, or:

$$\frac{\text{Price of stock per share}}{\text{Annual earnings per share}} = \text{Price-Earnings Ratio}$$

The P/E ratio is probably the most popular and useful measure of a stock's value. you can use it to compare the performance of a particular stock to the performance of the market as a whole or to the stock of other companies in the same industry. Or you can compare current P/E to historical P/Es. It's like today's temperature: You can compare it to yesterday's temperature, the temperature on the same day last year, or the highest and lowest temperatures on record. There are two caveats or adjustments that need to be made to the E part of it:

1. Some companies experience big swings in earnings. During a year of low earnings, the stock will have a very high P/E ratio. For example, assume a stock with $.10 in earnings is selling at $20 per share. This stock would have a P/E of 200! ($20 ÷ .10 = 200.) Anyone looking at the P/E ratio might conclude that this is a greatly overvalued (or overpriced) stock. But what if this represented the low in the company's business cycle, or the company just suffered a long strike? For this reason, analysts will "adjust" the earnings, either by using *normalized earnings* (what the company should earn in an average or normal year), or by estimating *pre-strike earnings*. Let's assume that in either case, these normalized earnings amount to $2.00 per share. Now the P/E ratio is a more realistic 10 ($20 divided by $2 = 10).

2. Some companies experience earnings during a year or quarter that will never happen again. Let's say the company above, for example, sells one of its divisions and reports earnings of $4.00. If we didn't adjust for these one-time earnings, the resulting P/E ratio of 5 ($20 ÷ $4 = 5) might mislead investors to assume the stock was very underpriced and a really good buy.

# Look into My P/E Crystal Ball

P/E ratios are very useful because they allow us to examine how a company has performed over time and make intelligent decisions about whether to buy or sell its stock. For instance, we can compare current to historical P/E ratios. We can also compare a company's current P/E ratio to the performance of the market as a whole (using the S&P 500's P/E, for example). This comparison is called the *relative P/E*. All of this information is listed in the newspaper.

Let's look at a simple example: Scooby Inc. makes Scoobies, and although the demand for Scoobies ebbs and flows (it's especially high just before Christmas), it doesn't fluctuate enough to require us to make an adjustment or normalize earnings.

## Scooby Inc.

| 10-Year P/E Range | 10-Year Relative P/E Range |
| --- | --- |
| 20–10 | 1.2–0.8 |
| **Current P/E** | **Current Relative P/E** |
| 12 | 1.0 |

Take a look at the first column. Over 10 years, the P/E for Scooby Inc. has varied from 20 to 10. The current P/E is 12. So, we can conclude that Scooby is selling close to its historical low P/E of 10. Hmm...this might be a good time to buy, because we can expect that Scooby stock will bounce back from this low.

The second column, however, tells us that the relative P/E of 1.0 is smack in the middle of the historical relative P/E range of 1.2–0.8. Hmm…maybe Scooby Inc. won't bounce back from this low. We'll have to do more research before deciding whether or not to buy this stock. We'll need to investigate whether earnings are increasing or decreasing, for example.

If you are going to get involved with trading individual stocks, an understanding of P/E ratios is crucial. The point is that the P/E is only useful when compared to other P/Es—be they historical or market figures. It's not a stand-alone number.

# Should You Play with the Big Kids or Just Get a Piggyback Ride?

Before you dive headlong onto the trading floor, let's think for a moment about how much time you're willing to invest in, well, investing. Only you can decide how much time and energy you're willing to devote to it. The great thing is you have options. Let's take a look at them now.

## *Take the Easy Route*

If you want to buy individual stocks, you'll be competing with full-time professionals who live and breathe P/E ratios and have the latest research and the finest analysts at their disposal. Just because you like to drive, does it make sense to drive in the Indy 500? Not only are you very unlikely to win, but you also could get hurt.

Owning a single stock or a limited number of stocks subjects you to an unhealthy degree of market risk. When the stock market is at an all-time high, there is always at least one stock that is selling at a new low for the year. Can you guarantee that you will not own that stock?

The best way to minimize market risk is to own a broadly diversified list of common stocks, spreading the risk out over 25 to 50 stocks. One bad apple out of 50 is acceptable; one out of one is not.

So, when it comes to your IRAs, 401(k)s, and other tax-deferred investments, stick with stock mutual funds. When you buy into a mutual fund you are buying shares in the fund, and the fund owns hundreds of stocks. Through the fund, you own those hundreds of stocks, too. Now, that's diversification. And you didn't have to do any of the hard work.

### Fiscal Facts

Prior to 1957, Standard and Poor's service used two indexes, a daily and a weekly index of 90 stocks. In 1957, S&P scrapped these indexes for a modern index of 500 stocks, calculated by a high-speed electronic computer. It is based on 425 industrials, 25 railroads, and 50 utilities. The index is carefully weighted according to the importance of the various stocks used. The 500 stocks represent the prices of shares comprising from 90 to 95 percent of the value of New York Stock Exchange common stock issues held by investors.

We'll dig into how to mix and match mutual funds in your portfolio to meet your investment needs in Chapter 12, "Why Mutual Funds Have Ruled the '90s."

## Creating Your Own Stock Index Fund

You can also consider buying and holding your own individual securities, with the emphasis on buying and holding. Remember, the more you trade your stock, the more taxable capital gains you could generate (go back to Chapter 8 to review how capital gains work if you need to). You could wind up owing a lot of tax and really eating into your profits.

Above all, keep in mind that if you want to own individual stocks, the idea is not to compete with professional traders. Trust us, if you try, you'll give yourself an ulcer. Most professional traders have ulcers, for that matter! Not to mention a pathological inability to sleep through the night without calling Tokyo.

**Super Strategy**

A better strategy might be to create your own personal *index fund*. An index fund is a mutual fund that mimics an index, such as the S&P 500, by buying the same stock in the same proportion as the index. The fund requires very little management: You simply buy the stock and hold it. No trades, no capital gains tax. You could purchase all 30 stocks in the Dow Jones Industrials index, for example, or the Dow Jones Composite of 65 stocks (30 industrials, 20 transportation stocks, and 15 utilities). The names of these stocks appear in *The Wall Street Journal*, C Section, Page C3 or C5 under the heading "The Dow Jones Averages."

## Just Buy Large-Cap Stocks

Similarly, you could select the 25 or 50 largest stocks in the S&P 500 index. By largest, we mean the stocks of companies with the most amount of money circulating in the stock market. This amount is called the *market capitalization* of a corporation. It equals the number of shares outstanding times the stock's market price. General Electric is currently the largest market capitalization stock (or, large-cap stock) listed on the stock exchange, with over $300 billion of its stock outstanding (being bought and sold on the market). The company with the largest market capitalization listed on NASDAQ is Microsoft, which also has about $300 billion of its stock circulating.

You would be surprised at how much of the S&P 500 index you could own by just owning the 25 or 50 largest stocks in the index. The top 50 stocks in the S&P 500 index account for over half of the index's total value. So, to set up your own index, you could just buy those stocks—rather than all 500 in the index.

Alternatively, you could buy the 25 to 50 largest stocks in the S&P Barra Growth Index. This index represents the most rapidly growing stocks in the S&P 500. This index currently contains 148 names. You would be surprised at how much of each index you can capture just by owning the 25 or 50 largest stocks.

|  | Top 25 Stocks as % of the index | Top 50 Stocks as % of the index |
|---|---|---|
| **S&P 500** | 31.1% | 50.8% |
| **S&P Barra Growth** | 59.1% | 79.9% |

Here are lists of the top 25 and 50 stocks currently held by the S&P Index and the S&P Barra Growth Index. To get a current list, contact Standard & Poor's at 1-800-852-1641.

## S&P 500 Index (500 Members)

| Top 25 | Top 50 |
|---|---|
| (1) General Electric | (26) Citicorp |
| (2) Microsoft Corp. | (27) Ford Motor Co. |
| (3) Coca-Cola Co. | (28) Schering-Plough |
| (4) Exxon Corp. | (29) American Home Products |
| (5) Merck & Co. | (30) Bellsouth Corp. |
| (6) Pfizer Inc. | (31) Fannie Mae |
| (7) Wal-Mart Stores | (32) Gillette Co. |
| (8) Intel Corp. | (33) Pepsico Inc. |
| (9) Procter & Gamble | (34) Abbott Labs |
| (10) Royal Dutch Petroleum | (35) Chase Manhattan Corp. |
| (11) Bristol-Myers Squibb | (36) BankAmerica Corp. |
| (12) International Business Machines | (37) Home Depot Inc. |
| (13) Lucent Technology Inc. | (38) Mobil Corp. |
| (14) American International Group | (39) Warner-Lambert |
| (15) Johnson & Johnson | (40) Dell Computer |
| (16) Philip Morris Co. | (41) Hewlett-Packard |
| (17) Cisco Systems | (42) First Union Corp. |
| (18) AT&T Corp. | (43) Chevron Corp. |
| (19) DuPont (E.I.) | (44) GTE Corp. |

*continues*

| Top 25 | Top 50 |
| --- | --- |
| (20) Nationsbank Corp. | (45) Morgan Stanley |
| (21) SBC Communications | (46) Unilever |
| (22) Travelers Group | (47) WorldCom Inc. |
| (23) Bell Atlantic | (48) American Express |
| (24) Disney (Walt) Co. | (49) Time Warner Inc. |
| (25) Lilly (Eli) | (50) Ameritech Corp. |

## S&P Barra Growth Index (148) Members)

| Top 25 | Top 50 |
| --- | --- |
| (1) General Electric | (26) Home Depot Inc. |
| (2) Microsoft Corp. | (27) Pepsico Inc. |
| (3) Coca-Cola Co. | (28) Dell Computer |
| (4) Merck & Co. | (29) Warner-Lambert |
| (5) Pfizer Inc. | (30) GTE Corp. |
| (6) Wal-Mart Stores | (31) Morgan Stanley |
| (7) Intel Corp. | (32) American Express |
| (8) Procter & Gamble | (33) Unilever |
| (9) Bristol-Myers Squibb | (34) Ameritech Corp. |
| (10) Lucent Technology Inc. | (35) Compaq Computer |
| (11) American International Group | (36) Tyco International Ltd. |
| (12) Johnson & Johnson | (37) Schlumberger Ltd. |
| (13) Philip Morris Co. | (38) Minnesota Mining & Mfg. |
| (14) Cisco Systems | (39) Monsanto Co. |
| (15) DuPont (E.I.) | (40) Xerox Corp. |
| (16) Lilly (Eli) | (41) Airtouch Communications |
| (17) Bell Atlantic | (42) US Bancorp |
| (18) SBC Communications | (43) Computer Assoc. |
| (19) Schering-Plough | (44) Medtronic Inc. |
| (20) American Home Products | (45) Northern Telecom |
| (21) Fannie Mae | (46) Sara Lee Corp. |
| (22) Gillette Co. | (47) Colgate Palmolive |
| (23) Chase Manhattan Corp. | (48) Kimberly-Clark |
| (24) Abbott Labs | (49) Gap Inc. |
| (25) Hewlett-Packard | (50) Campbell Soup Co. |

## How to Manage Your Index Fund: Leave It Alone!

Once you've created your personal index, what do you do? Nothing. Absolutely nothing. Don't execute a single trade. Just collect the dividends and invest them in a taxable or tax-free money market fund. One caution: This strategy only works if you are investing a large sum at one time. If you are investing $100–$400 per month, you can't really buy 25–50 stocks at a time. If that is your situation, you can still participate in an index by buying an index mutual fund. More on those in Chapter 12.

## The Best Ways to React to Blips

If you believe the newspapers, we should hold our collective breath every time the stock market takes a plunge and breathe a collective sigh of relief the minute the Dow Jones Average heads back up.

As a long-term investor, though, you should have absolutely no interest in and no concern for short-term blips in the market. Just keep breathing, no matter what! Whether the market is up or down today, last week or next month is irrelevant to your long-term game plan. In fact, ignore the financial section of the newspapers entirely (once you have shown everybody how you can read it).

By the same token, don't torture yourself following the daily ups and downs of your mutual funds. Just check on them once every three months. Each calendar quarter the papers publish quarterly mutual fund results. And you will most likely be able to access each of your fund's quarterly reports.

The most important thing you can do with this quarterly information is not react to it. Remember, you are in this for the long haul, and over time quarterly ups and downs mean nada.

# Asset Allocation/Rebalancing

Dollar cost averaging is a handy concept to help you keep your investments on target. When you invest, you allocate your money among various types of ventures according to percentages that you set as goals.

For instance, assume that last year you had a $100,000 portfolio and you decided to invest 50 percent in stocks and 50 percent in bonds. Obviously, you end up with $50,000 in both stocks and

### Investor's Idiom

There's a very complicated principle behind dollar cost averaging that we call K.I.S.S.—Keep It Simple, Stupid!

### Crash Alert

Applying dollar cost averaging to your portfolio is only an effective strategy for tax-deferred accounts. If your portfolio is not tax-sheltered, cashing in some of your stock to buy bonds and rebalancing your portfolio could cause you to owe a lot of capital gains tax.

bonds. Well, last year was a very good year for stocks, but not so good for bonds. Let's say that by now your investment in stocks has grown to $72,000, but you took a bit of a loss in bonds, and are left with $48,000 there. Your total portfolio is $72,000 + $48,000 = $120,000.

It's great that you've made money, but now your portfolio is a little out of whack. You definitely have more than 50 percent invested in stock and less than 50 percent invested in bonds. Time to rebalance. In this case, you need to sell some stock and buy some bonds in order to split your $120,000 50/50 between stocks and bonds. You should rebalance so you have $60,000 in stocks and $60,000 in bonds. You've used dollar cost averaging to figure out where the scales tipped and to rebalance your investments so you stay on track. Once a year, on your birthday (there's that day again), check to see if your stock or bond portion is out of balance and needs to be rebalanced.

# How Much Stock Should Be in Your Portfolio?

According to Ibbotson Associates (a firm specializing in financial statistics), common stocks have provided an average return of 13 percent over the last 72 years. This is more than twice the return for long-term Treasury bonds (5.6 percent average) and three times the average 3.86 percent return for T-bills. It's also four times the average inflation rate of 3.2 percent for the same period.

So, the evidence is overwhelming that you should keep a significant portion of your assets in common stocks—if you are at least 10 years from your planned retirement age. The simple rule is the longer time you have until you retire, the more you should have in common stocks. Here are some guides for how you should consider allocating your assets at different ages.

|  | Age 17–35 | Age 36–45 | Age 46–55 |
|---|---|---|---|
| **Stocks** | 100% | 70% | 50% |
| **Bonds** | 0% | 30% | 50% |
| **Bills** | 0% | 0% | 0% |

Another easy rule is: Multiply the number of years until you retire by two to get the percentage of your assets you should keep in stock.

| Age | Years to Retirement × 2 = | Stock % |
|---|---|---|
| up to 25 | 40 × 2 | 80% |
| 30 | 35 × 2 | 70% |
| 35 | 30 × 2 | 60% |
| 40 | 25 × 2 | 50% |
| 45 | 20 × 2 | 40% |
| 50 | 15 × 2 | 30% |
| 55 | 10 × 2 | 20% |

Both of these rules of thumb reflect two principles that should be the guiding light behind all of your retirement investing:

1.  The further you are from retirement, the more of your assets should be invested in stock.

2.  Change your stock/bond ratio no more frequently than every five years. You're not a professional investor, so you shouldn't be reacting to every zig and zag in the markets. Stay the course and you'll do fine.

What if you're starting to invest just before a "change point"—at age 44, for example? Start with the allocation recommendations for the next closest age bracket—45 to 50, in this case.

### Super Strategy

What if you reach a five-year mark and the table calls for you to cut back on stocks, but the market is weak and you are concerned that you won't get a good price for them? Because you're not a professional investor, go ahead and sell the stock anyway. If you're truly convinced that stocks have declined substantially and you wish to wait a year, go ahead, but don't defer your decision more than a year.

## If You're over 55

If you are over 55 or fewer than 10 years from retirement, you're dealing with the biggest risk in stocks, which is their volatility. Although over the long run stocks do very well, a dip right before you need your money can trash your retirement. You can only reduce this risk by reducing the percentage of your assets in stocks. On the other hand, only stocks offer some protection against inflation. And they can really grow. Therefore, it's wise to keep some equity in your portfolio even after you retire. How much? That's up to you. At least 10 to 20 percent is great, if you can swing it and are comfortable with that level of risk.

# Dollar Cost Averaging, or "How to Own Stocks and Stay Happy"

But how do you avoid the emotional roller coaster that is so much a part of the stock market? By staying well diversified and remembering that over the long haul, market ups are great and market downs are buying opportunities—so they're great, too. Ignore the histrionic reports in newspapers and on TV when the Dow Jones takes a dive. It will recover; it just may take awhile. As long as you have the time to ride it out, your portfolio will be fine.

After all, market drops are great buying opportunities. Assume you invest $300 per month in stock mutual funds. Market goes up? Great, you're worth more. Market goes down? Great, you can buy more shares with the same amount of money (think of this as the financial equivalent of a white sale). Let's say you bought $300 of a $10 fund last month, or 30 shares.

The fund declines 10 percent: Cool, $300 buys you 33 shares this month ($300 ÷ $10 × .9 = $9 = 33). Is this a great game or what?

You now have under your belt two of the great secrets to successful investing:

1. Rebalance your portfolio from time to time using dollar cost averaging.
2. Don't sweat the stock market's ups and downs.

And the hits just keep coming! If you're still frothing at the mouth to get into buying individual stocks, read the next chapter.

---

### The Least You Need to Know

➤ Bulls believe stock prices are going to rise; bears think stock prices are going to fall. You can ignore both by using dollar cost averaging.

➤ Stock investors try to find and buy undervalued stocks, because the stock price should eventually rise to more accurately reflect its value.

➤ Unless you have a lot of money to invest in a wide range of individual stocks, stick with stock mutual funds because they provide greater diversification.

➤ Set percentages for how you want to allocate your assets and rebalance your portfolio once a year. And only change your stock/bond ratio every five years.

➤ The further you are from retirement, the more of your assets should be invested in stock.

---

# Chapter 10

# So You Want to Play with Stocks

## In This Chapter

➤ Tips for trading like a pro

➤ What makes a stock worth buying

➤ How to glean the gold from annual reports

➤ Using a broker to place a trade

If you are an amateur investor, there are only three reasons to own individual stocks:

1. Your employer is a publicly traded company, and you want to own a few shares so you can keep current on company developments. If this is the case, see if your employer offers a stock purchase plan (which usually sells the stock at a discount price). Buy the minimum number of shares.

2. A relative passed away, leaving you shares of ABC Corporation with this admonition: "Whatever you do, don't sell ABC Corporation." If your conscience won't let you sell, give the shares to your favorite charity and take the tax deduction.

3. You love the action. Some people play the horses, some people play roulette or poker, some people play the office pool, and you play the stock market. Okay, we all have our vices; admit it to yourself (and your spouse), control it as best you can, and get on with your life. Just don't call what you're doing investing. It's entertainment—pay for it out of your entertainment budget.

You might also buy individual stocks for the reason we discussed in the previous chapter: to invest a lump sum in a taxable portfolio for retirement purposes. But this won't satisfy a desire to tangle with the pros in the stock market, as you're not supposed to trade these stocks. Remember...?

Still not persuaded? Still want to trade like a pro? Okay, here we go!

# Tips for Trading Like a Pro

Do:

➤ Use your broker to execute your trades, not to do your research. After all, paying full commission to a broker is like paying list price for a car.

➤ Negotiate your broker's commission before, not after, placing the order.

➤ Choose carefully between a full-service broker versus a discount/deep discount broker. If you feel you are getting your money's worth from a full-service broker, God bless, but you probably don't need or want his/her suggestions and reports. At least, not enough to pay for 'em.

➤ Avoid speculative securities. Initial public offerings (IPOs), *penny stocks*, and "hot tip" stocks aren't worth the risk. Even the best traders don't buy all their stocks at what turn out to be low prices; mistakes are part of the business. But good quality stocks recover and eventually go on to new highs; losers just curl up and die. IPO's are simple to deal with: The "hot" ones go to large institutional customers; the little person might get a few shares if he/she is lucky. If you are offered a good chunk of an IPO, odds are the broker was unable to unload all the shares to institutional customers and is calling with a "hot tip" because he's got to get rid of them somehow. Penny stocks are a speculator's dream. A $40 stock that goes up an eighth equals a yawn, but a $1 stock up $1/8$ equals a 12.5 percent gain! There's also the ego boost of saying "I just put away 10,000 shares of X." But "up $1/8$" can quickly become "down $1/8$." And wait until you see the commission on 10,000 shares! Temptation, get thee hence!

**Investor's Idiom**

*Penny stocks* are stocks that are selling for a very low price—typically one, two, or three dollars.

Regarding hot tips in general, please face facts: You're a small player, and when the hot tip gets all the way down the chain to you, it'll be lukewarm at best. The rule of thumb is: If an investment seems too good to be true, it *is* too good to be true.

# If You Buy It, You'd Better Love It

Ideally, you should buy stocks that you never have to sell. We say this because you must pay taxes every time you sell a stock for a profit.

If you paid $10,000 for a stock, held it for a year and sold it for $15,000, you would have $14,000 to reinvest—not $15,000. The difference is the long-term capital gains tax (e.g. 20 percent) on your $5,000 profit. If you had sold it before a year was up, you'd have a short-term capital gains tax (up to 39.6 percent). Depending on your tax bracket, that can be a huge bite out of your profit. In addition, there are commission costs for both the sale and the subsequent purchase. Not to mention state and local taxes.

### Super Strategy

Obviously, there are good reasons sometimes to sell a stock. Maybe you made a mistake in the first place, or the company has fallen apart. But your best bet is to buy the stocks of stable, high-quality companies that you'll feel comfortable owning for a long time. If they pay a modest but growing cash dividend, so much the better.

# The Biggest "Do" of All

Here's the "Big Daddy Do" for amateur investors: Limit your investments to quality companies. What's a quality company? Below are the characteristics that make a company worthy of your precious investment dollars:

### Fiscal Facts

The top 10 NASDAQ stocks, as of 7/13/98, are Microsoft, Intel, Cisco, Dell, WorldCom, MCI, Oracle, TeleCommunications, Inc., Sun Microsystems, and Amgen. Nearly half the companies trading on NASDAQ are technology companies.

1. Market leadership. If you want to buy stock in a certain industry, buy the market leader— buying number two or number three is not worth the aggravation. How can you tell if a company is the market leader? When size, marketing power, and cost control make it the most profitable company in its industry; when its new products or services are more readily accepted in the marketplace than the competition's; when it's the name investors buy when they want to participate in the industry; and when it's the last stock to be sold (if it ever is sold) when investors look to reduce industry exposure.

2. A strong balance sheet. Professional investors don't like to be blindsided by a company that suddenly develops credit problems. A strong balance sheet (more assets than liabilities) ensures a high credit rating, which in turn ensures that the company pays low interest rates when it does borrow. A strong balance sheet also enables the company to quickly take advantage of acquisition opportunities.

Ideally, an industrial company would have no debt, but this is a rarity. To evaluate a company's debt position, take a look at its debt to total capitalization ratio. This ratio is found in the annual report and should be between 25–30 percent. To figure it out for yourself, use this formula:

$$\frac{\text{long-term debt}}{\text{long-term debt + preferred stock + common stock + retained earnings}}$$

3. A consistent and seasoned track record. Any company whose stock you seek to own should have at least a 10-year public (not private) record to analyze. Look for how well or poorly the company did in previous industry and/or general economic downturns. Do revenues and earnings increase each and every year? Nine years out of ten? At least four years out of five?

**Crash Alert**

Be leery of corporations that buy back shares each year, irrespective of stock price levels. In some cases, they even borrow money to make the purchases. This is just a maneuver to improve the stock price.

Be careful of companies with above-average earnings growth (+10–20 percent) but only average or below average (+3–5 percent) revenue growth. This may indicate that management is trying to improve the bottom line by raising prices or cutting costs. This will only keep the company profitable for so long if revenues aren't increasing.

Here's a neat rule: Look for companies where unit sales (e.g., the number of widgets sold per year) are growing at least 50 percent faster than the real, or inflation-adjusted, gross domestic product (GDP) in this country. The GDP is reported quarterly in newspapers and on TV newscasts.

4. A high reinvestment rate. What does the company do with the money it makes? Does it pay out a significant sum to shareholders in the form of cash dividends? Companies that pay out a high percent of earnings to stockholders as cash dividends are telling you, by their actions, they do not view the future of the company with much favor. If they did, they would reinvest those dollars back into the business. Does it buy back a significant number of shares, or does it reinvest a significant portion back into the business? When a company buys back its own shares, it's artificially forcing up the stock price by decreasing the amount of stock outstanding. Sometimes management will do this to protect a stock that has been pummeled by investors for what management believes to be short-term or transitory reasons.

# Researching Individual Stocks

There are good research resources available to the individual investor, many at your local library. In addition, if you hire a full-service broker, you can indirectly avail yourself of his or her research department.

In our opinion, the two most basic, cost-effective, and objective research tools are the *Value Line Investment Survey* and *Standard & Poor's Stock Guides*. Both may be available at your local library, but if not, or if you wish to have your own personal copies, we have provided subscriber numbers below (aren't we nice?).

## *The Priceless Value of Value Line*

The basic Value Line service covers approximately 1,700 stocks. For each stock, Value Line provides two rankings: timeliness and safety. Of the two, pay particular attention to safety. Stocks are ranked on a 1–5 basis, with 1 being the safest. Don't consider any stock with less than a 2 rating.

Value Line also provides scores for four other key indicators:

➤ financial strength

➤ stock price stability

➤ stock price growth persistence

➤ earnings predictability

Value Line includes, in addition to the rankings and key indicators cited above, a great deal of relevant statistical and narrative information. Value Line reports are updated regularly. The individual company write-ups will take some getting used to, but after awhile you will find that you can easily determine a company's earnings growth rate and the consistency of that growth rate.

Use Value Line to help you select at least 25 stocks that:

1. are safe or very safe (remember, that means a ranking of 1 or 2)

2. are growing at an above-average rate

3. are growing consistently and steadily

What does "above average" mean? We suggest you look for a minimum of 8 percent and, ideally, 10 percent growth. And keep an eye on consistency. For a 10 percent grower, 10 percent a year is perfect but rarely achieved. A range of 8–12 percent is very consistent. From 6–14 percent is acceptable. But if the company's earnings swing between 0 percent and 30 percent, for example, it's too volatile to be in your portfolio.

To subscribe to Value Line, call 1-800-833-0046. A one-year subscription costs $570.

## S&P Stock Guides: Another Great Tool

Standard & Poor's Stock Guides (Bond Guides are also available) are an excellent research tool. The guides come out monthly and cover over 7,000 stocks, as well as mutual funds and variable annuity/life investments. The guides are not pocket-sized, but at 5" × 8" fit nicely into briefcases or pocketbooks.

You can order by calling 1-800-221-5277, or visit their web site at **http://www. stockinfo.standardpoor.com**.

## The Best Newspapers for Stock Info

Finally, two newspapers, *Investors Business Daily* and *The Wall Street Journal*, do an excellent job of tracking the stock market and individual stocks. Either may be available at your local library. To order a subscription to the *Journal*, call 1-800-521-2170, ext. 247. The Internet address is **http://wsj.com**. To subscribe to *IBD*, call 1-800-547-1919.

If you simply must follow the market during the day, both CNBC and Bloomberg Information TV do a good job of keeping you current. For a nightly wrap-up, check out PBS's Nightly Business Report.

### Investor's Idiom

A corporation is expected to issue an *annual report* once a year that includes the company's financial statements—income statement, balance sheet, cash flow statement, etc. The company is also required to file a *10-K report* with the Securities and Exchange Commission (SEC). The 10-K is the same information in the annual report, minus pictures and narrative. A company must also file an *8-K report* with the SEC within 30 days regarding any event that could affect the company's performance. The *SEC* is an agency that was founded by Congress in 1933 after the 1929 stock market crash to regulate the stock market and protect investors.

# All the News That's Fit to Print: Company Annual Reports

The most valuable research you can get your hands on is provided by the companies themselves. Once you purchase individual equities, the company (or your brokerage firm) will begin stuffing your mailbox with quarterly and annual reports.

If you want those reports before you purchase a stock, check the stock tables in *The Wall Street Journal*'s Section C. You will find a three-leaf clover–type symbol next to those companies that provide a free annual and free current quarterly report. To obtain these reports, *call The Wall Street Journal*'s Annual Reports Club at 1-800-654-2582, fax your request to 1-800-965-5679, or order via the Internet at **http://www.icbinc.com**.

Annual reports and quarterly reports are like report cards. Avoid the verbiage and the pretty pictures, and you'll be able to tease out trends from the financial statements. The *10-K* is the annual report equivalent filed with the *SEC*. It's sometimes more revealing than the corporate reports to shareholders and comes without the rosey verbiage.

Finally, the *8-K* form is a report that a corporation's managers must file with the SEC within 30 days of any event that might affect the financial status or share price of the company.

## Analyzing a Company's Annual Report

When that annual report arrives in the mail, skip all the narrative and pictures and turn straight to the Income Statement near the back (also called the Profit/Loss Statement). Below is a guide for how to analyze each item of the Income Statement—'cause there's gold in them thar hills! (While you're at it, take a quick gander again at the personal income statement you developed in Chapter 4. It's basically the same.)

1.  Gross or Total Revenues: For quarterly reports, how do revenues compare with the previous quarter and the same quarter in the previous year? For annual reports, how do they compare to last year, five years ago, 10 years ago? You are looking for changes or breaks in the normal patterns, up or down. If you find any, scan the text for explanations. If you aren't satisfied with them, call the company, ask for the investor relations officer (IRO) and introduce yourself as a shareholder with questions. If there is no IRO, or you are still not satisfied, go progressively up the line: treasurer, financial vice president, president. Remember, you are a shareholder, an owner; act like one.

2.  Gross Profit: This figure is the result of subtracting the cost of goods from the actual revenues. Cost of goods sold is the cost of making each additional unit of whatever's being sold. Gross profit is an indication of manufacturing efficiency: Is it improving or deteriorating? Again, compare the numbers for previous years and quarters. If you really want to get fancy, divide gross profit into revenue and multiply by 100 to get a percentage called "gross profit margin." You can analyze every item on the income statement this way—by dividing it into revenue. This way you can see how each item looks as a percentage of revenue. If gross profit is only 5 percent of revenue, for example, where's all the revenue money going? Why isn't gross profit higher?

3.  Selling, General, and Administrative Expense (SG&A): Again, compare to past periods. Any big changes? Divide this expense (SG&A) into revenue.

    If the resulting percentage is very high, maybe that's your answer for why gross profit is low—because the company has very high expenses.

4.  Research & Development (R&D): Sometimes this item is included in SG&A; sometimes it's broken out separately. For some companies (such as technology companies), this is a critical expenditure; it could make or break future growth

opportunities. Look to see if R&D is rising in line with revenues; if not, the company may be shortchanging its future to keep its current earnings looking attractive.

5. Earnings Before Interest, Depreciation, and Amortization (referred to as EBIDA and pronounced "E-bah-dah"): the current trendy figure used to measure a company's profitability and efficiency.

6. Pre-Tax Earnings: Earnings before taxes; again, divide into revenues to obtain pre-tax margins.

7. Tax Rate: Is the tax rate rising or falling? If falling, management may have manipulated it to cover up declining revenues.

8. Net Income: Income after taxes. Any cash dividends on common stock will be paid from this sum.

There you go. You're now your own security analyst! It's kind of like being a detective: looking for clues in all the right (or wrong) places. As you go through this exercise for the first time, think how each of these categories relate to your personal income statement.

## Analyzing the Balance Sheet

Just like your personal balance sheet, a corporate balance sheet in an annual report is broken down between assets and liabilities, and each of these categories, in turn, are divided into short- (or current) and long-term assets and liabilities. Like so:

| Assets | Liabilities |
|---|---|
| *Current Assets* | *Current Liabilities* |
| Cash & Marketable Securities | Accounts Payable |
| Accounts Receivable | Debt due w/in 12 mos. |
| *Long-term Assets* | *Long-term Debt* |
| Plant | Mortgages |
| Equipment | Debentures |
| Other | **Shareholders Equity** |
| Goodwill | Preferred Stock |
| | *Common:* |
| | Par Value |
| | Paid in Capital |
| | Retained Earnings |
| Total Assets | Total Liabilities and Shareholders Equity |

The balance sheet contains all the information you need (i.e., is the company carrying lots of debt? What kind of cash is available?) to analyze a company's financial strength and financing strategies. Analysts look at several ratios when examining a balance sheet. These ratios indicate the amount of long-term debt the company is carrying and how it relates to the amount of equity outstanding.

Debt-to-Equity ratio: Total Debt/Total Equity

Debt ratio: Total Debt/Total Assets

Current ratio: Current Assets/Current Liabilities

Analysts also watch for increases or decreases in cash, accounts receivable, and accounts payable.

# How to Use a Broker to Place a Trade

Once you've decided what stocks you want to buy, you'll need a broker. *Broker* is a generic name for the person in the middle who facilitates trades between buyers and sellers. Many brokerage firms have created more impressive titles such as "registered representative" (because the brokers are registered with the Securities and Exchange Commission and represent their firm), sometimes shortened to "RR." "Account executive" (AE) is another popular title.

Find a *full-service*, *discount*, or *deep discount broker* the same way you would find an insurance agent—by asking friends and relatives to recommend someone or by looking in the Yellow Pages under Stock and Bond Brokers. However, this still may seem like too much work for you. If either of these options don't pan out for you, you might want to contact your local bank, as banks increasingly offer a wide variety of investment services.

A full-service broker's tasks are the following:

1. to broker a trade.

2. to serve as an investment resource for the customer—calling the customer with stock or bond recommendations, for example.

3. to move stock "off the shelves" that his or her firm has brought to market for a corporation. There have been cases where brokers push bad products in exchange for bonuses from the company, or just to earn a fat commission.

Sometimes #3 is the only reason for #2! Discount, and especially deep discount, brokers perform only role #1.

**Investor's Idiom**

A *broker* will act as an intermediary between you and the stock market. He or she will seek out buyers for stock you want to sell and find sellers of stock you want to buy. *Full-service brokers* also provide research and make recommendations. *Discount* and *deep-discount brokers* are services that simply execute trades.

# *Placing an Order with Your Broker*

Think of the order you give to your broker as falling within one of three forms:

1. The Market Order. This instructs the broker to buy or sell at whatever the current market price is, no matter where it goes before your order is filled. You can expect that your broker will complete trades of 1,000 shares or less at or very close to the last trading price recorded. Such orders are typically executed electronically. You can usually get your price confirmed before you hang up after placing the order with your broker. Larger orders of 25,000+ shares may have to be "worked." For example, if ABC stock is moving up and you place an order to buy 50,000 shares of that stock, which was trading at 45, you may receive a report from your broker that you purchased:

   10,000 shares at $45^1/_8$

   15,000 shares at $45^1/_4$

   10,000 shares at $45^3/_8$

   At this point, your broker may say: "I can fill the balance at $45^3/_4$." Now it's your decision: Do you want to fill at that price or step aside and see if the price declines? If you go ahead, your broker would most likely report the balance of the trade as:

   100 shares at $45^1/_2$

   100 shares at $45^5/_8$

   14,800 shares at $45^3/_4$

   Your average stock price (before commissions) would be $45.40.

2. The Limit Order to Buy or Sell. Using the above example, you might conclude that ABC stock will settle down in price and instruct your broker to "buy 50,000 shares of ABC with a 45 limit." Next, you must tell the broker if this is a day order (i.e., either filled that day or canceled) or "good 'til canceled" (referred to as GTC). That means the order will stay open until the broker fills it or you cancel it.

   The problem with GTCs is you can forget you placed them. Maybe a few weeks later you'll buy alternative stock XYZ only to receive a follow-up call from your broker stating that "we just filled your GTC on ABC." Whoops, a little short on money? It's easier to stay on top of things if you cancel and reenter your order each day, although your broker won't appreciate the extra work.

3. The Stop or Stop Loss Order. Let's say you bought ABC stock at 30, saw it shoot up to $45^3/_4$, and it has now backed down to 42. At this point, you may be more willing to lock in a gain rather than roll the dice to see if it crests the $45^3/_4$ high again. So, you instruct your broker to place a stop loss order to sell at $40. If the stock goes up, great; if it goes down, you're "out" at 40.

Unless you are a professional investor dealing with large orders, our advice would be to use market orders. Of the three, there isn't the margin of error that exists in the latter two choices. You're still getting in on the action, but you're letting a professional do most of the work.

## Discount Brokers

Discount/deep-discount brokers perform a single task: They execute your order, be it market, limit, or whatever. In some cases, you don't even talk to a human being. If you know what you want to do and don't have a large or otherwise difficult order, go the discount route. There's one caveat, though: Once you choose a discount broker, stick with him or her. Otherwise, you'll be reconciling statements from at least two different brokerage firms, and that's just no fun. You want to keep things as simple as possible, right? Right!

The advantage of a discount broker is a lower commission rate. Period. No free toasters, no hand-holding, no "hot tips." If this is all you want from a broker, go for it.

# When Should You Buy Stock?

It depends on how much money you have and how much time you want to devote to managing your individual stock holdings. We're going to assume your answer to both questions is: "Not much."

If you have selected your stocks but can only afford to purchase a round lot (100 shares) of each, go ahead and buy. If you can buy, say, 200 shares of each, buy 100 now and the rest:

➤ on your anniversary date—usually your birthday

➤ or if the stock declines 10 percent from your purchase price, whichever comes first

**Super Strategy**

If you set aside an additional sum each year to purchase stocks, or if you plan to reinvest your dividends, pick an annual portfolio anniversary date. Avoid vacation months, holiday months, or January, which is generally a strong month for stock prices because institutions are buying stocks for their pension and profit-sharing plans that month. Pick your birthday month, or, if your birthday clashes with any of the above stipulations, an "interim" time like late October–early November.

## *Rebalancing Your Stock Holdings*

If you look at the stocks you've purchased, they probably fall into a few different categories. For instance, some might be "energy" (i.e., oil companies) or "technology" (i.e., software manufacturers). These categories are called sectors. A *sector* is a particular segment of the economy. Now, when your portfolio anniversary comes up, take a look at how each stock you hold in each sector has performed.

Now, stick with us here. We're going to tell you to do something that might not seem like the obvious choice: If you plan to purchase more stocks, put more money into the stocks that did poorly. Why? So that you maintain positions for each sector that are comparable. This is another example of dollar cost averaging.

Let's say you started with $10,000 and split it evenly, buying $2,500 worth of stock in each of four different sectors: technology, health care, energy, and finance. By the end of the first year, maybe your technology stocks are now worth $3,000, health care stocks dropped to $2,000, energy shot up to $4,000, and your finance stocks held steady at $2,500. Your portfolio is now worth $12,000, but you no longer own an even 25 percent in each sector.

| | |
|---|---|
| $3,000 | (technology) |
| + $2,000 | (health care) |
| + $4,500 | (energy) |
| + $2,500 | (finance) |
| = $12,000 | |

We're suggesting that you rebalance your portfolio so that you again own 25 percent in each sector. With a $12,000 portfolio, that would mean putting $12,000 × .25, or $3,000, into each sector. You'll have to sell off some of your energy stocks to beef up your holdings in health care and finance.

Professionals might disagree with this approach, arguing that you should pour money into your "winners" and less into your "losers." This is fine for professionals whose job it is to carefully research their holdings. Right now, you're a rookie and your one big asset is (yes, you guessed it) time. As long as you stick with top quality investments, the time you invest in them is more than likely to pay off. You may not have as many big winners, but, by the same token, you should have fewer (and maybe no) losers.

# Diversifying Your Stock Portfolio: How Many Holdings Are Enough?

We mentioned in a previous chapter that you need at least 25 stocks to achieve an acceptable degree of diversification. That doesn't mean that owning 25 drug stocks will give you diversification, however! You need diversification by number (25+), and by sector or type.

Let's look at how the S&P 500 is weighted by sector, and compare this to four tax-advantaged portfolios we've set up:

## Diversification

| Sector Weighting | S&P 500 | S&P 500 | | S&P Barra Growth | |
|---|---|---|---|---|---|
| | | Top 25(1) | Top 50(1) | Top 25(1) | Top 50(1) |
| 1. Basic Materials | 3.6% | 4 | 2 | 4 | 4 |
| 2. Capital Goods | 7.5 | 4 | 2 | 4 | 4 |
| 3. Consumer Cyclical | 9.4 | 8 | 10 | 4 | 6 |
| 4. Consumer Staples | 14.9 | 12 | 12 | 16 | 20 |
| 5. Energy | 6.8 | 8 | 8 | 0 | 2 |
| 6. Finance | 17.9 | 12 | 20 | 12 | 12 |
| 7. Health care | 11.8 | 20 | 18 | 32 | 20 |
| 8. Technology | 15.9 | 20 | 14 | 20 | 20 |
| 9. Communication Serv. | 7.1 | 12 | 14 | 8 | 10 |
| 10. Utilities | 3.0 | 0 | 0 | 0 | 0 |
| 11. Transportation | 1.0 | 0 | 0 | 0 | 0 |
| 12. Misc. | 1.0 | 0 | 0 | 0 | 0 |
| **Total** | 100.0 | 100.0 | 100.0 | 100.0 | 100.0 |

*(1) Equal weighted*

As you can see, our four model portfolios own stock in at least 8 of the 12 sectors that are available in the market. This is so we won't be zigging when the market is zagging.

If you select individual securities for your portfolios, be sure to line them up by sector as shown above to make sure you have good diversification. Keep in mind the following rule of thumb: For each of the five biggest sectors of the S&P 500, try not to own more than two times the percentage amount of stock that the S&P 500 owns. And make sure you don't own less than half of what the S&P 500 owns in each of those same five sectors.

Okay, if you want to play with stocks, at least we've done our best to goof-proof you!

## The Least You Need to Know

➤ Save bucks by using a discount broker to execute your trades, not to research them.

➤ Avoid IPOs, penny stock, "hot tips," and other speculative trades.

➤ Only buy quality stocks that you feel comfortable owning for a long time.

➤ The best research tools are Value Line, *S&P Stock Guides*, *Investor's Business Daily*, *The Wall Street Journal*, and company annual reports.

➤ In general, stick with market orders when having your broker execute a trade.

➤ Rebalance your portfolio once a year.

# Chapter 11

# Slow and Steady Wins the Race: Fixed-Income Securities

## In This Chapter

➤ What are fixed-income securities?

➤ Using fixed-income securities to protect your portfolio

➤ The lowdown on bonds

➤ How to buy Treasury bonds

➤ What to buy and what to avoid

Maybe you're not the type that likes to take big chances. You like to know what's coming around the corner, and, if you can't, you at least like to have a back-up plan to deal with life's little boomerangs. If this is you, there are two words you need to remember: fixed income. A fixed-income security entitles you to regular fixed payments of interest income on your investments. If you don't like taking chances, fixed-income securities are a great place to park your investing dollars. If you do have designs on the stock market, then they're a great way to balance out your portfolio. In this chapter, we're going to give you the lowdown on fixed-income securities and how they can benefit you.

## What Are Fixed-Income Securities for?

Bonds and notes are fixed-income securities that corporations and governments issue in order to borrow money. When corporations raise money using fixed-income securities, it's called *debt financing*. When they issue stock to raise money, it's called *equity financing*. Basically, you agree to lend a sum of money and the borrower gives you a

### Investor's Idiom

*Bonds*, *notes*, and *bills* are all IOUs that corporations and governments issue when they want to borrow money. The IOU promises to pay interest and the amount borrowed on a specified date. These IOUs are called bonds when the specified date is longer than 10 years from the date the bond is issued. When the maturity date is between one and ten years from issuance, the IOU is a note. When it's under one year, the IOU is called a bill.

fixed-income security that promises that the borrower will make specified interest payments to you and return the full amount borrowed when the security matures. The amount of income, the timing of the payments, and the maturity date are all spelled out.

Bonds and other fixed-income securities really balance out the risk of carrying stocks in your portfolio. Unless you lend money to a borrower with lousy credit, you can count on getting your money back when the fixed-income security matures. Plus, you earn all that interest income.

When the stock market is tanking, it can be a great relief to know that you have some of your money in nice, safe bonds. Even better, when the stock market is performing miserably, the bond market tends to do really well, and vice versa. This seesaw effect keeps your portfolio on an even keel when you own both stocks and bonds.

Since fixed-income investments play such an important balancing role in your portfolio, let's take a closer look at them.

## When Do You Get That Groovy Interest Income?

Most, but not all, fixed-income securities pay interest twice a year (on the annual anniversary of the original issue date, and again six months later). For example, five-year U.S. Treasury notes yielding 6.625 percent and due April 30, 2002, pay interest on April 30 and November 30 each year. Plus, the Treasury will pay you back the amount you lent it (your principal) on the maturity date, April 30, 2002.

### Beware the Call Feature

Some fixed-income investments include a "call" feature. What is this? Well, let's say you have a home mortgage. This is essentially a fixed-income security you sold to your bank. You, as the borrower, agreed to make fixed monthly payments and to pay off the principal by a final maturity date. You have, however, the right to pay off your mortgage in advance and to refinance your mortgage to take advantage of declining interest rates. This right is the "call" feature. You can "call" your mortgage anytime and pay it off. Some U.S. Government bond issues and the vast majority of corporate and municipal issues also have call features. These give the issuer/borrower the right to pay off ("redeem") the bonds issued.

Why would the borrower want this right? Well, let's go back to our example of Treasury notes paying 6.625 percent interest and maturing in 2002, and pretend the issue is callable. Now, what if interest rates declined to 4 percent? The Treasury would love to be able to pay off the note at 6.625 percent and issue a new note. It would save so much interest!

This would be a drag for you, though, because now you no longer have a 6.625 percent note. Sure you got your principal back, but now if you want to re-invest it, the best you'll do is a new Treasury note at 4 percent. Your interest income has been drastically reduced by this swift move and there's not one thing you can do about it. Boo hoo!

Now, let's assume that rates increase to 8 percent. You would be very pleased if the Treasury would call your note so you can reinvest at 8 percent, but the Treasury sure doesn't want to pay 8 percent when it's got you locked in at 6.625 percent.

In this case, the Treasury would not exercise the call right.

**Crash Alert**

Call features only benefit the original issuer; they never benefit the purchaser or owner. Therefore, either don't buy any issues with a call feature, or be very careful about incorporating them into your bond portfolio.

## Sinkers

Now, let's return to the example of a mortgage. Your monthly payments may stay the same over the life of the mortgage, but as you get closer to maturity some of the monthly payment is interest and some of it starts paying off the principal. The amount of interest income going to the bank is declining. Some corporations issue bonds that do the same thing—the part of the payment that is devoted to interest gets smaller and smaller as the bond gets closer to maturity. These are called sinking fund payments, or "sinkers."

Here's an example of what you receive each six months for a $100,000 purchase of a 6 percent corporate bond due in 10 years with a mandatory sinking fund starting in year five.

| Year | | Interest | Principal | Total |
|------|------|----------|-----------|-------|
| 4/30/97 | 1A | (Issue Date) | | |
| | 1B | $ 3,000 | | $ 3,000 |
| 4/30/98 | 2A | 3,000 | | 3,000 |
| | 2B | 3,000 | | 3,000 |
| 4/30/99 | 3A | 3,000 | | 3,000 |
| | 3B | 3,000 | | 3,000 |
| 4/30/00 | 4A | 3,000 | | 3,000 |
| | 4B | 3,000 | | 3,000 |
| 4/30/01 | 5A | 3,000 | | 3,000 |
| | 5B | 3,000 | | 3,000 |
| 4/30/02 | 6A | 3,000 | $10,000 | 13,000 |
| | 6B | 3,000 | | 3,000 |

*continues*

*continued*

| Year | | Interest | Principal | Total |
|------|------|---------|-----------|-------|
| 4/30/03 | 7A | 3,000 | 10,000 | 13,000 |
| | 7B | 3,000 | | 3,000 |
| 4/30/04 | 8A | 3,000 | 10,000 | 13,000 |
| | 8B | 3,000 | | 3,000 |
| 4/30/05 | 9A | 3,000 | 10,000 | 13,000 |
| | 9B | 3,000 | | 3,000 |
| 4/30/06 | 10A | 3,000 | 10,000 | 13,000 |
| | 10B | 3,000 | | 3,000 |
| 4/30/07 | 11A | 3,000 | 50,000 | 53,000 |
| | | $60,000 | $100,000 | $160,000 |

Is this a good deal for you? Well, because you are getting some of your principal paid back before maturity, you are faced with the reinvestment rate issue. Unless you are living off the principal and interest, you have to reinvest your interest and sinking fund payments back into the bond market. If rates go down, it's a bad deal for you. If rates go up, it's a good deal for you.

### Super Strategy

To paraphrase Will Rogers, "It's not the return *on* your principal, it's the return *of* your principal...." When buying fixed-income securities, don't just look for notes and bonds with the highest interest rates. If a borrower is willing to pay high interest rates, its credit must not be very good. "Junk" bonds, for example, are high-yielding bonds from corporations with lousy credit ratings. They may pay a lot of interest but the risk that you will never be paid back part or all of your principal is also very high—too high to risk. The highest yield, per se, cannot be your objective; it must be the highest yield on the highest quality bonds.

## The Wonderful World of Bond (No, Not James)

The bond is a popular form of fixed-income security. But in the world of finance, you've probably heard the term tossed around with stocks as if they're one and the same: "Stocksnbonds, stocksnbonds." Well, obviously, they're not.

For one, when you buy a stock you are buying equity—ownership in the company that issued the stock. You are now an owner, entitled to share in the profits and to suffer the losses of the company. The company may or may not pay you dividends, depending on whether or not profits rise. The price of the stock you own may or may not rise. If it does, you could sell it and get your investment back many times over. But when you buy a bond, you are buying debt. You are not an owner; you are lending money to the company (or government) and it has agreed to pay you interest and to pay you back at a certain date. You are promised a specific return (the interest) on your investment, as well as the eventual return of your investment. Because you are not an owner, you are not entitled to a share of the company's profits, nor are you expected to suffer its losses. No matter how bad things get, the company is expected to honor its promise to pay you interest and return your principal at maturity.

Unlike bondholders, stockholders are not guaranteed a specific rate of return or that they will even get their investment back. On the other hand, a stockholder might make a huge return on investment if the company in which he or she owns stock starts to take off. A bondholder will never share in that possibility. Stocks are riskier investments than bonds, but offer the possibility of higher returns.

## How Inflation Erodes Bonds

One more thing: We mentioned in Chapter 1 that inflation is a general rise in prices. When prices rise, it costs more money to buy the same thing. It's no fun when it costs $100 to buy the same bag of groceries you bought last year for $75—especially if you didn't get a raise.

Stock prices typically rise with inflation, so the value of stock you own is somewhat protected from inflation. Bonds, on the other hand, offer no protection against inflation because a $1,000 bond bought today will only pay the bondholder $1,000 at maturity. If that $1,000 only buys $750 worth of groceries due to inflation, the value of the bond has been eroded by inflation. This is why bond prices typically decline when investors hear economic news that causes them to worry about inflation.

**Fiscal Facts**

Here's a handy chart illustrating the differences between stocks and bonds:

**Stock**

equity—investor is owner
entitles investor to share in the
   company's profits—if there are any
unlimited upside/downside
value not eroded by inflation

**Bond**

debt—investor is lender
return of principal
limited upside/downside
value eroded by inflation

**Fiscal Facts**

Each of the two world wars occurred just before a major turning
point in the history of bond yields.
World War I was accompanied by
high and rising yields, and so was
every earlier great war of modern
times. World War II, in contrast, was
accompanied by low and declining
bond yields. World War II ended
one year before bond yields reached
their lowest point this century. In
1946, one issue of the long government bond sold yielding only 1.93
percent. (Source: *A History of
Interest Rates*, pp. 332–334)

## When Do You Want Bonds in Your Portfolio?

There are three reasons to own bonds:

1. To meet current income needs. Bonds provide high current income. This is why, as you approach and eventually reach retirement, bonds will play an increasingly important role in your portfolio. You should be able to live off the income they generate when you no longer earn a salary.

2. To reduce the volatility or risk in your portfolio.

3. In the unlikely event of another depression like the one that decimated stock prices between 1929 and 1932, having bonds in your portfolio can cushion the blow when your stocks take a hit.

Let's look an example. Let's say there are two portfolios: One is invested 100 percent in equities, and the other has 20 percent in bonds that pay 6 percent annual interest and 80 percent in stocks.

| Portfolio One (100% Equities) | | | | Portfolio Two (20% Bonds/80% Equities) | | | |
|---|---|---|---|---|---|---|---|
| Bond Return | Equity Return | Total Return | Index Nos. | Bond Return | Equity Return | Total Return | Index Nos. |
| - | +10 | +10 | +1.010 | +6 | +10 | +9.2 | +1.092 |
| - | 0 | 0 | +1.10 | +6 | 0 | +1.2 | +1.105 |
| - | +20 | +20 | +1.32 | +6 | +20 | +17.2 | +1.295 |
| - | -10 | -10 | +1.188 | +6 | -10 | -6.8 | +1.207 |
| - | +30 | +30 | +1.544 | +6 | +30 | +25.2 | +1.511 |
| Total Return | | +50 | | | | +46 | |
| Average | | +10.0% | | | | +9.2% | |
| Compound Annual | | +9.1% | | | | +8.6% | |

The portfolio with bonds returns 8.6 percent. The portfolio invested exclusively in stock earns 0.5 percent more (9.1 percent) but it is much more volatile. Is it worth that small 0.5 percent difference to invest in bonds and have a more stable portfolio—especially as you get closer to retirement age?

## How to Read a Bond Table

Like stocks, bonds are also listed in tables in the financial section of newspapers. Bond tables are useful for two reasons:

1. If you own a bond and want to sell it, chances are the price is going to be different than what you paid for it. You need to know how different.

2. Most bonds are already outstanding. Therefore, most of your bond purchases will be of bonds that have already been issued and are trading on the bond market. If you are going to buy an outstanding bond, you need to know its price and current yield.

A bond table is a handy way to adjust to changes in bond yields and/or prices. When bonds are first issued, they are priced to sell at *par*, or 100. As they trade, their price moves above or below 100, depending on the demand for the bonds. If a bond's price falls below 100, it is considered to be selling at a discount. If it rises above 100, it is selling at a premium. Bonds trade in "32nds"; 1/32, 2/32 price movements. For example, on August 15, 1998, the Treasury sold five-year notes that mature on 8/15/03 and pay $5\frac{1}{4}$ percent interest. By August 17, 1998, the notes were trading at a discount price of 99 22/32 bid/23/32 asked, with a yield of 5.3148 percent. Bid is what a dealer is willing to pay for your bond; asked is the price a dealer is willing to sell the bond for.

If the yield fell 30 basis points (.30 percent), what would the price of the bond be? Look down the yield scale to 5.0148 and over to the price column to see 101.027. That's the price. Alternatively, if the yield rises to 5.6148, the price is 98.4305.

What if you know the price but want to determine the yield? Look under the price column to find your price, then across to the correct yield. In this case, a price of 98.60 equals a yield of 5.5748 percent.

**Investor's Idiom**

*Par* is the original price of a bond, note or bill. It is also the amount that the security will pay back at maturity and is referred to as 100. Between issuance and maturity, a fixed-income security may be bought and sold, with its price rising or falling depending on interest rates and other factors. If a bond's price is over 100, the bond is said to be trading at a *premium*. If the price falls below 100, the bond is trading at a *discount*.

# Corporate Debt—An Unwise Choice for Small Investors

Corporations issue bonds and notes, but these are not wise investments for individual investors like you. Why not? Well, since you asked so nicely...

1. Because corporate debt typically includes call features and/or sinking fund provisions—musts to avoid. Some corporations also issue a hybrid security called a convertible debenture. A convertible claims to give you participation in both the bond market and the stock market. Unfortunately, you just get two watered-down products: 1) a coupon that pays less interest income than a plain old bond and 2) a chance to buy the company's stock that doesn't kick in unless the stock price rises at least 20–25 percent. Avoid convertibles and leave the field to the experts who specialize in this product.

2. Because most corporations have fluctuating credit ratings. You might buy bonds from a company with a triple AAA rating, only to find that a few years later the company has made some bad business decisions and has had its credit rating downgraded to A or even BBB. Yikes, now you have to worry about whether the company will be able to honor its promise to give you back your principal at maturity.

3. Outstanding corporate debt typically sells in individual units of 100 bonds ($100,000). Do you want to sink that kind of money into one company's bonds? Not unless you have millions to invest, in which case you don't need this book, you need your own private financial advisor.

4. Corporate debt is primarily traded over the counter instead of on the New York Stock Exchange or American Stock Exchange, which are more accessible to individual investors. The NYSE might trade around $10 million in bonds on any given day. Amex only does around $750,000. Meanwhile, roughly $100 million a day in corporate bonds is traded in the over-the-counter market. That's a market that small investors don't really have access to, and those bonds aren't quoted in the newspaper bond tables, either.

For all these reasons, corporate bonds are not a good choice for individual investors—meaning you.

Here is a very rough approximation of the spreads between debt issued by the Treasury, federal government sponsored agencies like the Federal National Mortgage Association (FNMA) and the Government National Mortgage Association (GNMA), and some triple-AAA corporations as of 8/14/98. As you can see, you won't make that much more money buying corporate bonds and you take on a lot more risk and aggravation. Stick with Treasury and government agency paper.

## Spread (Basis Point Difference)

| Issuer | Issue | Yield | V. T-Notes |
|---|---|---|---|
| US Treasury | 5–3/8%, 6/2003 | 5.35 | |
| FNMA | 5.45%, 10/2003 | 5.67 | +32 |
| Bell South | 6.25%, 2003 | 6.10 | +65 (AAA) |
| US Treasury | 5–1/2%, 2/2008 | 5.44 | |
| Int'l Am. Dev. Bank | 6.63%, 3/2007 | 5.70 | +26 |
| GMAC | 6–1/8%, 2008 | 6.20 | +76 (A–) |

# Okay, Corporate Debt Is Out—What Should I Buy?

Don't feel too bad about staying away from the tantalizing array of corporate debt out there. The U.S. Government issues plenty of options that are much healthier for your portfolio.

U.S. Government debt is issued by:

➤ The Treasury Department

➤ Government and Quasi-Government Agencies

U.S. Treasury debt takes one of three forms:

1. Treasury bills (out to one-year maturity)
2. Treasury notes (two-to-10 year maturities)
3. Treasury bonds (maturities beyond 10 years)

Best of all, U.S. Treasury debt is backed by the "full faith and credit" of the U.S. Government. In other words, it's super safe!

There are also two other forms of Treasury debt:

1. Treasury STRIPs—you met these in Chapter 5. STRIPs are Treasury notes and bonds "stripped" down to their individual coupons and maturity. These are sold at a discount like Treasury bills, and are very useful if you know you will need a sum of money by a certain date (college tuition, for example).

2. Treasury debt also appears as inflation-indexed notes and bonds. These include an inflation adjustment, which you get when the bond matures. So if you buy a $10,000 inflation-indexed bond and inflation has risen by 10 percent by the time the bond matures, you'll get your $10,000 principal back plus a $1000 inflation adjustment.

## How to Buy Treasuries

Treasury securities are easy to purchase at regular Treasury auctions. There are weekly T-bill auctions, monthly one-year T-bill auctions and quarterly Treasury note and bond auctions. Check your local newspaper or *The Wall Street Journal* for advance notices, which usually appear five to seven days before an auction. You can either deal directly with your nearest Federal Reserve Bank or ask your banker or broker to make purchases for you for a small service fee of around $25. All Treasury securities can now be purchased in $1,000 denominations.

## Buying Outstanding Treasuries

Besides buying Treasuries at auction, you can also buy outstanding Treasuries on the market. They will be trading either at a discount or a premium. Currently, most Treasury notes and bonds are selling at a premium, because interest rates have been declining for a long time (when interest rates fall, bond prices rise).

What does this mean to you? Well, a bond or note is selling at a premium because it pays a higher interest rate than current new notes or bonds. So if you buy an outstanding Treasury at a premium, you will get higher interest income than you would from the new Treasuries being auctioned. On the other hand, you don't get all your principal back when you buy a Treasury that is trading at a premium. Remember, the principal is the amount that the borrower originally borrowed. If you buy a $10,000 Treasury note at a premium, it'll cost more than $10,000, but $10,000 is all you get paid back at maturity.

A discount bond works in just the opposite manner. Let's say you purchase a Treasury bond trading at 96, or $9,600. You'll receive $10,000 at maturity, for a gain of $400. However, you'll get interest income from this note for around $400–$600 less than the current rate. Is it worth it to receive less income in return for greater principal return? That depends on what's more important to you—some people want income, some want a greater return in the long run.

If the answer to either question is no, just buy at the auctions.

### Investor's Idiom

Starting in September 1998, the Treasury will begin selling *Series I savings bonds*, which are inflation adjusted.

## Savings Bonds

The Treasury also issues savings bonds, which take one of two forms: *EE* or *HH*. *Series EE* bonds are purchased at half-price and their value eventually rises to par. You'd pay $5,000 for a $10,000 EE bond, for example. It's value will eventually rise to $10,000. When it gets to that point, however, depends on interest rates. Instead of receiving interest income from an EE bond, the interest income is added to the value of the bond, causing it to rise until you redeem it. If rates are high, the bond's value will increase quickly. If rates are low, it will grow more slowly. You do have to hold the bond for at least five years to avoid paying a three-month interest penalty. There are now also inflation-indexed savings bonds.

*Series HH* bonds are issued at face value (in other words, if the bond is for $10,000, you pay the full $10,000 for it) and earn interest by a pre-stated formula.

EE savings bonds are a good choice for college savings accounts, provided you purchase them at least five years before redeeming them. Unlike regular bonds, you don't have to report any income for tax purposes until you cash them in. This makes EE savings bonds great for taxable portfolios, like college funds. EE savings bonds are also a great gift for kids from relatives and can be purchased in denominations as low as $5.

Plus, EE savings bonds are no-brainers because you don't have to reinvest interest income every six months, as you do with Treasury notes and bonds.

# Agency-O-Rama

There are a host of government agency and quasi-agencies (agencies created by an act of Congress, like FNMA) that issue debt (both bonds and notes), including:

1. The Federal National Mortgage Association (known as "Fannie Mae"). FNMA is a quasi-agency. Its debt is an implied (but not a guaranteed) obligation of the federal government. The agency's stock trades publicly on the New York Stock Exchange under the ticker symbol FNM.

2. Federal Home Loan Mortgage Corp. ("Freddie Mac"). Like Fannie Mae, Freddie Mac is a quasi-agency/private corporation with stock listed on the New York Stock Exchange (symbol FRE).

3. Student Loan Marketing Association ("Sallie Mae"). Sallie Mae is the third and last of the three public/private corporations. Its ticker symbol is STU, but the name changed recently to SLM Holding.

4. Government National Mortgage Association ("Ginnie Mae") issues bonds that return both principal and interest, just as you pay your monthly mortgage in a single sum to cover both principal and interest. GNMAs are federally guaranteed. This is the only quasi-agency that enjoys this privilege. "Ginnie Mae" bonds are an example of a class of bonds called mortgage-backed securities (MBS). The MBS is a debt instrument with a pool of real estate loans (perhaps your mortgage included) representing the underlying collateral. As principal and interest payments are paid into the pool, they, in turn, are paid out to GNMA bondholders. Mortgage-backed certificates are issued by banks and insured by private mortgage insurance companies.

5. Resolution Funding Corporation (RFC). These bonds are guaranteed as to principal, but not interest, and were issued to help resolve the Savings & Loan crisis of the late 1980s/early 1990s.

And a host of others.

# CDs: A Viable Alternative to Government Debt

If you do want the guarantee of the federal government and aren't willing to venture into buying Treasuries, consider your old pal the CD again for the fixed-income segment of your portfolio. After all, CDs can be purchased in maturities up to 10 years, and for specific sums once you clear the minimum (usually $1,000). And the first $100,000 is completely guaranteed by the federal government.

CD rates tend to be competitive with government paper, but you may need to shop around. The only problem with CDs is the penalty you incur (usually three to six months of interest, depending upon maturity) if you sell prior to maturity. With that caveat, CDs offer an interesting alternative to government securities. And, if you buy at your local bank, you have the added convenience factor.

---

### The Least You Need to Know

➤ A fixed-income security pays you interest income when you lend a sum to a borrower, who promises to pay back the loan on a specific date called the "maturity date."

➤ When the stock prices are falling, bond prices tend to rise, so having bonds in your portfolio can counteract declines in the value of your stock.

➤ Avoid call features, sinkers, and corporate debt.

➤ Buy Treasury bills, notes, and bonds and government agency paper for the fixed-income segment of your portfolio.

---

# Chapter 12

# Why Mutual Funds Have Ruled the '90s

---

**In This Chapter**

➤ Picking winning funds

➤ How to avoid unnecessary fees

➤ Contact numbers for some excellent funds

➤ Managing several funds at a time

---

If you were to make a list of growth businesses for the 1990s, you'd have to place the mutual funds business at or close to the top. Although the first mutual funds were created before the 1929 stock market crash, mutual funds have truly exploded in popularity during the present decade.

Why are mutual funds finally so popular? There are a few reasons:

1. Mutual funds have become the product of choice for 401(k) plans, and both asset growth and dollars for those plans now exceed every other type of retirement plan.

2. Some mutual fund firms have developed enough critical mass to justify advertising on—gasp—television during prime time, reaching all those Must-See-TV *Friends* and *ER* and *Frasier*-watching folks who probably have a little extra cash to burn, and

3. Some mutual fund managers actually have become cult figures who are frequently quoted and interviewed in major publications nationwide.

Still don't see why mutual funds are the hot ticket? Let's delve a little deeper. In this chapter, we're going to show you what mutual funds are and (more important) what they can do for you.

# What Exactly Are Mutual Funds?

A mutual fund is a company that invests on behalf of customers who deposit money with it. The "customers" may be individual investors like you, or even big companies. Either way, the mutual fund company pools the money it collects and manages it with investment objectives that are carefully spelled out.

For example, one fund might invest only in technology stocks. Another might invest in small, emerging companies. Another might have holdings that mimic the S&P 500 index. As you learned in Chapter 9, a fund that mimics an index is called an *index fund*. It is passively, not actively, managed—meaning that the fund's managers do very little except make sure the fund's holdings stay in proportion to the index it mimics.When you buy "shares" in a mutual fund, you own a piece of its investments proportional to the amount you've invested. Because the mutual fund is investing millions of dollars, it can develop a very diversified portfolio. By investing in a mutual fund, you achieve a level of diversification for your own portfolio that you could never afford to create by yourself.

# Open-End and Closed-End Funds

All mutual funds are collective investment funds or portfolios registered with the Securities & Exchange Commission (SEC) under the Investment Advisors Act of 1940 ("The 40 Act"). Most mutual funds are *open end*. This means that they are always open to accepting more deposits from more customers and can continue to grow in size with no upper limit. Some funds are *closed*, meaning they accept no more deposits after their initial offering. Closed-end funds only sell a fixed number of shares—like a corporation does when it makes an offering. And, like many corporation's shares, closed-end funds are primarily listed and traded on the New York Stock Exchange or the American Stock Exchange. Closed-end funds only hold around 2 to 3 percent of the total assets invested in mutual funds.

**Investor's Idiom**

*Net asset value* (NAV) is the dollar value of all the marketable securities (stocks, for example) owned by a mutual fund, less expenses, and divided by the number of the fund's shares outstanding. When you want to buy shares in an open-end mutual fund, the price you will pay is based on the net asset value. Because the shares of a closed-end fund trade on the market, however, its share price may differ from its NAV.

You can buy shares in a mutual fund by contacting its distributor. (We provide some contact numbers later in this chapter.) The price you'll pay for shares is based on the net asset value that day, provided your order is received and accepted before the close of business (currently 4:00 p.m.). Orders received after 4:00 p.m. are priced at the next day's *net asset value (NAV)* figure.

With a closed-end fund, though, differences can develop between a share's net asset value and its market price because shareholders are competing to buy a fixed number of shares.

If the shares are selling above the net asset value, they are selling at a "premium." In contrast, shares trading below NAV are said to be selling at a "discount." Some closed-end funds sell at a discount of 20 percent or greater.

If you buy shares in a fund that's selling at a hefty discount and later the fund's share price bounces back, you could make a tidy profit. So, if you are interested in closed-end funds:

➤ stick with discounts

➤ study the historical discount range to determine whether the current price is at the top, middle, or low end of the historical discount range

Why would a fund choose to be closed rather than open? Fund managers are concerned with sell-offs that could be triggered by bad news or other events. For this reason, emerging market equity funds, specialized equity funds, and municipal bond (especially state-specific) funds tend to be set up as closed-end funds—because these types of funds are highly specialized and, therefore, vulnerable to bad news. With a closed fund, holders of the shares who wish to sell don't turn to the fund, but to the market. This protects the fund managers from having to raise the money to buy back shares in the event of a sell-off.

**Crash Alert**

Sometimes closed-end funds become open-end funds, thereby eliminating the discount that may have made them an attractive buy in the first place. You can check the current premium or discount by looking in the Monday *Wall Street Journal* (Section C near the back); also in the Sunday *New York Times* "Money & Business" section (again, near the back).

# Avoid Load Funds

Do you simply pay the NAV times the number of shares you want to purchase when you buy shares in an open-end mutual fund? Not always. Some funds deduct a sales charge from your principal; this is referred to as a "front-end load." Funds that charge this fee are called "load" funds. Loads currently approximate up to 5.0–5.5 percent of your investment and go to whomever sold you the fund (your broker, for example); they do not go to the fund itself.

Funds that do not charge this fee are called "no load" funds—and they are a much better deal. Here is a simple example of how front-end load can hurt your investment. Let's say you purchase $10,000 of a fund with a NAV of $10.00 and a 5 percent load:

|  | Load Fund | No Load Fund |
|---|---|---|
| Principal Amount | $10,000 | $10,000 |
| Less Sales Commission | $500 | $0 |
| Net Available | $9,500 | $10,000 |
| Net Asset Value | $10 | $10 |
| Number of Shares | 950 | 1,000 |

If you buy the load fund, you lose $500 or 5 percent of your principal before it even has a chance to work for you! Think twice before buying a load fund.

## Back-End Loads and 12b-1 Fees

Some funds also charge you when you redeem (sell) your shares. This charge is referred to as *back-end* or *back-door load*. It is also called a *deferred sales charge*. The intent here is to penalize investors who make frequent fund purchases and sales.

Back-end load may run as high as 6–7 percent of the amount you sell in the first year, scaling down to zero by, say, the seventh year. This charge, if applicable, is deducted from your gross proceeds when you make the sale. Again, these charges do not go to the fund company, but to whomever makes the transaction for you.

**Investor's Idiom**

A *prospectus* is a legal document prepared by a mutual fund and sent out to potential investors that describes the fund and its operations.

Finally, many funds charge a shareholding servicing fee, often referred to as a *12b-1* fee. This fee, limited to .25 percent, is used as an inducement to brokers who have helped or may help sell fund shares. It is vital that you learn before purchasing shares in a fund whether it charges front- or back-end load, and/or a 12b-1 fee. It's your money, after all! Simply ask your broker, call the fund company, or request its prospectus.

## Index and Tax-Advantaged Funds

If you can shelter all the dollars you want to invest in IRAs and 401(k)s, great. But if you put some of your money directly into equity mutual funds, without the shelter of an IRA, you will have to pay taxes on any gains the fund makes. Even if you immediately reinvest any dividends or gains from the fund, you will have to pay taxes to Uncle Sam on them. Bummer.

To avoid this situation, you can limit your mutual fund holdings to one of two types of stock funds: index funds and tax-advantaged funds.

➤ Index funds mimic the behavior of stocks in a particular index (such as the S&P 500). The fund just buys the stocks in the index in the same proportion as they appear in the index and holds them. Since there are few trades, few capital gains are generated for you to pay taxes on.

➤ Tax-advantaged funds make a conscious effort to minimize taxes by minimizing trading. The fund managers don't completely ignore opportunities to improve the portfolio by buying and selling, but they do it as little as possible to avoid generating taxable capital gains. The fund managers will also attempt to offset gains with losses whenever possible—again, to reduce taxes.

> **Super Strategy**
>
> There are only a handful of tax-advantaged funds available at this time, but they could be useful for your portfolio if you can't shelter all your investment income in 401(k)s and IRAs. Keep an eye on the financial pages for further developments.

# What's Out There in the Fund Universe?

There are over 9,000 open-end funds currently operating. Morningstar recently broke them down as follows:

| | |
|---|---|
| Domestic Equity Funds | 4,048 |
| International Equity Funds | 1,259 |
| Taxable Bond Funds | 1,924 |
| Municipal Bond Funds | 1,818 |
| Index Funds & Other | 252 |
| TOTAL | 9,301 |

Open-end funds are listed by the National Association of Securities Dealers (NASD) once they have at least 1,000 shareholders or net assets of $25 million. Money market funds, which we discussed in Chapter 3, number about 1,300, of which 875 are taxable and 425 are tax free (either general or state specific). There is a listing each Thursday in *The Wall Street Journal* (Section C near the back), which tells you the average maturity of the fund, its seven-day yield, and total assets of the fund.

# Why Funds Are a Great Investment Option

There are several key reasons why you should consider mutual funds:

1. Professional Management. The manager of a given mutual fund may not be more intelligent or luckier than you, but he or she can devote full-time attention to what you can, at best, only give a portion of your time. In addition, professional investment management has access to research and to market information that would either not be available to you at all or only after a time delay—and timing is crucial when making investment decisions. In addition, corporate "road shows" stop off at various professional management offices to bring them up to date, but don't expect them to come knocking on your door. Finally, influential Wall Street professionals share their opinions first with large, commission-generating customers—like mutual fund managers.

2. Instant Diversification. We've shared with you the importance of diversification. To achieve even bare-bone diversification, you would need 25 sector-diversified equities and at least 10 different bond issues (unless you limit your bond portion to governments), at $100,000 each. Want to add some international stock? Prepare to add at least 50 more. Get the picture?

### Super Strategy

The ultimate diversified portfolio is *the index fund*. This is a mutual fund set up to mimic an index, such as our old pal the S&P 500 or other indices like the Russell 2000 Small Cap Index and the Wilshire 5000 Index. Can you afford to buy all 500 stocks in the S&P 500? Probably not, but a mutual fund can. And by buying shares in that fund, now you can, too.

3. Low Costs. We've pointed out layered fund expenses such as front- and back-end loads and 12b-1 fees. Funds also charge management expense fees that approximate 50–75 basis points (.50–.75 percent), and go as high as 75–150 basis points for some equity funds. If you stick to no-load funds that keep expenses low, however, you'll find that investing in mutual funds is a great deal cheaper than investing in stocks on your own and paying commissions and transaction costs. Some index mutual funds have expenses as low as 20 basis points (.2 percent). Try topping that!

4. Terrific Variety. Whatever you want, the fund industry offers. Want to invest in Japanese companies? Health care? New Jersey municipal bonds? Indonesian utilities? There's a fund somewhere doing just that.

### Investor's Idiom

There are 100 *basis* points in one percentage point. So, 100 basis points = 1%.

5. Ease and Convenience. Usually, you can complete your transaction with one phone call and a minimum of paperwork. And if you stay within a particular fund "family," you can switch funds with no—or at the very least, minimal—expense, over the phone.

These are some of the more significant reasons why mutual funds have reached unparalleled popularity in this country (other than those prime-time TV ads). You just have to use your head (and our advice) in making your selections. Start by requesting annual and quarterly reports and prospectuses from funds that interest you. And actually read them before you buy!

# How to Pick a Winning Fund

How do you pick a fund? Well, for starters, don't read those glossy financial magazines with the eye-catching headlines screaming from the newsstand about can't-lose mutual funds. Okay, read them if you must, but take a look at who's buying the ads that keep these mags afloat. That's right: mutual funds.

We have a better suggestion. Simply apply the criteria below, and you'll make excellent choices.

1. Performance. Is the fund rate of return above average for its category for the latest one, three, and five years? Notice that we are not recommending that you buy the funds with the highest return or even the ones in the top 10 percent. We prefer to sacrifice some historical returns for consistency. Don't run out and buy a fund that just hit a home run; it might strike out the year after you buy it. Better to seek funds that consistently hit singles and doubles. If you get consistent above-average returns, you'll get superior results over the long haul.

2. Management. Make sure that the same team has been managing the fund for at least the last five years. When a fund changes managers, you simply don't know whether the new management will do better or worse. You also may not be able to find out the track record of the new manager. Just stick with funds that have retained the same management for at least five years.

3. Size. With index funds, go for the largest size fund because it would (or should) have the lowest expenses. But with actively managed funds, avoid unproven funds of small size, as well as very large, ponderous funds that may lack the flexibility to move from stock to stock or industry to industry as conditions warrant. Just for you, we've arbitrarily selected a range of $250 million to $5 billion.

4. No Load. You know our feelings on this. We want to start with $1 working for us, not 95¢.

5. Expense Ratios. We expect the administrator and the investment advisor for the fund to make a profit. But we don't want that green monster called greed to rear its ugly head. Stick with funds that keep expenses under:

   1.25% for equity funds

   0.75% for fixed-income funds

   0.50% for lower yielding fixed-income funds (municipal bond funds and intermediate-term taxable bonds)

**159**

# Check Out These Funds

We applied the above criteria to Morningstar Principia software to develop the following list of funds that we like.

We have included the telephone number in the event you wish to contact the fund directly for literature. We have excluded short-term bond funds, along with emerging country funds (which should only be purchased in closed-end format, as discussed previously). Finally, we have eliminated any funds that you, as a retail investor, would not be eligible to purchase.

### Large-Cap Growth

Columbia Growth   800-547-1707
Harbor Capital Appreciation   800-422-1050
Vanguard Index Growth   800-662-7447

### Large Value

Clipper   800-776-5033
Kemper Value S   800-621-1048
Preferred Value   800-662-4769
Vanguard Growth & Income   800-662-7447
Vanguard Index Value   800-662-7447

### Large-Cap Blend (Value and Growth)

BT Investment Equity 500 Index   800-730-1313
T. Rowe Price Blue Chip Growth   800-638-5660
T. Rowe Price Equity Index   800-638-5660
Torray   800-443-3036
Vanguard/Morgan Growth   800-662-7447

### Mid-Cap Growth

T. Rowe Price Mid-Cap Growth   800-638-5660
T. Rowe Price New America Growth   800-638-5660
William Blair Growth   800-742-7272

### Mid-Cap Value

Homestead Value   800-258-3030

### Mid-Cap Blend (Value and Growth)

Excelsior Value & Restruct   800-446-1012
Nicholas II   800-227-5987
Strong Opportunity   800-368-1030
Vanguard Index Extended Market   800-662-7447

### Small Growth

Janus Enterprise   800-525-8983
Warburg Pincus Emerging Growth   800-927-2874

**Small Value**

FAM Value   800-932-3271

**Small Blend (Value and Growth)**

Acorn   800-922-6769
Nicholas Limited Edition   800-227-5987
Safeco Growth No Load   800-426-6730
T. Rowe Price Small Cap Stock   800-638-5660

**Foreign Stock**

Acorn International   800-922-6769
Fidelity Diversified International   800-544-8888
Preferred International   800-662-4769
Scudder International   800-225-2470

**Long Government**

American Cent-Ben Tar Mat 2020   800-345-2021
(Treasuries)
Vanguard F/I L/T U.S. Treasury   800-662-7447

**Intermediate Government**

T. Rowe Price GNMA (Mortgage)   800-638-5660
Vanguard F/I Inter-Term US (Treasury)   800-662-7447

**Long-Term Bond**

USAA Income   800-382-8722

**Intermediate-Term Bonds**

Dodge & Cox Income   800-621-3979

**Muni National Long**

USAA Tax-Exempt Long-Term   800-382-8722
Vanguard Muni High Yield   800-662-7447
Vanguard Muni Long-Term   800-662-7447

**Muni National Intermediate**

USAA Tax-Exempt Interm-Term   800-382-8722

Don't be concerned with the short list of fixed income (bond) funds we've provided. We like mutual funds for equities, but recommend that you buy individual government securities (or municipals) for the bond portion of your portfolio. There are two problems with bond funds:

1. Much of the yield is eaten up by management fees.

2. When you buy into a bond fund, you can't stagger interest income to meet your individual income needs the way you can when you buy individual bonds, and you know their maturity dates. We really like the idea of buying bonds of different maturities so that after you retire, you have interest income coming in every month that matches up with your monthly expenses.

At the end of each quarter, newspapers such as *The New York Times* and *The Wall Street Journal* publish a special supplement on mutual funds. These special supplements provide a wealth of information on many funds, including phone numbers, fund objectives, assets under management, sales charges (if any), expenses, and NAV and performance results. Use these supplements to do your own screening!

# Money Market Funds

With respect to both taxable and tax-free money market funds, we used a much simpler screening process: Qualified funds had expense ratios under 50 basis points (0.5 percent) and assets over $500 million. This is a good list of retail funds you can use that are large and have low expense ratios. Each list is alphabetical.

| Assets ($ millions) | Fund Name |
| --- | --- |
| ***U.S. Treasury Funds*** | |
| $3,101.6 | Benham/Capital Presv Fund I |
| 1,905.6 | Fidelity Spartan US Treas MMF |
| 4,107.8 | Vanguard Admiral/US Treas MMF |
| 3,494.7 | Vanguard Treasury Fund/Treas MMP |
| ***U.S. Government & Agencies Funds*** | |
| 772.8 | Fidelity Spartan US Govt MMF |
| 1,275.5 | Fidelity US Govt Reserves |
| 932.9 | SSgA US Govt MMF/Cl A |
| 3,722.5 | Vanguard MMR/Federal Port |
| 671.9 | Zurich Government Money Fund |
| ***General Money Market Funds*** | |
| 10,521.2 | Dean Witter/Active Assets MT |
| 3,698.0 | IDS Cash Management Fund |
| 2.662.5 | J.P. Morgan Prime MMF |
| 5,548.8 | SSgA Money Market Fund/Cl A |
| 1,467.3 | T. Rowe Price Summit Cash Reserves |
| 2,397.9 | USAA Money Market Fund |
| 29,257.1 | Vanguard MR/Prime Port/Retail |
| 4,516.5 | Zurich Money Market Fund |

| Assets ($ millions) | Fund Name |
| --- | --- |
| *Tax-Free Money Funds* | |
| 4,774.9 | Fidelity Municipal MMF |
| 1,197.5 | J.P. Morgan Tax-Exempt MMF |
| 1,595.4 | USAA Tax Exempt MMF |
| 5,721.3 | Vanguard Muni Bond/MMF |
| 806.6 | Zurich Tax-Free Money Fund |

*(Source: IBC Financial Data, Inc./290 Eliot St., P.O. Box 9104, Ashland, MA 01721-9104, 508/881-2800,* http://www.ibc.data.com)

Space does not permit us to list state-specific funds, which may well be the first choice for those in higher tax brackets and high-tax states. But the above list at least provides a starting point.

# Variable Annuity: A Mutual Fund Wrapped Around an Insurance Contract

Approximately 50 insurance companies offer at least 900 different variable annuity funds. An annuity promises to provide a sum in an annual or other regular (e.g., monthly) interval. A fixed annuity is for a fixed amount. A variable annuity provides an undetermined amount that depends upon the return of the underlying mutual fund.

Since a variable annuity is a mutual fund wrapped around an insurance contract, the "variable" depends upon how well the fund performs. Are variable annuities a good deal?

Variable annuities are like traditional IRAs, in the sense that they are tax-deferred funds subject to ordinary income taxes (up to 39.6 percent) when funds are withdrawn. Until withdrawn, variable annuity funds grow uninhibited by taxes. Unlike the traditional IRA, however, there is no limit to how much you can contribute to a variable annuity each year. In addition, when you do retire, you can convert a variable annuity to a fixed annuity. Probably a majority of annuities are held in our old friend, the 403(b) plan. The biggest drawback, in our opinion, is that if you buy a variable annuity, you have to pay not only the underlying mutual fund expenses but an additional fee of typically 1.1 percent for the *death benefit*. The death benefit guarantees that the holder's heirs will receive at least the principal back in the event of a market meltdown. But is that worth 1.1 percent each and every year? We don't think so.

**Fiscal Facts**

According to Morningstar, there are more than 9,300 funds (excluding money market funds). That's greater than the number of stocks listed on the New York, American, and NASDAQ exchanges.

If you wish to follow variable annuities, check the Monday *Wall Street Journal* (Section C near the back).

# Lifestyle and Tax-Efficient Funds

Two other new types of funds deserve mention. One is the so-called lifestyle fund. This fund allows you to set a target retirement date, and, as you approach that date, the asset allocation automatically shifts to less equity exposure. Be aware that a generic stock/bond ratio might not be appropriate for most investors because the ratio makes assumptions that might not apply to your age or risk tolerance. Nevertheless, the automatic asset allocation rebalancing concept is appealing. Vanguard seems to be the leader at this point.

We are wholeheartedly enthusiastic about a new concept that we discussed earlier for individual investing: so-called tax-efficient (or tax-managed, tax-preferred, etc.) funds. The concept is only several years old, with no more than 40 funds available at present. Once again, Vanguard is the leader and should be contacted if you have further questions.

With actively managed equity funds posting such strong gains these days, tax-efficient funds could be a good choice for your taxable investments. Vanguard currently offers the Vanguard Tax-Managed Growth and Income Fund and the Vanguard Tax-Managed Capital Appreciation Fund.

# Pick a Date to Rebalance Your Mutual Fund Holdings Annually

Well, by now you know what date that is. That's right, your birthday (unless it falls in January or near a big holiday). But what are you going to rebalance, and which portfolio(s)?

For your tax-deferred accounts (IRAs, 401(k)s, etc.), any actions you take will not trigger a tax bite. So, if you are in equity mutual funds, rebalance them back to your original targets or your revised targets. This should only be necessary if the stock market has gone up or down significantly in the previous 12 months. Of course, if you have hit one of those rebalancing years we discussed in Chapter 10 and it's time to reduce your equity exposure, make the move irrespective of what the market has done.

If you have just one equity mutual fund, this is a fairly simple procedure: Sell some of your equity fund and use the proceeds to buy Treasury notes or bonds or shares in a bond fund. But what if you have more than one equity fund? Then you have to rebalance these funds within the equity portion. Let's say your portfolio of equity mutual funds looks like this:

|                    | Initial Target | Current |
|--------------------|:--------------:|:-------:|
| Large-Cap Growth   | 30%            | 33%     |
| Large-Cap Value    | 30%            | 33%     |
| Mid-Cap Growth     | 10%            | 10%     |
| Mid-Cap Value      | 5%             | 5%      |
| Small-Cap Growth   | 5%             | 4%      |
| Small-Cap Value    | 5%             | 4%      |
| International      | 10%            | 8%      |
| Emerging Markets   | 5%             | 3%      |
| Total              | 100%           | 100%    |

First and foremost, figure out how much the equity segment of your portfolio is worth in dollars, then rebalance the individual equity funds so the percentage invested in each corresponds to your original target.

## Rebalancing Taxable Accounts

With taxable accounts, the goal is to generate as few capital gains as possible. That's why we recommend passive equity holdings and/or index funds, which minimize taxes—if nothing's being sold, no capital gains are being generated. You don't want to sell equities in a taxable account unless you are at a milestone year (you might be approaching first-year college expenses, for example). If the equities in your taxable accounts have declined significantly, however, you do want to rebalance upward. Use the proceeds from bond or bond fund sales, which should generate minimal capital gains. That's all there is to it!

---

### The Least You Need to Know

➤ A mutual fund is a company that invests on behalf of customers who deposit money with it.

➤ Look for open-end funds that keep expenses low and don't charge load or 12b-1 fees.

➤ Mutual funds are great for the equity portion of your portfolio, but for the fixed-income portion skip bond funds and buy individual bonds.

➤ Keep an eye out for developments in lifestyle and tax-efficient funds; these could be good buys.

---

# Part 4
# Rolling with Life's Changes

In investing money, the amount of interest you want should depend on whether you want to eat well or sleep well.

—J. Kenfield Morley

*Life is full of transitions, shocks, and assorted doozies. Our happiness, in fact, has little to do with avoiding life's changes and everything to do with being prepared to roll with them.*

*Properly managed investments can make transitions like buying a home or retiring a lot smoother. Knowing how to handle exciting developments that affect your investments, such as changing jobs or inheriting money, can ease the stress that even the most positive events can cause. And it's crucial to know how to protect your assets from potentially devastating events like divorce.*

*This part is a primer on how to manage your investments through all the biggies: marriage, divorce, buying a home, educating your kids, inheriting money, changing jobs, and, yep, even that final spooky transition we'd all rather pretend is never going to happen. At least not to us.*

*Hey, get ready to lead an exciting financial life!*

# Chapter 13

# Work Smart, Not Just Hard: Getting the Max from Your Job

## In This Chapter

➤ Five vital questions for a new employer

➤ When your Social Security benefits can be taxed

➤ The changing retirement age

➤ How Medicare works

Are you one of those people who ignore every memo and form about complicated-sounding things like 401(k)s and vesting that come across your desk? Do you figure that if you ignore them, maybe they'll go away? Well, what's going away is your opportunity to squeeze the most dollars possible out of your job.

Now that we've got your attention…think of this chapter as your personal machete. Use it to cut through the thickets of paper and nonsense that many corporate human resource departments love to erect between you and simple answers about how to best handle the retirement benefits offered by your employer. And, if you're self-employed or thinking about becoming self-employed, we'll show you how to set up your own retirement account and get a major tax break in the process.

## What to Ask a New Employer

There are five topics you must discuss with personnel immediately when you start a job at a new company. Make an appointment ASAP with a human resources person. You'll shock and amaze him or her if you walk in there with these questions under your hat:

1. "Do you have a pension plan, and, if so, when am I eligible to participate?"

   Typically, each credited year requires 1,000 hours of work. If you start work before June 30, therefore, you will probably be eligible that year. If your hire date is much later than that, you will probably not be eligible until the following year. Find out if you will qualify in year one of your employment. How long will you have to work at the company until you are fully vested? Five years is typical.

2. "Can I transfer the money in my existing 401(k) plan to your 401(k)plan? How exactly do I do that? When can I start to participate in your plan? What are the investment choices offered by your 401(k) plan? Does the employer contribute and to what degree?"

   Get very specific answers here so you don't risk leaving the assets in your current 401(k) plan unsheltered. As we discussed in Chapter 5, you typically only have 60 days to get this together before the IRS can swoop in. You usually will be able to participate in your new employer's 401(k) plan after you've been there one year.

3. "Is there a bonus or incentive plan? How general or specific is it? Is it tied to my job performance or the performance of the company or my department as a whole? When will I be informed of the amount? When is it paid to me? Do I have to be a full-time employee when the checks are passed out?"

   It's better to have a bonus that's tied directly to your own performance, not to the performance of others. That way you control your own destiny. Bear in mind, also, that you don't want to screw yourself out of a big bonus or incentive check at your current job by leaving to take a new one. Before you leave, check out any pertinent dates. If waiting a few weeks to start your new job will keep you from losing money, you could either arrange that or negotiate a sign-on bonus with your new employer.

4. "Are there stock options? Am I eligible for them?"

   If the answer to both questions is yes, get the details. Normally, if you are eligible, stock options would have already been dangled as incentive to get you on board in the first place and would have been included in your hiring agreement.

5. "Does the company have a health plan? When do I and my family become eligible? Is there a choice of plans, or just one?"

   You want to know what kind of choice you have. There may be just one HMO, several alternative HMOs, or a traditional plan. There may be some variation that allows you to opt in or out of your HMO. Typically, you are eligible on the first of each month.

**Super Strategy**

When you start a new job, meet with your human resources contact right away to ask about the company's:

➤ pension plan

➤ 401(k) plan and whether you can transfer money from your existing 401(k) into it

➤ bonus or incentive plans

➤ stock options

➤ health plan

Also check with HR at your old job to make sure that you aren't forfeiting a bonus or incentive check by leaving. Sometimes just postponing your departure a few weeks can make a big difference.

# Transferring Retirement Accounts

As we mentioned in Chapter 5, you have three options with your 401(k) plan when you change jobs:

1. Keep it with your previous employer, if it will allow you to do so (and many do).
2. Transfer it to your new employer, provided that it is willing to take your assets (almost all will).
3. Create an IRA rollover with a bank or broker.

If you choose option #2 or #3, remember that you have only 60 days to get this done; otherwise, the Feds will assume you are taking a distribution and hit you with taxes and, potentially, penalties. Given the choice, most people are most comfortable with option #2; when people leave a firm, they like it to be a clean break. Option #3 is really for those who can't do #2 or #1.

# So You're Your Own Boss

If you are self-employed, you have to provide for yourself benefits that employers normally provide, such as retirement planning and health insurance. You should also carefully research all aspects of working from home. You'll want to maximize your business tax deductions to offset the fringe benefits lost when you leave an employer to set up your own business, such as health insurance, pension plan, sick leave, and vacations.

## Setting Up Your Own Retirement Plan

One great way to both reduce your taxes and provide an important employment benefit for yourself is to set up your own retirement plan. As we discussed in Chapter 5, you can choose from the following plans:

➤ SEP-IRA

➤ SIMPLE-IRA

➤ Keogh (which will probably be referred to by your banker simply as a defined contribution plan, or D.C.)

### Fiscal Facts

When you work for a company that provides health insurance, retirement plans, and other benefits, these fringe benefits are worth between 25 percent to 50 percent of your salary. If your salary is $40,000, for example, your benefits are worth between $10,000 and $20,000.

(Source: Paul and Sarah Edwards, authors of *Working from Home*, G.P. Putnam's Sons, 1994)

Any bank, mutual fund, brokerage firm, or insurance company will be delighted to provide you with the forms you need to open these plans—especially if you are thinking of keeping your assets with their institution. SEPs and SIMPLEs are very easy to open yourself, but you'll need help with the rather complicated paperwork required to set up a Keogh.

If you've been self-employed for a while but haven't gotten around to setting up your retirement plan, boy, have you been missing out on a major deduction on your federal income tax! You can contribute to a SEP or SIMPLE—and then deduct from your income tax—either 13.04 percent of your *net earnings* from self-employment up to $150,000, or $19,565. (Note: This amount is adjusted every year to account for inflation.)

### Investor's Idiom

*Net earnings* from self-employment are the amount of income on which you pay self-employment tax, minus the tax itself. Self-employment tax, if you recall from Chapter 8, is what self-employed people have to pay into Social Security because they don't have an employer contributing on their behalf.

Anyway, if you take advantage of this situation, you can slice your taxes and build a strong retirement account at the same time. Let's say your net earnings on self-employment—after you deduct business and home-office deductions and the self-employment tax—is $25,000 and your federal income tax rate is 28 percent. Your federal income tax will be $25,000 × .28 = $7,000.

Now, what if you invest 13.04 percent of that $25,000 in a SEP-IRA? You would invest $25,000 × .1304 = $3,260. And you can deduct that $3,260 from the $25,000 you earned. Now you owe federal income tax on $25,000 − $3,260 = $21,740. Gosh, your tax rate just dropped from 28 percent to 15 percent, because that deduction dropped you into a lower tax bracket. Now the amount of federal income tax you owe is only $21,740 × .15 = $3,261. That's a lot easier to fork over to Uncle Sam than $7,000, plus you've tucked away $3,260 to grow tax-deferred until you retire.

### Super Strategy

If you are self-employed and haven't opened a SEP or SIMPLE account yet, get thee to a bank immediately! You are missing out on a huge opportunity to shelter your hard-earned bucks from Uncle Sam. If you invest the maximum 13.04 percent of your earnings in a SEP-IRA, for example, you can deduct your entire investment from your income. This swift move will slice your income tax, plus that precious money is now sheltered under an IRA where it can peacefully grow tax-deferred until you retire.

## Retirement...At Last!

Whether you work for a big corporation or yourself, if you're doing well, you may be tempted to consider retiring early. Should you retire early? It sounds great, but remember:

### Fiscal Facts

Where do your Social Security tax dollars go? Out of every $1:

➤ 70¢ goes to a trust fund to pay retirees

➤ 19¢ goes to a trust fund to pay Medicare beneficiaries

➤ 11¢ goes to a trust fund to pay benefits to qualified disabled people

1. Your benefits from Social Security and your employer's retirement plan will be reduced or even become nonexistent, depending on when you decide to retire. This means your own retirement portfolio will have to be that much larger.

2. Retiring early means your retirement dollars will have to last longer. Again, this means you'll need to accumulate more assets that will generate retirement income.

## How the Retirement Age You Choose Affects Social Security

Let's look specifically at Social Security. The earliest you can start receiving benefits is age 62. And, at age 62, you will only receive about 80 percent of what you would have received had you waited until age 65 to retire.

Starting 2003, the full retirement age will be increased in steps until it reaches age 67. *Full retirement age* is the age at which you can expect to get full (but not necessarily maximum) benefits. Those born in 1937 or earlier will not be affected by the increase in the full retirement age.

Those born in 1938 will have full retirement age defined as 65 years and 2 months. Add two months for each year after 1938 that you were born. For those born in 1960 and later, 67 will be the full retirement age. If you were born in 1960 and want to take early retirement at age 62, your benefit will only be 70 percent of the age 67 full benefit. Find yourself on the table below, compliments of the Social Security Administration:

## Age to Receive Full Social Security Benefits

| Year of Birth | Full Retirement Age |
| --- | --- |
| 1937 or earlier | 65 |
| 1938 | 65 and 2 months |
| 1939 | 65 and 4 months |
| 1940 | 65 and 6 months |
| 1941 | 65 and 8 months |
| 1942 | 65 and 10 months |
| 1943–1954 | 66 |
| 1955 | 66 and 2 months |
| 1956 | 66 and 4 months |
| 1957 | 66 and 6 months |
| 1958 | 66 and 8 months |
| 1959 | 66 and 10 months |
| 1960 and later | 67 |

### Investor's Idiom

*Combined income* is adjusted gross income (remember that?) plus non-taxable interest (interest on municipal bonds, for example) plus half of your Social Security benefits. It's just another way to hit up the fat cats!

# Pay Tax on Social Security Benefits? Sad, but True

Are your Social Security benefits taxable? In some cases they are. Here's the gist of it:

If you file your federal tax return as an individual and your combined income is between $25,000–$34,000, you may have to pay taxes on 50 percent of your Social Security benefits. If your *combined income* is above $34,000, up to 85 percent of your Social Security benefits are subject to tax. If you file a joint return, the numbers are $32,000–$44,000 (up to 50 percent) and over $44,000 (up to 85 percent).

About 20 percent of the people receiving Social Security pay taxes on their benefits. Each year recipients receive a Social Security Benefit Statement (Form SSA-1099). Use this form when filling out your federal income tax to determine if any of your benefits are subject to tax.

# Can You Work and Still Collect Social Security?

Can you work and still get all your Social Security benefits? It depends on your age and the amount. If you are under 65, the earnings limit is $8,640. And "earnings" are limited to wages and self-employment income. Income from investments and other sources is excluded.

What happens if you earn more than that? Your Social Security check will be cut by $1 for $2 you earn over the limit. Another reason to think twice about retiring early! For those aged 65–69, the earnings limit is $13,500, and "only" one dollar for every three dollars over the limit will be deducted. If you're 70 and over? No problem, you're in the clear.

# Advantages to Delaying Retirement

What if you choose to delay retirement? There are some advantages. Depending on when you were born, your eventual annual Social Security benefits will be increased from 3 percent (for those born before 1925) to 8 percent (for those born in 1943 or later). But, if you do decide to retire after age 65, please sign up for Medicare at age 65; otherwise, your medical insurance could cost more.

Your spouse is also eligible to receive benefits at his or her full retirement age, which is currently 65. How much? Either 50 percent of your benefits or his or her actual earned benefits, whichever is higher. Your spouse can begin collecting benefits as early as age 62, but they will be reduced roughly 4 percent per year before full retirement age.

# When and How to Apply for Your SS Benefits

Apply for Social Security benefits three months before the date you want the benefits to start. The Social Security Administration recommends that you discuss your plans with one of their representatives the year before you plan to retire.

Remember, the rules are not simple or straightforward, and are subject to change. What do you need to apply for benefits? Plan on having to present the following:

➤ Your Social Security number

➤ Your birth certificate (original or certified copy)

➤ Your latest W-2 or self-employment tax return

➤ Your military discharge papers

➤ Your bank name and account number (if you want to arrange direct deposit of your benefits)

# How Does Medicare Work?

We've mentioned Medicare a few times. What's that all about? Medicare is a federal health insurance plan for people 65 and older (plus people qualified as being disabled, regardless of age). Medicare is divided into two parts: Part A and Part B. Part A is hospital insurance and Part B is for medical insurance—it covers doctor visits and other nonhospital expenses.

## Part A and a Hospital Stay

Part A is what part of the Social Security deductions from your paycheck were going to for all those years. So, you have already paid for it. However, "it" does not cover all of your hospital room and board charge. The difference is covered by coinsurance payments that either you or your insurance company must pay. You will also have to cover an annual deductible. If you arrange for your Social Security benefits to begin at age 65, you are automatically enrolled in Medicare Part A. If you choose to retire after your 65th birthday, be sure to sign up for Medicare at age 65; otherwise you won't be enrolled in Medicare Part A.

## How to Pay for the Expenses Medicare Doesn't Cover

Part B of Medicare is optional. "Optional" is a misleading word, however, because you will be automatically enrolled—and the premium deducted from your monthly Social Security benefit check—unless you proactively opt out. If you opt in, the premium will not cover all your expenses. What's missing?

**Crash Alert**

Retiree health insurance offered by your employer may be another option you can use to cover the gap in Medicare coverage. Carefully check to make sure, however, that your employer's retiree health insurance being offered will provide the same benefits and roughly the same coverage you enjoy now. If not, you could end up in a pickle, looking for insurance at age 70–75 with possible pre-existing conditions. This client profile does not appeal to insurance companies.

First there is an annual deductible. Second, in many instances, there is an 80/20 split: Medicare pays 80 percent, and you or (your insurance company) pay the remaining 20 percent. The question becomes this: Do you want to pay for the necessary coinsurance, or do you want to select one of the 10 existing Medicare supplement policies? If you choose one of the latter, they basically cover your coinsurance for both parts A and B, but charge you a premium. But wait, there's a third option: You can go the HMO route. The HMOs are cheaper but restrict you to specific doctors and procedures.

## Medicare Is in Flux

Medicare is in the process of being restructured and refinanced, which for you will mean higher premiums, deductibles, coinsurance, etc.

If you want more information on Medicare, call Social Security at 1-800-772-1213 and request Publication No. 05-10043 (Medicare), which explains Medicare hospital and medical insurance.

We also recommend an excellent article in the September 1998 issue of *Consumer Reports* entitled "Medicare: New Choices, New Worries." Reprints of this special report are available for $3 per copy. Call 1-800-766-9988 or visit Consumer Reports' Web site at **www.consumerreports.org**.

# What About Lump-Sum Retirement Benefits?

When you do announce your retirement, your employer may very well offer you the option of receiving your defined benefit annuity in a single lump-sum payment. Essentially, your employer will take an interest rate provided by the federal government and apply it to your monthly benefit. You can either reject the option, or take the lump-sum and turn it over to an insurance company, or invest it yourself. Just remember to confirm that your monthly income is going to be noticeably increased by going the lump-sum route. If that's not the case, sit back, relax, and enjoy the monthly checks from your employer's plan administrator.

## Taking Your Home As a "Lump Sum"

Much has been written about a strategy where a bank or mortgage company buys your home (freeing up capital for you), and you pay the equivalent of a lease or rental fee. In other words, you would free up equity in your home while still enjoying living there. Although this is a reasonable option, we think you should give at least equal weight to the idea of selling your home and "downsizing" into a residence that is less expensive to own and maintain. Check with your local realtor to see whether either of these options—or just staying put—makes the most sense (and dollars) to you.

---

### The Least You Need to Know

➤ When you start a new job, ask right away about the company's pension and 401(k) plans, incentive plans, stock options, and health plans.

➤ If you're self-employed, any bank, mutual fund, brokerage, or insurance company will be happy to help you set up your own retirement plan.

➤ Starting in 2003, the full retirement age will be increased in steps until it reaches 67.

➤ If your combined income is over $34,000, up to 85 percent of your Social Security benefits may be taxed.

➤ You will need some form of health insurance after retirement to cover expenses not paid by Medicare.

---

# Chapter 14

# The Ramifications of Romance

> ### In This Chapter
>
> ➤ Using a pre-nup to avoid financial disaster
>
> ➤ Should you keep bank accounts and investments separate?
>
> ➤ The marriage tax
>
> ➤ Untangling assets after divorce

It's hard to think about money and love at the same time—but both have the ability to make us either turn green and act nuts or feel very secure and happy. Money and love are inescapably intertwined once two people marry. Every financial move you make is affected by your marital status, from how you choose to bank and invest, to how you protect your assets and the amount of tax you pay. In this chapter we will go over the financial ramifications of romance.

## When You Need a Pre-Nup

We've all been bombarded with tabloid tales about this or that wealthy celebrity who invokes a pre-nuptial agreement when the wedding of the year turns into the divorce of the decade. What is a pre-nup, exactly? A *pre-nuptial agreement* is a legal document, signed by both parties, stating "that is yours and this is mine." With roughly half of all marriages ending in divorce, and with roughly half of the assets usually going to each party, you can understand why a wealthy spouse whose mate is not exactly flush would demand a pre-nup.

But what about you? You're going to tell us you're not wealthy, but are you bringing something into the marriage that could eventually represent substantial wealth? A patented idea? Shares in your business—which could grow to become a regional or national chain? The great American novel in your desk drawer that finally finds its way to a supportive publisher? And what about those personal items handed down from generation to generation in your family? Or how about stock options that have no particular value at the time of marriage but will be worth a great deal some years hence?

**Investor's Idiom**

A *pre-nuptial* agreement is a legally binding document signed by two people before they get married. Most pre-nuptial agreements simply spell out who owns what and who will get what in the event the marriage ends in a divorce. A few pre-nuptial agreements that have made the news lately go into great detail, even specifying how often the couple will have sex or see their in-laws!

## What Can Happen If You Don't Have a Pre-Nup

Without a pre-nuptial agreement, you and your spouse will be subject to the property-settlement laws of the state in which you reside. In eight states (Arizona, California, Idaho, Louisiana, Nevada, New Mexico, Texas, and Washington) all assets ruled to be marital property by the court will be split 50–50—even if one partner earned all the money.

In the other states, marital property division is up to the judge. And, surprisingly, even assets acquired before the marriage, such as a house, stock, or even a business are thrown into the pot. In some states, even a professional degree earned during a marriage is included. If you become a doctor, lawyer, or accountant during the marriage, for example, your spouse might be able to claim half your earnings stemming from that degree.

We are not suggesting you turn to your spouse and say, "Honey, we need a pre-nup." That's a hard sell, and frankly, after you're married it's too late. It's even too late if you wait until just before the wedding. Many courts will throw out a pre-nup that one party can prove he or she was pressured to sign because the wedding was already planned.

But before your marriage, be it your first, third, or fifth, we suggest you talk seriously with your lawyer about a pre-nuptial agreement. This applies to women as well as men; if you and/or your soon-to-be spouse have or expect to earn a lot of money, hammer out a pre-nup before you say "I do." It could save a lot of pain and anguish later on.

# The Marriage Tax

The tax code was drawn up back in the day when one spouse worked and the other (guess which one?) stayed home and took care of the kids. So, marriage got a favorable treatment under the tax code. The numbers looked roughly like this:

| Status | Taxable Income | Tax Due |
|---|---|---|
| Single | $50,000 | $10,880 |
| Married, Filing Jointly | $50,000 | $8,787 |

Today, both spouses are much more likely to work, yet the marriage tax break persists—but it only works for families with one breadwinner. Working couples who get married get slammed. Below take a look at how two people, both earning $50,000, will be affected if they get married and both continue to work.

| Status | Income Total | Income/Income Tax |
|---|---|---|
| Two Single People | $50,000 + $50,000= | $100,000/$21,760 |
| Married, Filing Jointly | $100,000= | $100,000/$22,880 |
| Married, Filing Sep. | $50,000 + $50,000= | $100,000/$22,880 |

A couple will be penalized $1,120 if they get married! Clearly, if you are both going to work, the tax code suggests that you don't get married. If this offends you (and it should), write to your congressional representatives.

# Joint Bank Accounts

You may be penalized on your income tax if you get married, but at least it's cheaper to bank. Unless one of you is living a secret life or the two of you have trouble communicating, there is no reason to keep separate checking accounts.

The main advantage of one vs. several checking accounts is the savings on monthly service charges and fees. In addition, if you have the type of account that pays a minimum interest rate for minimum balances, it's obviously easier to meet the minimum balance requirement when you combine assets in one account. An exception needs to be made if you are a principal or sole proprietor of a business; in that case, a separate business checking account is a must.

**Crash Alert**

If you and your spouse decide to share a checking account, we can't stress enough the importance of communication. Make it a habit to to go over checks written and deposits/withdrawals made on a daily basis to avoid messy and expensive overdraft charges. And if your marriage should fall on the rocks and you separate, immediately dissolve any joint checking accounts.

# Should You Keep Separate Investment Portfolios?

Whether you keep separate or joint investment portfolios depends on the type of account. Some accounts, like IRAs, must be legally kept separate. The same applies to any 401(k) or 403(b) retirement plan, or a defined benefit (pension) plan: The employee is the sole legal owner.

181

For taxable accounts, however, a joint name is preferable, for three reasons.

1. Most investment advisors and planners charge a fee based on a percentage of your assets, and the greater the assets the lower the fee. An advisor may charge 2 percent to manage $500,000, and only 1 percent on $1 million, for example. Also, most, if not all, financial planners charge a minimum dollar fee, and you wouldn't want to pay two minimum fees.

2. Even if you don't use an investment advisor or counselor, it's still easier to balance and manage a single portfolio, rather than two or more. We strongly suggest you stick with one broker for the same reason. Less confusing!

3. One spouse is usually going to be less investment savvy than the other. The spouse who takes less naturally to investing is always going to be tempted to say, "Oh, I let Fred/Mary take care of that." But what happens to that spouse if financially astute Fred or Mary is no longer around? Far too many elderly widows have found themselves in exactly this vulnerable position, easy prey to the con artists who unfortunately exist in the investment business. Joint ownership confers upon the other party both the right and the obligation to know what is going on with their investments.

**Super Strategy**

If you and your spouse separate, make no changes in the joint ownership of your taxable accounts. You don't want to pay taxes if there is the slightest chance of a reconciliation. If you proceed to divorce, your assets will be separated as part of the terms of the divorce decree.

# Untangling Your Assets During Divorce

Suppose you have moved, gradually or precipitously, from blissful wedlock to separate padlocks. Who gets what and how? Generally, you (and your lawyer) will look to the laws of the state in which you plan to file for divorce. As we mentioned, eight states split all marital assets 50–50. Some states will favor the wife, especially if she is non-working and a mother.

## Handling the House

How easy or difficult the division of property will be depends upon the complexity of the assets and the attitudes of the individuals getting divorced. But, as a general rule, estimate the value of each asset and assume that each party will get half.

For many couples, their home is their biggest asset. To divide this asset or give it to one party, you'll need to have it appraised. One of the first calls you should make, therefore, is to your realtor. And don't even bother with secrecy; everyone probably knows what's happened.

## Divvying Up Other Assets

The most difficult types of assets to deal with are family heirlooms and compensation-related issues like stock options and family businesses.

➤ First, you should each make a list of your individual assets and place a fair market value on each (to the best of your ability).

➤ Next, you and your lawyer should sit down with your soon-to-be ex-spouse and his or her lawyer to reconcile any differences.

Family heirlooms that have been in your family will generally go to you; but you may or may not have to give up something in return. A lot depends on your spouse's attitude.

Stock options are a bear: What were they worth at the time of the marriage? What are they worth now? What could they be worth? Just give your lawyer the facts and let him or her deal with the issue. If it can be negotiated, great; if not, you may have to litigate. State laws vary on this specific asset, but best to assume that stock options are one of the marital assets subject to distribution in a divorce. If it turns out otherwise, lucky you.

Provide your lawyer with the date and amount of options granted, and the date and price at which they can be exercised. You'll also need to obtain, in writing, a statement from your employer regarding whether the options are a basic part of your compensation package, or an incentive for future efforts.

# Negotiate with Your Head, Not Your Spleen

If you've seen the movie "The War of the Roses," you have some inkling of the dark side of divorce. Sometimes two people can be zipping through an amicable divorce until she decides she wants half of the Simon and Garfunkel collection and he insists on keeping the dog—with no visitation rights. And then comes that killer statement: "Well, if you're going to be that way…," and everything unravels.

The chances that you and your lawyer are going to pull the wool over the eyes of your spouse and his or her lawyer are pretty small. So, be reasonable and fair. Where there is an asset or issue that you feel quite strongly about, be firm but convey the firmness via your lawyer. The more obstreperous things become, the longer the process takes, and lawyers charge by the hour. It's your money.

Unless you have a very amicable divorce pending (whatever that is), move out of the house immediately. You can arrange to come back and do your inventory and obtain necessary clothing at a mutually agreed upon time and date. It's a good idea to agree on that time and date before leaving.

### Super Strategy

Divorce between two working spouses without children is (or should be) straightforward. Add a child or children and emotional pain enters the equation. Change one spouse to non-working, add children and a long marriage, and you have a really difficult situation. But our advice is the same in every divorce situation: keep your cool, be fair, be firm when you feel strongly about an issue or asset, and keep it lawyer to lawyer.

## Other Divorce Options

Before you go the divorce route, please try a separation (legal or informal). With a little time and a little space, along with a fuller understanding of the dollar and emotional costs involved, many marriages can be repaired. Joint therapy and/or marriage counseling can also help repair the torn fabric of a marriage.

If divorce is inevitable and feelings are amicable, think about "no-fault" divorce. The two of you simply go before the judge and say it was no one's fault that the marriage failed. This can save a lot in legal fees, and you'll be unhitched that much faster.

### The Least You Need to Know

➤ You need a pre-nuptial agreement if you are bringing anything into a marriage that could eventually represent substantial wealth.

➤ If you don't have a pre-nup, you will be subject to the property settlement laws of your state if you get divorced.

➤ If both you and your intended work, the tax code will actually penalize you for getting married.

➤ Married couples should keep their tax-deferred retirement accounts separate but share taxable investment accounts jointly.

# Chapter 15

# Home Ownership: What You Need to Know

---

### In This Chapter

➤ Down payment dos and don'ts

➤ Timing the real estate market

➤ Owning vs. renting

➤ Choosing between fixed-rate and adjustable-rate mortgages

---

Most everyone starts adult life renting rather than owning. The reason is simple: It's cheaper! Initially, you may not even be able to afford to rent on your own, hence your roommates and their socks on the living room floor. But some 5 to 10 years after you enter the work force, with perhaps marriage and children either present or on the way, the subject of purchasing your own home needs to be reviewed. In this chapter we will run you through key questions to ask yourself before you make the big life change from lowly renter to king or queen of your castle.

## The Down Payment

Do you have the down payment necessary to buy a home? You will need to put down at least 10 percent, and in some cases up to 20 percent, of the purchase price of the home in order to obtain mortgage approval. There are also some first-time homebuyer programs that don't require such high downpayments—for example, VA loans and HUD programs.

Here are the best sources for your down payment, in order of preference:

1. Savings. You planned ahead by putting aside the savings for 10 percent down, and you're ready to go.

2. A loan from good old Mom and Dad (or your spouse's mom and dad). "We can pay it back at our convenience? At 0 percent interest?" Or how 'bout: "It's a gift? We couldn't possibly…well, if you insist!"

3. Tapping your retirement plans (Roth IRA, 401(k), etc.). Borrowing from the Roth IRA is preferable, but the program just started so even if you have one, there's probably not much money in it yet. If you borrow from your 401(k), it's considered a loan that you must pay back.

Do not borrow the money for your down payment. The cost of carrying what amounts to a first and second mortgage will most likely overtax you financially. If you approach your mortgage banker already carrying a debt like that, you might be turned down for the mortgage, anyway.

**Super Strategy**

Consider moving through a series of steps toward owning your dream home. Most people end up doing this: rental to condo to town house to starter home to the big comfy house in the 'burbs. Skipping any of these steps may leave you financially strapped.

# Timing Is Everything

The next question to ask is: What's the real estate market like? Hot, medium, or cold? If it's hot, you run the risk of paying inflated prices, potentially coming in at the top of the market. This translates to a higher down payment and higher monthly payments (principal, interest, and, in many cases, real estate taxes). If you then have to move for any reason, you run the risk of having to sell at a loss.

If possible, follow your local real estate market for several years before even considering home ownership. Most local newspapers carry charts or tables that show you whether home sales in your area are trending up or down, and to what degree. You can also get a feel by going to open houses and requesting sales literature on around a dozen homes that might meet your needs.

Specifically, you'll want to observe two indicators:

1. Has the asking price been reduced, and, if yes, how much and how many times?

2. How many days has the house been on the market?

In a "hot" market, homes are gobbled up in a matter of days, and the buyer pays the asking price. In a really hot market, with two or more buyers vying for the same property, the "winner" ends up paying more than the asking price. You definitely do not want to make your first home purchase in this environment.

You should also check out mortgage interest rates, but home prices are a more important indicator of whether or not it's the right time to buy. High mortgage rates and high home prices often go hand-in-hand—but not always. In August 1998, for example, we saw higher home prices and lower mortgage rates. Three years ago the trend was higher mortgage rates and lower home prices.

### Super Strategy

A good rule of thumb: If you can handle the monthly payments on the home you want and you think it's selling at a good price, don't concern yourself with mortgage rates. Just focus on home prices. Don't forget, you can always re-finance your mortgage if and when rates fall.

# Evaluate Your Mortgage-Worthiness Before a Banker Does

Once you start to keep tabs on the real estate market, make it a point to sit down with a mortgage banker and determine what he or she looks for in a successful applicant, so you can compare that profile to your present situation. If you can't find a mortgage banker willing to do this, go to a knowledgeable and experienced real estate broker. Basically, if you present your personal balance sheet and income statement (which you learned how to create in Chapter 4), the expert can tell you if you could qualify for a mortgage and how large a mortgage you could handle. If you don't qualify, you can spend the next few years both following the local real estate market and getting in better financial shape.

# Compare Renting to Owning

If you are thinking about buying a home, sit down and calculate the total cost of home ownership vs. renting. When you rent, you pay a monthly rental fee and utilities. You may also pay for parking and laundry. That's about it. Home ownership, on the other hand, is not just about a monthly mortgage payment and taxes. There are many expenses you may not have considered, such as:

➤ outside maintenance—yard work, painting, and equipment such as a lawn mower and leaf and snow blowers.

➤ inside maintenance—carpet cleaning, floor sanding and coating, appliance maintenance, plumbing repairs, painting, and papering.

➤ major repairs and replacements. Retain an inspection service to ascertain the expected life of your hot water heater, roof, siding, deck, etc. People stay in one home an average of five years, so for anything that will probably need to be replaced within five years, determine the cost and divide it by 60. Add this cost to your monthly payments.

On the bright side, your interest and taxes on a home are tax deductible, and you are gradually building up equity (ownership!) in your home. In addition, you won't be hit with yearly rent increases.

# Over Time, Owning Should Save You Money

It's hard to come up with a specific example that is applicable to everyone, so let's make some broad assumptions and compare renting to owning over a 60-month (five-year) time frame:

| Per Month | Rent | Purchase |
|---|---|---|
| Rent: $2,000 × (4% annual increase ÷ 2) = | $2,217 | |
| Parking | 160 | |
| Utilities | 100 | 200 |
| Laundry | 24 | 12 |
| Principal & Interest* | | 1,347 |
| Transportation | 50 | 200 |
| Maintenance | | 100 |
| Homeowners Insurance | | 50 |
| Repairs | | 250 |
| Taxes | | 300 |
| Tax/Interest Deductions = 1,300 + 300 × .31 = 496 × .12 = | | −41 |
| Totals | 2,551 | 2,418 |

*Assumptions: $225,000 purchase price, 10% down, the balance financed at $7^1/_8$% over 30 years.*

In this example, we have a pretty clear-cut case favoring purchase. Your case may be different.

# Renting Pluses

Although it's generally considered preferable to buy, continuing to rent is definitely preferable to buying the wrong home at the wrong price at the wrong time in the real estate market. That's why we suggest spending several years watching the market and getting a feel for what constitutes a bargain in your price range and your area.

Owning your own home has always been considered part of the American Dream, but for people who bought when the real estate market peaked in the 1980s and suffered huge losses when they needed to move, the American Dream turned into a nightmare.

Remember, you're in charge; you decide when the time is right, and another year or two in a rental is not the end of the world. Be cool.

# How Much of Your Income Should You Spend on Housing?

Twenty-five percent of your gross income is a reasonable sum to spend on housing. Some experts use up to 33 percent, but let's be conservative! Our recommendation means that someone earning $100,000 can afford roughly $2,000 per month for housing. Assuming a $7^{1}/_{8}$ percent mortgage rate and a 30-year mortgage, principal and interest would equate to roughly $1,685 per month on a $250,000 mortgage, leaving $315 per month for taxes. That feels about right. And with 10 percent down and closing costs, you're looking at a $275,000 purchase. Naturally, taxes vary, as do home prices and what you get for your money. That $275,000 probably buys you a lot in Nebraska or North Dakota, but little (if anything) in San Francisco.

**Fiscal Facts**

The Consumer Price Index (CPI) is a group of prices that are followed by economists in order to gauge whether inflation is on the rise or waning. The CPI is probably the most well-known and widely reported inflation number we have. What is not well-known is that housing prices for both rental and owned residences makes up 40 percent of the CPI.

# Fixed Rate vs. Adjustable Rate Mortgage

Your mortgage banker may offer you a choice between:

1. A fixed-rate mortgage that locks you into a given interest rate for the life of the mortgage, which is traditionally 30 years, or

2. An adjustable rate mortgage.

How long you intend to stay in the house is the key to your decision. An adjustable rate mortgage can be a good deal if you plan to stay in your house for no more than five years, and if the rate is sufficiently below the 30-year rate for a fixed-rate mortgage.

### Investor's Idiom

An *adjustable-rate mortgage* (ARM) is priced off the yield for the 10-year Treasury note. Since the yield on the note changes every six months, so will the interest rate on your ARM. And when short-term rates are lower than long-term rates, you may get a better deal with an ARM than with a long-term fixed mortgage. How much the ARM rate fluctuates over the duration of your mortgage depends on interest rates in general and the product itself. Most ARMs have a lifetime cap, above which the rate cannot rise.

If the adjustable rate is not at least 200 basis points (2.0 percent) below the 30-year rate, it's not worth the risk of escalating interest rates to commit to it. Right now, for example, short-term and long-term interest rates are all very low and there's not much difference between them, so few new home owners are taking out adjustable rate mortgages.

# The Costs of Closing

When you buy your first home, be prepared to cover closing costs of around 3 percent of the price of the house before the keys are yours. Closing costs vary from state to state, depending on whether the state says attorneys are required to handle the closing and on real estate tax rates.

Following is a summary of a typical closing statement. Looking just at the columns pertaining to the buyer, we see that the buyer ends up paying over $6,000 in closing/settlement costs.

**Line:**

| 101 | Contract sales price | $252,000.00 | The amount you agreed to pay for the home |
|---|---|---|---|
| 103 | Settlement charges | 6,384.81 | Detailed below |
| 120 | Gross amount due from buyer | 258,384.81 | Total of lines 101 and 103 |

**Less:**

| 201 | Deposit of earnest money | 25,300.00 | Down payment |
|---|---|---|---|
| 202 | Principal amount of new loan | 100,000.00 | The buyer's new mortgage |
| 220 | Total paid by buyer | 125,300.00 | Total of lines 201+ 202 |
| 303 | Additional cash from buyer | 133,084.81 | Sum buyer must come up with at closing Summary of Settlement Charges (Line 103) |
| 802 | Loan discount | 2,000.00 | Buyer paid "points" (two) to get lower mortgage rate |
| 904 | Three Months real estate taxes | 1,548.22 | Three Months real estate taxes |
| 905 | | 6.94 | Property overlaps two municipalities |

| 1107 | Attorney's fees | 950.00 | For the "closing" |
|------|-----------------|--------|-------------------|
| 1108 | Title insurance | 1,708.00 | Required |
| 1201 | Recording fees | 70.00 | Required |
| 1204 | Notice of settlement | 16.00 | Required |
| 1303 | Faxes | 45.65 | |
| 1304 | UPS | 40.00 | |
| 1400 | Total Settlement Charges | 6,384.81 | Lines 802–1304 |

# Second Mortgages—Pros and Pitfalls

Once you own a home, you will be bombarded with offers to place a second mortgage on your home. Second mortgages are tax deductible, but they place you in a financial straight jacket. With a second mortgage, you sign for a fixed-rate loan for the full amount of equity in your home. You might not need or use all the money, but you sure are paying interest on it.

A home equity loan is a better deal because it is a revolving line of credit—you only pay for what you use (like a charge card), and you can still deduct the interest from your taxes. A second mortgage is either a desperation step for someone who wants to finance a dramatic career shift, or a short-term means of coming up with the down payment on your first (starter) home. Do not enter into it lightly.

# Pluses to Paying Off Your Mortgage

Mortgage (or rent) represents the largest single expenditure for the average tax payer. It's wise, therefore, to try to retire your mortgage before you retire yourself. There are three ways to accomplish this:

1. Stay in your home for 15–30 years and pay off the mortgage.
2. Pay off half the mortgage, sell your home and buy a condo/town house at half the price of your former home.
3. Benefit from escalating home values. If your home rises in value 50 percent in five years, for example, sell your home and buy a condo/town house at half the price.

# Should You Shorten Your Mortgage?

Moving from a 30-year to a 15-year mortgage can make a big difference. Here's an example, using a 60-month occupancy assumption and a $200,000 mortgage. The figures are very rough and just for purposes of illustration.

30-year mortgage, $7^1/8$%*, monthly principal & interest = $1,347

15-year mortgage, $6^7/8$%*, monthly principal & interest = $1,783

Difference per month = $436

Increased Equity of $436 × 60 = $26,160

*You can get a rough approximation by adding or subtracting $15 for each $1/8$ percent rate up or down.*

In essence, making a bigger monthly mortgage payment goes a long way toward building equity and reducing the mortgage on your property. Question: Is it better to save/invest this way as opposed to contributing $436 to your 401(k) or IRA? Probably not. In fact, if all you did was to invest $436 per month in a 4 percent tax-free municipal bond, your principal would amount to approximately $29,000 by the end of five years.

Remember in Chapter 8 when we talked about how many people make the mistake of over-withholding their taxes when it would be better for them to withhold the minimum and invest the difference? Choosing a 15-year over a 30-year mortgage is a similar situation. The 15-year mortgage just forces you to save. It might be better to take the longer mortgage and its smaller mortgage payments and invest the $436 that you save each month into a tax-deferred investment. This way you get the tax break and the benefits of compound interest. Opt for additional retirement savings, and pay the mortgage off sooner that way.

# The Relocation Package

If you are moving to take a new job or because you've been transferred by a new employer, look into whether your firm offers a "relocation package." Some aspects of a relocation package may be classified as compensation, meaning you'll have to pay income tax on it, but that's still better than paying all moving expenses out of pocket. The "job relo" may include any or all of the following:

1. Prepaid moving services

2. Special financing rates

3. Purchase of your existing home (or the sub-leasing of an apartment for you in the new area until you sell your home)

4. A "buyer's broker" paid for by your employer

If you don't have a job relo, go to a reputable real estate firm and ask for a licensed realtor with at least five years experience. Be specific about your housing needs, such as size, style, price range, transportation, and schools. If good schools are an important part of your decision, ask the realtor for the names of the best school systems and cross-check the list with your employer. And bore in on real estate taxes. Remember, it's not the current taxes that matter, it's what your tax bill will be if you purchase the property.

Should you use a "buyer's broker"? Before answering that question, let's make sure you understand who pays and who receives residential real estate commissions. A typical real estate commission of, say, 6 percent is split 3 percent to the listing broker (and his/her firm) and 3 percent to the selling broker (and his/her firm). The 6 percent is paid by the home seller. The selling broker is a sub-agent who represents the seller, not you. You are free to go to as many brokers as you wish to be shown properties.

When you use a buyer's broker, on the other hand, you sign a written contract with a specific broker who will represent you, the buyer. You, in turn, agree to only work with that broker. That 3 percent selling commission still comes from the seller's proceeds, only it goes to your buyer's broker. We think tilting the odds a little away from the seller and toward the buyer makes sense, so we recommend that you use a buyer's broker.

**Crash Alert**

Choosing the 30-year over the 15-year mortgage is financially sound if you really, truly have the discipline to invest what you would have had to pay monthly on the 15-year mortgage in your retirement account. If you find you're just spending that extra few hundred dollars a month, then opt for the 15-year mortgage.

# Renting Out Your Home When You Move

Nobody wants to be temporarily owning two homes: the one you just purchased and the one that hasn't sold yet. But that situation arises more often than not. And if the prospective buyer knows your situation, you've lost some negotiating leverage.

What to do? Well, it depends primarily on market conditions and secondarily on your particular property. If the market is strong (or even stable), the economy is decent, and you have a tract home, one to two months of patience will probably pay off. Check with your broker to make sure your home is competitively priced; this is no time to be reaching for top dollar. Chances are, you know by the number of "showings" and offers (if any) whether or not you have a problem. If the market or the economy is weak, or if you have an atypical home (say, an offbeat architectural style or a less-than-accessible location), you may want to consider renting it out or renting it with an option to buy.

If you decide to rent your property, plan on offering a one- to two-year rental; shorter-term rental tenants are less likely to take care of your property. And remember, your end objective is still to sell your home. The complication is that you have to maintain your property while being geographically removed.

Unless you already have a willing tenant, you'll need to retain a broker to list your property as a rental. Typically, they will receive, up front, 10 percent of the yearly rent.

# Real Estate Agents

We've all heard stories about how Jack and Mary sold their home themselves and saved $6,000, $12,000, or $18,000. What you don't hear about are the Bills and Nancys who overpriced their home, were excluded from multiple listing and relocation sources, and had no marketing plan. Their home sat on the market for months with few showings and no offers.

Not only do you waste time in this situation, you get a reputation for having an overpriced home. When you do get showings, it may simply be brokers using your home to show how attractive another property is on a price basis. We strongly urge you to get a broker; just be sure he/she is experienced. Ask for references and determine how much property the broker has sold during each of the previous three years. A good broker is worth more than the cost of the commission. Make sure your house is presentable, and don't restrict access to potential buyers.

If you are buying, by all means sign up with a buyer's broker. As we said, it's the only way to at least partially even the odds.

# Closing the Deal

In a seller's market, you will get one or more offers at or very close to your asking price in a very short period of time. Lucky you! Make sure all parties agree to your closing terms, and let the process sort out the highest bidder.

In a buyer's market, you (and your broker) will have to "walk up" the bid. A low bid may be insulting, but don't let personal feelings get in the way of a business deal. Come down a little on your asking price and see what the prospective buyer does. Chances are the buyer was just trying to judge your level of desperation. After a few more rounds of this, your broker will offer this famous phrase: "Let's split the difference." Now, your soul-searching begins. Yes…no…maybe? It's a fine line between keeping the negotiations going and killing the deal. Listen to your broker, and good luck!

---

### The Least You Need to Know

➤ Don't borrow the money for your down payment; you might get turned down for a mortgage.

➤ Try to follow your local real estate market for several years before buying a home.

➤ Evaluate your mortgage-worthiness before a banker does.

➤ Continuing to rent is definitely preferable to buying the wrong home at the wrong price and time.

➤ Retire your mortgage before you retire yourself.

➤ If you must relocate because of your job, see if you can have your company pick up the expenses of moving.

---

# Chapter 16

# Educating the Little Rascals

---

## In This Chapter

➤ Setting up educational funds

➤ Withdrawing from a Roth IRA to pay for college

➤ The Education IRA and EE savings bonds

➤ Evaluating qualified tuition programs

---

When it comes to educating your children (or grandchildren), there's both good and bad news. The bad news is that college expenses are continuing to grow by at least two times the overall inflation rate in this country. The good news is that an increasing percentage of college enrollees are getting financial aid. In addition, several new options have been unveiled—such as the Roth IRA and the Education IRA—that will make saving for college easier than ever.

Expenses for college vary dramatically, depending upon whether your child attends a state school or a private college or university. Gross expenses include tuition and fees, room and board, and books and supplies. Figure on spending roughly $10,000–$12,000 per year in gross expenses for a state school, if you reside in state. Add $3,000–$4,000 if you live out of state. Ivy League schools average around $30,000–$32,000.

These are just ballpark figures, of course, but they give you an idea of the magnitude of the challenge faced by families trying to put several kids through college. And assume inflation will add roughly 3–5 percent per year, or roughly twice the Consumer Price Index, to these figures.

# Put Your Financial Security First

Many parents go into debt to pay for their children's education. This is understandable, but financially questionable. Of course, you need to try your best to provide a good education for your children. But jeopardizing your retirement assets to bolster educational assets is not the answer. As we suggested in Chapter 3, of the 10 percent you should be saving out of your salary, commit 8 percent to your retirement and 2 percent to your children's education.

Your child has many options at age 18: college first; work, then college; work-study program; no college; the military; etc. Your retirement only has two options; either you have the money to retire or you don't. And don't forget two other issues:

1. Where your child goes to college is driven more by his or her academic and extracurricular accomplishments than by your checking account.

2. Your child is capable of contributing to his or her college education via summer or part-time work, and probably will be a better person for doing so.

**Super Strategy**

Involve your child in the decision about where to go to college by getting him or her a copy of a great reference guide: *The College Handbook*, published by the College Entrance Examination Board. The handbook profiles 3,215 colleges and will definitely get you and your soon-to-be campus star excited and motivated.

# Setting Up Educational Funds

Set up educational funds for each of your children as soon as they are born…or you can start now! There are three questions that need to be answered when setting up funds for college education:

1. Which fund or funds are most appropriate? Your best choices include:

   ➤ Traditional IRA

   ➤ Roth IRA

   ➤ Education IRA

   ➤ EE savings bonds (alone or as part of an IRA)

2. What scholarships, grants, and loans are available for student expenses or reimbursement? Presently, programs available include:

   ➤ Hope Scholarships

   ➤ Pell Grants

   ➤ Lifetime Learning Credits

   ➤ Student loans

   ➤ Qualified tuition programs

   ➤ Employer-paid educational assistance

3. Finally, should the securities or other assets you intend to save be in your name or the child's name?

Let's look at the fund options first.

## Using a Traditional IRA to Save for College

Presently, each working or nonworking spouse can contribute up to $2,000 per year to a traditional IRA. Previously, nonworking spouses were limited to $250. For the full contribution to be deductible under the Taxpayer Relief Act of 1997, the contributor must have an adjusted gross income (AGI, remember that?) of under $30,000 ($50,000 for a joint return). After $30,000, the contribution's deductibility is phased out incrementally, so that by $40,000, none of it is deductible.

The phase-out ranges move up over the next 10 years as follows:

| Year | Status: | Single | Joint |
|------|---------|--------|-------|
| 1998 | | $30–40,000 | $50–60,000 |
| 1999 | | $31–41,000 | $51–61,000 |
| 2000 | | $32–42,000 | $52–62,000 |
| 2001 | | $33–43,000 | $53–63,000 |
| 2002 | | $34–44,000 | $54–64,000 |
| 2003 | | $40–50,000 | $60–70,000 |
| 2004 | | $45–55,000 | $65–75,000 |
| 2005 | | $50–60,000 | $70–80,000 |
| 2006 | | $50–60,000 | $75–85,000 |
| 2007+ | | $50–60,000 | $80–100,000 |

In addition, beginning in 1998, if one spouse does not actively participate in an employer-sponsored plan, he or she may still make a deductible IRA contribution if the couple's adjusted gross income is $150,000 or less.

Most interesting for our purposes in this chapter, the 10 percent additional tax on withdrawals from a traditional IRA before age 59$^1/_2$ can now be waived for qualified higher education expenses. "Qualified" expenses include tuition, room and board, books, fees, and supplies. These changes put a lot more muscle in the traditional IRA, particularly when applied to educational expenses.

## Advantages of the Roth IRA

The Roth IRA was introduced during the 1998 tax year. It offers some great options for families saving for college.

1. Funds can be withdrawn tax-free after five years under certain circumstances. Previously, investment earnings were taxable at the time of withdrawal. Funds can be withdrawn tax-free:

   a. On or after age 59$^1/_2$

   b. For a beneficiary after the death of the contributor

   c. For a "qualified special purpose"

   This includes qualified higher education expenses, as discussed above, and up to $10,000 toward the purchase of the principal residence of a first-time homeowner.

2. There is no mandatory distribution starting at age 70$^1/_2$, as with traditional IRA's.

3. You can contribute to the Roth for as long as you wish. With the traditional IRA you have to stop contributing before reaching the age 70$^1/_2$.

Those are the positives. There are two negatives:

1. The total amount that an individual can contribute to a Roth and other IRAs is $2,000 (excluding Education IRAs—more about those below).

2. Contributions are limited by your adjustable gross income. Once your AGI hits $95,000, the amount you can contribute starts to decline, reaching zero at $110,000. (The limits kick in between $150,000–$160,000 for joint filers.)

**Investor's Idiom**

*The Education IRA* was introduced in 1998. Contributions are limited to only $500 per year, per beneficiary, and grow tax-deferred. You can make contributions annually until your kids hit 18. Withdrawals for qualified educational purposes are tax-free.

## New in '98: The Education IRA

The Education IRA was also introduced in 1998. Contributions are tax-deferred, but not deductible and are limited to only $500 per year, per beneficiary (little rascal). You can make contributions annually until your little rascal(s) becomes 18. Withdrawals for qualified educational purposes are tax-free.

As with the Roth IRA, there's an adjusted gross income (AGI) phase-out for eligibility. The phase-out ranges are $95,000–$110,000 for an individual and $150,000–$160,000 for a joint return.

## EE Savings Bonds

EE savings bonds can be either plugged into Education or Roth IRAs, or used on their own to save for college. There are some disadvantages to using savings bonds, however:

➤ The yield is fixed at 90 percent of a five-year Treasury note, with the yield recalculated every six months. If Treasury note rates fall, so does the rate on your bond. If the five-year Treasury note is yielding 5 percent, the EE Savings Bond is yielding 4.5 percent. But if six months later, the Treasury note yield drops to 4.5 percent, your bond starts earning only 4.05 percent. Of course, the yields could go up, too!

➤ Although you can redeem (cash in) an EE savings bond after six months, you will pay a three-month interest penalty unless you wait five years to redeem it. To avoid the penalty, you have to really plan ahead when using EE savings bonds for college. You'll need to stop purchasing the bonds five years before the last college bills come due.

➤ You also have to deal with a limit of $15,000 purchase price per purchaser per year. If you remember from our discussion of EE savings bonds in Chapter 11, you buy the bonds at half price and wait for them to rise to full price at maturity. So a $15,000 EE savings bond will eventually be worth $30,000.

EE savings bonds do have some great advantages:

➤ You can purchase them with as little as $25. They are perfect for that $500 limit on contributions to Educational IRAs.

➤ They make great gifts from relatives.

➤ The interest income on an EE savings bond is free of state and local taxes. The federal taxes on interest income are due only when the EE savings bond is redeemed. And, in some instances, there is a tax exclusion if the proceeds are being used for postsecondary education.

**Crash Alert**

The $500 annual contribution limit per child really cuts the investment options for your Education IRA, as most mutual funds have minimums greater than $500, and treasury securities and bank certificates of deposit have $1,000 minimums. This restricts—but does not negate—the favorable aspects of this education expense tool.

Cool, but how does this work? First of all, the exclusion is limited to tuition and required fees. In this case, it may not be applied to room, board, or books. Second, the bonds must be registered in the name of the taxpayer, not the child, although the child can be named as beneficiary.

In addition, the qualified tuition and fees paid must be equal to or greater than the amount of money received when the bonds are cashed in. If you pay tuition and fees of $5,000 and the bond proceeds are no more than $5,000, you're qualified for the exclusion. If tuition and fees are $4,000 and the bond proceeds are $5,000, you can deduct only that ratio ($4,000 ÷ $5,000 = 80 percent) of the interest income on the bonds (not the principal). Don't you love how confusing the IRS can make things?

Finally, to qualify for the tax exclusion, you have to earn less than the modified AGI limits. For 1997, the range of modified adjusted gross income is $76,250–$106,250 for couples filing jointly and $50,850–$65,850 for single filers. In other words, you can get full exclusion if you earn under $76,250, and partial exclusion scaling down to zero once you earn over $106,250. Did you notice that we tucked in the word "modified"?

In this case, modified AGI is AGI plus the interest earned on the redeemed bonds. Ah, the tax code! But wait: there's another neat way to use EE savings bonds for a child's college expense. Buy the bonds in the child's name and file a tax return with the child's Social Security number. Then report the accrued (earned but not received) interest income on the bonds for that year. You won't need to file again and no tax is due unless or until the child's total income exceeds the threshold for taxes owed (e.g., $650). If tax is owed, it is at the parent's rate for children under age 14 and at the child's rate at age 14 or older.

It is unfortunate that the regulations on EE savings bonds are so complicated because they have a lot to offer parents saving for college. But, that's the Feds for you.

# Qualified Tuition Programs

Public or private schools may now establish tax-exempt prepaid tuition programs. Prior to 1998, these programs had to be state-sponsored. Withdrawals from qualified programs may be made for tuition, fees, room and board, books and supplies. You can't contribute to both qualified tuition programs and an Education IRA in the same year, however.

Among the various plans offered, the one that grabbed our attention is the UNIQUE College Investing Plan, sponsored by the State of New Hampshire and managed by Fidelity Investments. If you would like more information than we've highlighted below, contact the Unique Plan at 1-800-544-1722.

The Unique Plan works like this:

1. The parents open a brokerage account with Fidelity Brokerage with a minimum of $1,000. As an alternative, you can sign up for Fidelity Automatic Account Builder (FAAB), with automatic transfers from your checking account of as little as $50 per month. All contributions must be in cash (i.e., by check).

2. Your funds are invested in a "lifestyle" portfolio consisting of Fidelity Mutual Funds. Remember lifestyle funds from Chapter 12? These are funds that

automatically shift the allocation of your assets between equity and fixed income as you age.

The Fidelity portfolio is similar, in that it shifts the assets in your Unique Plan account between equity, bond, and money market funds as the beneficiary (your child) ages. A newborn might be invested 88 percent equity/12 percent bonds, while at college age the ratios might shift to 20 percent equity/40 percent bonds/ 40 percent short-term bonds and money market—freeing up funds to pay for college. The stock/bond ratio for your child would be dependent upon his or her age upon entering the program.

3.  Fidelity uses no-load mutual funds, so the account will be charged only the operating expenses for each mutual fund. In addition, there is a fee of 0.30% of your account assets per year and a $30 annual maintenance fee (waived for accounts over $25,000 or if you sign up for FAAB).

4.  You can increase your monthly contributions with FAAB at any time if you start earning more money or decide that you've underestimated potential education costs.

5.  Earnings grow tax-deferred until they are distributed. If the distributions are for qualified educational expenses, they are taxed at the beneficiary's (your child's) rate. This is true of federal taxes; check with your state to determine state tax status.

6.  There is no adjusted gross income (AGI) to restrict or to pre-qualify you.

7.  Multiple accounts can be opened for your child by grandparents and other relatives. Joint accounts are not allowed, however. As of 1999, the most you can invest in each account per beneficiary is $105,545.

8.  You can change the beneficiary to another child. If you distribute the assets to someone besides the designated beneficiary, however, or if the funds are not used to pay qualified education expenses, you will be socked with state and federal taxes, as well as a 10 percent penalty.

9.  Contributions are considered completed gifts, so the value of an account won't be included in the donor's estate when he or she dies. You can also give up to $50,000 in one year without gift tax as long as you opt to apply the $10,000 annual exclusion over five years.

10. If you invest in the UNIQUE Plan and an Education IRA totaling more than $500, the amount in the IRA is subject to a 6 percent penalty tax. So choose one or the other. Your child can still benefit from Hope Scholarship and Lifetime Learning Credits, which are discussed below.

11. You can use the assets to pay for qualified education expenses at any accredited institution of higher learning, not just New Hampshire schools.

This is just a summary of the Unique Plan. You will want to delve more deeply into the matter before proceeding, but it looks pretty nifty to us.

# New Income Tax Credits for Education Expenses

As we said at the beginning of this chapter, there are all kinds of ways to defray expenses for college—and more are coming on line all the time. Several new credits are now allowed by the IRS, for example.

## The Hope Scholarship Credit

Starting in 1998, the Hope Scholarship Credit allows parents to take a credit against federal income taxes for tuition and related expenses. The credit is limited to the first two years of college and consists of 100 percent of the first $1,000 of qualified expenses, and 50 percent of the second $1,000. Thus, the maximum credit you can take in the first two years is $1,500 per year. You must also meet a modified AGI of $40,000–$50,000 (single) or $80,000–$100,000 (joint).

## Lifetime Learning Credits

Lifetime Learning Credits were also introduced in 1998. These are credits you can take for education expenses that are not eligible for the Hope credit. Included are expenses incurred to acquire or improve job skills. The credit is 20 percent of expenses up to $5,000 before 2003, and $10,000 thereafter. The Lifetime has income credit phase-outs on AGI identical to the Hope.

## The Education-Loan Interest Deduction

Qualified parents can now deduct interest paid on loans taken out expressly to pay college costs. The interest paid for the first 60 months can be deducted, with the maximums being:

| | |
|---|---|
| 1998 | $1,000 |
| 1999 | $1,500 |
| 2000 | $2,000 |
| 2001+ | $2,500 |

As usual, the deduction comes with the dreaded AGI limits, which are slightly different than elsewhere: $40,000–$55,000 for individual and $60,000–$75,000 for joint.

# Other Options

We have no intention of exploring every conceivable option for financing your kids' education in this chapter. Our intention was to primarily explore investment options.

But do take a look at two other important prospects:

1. Student loans from the government's "Sallie Mae" program (202-333-8000). These are student loans at very reasonable interest rates—presently 7–8 percent. Approximately 8 million students participate in this program per year.

2. Scholarships. First, check with the college your child wants to attend to find out whether he or she is eligible to apply for any scholarships. Definitely call local organizations such as the Rotary Club or Kiwanis, which often sponsor scholarships for deserving students. Remember that grants or scholarships do not have to be repaid, loans do. Your college can also help you determine whether your child qualifies for financial assistance in the form of Pell grants or other government-sponsored grants. Financial aid is defined in terms of demonstrated need; total college expense less family contribution equals demonstrated need.

# Sorting Out All the Options

Now, how do you sort out all these complicated alternatives? It seems that the best tax-incentive alternatives are available to low-income parents, who may also be most likely to obtain scholarship dollars for their child.

On the other hand, these parents face a level of complexity that would challenge an accountant. Parents over the AGI limits, meanwhile, can feel very frustrated. Let's list the alternatives we've discussed on a best-to-worst basis, both for those with a qualifying AGI and those above it.

If you earn at or below the AGI minimum:

1. Education IRA—Benefit specific (education) and ideal for larger families.
2. Roth IRA—Not education specific, but same qualifications and benefits.
3. EE savings bonds—Register in your name; also request gifts in child's name. Not all education expenses covered.
4. Scholarships—Must pursue and apply shortly before matriculation.
5. Hope/Lifetime Credits—If you have to borrow, use these tax deductions.
6. Student Loans—Last resort.

If your earnings are over the AGI Minimum:

1. Traditional IRA—Use the education expense option.
2. Qualified tuition programs—Choose the variable option over the fixed one; this gives you a better shot over time at making more money.
3. EE savings bonds—Keep in child's name; ditto for gifts; don't bother with annual tax filing.
4. Taxable portfolio—Invest in index equity funds or passive equities; mix with EE bonds.
5. Hope/Lifetime Credits—See if you qualify.
6. Student Loans—See Sallie as a last resort.

Finally, encourage your little rascal to study hard!

## Sorting Out the AGI Level Morass

When you start looking into financing your kids' education, it seems every option has different rules about income limits. The chart below is a useful reference:

| Program | Individual Tax Return | | Joint Tax Return | |
|---|---|---|---|---|
| | Eligible below | Not eligible above | Eligible below | Not eligible above |
| Traditional IRA: | $30,000 | $40,000 | $50,000 | $60,000 (for $2,000 deduction) |
| Traditional IRA (nonworking spouse) | N/A | N/A | $150,000 | $160,000 |
| Roth IRA: | $95,000 | $110,000 | $150,000 | $160,000 ($2,000 max allowed b/w Trad. and Roth) |
| Education IRA: | $95,000 | $110,000 | $150,000 | $150,000 ($500 per child) |
| EE Savings Bonds: | $50,850 | $65,850 | $76,250 | $106,250 (in your name, for interest deduction only) |
| Hope/Lifetime Credits: | $40,000 | $50,000 | $80,000 | $100,000 |

## In Whose Name?

Parents ask us all the time whether they should keep education funds in their name or in the kid's name. This issue revolves around taxes vs. trust. If the assets are put in the child's name, the tax bite is going to be less. But if the assets are in the child's name, the child can choose to cash them in and move to Bali to study puppetry, rather than attend your alma mater. The very thought sends some parents into a spin. Then again, the young woman who designed the award-winning sets for Disney's Broadway production of *The Lion King* went to Bali to study puppetry, to the probable mortification of her parents—and she's doing awfully well! If the assets are in the child's name, it can reduce a child's financial aid eligibility.

We come down on the side of holding taxable education assets in the child's name, for the lower tax hit. If you are concerned that your child might abuse these assets, your problems are far greater than financing a college education.

## The Least You Need to Know

➤ We've said it before, we'll say it again; don't jeopardize your retirement to pay for your kids' education.

➤ Put your education savings in traditional, Roth, and Education IRAs and EE savings bonds.

➤ Qualified tuition programs are tax-exempt, prepaid tuition programs; one of the most interesting is the Unique College Investing Plan.

➤ Several new income tax credits are now allowed by the IRS for education expenses.

➤ Hold taxable education dollars in your child's name for a smaller tax bite.

# Chapter 17

# Covering Your Assets

> ### In This Chapter
>
> ➤ Determining your insurance needs
>
> ➤ Life insurance simplified
>
> ➤ Insuring your home and other assets

You might not think of insurance as related to investment, but a single uninsured catastrophe can wipe out years of gains in your portfolio. Making sure you have adequate medical, home, auto, and life insurance is an important piece of your life as a savvy investor. You don't want to ever have to sell off great-performing stocks, or worse, dip into your retirement accounts to cover a hospital bill or buy a new car because you didn't have your assets covered. We've already discussed auto and health insurance in Chapters 6 and 13, respectively, so in this chapter we'll focus mostly on life insurance.

# Don't Insure What You Can Afford to Replace

If you think of insurance as an offset to a catastrophe, you will save a lot in insurance premiums. Take your car as an example (before we get to your life). Most insurers offer you a deductible on collision insurance ranging from $100 to $1,000. In other words, you pay out of your own pocket for the first $100 or the first $1,000 of damage.

If your snazzy new auto is worth $30,000, what will your premiums be? Well, depending upon the insurer, the $100 deductible policy will cost you around $1,600, and the $1,000 deductible policy will cost you $660. You save roughly $1,000 per annum. In the first year, the extra cost of a collision (which is the difference in deductibles) is almost exactly offset by the lower premium! Admittedly, this data is from New Jersey, where auto insurance is very pricey. But the principle still stands.

You know we've got a rule of thumb for you, and here it is: Take the difference between the collision premiums for the minimum and the maximum deductible, and divide it by the difference in deductibles.

Premium for max. deductible – premium for min. deductible
÷ maximum deductible – minimum deductible

If the resulting ratio is one-third or higher, opt for the maximum deductible.

### Super Strategy

Once you realize that you should carry coverage for catastrophes but not for every conceivable expense, you can save or reinvest the premium dollars saved. "Ah," you say, "but what if I have a catastrophe? How do I deal with a thousand dollar out-of-pocket expense, smart guy?" Well, remember the emergency fund? That, in part, is what it's for. Emergencies.

# Life Insurance Simplified

Life insurance has one purpose: to provide for your family in the event of your demise. Your beneficiary can use the proceeds of your life insurance policy to cover your funeral expenses, pay your estate taxes, and raise your children.

# Determining Your Insurance Needs

Far too many people carry far too much life insurance, giving rise to the popular expression "insurance poor." There are two ways to estimate how much life insurance you really need.

1. Make a list of expenses your family will need to cover if you die.

2. Figure out how much of your salary your family would need to replace if you die.

Here's an example of an expenses list.

Funeral expenses: $20,000

Outstanding debts: $5,000

Remaining mortgage: $100,000

College costs for children: $60,000

Annual minimum: ($50,000 ÷ .06 or 6%) $833,000–$1,018,000

Less: Stocks,bonds,insurance, etc.: $300,000–$718,000

Less: Social Security & other retirement benefits (if operable): $50,000

Net New Insurance Needs: $668,000

The "annual minimum" of $833,000 is the sum that will generate $50,000 a year in income for the family to live on if it's invested at 6 percent. This family will need life insurance coverage for $668,000 should the breadwinner(s) die.

To determine how much life insurance you need to replace your salary, simply multiply your present salary times the number of years your family will need it. If your family will need your $75,000 a year salary for 15 more years, for example, you'll need $1,125,000 in life insurance. We don't necessarily endorse either method of estimating your life insurance needs. But at least they will get you thinking.

## The Five Basic Types of Life Insurance

There are as many different types of life insurance policies as there are days in the year. And insurance agents sell them all, using every sales technique in the book. For the sake of simplicity (and your sanity), we are going to boil these down to five broad choices. It won't be easy going, but if you get through this next section, you'll be a lot more clued in than most people when you sit down with your insurance agent.

1. **Term Life.** The cheapest life insurance policies guarantee benefits only if you die before a specified term. They are called term life insurance policies. You pay X dollars in premiums and are insured for Y amount for Z years. If you die within the Z period, your beneficiaries get the Y amount. If you die after Z years, they get zip. The idea is to set Z years for a period after your kids are grown and able to take care of themselves.

    If this appeals to you, ask your insurance agent about declining term insurance. With this policy, the amount of protection decreases each year (just as your need does). Declining term insurance should be your cheapest option.

2. **Whole Life.** Whole life insurance is much more expensive than term insurance, but accumulates more value. A portion of your monthly premium goes to the insurer, who invests it on your behalf. Over time, compounding does its magic and the cash value of your policy grows exponentially. Upon your death, your family gets a death benefit plus the money that has accumulated in the policy.

3. **Joint Life and Survivorship.** Two popular variations used by two-worker families and business partnerships are joint life and survivorship. With joint life, two or more people are insured, and the face amount is paid upon the death of the first individual to the second individual. Survivorship policies are also called "second-to-die" insurance. With second-to-die, no payment from the insurance company is made until the second insured dies. Premiums are payable until the second death. Now, skip ahead to the estate-planning chapter: you die, your assets are sheltered by the marital deduction, but your surviving spouse's are not. The second-to-die policy can pay the taxes resulting from your spouse's death. This policy is also very popular with business partnerships.

4. **Universal Life.** This is a life insurance contract that, like whole life insurance, accumulates cash value. It is more flexible, however. The death benefit may be increased or decreased, and the premium changes to reflect that increase or decrease. A back-end load of around 7 percent is typically charged when you make any changes in your policy.

5. **Variable Life.** Variable life is a securities-based, whole life product. The insurance company sets up a separate account to hold the assets, which come from your premium payments, and invests them in common stocks, bonds, and/or money market securities. Because the value of the securities changes daily, so does your potential death benefit. The change is always on the upside, however. You are guaranteed the face amount of the policy. Premiums are fixed.

5A. **Variable Universal Life Policy.** This is like a Cadillac with all the options. It includes flexible premium payments, an adjustable death benefit, and two cash benefit options. The cash values are held in a separate account (as with a variable life policy), and the investment performance can affect the amount of the death benefit.

The policy holder may pay premiums in any amount and with whatever frequency (monthly, quarterly, etc.) he or she finds convenient. Loads are deducted from the premiums to cover sales and administrative expenses; and they can be either "front-end" or "back-end."

However—and it's a big "however"—there are monthly deductions from these separate accounts to pay for the insurance coverage provided by your policy. And if there is an insufficient sum in the accounts, the policy holder must deposit additional dollars to keep the policy in force.

Are you totally confused? Maybe this will help:

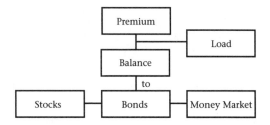

What do all these options cost? That's not easy to answer, but here's as good a comparison as you will find, compliments of Gary Katz of Sagemark Consulting, a member of Lincoln Financial group.

## Comparison Data

| Features | Type of Policy | | | |
| --- | --- | --- | --- | --- |
| | **Term** | **Permanent** | **Universal** | **Variable** |
| Death Benefit | Fixed, level | Fixed, level | Adjustable, level or increase | Depends upon performance; guaranteed minimum |
| Premiums | Fixed schedule, increasing | Fixed schedule, fixed amount | Flexible schedule, flexible amount | Fixed schedule, fixed amount |
| Cash Values | None | Fixed and guaranteed | Current interest plus guaranteed minimum | Depends upon performance |

# Annuities

Insurance companies also sell annuities, which, you learned in Chapter 5, are regular payments for the length of the life of the person who owns the annuity contract. Like life insurance, an annuity is a contract between the insurance company and the purchaser (you). This person is called the "annuitant." Typically, you would designate yourself the annuitant and name a beneficiary, who will receive whatever value is left over in the annuity when you die.

Here's the interesting difference between life insurance and annuities. With life insurance, the insurer is hoping that you will live long enough to pay enough premiums to more than cover the

**Crash Alert**

Life insurance is a commodity, so shop accordingly. You do want to be sure that the insurance carrier will be able to pay your death benefits, so always check into the financial capabilities of your insurer. A good way to start is to call your state insurance commissioner and see if any complaints or charges are outstanding.

death benefit. The longer you live, the better for the insurance company. With an annuity, on the other hand, the payments stop rather than start at death, so the shorter your life, the happier the insurance company. Kinda ghoulish, eh?

Importantly, for both fixed and variable annuities, your death benefit will at least equal the amount you paid for the contract. This is one of the features that insurers use to trumpet variable annuities over mutual funds. Your mutual funds, after all, could theoretically decline in value below what you put into them. A variable annuity, as we mentioned in Chapter 12, is basically a mutual fund with an insurance contract wrapped around it. You get to invest in the possibilities of growth with the underlying mutual fund, plus you are assured a defined death benefit. However, we think you're better off buying mutual funds for your portfolio and separate life insurance.

# Your Kids Don't Need Life Insurance

Insurance agents will use three reasons to sell you on life insurance for your kids:

1.  Premiums are low because of their young age.
2.  It guarantees their insurability in the event of major health problems.
3.  The cash value can be used for the child's education.

Okay, these are all valid reasons, but we just don't buy it. And we don't think you should. There are better ways to finance a child's education, as we discussed in Chapter 16. And if your child has major health problems, group health insurance, not life insurance, seems the more appropriate course.

## Disability Insurance Is a Must

Disability insurance, on the other hand, is a must—for you, not your kids. Disability insurance replaces your income if you are disabled and can't work. Short-term (e.g., three months) disability is usually a part of your group health plan, but you'll need to buy long-term disability insurance (LTD) to cover you should a disability prevent you from working for a long time. Some employers offer this insurance to employees; if yours doesn't, contact your insurance agent.

Plan on paying about $50–$100 per month for disability insurance. It's a small price to pay for a lot of peace of mind. LTD will serve as a salary substitute if you are ever disabled.

# Insuring Your Home and Other Assets

Finally, be sure to discuss homeowner's insurance with your agent. Your mortgage bank will require you to carry insurance at least equal to the outstanding mortgage. Your main concern should be coverage for fire, flood and wind damage.

Flood insurance, if you live in a flood plain, can be purchased most cheaply from the federal government. You may have seen articles about Topsail Island, one of the barrier islands off North Carolina. That's Hurricane Alley, and the people living there are in a continuing build/destroy/rebuild cycle. We can't imagine what they would do without flood insurance.

If you're not in a flood plain and the worse floods you face are one inch of water in the basement every 10 years, you don't need flood coverage. Fire will be your main concern. Be sure your coverage is for 100 percent of the current replacement value of your home.

### Super Strategy

When you insure the contents of your home, be sure to go from room to room with a camera. Use up the roll to prove what you have and what it looks like, and store it in your safe deposit box, not in your home.

If you own any important works of art or antiques, take out a fine arts policy. This insurance is not cheap, but it's the only protection available for such precious items.

As a property owner, you should also seriously consider taking out liability insurance. This is insurance that will protect you from being wiped out by any lawsuits brought by someone who slips on your sidewalk or is otherwise injured on your premises. An "umbrella" policy providing a million dollars of coverage for various liability issues will cost around $200 a year. It's well worth it for the peace of mind, which, after all, is what covering your assets is all about.

## The Least You Need to Know

➤ Don't insure what you can afford to replace.

➤ Life insurance has one purpose: to provide for your family in the event of your death.

➤ There are five basic types of life insurance: term, whole, joint, universal, and variable.

➤ Your kids don't need life insurance.

➤ Besides life and health insurance, you need disability and auto insurance. If you're a home owner, you will need homeowner's and liability insurance.

# Chapter 18

# Keeping Uncle Sam's Greedy Mitts Off Your Estate

---

### In This Chapter

➤ Probate-proofing your will

➤ Saving on estate taxes

➤ Cons of passing everything onto your spouse

➤ Trusts and gifts

---

Most people react to estate planning the same way they do to pre-nuptial agreements: "That's just for the wealthy." But it's definitely not. Don't assume, for example, that if you were to die, your spouse would automatically inherit your assets. Without a will, that's not guaranteed. And, without careful estate planning, the government—not your heirs or spouse—is likely to end up with at least half of your hard-earned assets. There are two main definitions of the word "estate":

1. A sizable piece of land with a large house. This is what most people associate with the word "estate."

2. All of one's possessions. This is what you should associate with the word "estate."

Do you care what happens to your estate—who gets what, and when? If you pay an accountant to make sure you pay the lowest possible income tax, does it not make sense to pay a tax/trust attorney to ensure that your estate will not take an unnecessary hit from estate taxes? Now, have we got your attention?

# Why You Don't Want to Die Without a Will

Let's start with the most basic estate-planning strategy: the will. A *will* is a legal document, signed by you and witnessed, that gives explicit directions as to who or what is to get whatever specific assets of yours you choose to list. If you have children under the age of 18, you would specify in your will a guardian whom you want to take care of them upon your death.

Technically, you don't need a lawyer to draw up a will, but we strongly recommend that you use one. If you die without a will, it is referred to as dying "intestate." That means the state (and even potentially an ex-spouse), rather than you, decides how and to whom your assets will be distributed.

"The state," in this case, is that part of the judicial system known as probate court. Without a will, the state may give some of your assets to heirs who do not need them, while others who do need them get less or none. Even scarier, if you are a single surviving spouse with children and you die without a will, the court, not you, will appoint a guardian for your children. Finally, dying intestate delays the distribution of your assets and adds to the expense. None of these scenarios sound too hot, do they?

**Investor's Idiom**

A *will* keeps your assets out of probate court, or probate. With a will, you legally designate who will get your assets and your *executor* (i.e., a person you appoint to carry out the provisions and directions of your will) makes sure that happens after you die. If you die without a will, or if your will is contested, your estate can end up in your state's probate court, to be fought over by anyone who can demonstrate a claim to your assets.

We feel very strongly that everyone with assets needs to have a will. It should be reviewed every year to reflect any changes in your personal, legal, or financial situation. And you know when, don't you? That's right, on your birthday. Except, from now on, we are no longer referring to it as your birthday. After all, we all reach a point in our adult life when we don't want to acknowledge the date of our birth any more. So, henceforth, we will refer to your birthday as your *Review Day*. Okay? Reviewing your will each Review Day will literally take five minutes. And changing your will, for whatever reason, is a simple matter requiring a phone call to your attorney. It's also a good idea for both you and your spouse to make out your wills at the same time, so you can make sure you're not expressing conflicting wishes—regarding your children, for example, which could cause problems if you both die at or near the same time.

One final matter you should address with your will is the naming of an executor. Your *executor* will distribute your assets as you have set forth in the will. Although you can name anyone, we suggest appointing a professional, such as your attorney or someone from your bank trust department, and a close family member (spouse or sibling) as co-executors. Believe us, this is not an honorary position!

# Probate: The Process of Administering Your Will

The next step in the estate planning process is coming up with ways to make sure your will doesn't end up in probate court. Probate is the process of administering your will (or divvying up your assets if you die intestate). Probating takes time, costs money and allows the public to view your personal assets (and you thought you had heard the last of your ex!). Fortunately, there are several ways to avoid probate court.

## Living Trust

Perhaps the best-known way to avoid probate court is the *living trust*.

A living trust is a legal document that allows you to designate someone to manage your assets if you die or are incapacitated. The trust is typically managed by a trustee for you and for whomever else (your spouse, usually) you wish to include. This document is especially important if you have health concerns that could leave you incapacitated, but is important for most people to have these days because of medical advances that have resulted in more people "living" in incapacitated states.

Often you serve as trustee for yourself with provisions for someone else (a professional) to serve in the event of your death or incapacitation. You can also name a friend or relative as trustee/co-trustee. Because you created the living trust, you can change it whenever you wish, just as you can modify your will. A will and living trust are often created and modified at the same time, and drawn up by the same estate-planning attorney.

## Joint Ownership

A simpler and less expensive way of avoiding probate is to keep some assets (home, securities, etc.) in joint ownership. Joint ownership does preclude several terrific estate-planning techniques that will reduce or eliminate state taxes. (We'll discuss those shortly.) Joint ownership is worth considering as an alternative to a living trust, however. Either joint ownership or the living trust are good first steps in the estate-planning process.

**Investor's Idiom**

One way to keep your estate out of probate court is to use a *living trust*, which names someone to actually manage your assets if you die or are incapacitated. The technical name for this trust is *inter vivos*—feel free to impress friends and neighbors with this phrase!

**Crash Alert**

If you create a living trust and choose to exclude specific assets for any reason, you can include or add them to the trust per the terms of your will. This is referred to as a "pour over" provision in your will. However, you will still need to have these specific assets probated since they were technically not in your living trust at your death.

Before we leave probate, let's mention one class of assets that are automatically excluded: beneficiary-designated accounts. When you designate a beneficiary for your

➤ Retirement accounts (IRAs, pensions, 401(k)s, SEPs, etc.)

➤ Life insurance policies

➤ Qualified tuition programs

the assets in these accounts bypass probate and go directly to your designated beneficiary: spouse, child, etc. These sums are still included in your taxable estate, however.

# How to Take the Bite Out of Estate Taxes

Now that we've taken care of the probate issue, let's proceed to ways to save on estate taxes. These taxes are among the most onerous in the U.S. tax system. They start at 37 percent (not far from the 39.6 percent top figure in the income tax code), and run up as high as 55 percent. It's a bummer to think that you might have a million dollars to leave to your kids, but the government could take half of it before the money even gets to them.

Fortunately, there is a new feature on the income tax return called the "unified credit," which can be used to offset gift and/or estate taxes. For 1997 this credit amounted to $192,800, which was the tax due on $600,000 in combined estate and gift transfers. Even better, the Taxpayer Relief Act of 1997 gradually increases the amount that may be exempted by using the unified credit. Here is the new schedule:

| Year | Amount Excluded |
| --- | --- |
| 1998 | $625,000 |
| 1999 | $650,000 |
| 2000–2001 | $675,000 |
| 2002–2003 | $700,000 |
| 2004 | $850,000 |
| 2005 | $950,000 |
| 2006+ | $1,000,000 |

So, in 1998, if your taxable estate and lifetime gifts do not exceed $625,000, your estate will not owe any estate taxes.

# They Can Tax That?!

Maybe you think you don't have to worry about estate planning because your estate isn't worth over $625,000. But take a close look at what's included in the definition of "estate." It adds up fast. Let's make a partial list:

➤ Taxable investments (stocks, bonds, mutual funds, CDs, money market accounts, etc.)

➤ Employer-sponsored retirement plan benefits

➤ All IRAs

➤ Personal residences less their mortgages

➤ Business/partnership interests

➤ Life insurance proceeds (at time of death)

➤ Automobiles, boats (less loans)

➤ Jewelry and collectibles (antique furniture, paintings, coins, stamps, etc.)

➤ Other items of value (clothing, furniture, etc.)

➤ Taxable lifetime gifts

**Fiscal Facts**

Federal Estate Tax Return Form 706 must generally be filed and taxes paid by the estate within nine months following the estate owner's death.

Does any of this look familiar? It should mimic what's on your personal balance sheet. (Have you gotten that together since Chapter 4? Nag, nag!)

**Super Strategy**

As you get older, the value of your estate is going to continue to increase. You may not be a millionaire now, but you may be in 2006 or 2016 or 2026. Start protecting your estate now. First, carefully estimate the value of your estate. Have jewelry, collectibles and other property appraised. Think about what gifts you want to make to charities and to family members. In short, use this chapter as inspiration to get organized—then, see your attorney!

Are there any deductions? Precious few. We've indicated some in our partial list (mortgages and car loans). Others include funeral expenses, transfers to charities of your choice, and the cost of administering your estate (trust bank fees and the like).

## Cons of Passing Everything onto Your Spouse

There is one big deduction you can take on your estate: the unlimited marital deduction. The tax code says that you may deduct from your estate the value of all assets that are transferred from you to your spouse, either directly (via a will) or in a trust. In that case, there would be no tax on your estate: zero, zip, nada.

"Now wait a minute," you're wondering. "First they scare us with 55 percent rates, then they tell us that if we pass on everything to our spouse, there's no tax. What gives?" Yes, Virginia, there is a catch.

If you pass away, your assets (and your share of any joint assets) pass to your spouse and there is no estate tax on your estate. But what happens when your spouse dies? Your spouse's estate won't be able to use the unlimited marital deduction because you're dust.

What if your spouse dies first? Then you get the unlimited marital deduction benefit on his or her estate—and your own estate loses that benefit. Yes, as the surviving spouse you still get the unified credit exclusion ($625,000 in 1998), but it has to apply to the total of both your and your deceased spouse's estate.

Are there any better options? Yes, and we will briefly outline a few of them for you in a minute, but first, let's bring up one more issue to make sure you are totally confused: The Generation Skipping Transfer Tax (GST).

## Watch That Generation Gap

The GST tax is an unbelievable 55 percent, tacked on top of other estate and gift taxes. This tax was intended to prevent Rockefeller-rich families from preserving their wealth by giving to grandchildren instead of to children and thereby skipping an entire generation of tax.

Presently, if your total gifts (directly or via trust accounts) exceed $1 million (or $2 million if the total is joint with your spouse), you're taxed at 55 percent on the excess. And you can't get around the GST tax by setting up a trust for your child that passes to your grandchild at the time of the child's death. Your child can set up the trust, however. The GST tax is another good reason to consult with an estate-planning attorney to make sure your family doesn't get bashed.

# Tax-Saving Alternatives

Now that we've made you aware of some of the ways Uncle Sam plans to get his mitts on your dough, let's get to the good part: tax-saving strategies.

## Gimme Shelter

A smarter way to use the unlimited marital deduction is to divide your assets in half and will only half to your spouse. Use the other half to set up a credit shelter trust

(CST). Your spouse gets all the income generated by the trust's investments during his or her lifetime. The principal goes to your children when your spouse dies. Ideally, the assets used to set up the CST will be no more than the exclusion amount ($625,000 in 1998) in the year of your death. At the time of your death, assets equal to the exclusion amount for that year go to create the CST, and the balance goes directly to your spouse via the unlimited marital deduction. At the time of your spouse's death, the CST is excluded from his or her estate. Voila! You've cut your and your spouse's estate tax bill in half.

## QTIP: No, Not the Kind You Stick in Your Ear

In addition to the CST, you can also set up, via your will, a second trust that qualifies for the marital deduction. What kind of trust qualifies? The most popular choice is called the Qualified Terminable Interest Property Trust, or "QTIP" for short.

With a QTIP, your spouse receives the income during his/her lifetime. At the time of your spouse's death, the assets pass on to whomever you've named in your will. The assets are still included in your spouse's estate, but you retain control of the assets "from the grave." The QTIP is great for a second marriage, for example, because you can make sure some of your assets reach the children of your first marriage after your second spouse dies.

## Charitable Trusts

There are two kinds of charitable trusts:

1. Charitable Remainder Trusts (CRTs)
2. Charitable Lead Trusts (CLTs)

With the CRT, you set up a trust for the charity of your choice, but you retain all rights to the income generated by the trust until you and/or your spouse dies. At that time, the assets go to the charity. You get a charitable gift deduction (Schedule A on IRS Form 1040) and the assets in the trust are excluded from your estate.

CRTs take one of two forms: either a Charitable Remainder Annuity Trust or a Charitable Remainder Unitrust. The former pays a fixed dollar sum to you each year; the latter pays you a fixed percentage of the assets.

Alternatively, the Charitable Lead Trust provides all income to the charity of your choice for a set period—20 years, for example. At the end of that period, the assets revert to whomever (son, granddaughters, etc.) you initially named as the remainder beneficiary.

You can establish a CRT or CLT:

➤ At the time of your death, via your will, protecting some of your estate from taxation.
➤ During your lifetime, improving both your income tax and estate tax situations.

**221**

# Other Ways to Reduce Estate Taxes

There are several other ways to cut estate taxes and make sure more of your hard-earned money goes to the people you love, not to the IRS. Again, we recommend that you consult an attorney, but at least if you read this chapter, you'll walk into the law office reasonably well informed (always a plus, especially if you're paying by the hour). Consulting a licensed CPA wouldn't hurt, either.

## Life (Saver!) Insurance

Life insurance can be used to pay any estate taxes, thereby nullifying the need for your heirs to sell estate assets to raise the cash for the tax bill. You can also create a life insurance trust to hold or purchase life insurance. At your death, the trustee would collect the proceeds and invest them for the benefit of whomever you named as beneficiaries. The proceeds won't be included in your estate as long as the policies are purchased at least three years before your death or transferred to the trust three years before death.

## The Gift That Keeps on Giving

Gifting is another nifty way to lessen the burden of your pesky Uncle Sam. You can give $10,000 per person per year ($20,000 if you're making a joint gift with your spouse). This is an excellent way to reduce your estate, and thereby reduce your potential estate tax. Giving appreciated or potentially appreciating assets such as stock or real estate is a particularly good idea.

If you make medical or educational payments on behalf of your heirs, these payments are excluded from your estate—provided you make payments directly to the source. Education is limited to tuition, and you must pay the college directly. Medical payments must be paid directly to the hospital, doctor, or clinic, or to the insurance company, if you are paying for medical insurance. These exclusions only apply when you make payment on behalf of others, not for yourself.

## Just a Little Token—Gifts to Minors' Trusts

You can also set up a trust for a child or grandchild and appoint a trustee (a parent, usually) to oversee the use of the funds in the trust. The trustee can pay out necessary sums for the minor's needs—college tuition, for example. At age 21 the child or grandchild has full access to the trust, however.

### Super Strategy

If it makes you nervous that your child or grandchild can get into a trust at age 21, you can set up a Crummy Powers trust. A Crummy Powers trust gives the child or grandchild access to the trust for only a few days each year to make withdrawals. Technically, the child or grandchild has access to the principal, but for a very limited number of days each year. How much damage can they do? Um....

## Personal Residence Trust

You might also talk to your attorney about transferring your home to a trust, while retaining the right to use the home for a specified number of years.

For a personal residence trust, you make a member of your family the beneficiary. If you die before the specified number of years is up, the residence stays in your estate. If you live beyond the specified time, you get an exclusion for one of the biggest assets in your estate. You only need to pay a competitive rent after you survive the trust term.

This is but a short list of some of the more popular measures to save on estate taxes. We urge you to seek professional assistance if you wish to pursue any of these options; individual state laws differ, federal law is subject to annual change and interpretation, and we can't possibly cover all of the nuances for each of these alternatives. Above all, don't put off estate planning. As we've said throughout this book: It's your money!

# What If You Inherit Money?

All this complicated talk about estate planning has probably got you wondering what to do should Uncle Fritz kick the bucket and leave you half of the $20,000 stuffed under his mattress.

When you inherit money, you will have two questions:

1. How much do I get?
2. How much do I owe?

# What to Do When Your Ship Comes In

The first question, if it involves financial assets, is easy to answer, as nearly all securities have public market values.

The second question is a little more complex. In most cases, the cost of securities you inherit will be marked up to "date of death" (DOD). This is good news. It means that if you sell them shortly after receiving them, you will owe little or no capital gains taxes.

Although DOD minimizes your potential taxes, it maximizes the deceased's estate value. Depending on the final sum and the manner in which the assets were set up, therefore, you may owe estate tax after the estate is settled.

When an estate is being settled, the executor is concerned with determining the value of each asset as quickly as possible, and distributing these assets as soon as possible. Normally, marketable financial assets are sold, so the executor is distributing cash to the heirs. However, the heirs may jointly request that some or all of the securities be distributed "in kind." This means that if the estate holds 400 shares of General Electric and there are four heirs, each heir will receive 100 shares of General Electric.

# Beyond Cash: Property, Businesses, and Valuables

Although most estates are valued on a date-of-death basis, the federal tax code also provides for an alternate valuation date: six months after the decedent's death. What's this alternate date for? Typically, the date is used if an estate is dominated by real estate or privately held businesses. The six-month leeway gives the executor time to hire an appraiser to estimate the "fair and sound value" of the estate. If the executor is able to "distribute, sell, exchange, or otherwise dispose" of the property within six months, it will be valued as of "date-of-death," not six months hence.

Household and personal items, such as watches, rings, antiques, paintings, etc., are considered what you probably consider them already: valuables. Their worth is estimated by the IRS's "willing buyer/willing seller" rule, which reads: "The price at which the property would change hands between a willing buyer and a willing seller, neither being under any compulsion to buy or to sell and both having reasonable knowledge of relevant facts."

If you didn't catch that, if just means the price is whatever the market will bear for the item(s) at the time, regardless of the circumstances under which they're being sold (i.e., the death of your great Aunt Tilly). The executor will most likely hire an appraiser to do an item-by-item, room-by-room appraisal. The appraisal will help you determine which items, if any, hold more than sentimental value. For those items, ask your insurance agent for a "fine arts" insurance policy.

# What to Do with the Dough

After the first two questions have been answered, you will have a third: "What should I do with the dough?" In order of priority, until the money runs out, do the following:

1. Pay off "bad" debt: credit cards, auto loans, etc.

2. Pay off student loans, if you have any.

3. Replenish emergency funds.

4. Bring retirement plan assets up to the level you've determined (using our handy guide, of course) they need to be to reach your retirement savings target.

5. Put the balance in educational funds, if you have children.

6. Pay down your mortgage with any remaining proceeds.

Please, do not do the following:

1. Buy a bigger house.

2. Buy that new luxury car.

3. Buy a boat, snowmobile, or any other large, expensive piece of recreational equipment for the heck of it.

If you want a treat, take a nice vacation. It's a lot less expensive and won't stick around to haunt you.

---

### The Least You Need to Know

➤ A will is a legal document, signed by you and witnessed, that gives explicit directions as to who or what is to get your assets.

➤ A living trust is a document that allows you to choose someone to manage your assets should you die or become incapacitated.

➤ Estate taxes are among the most onerous in the U.S. tax system; use a good attorney to help you protect your estate.

➤ You can reduce your estate (and therefore your estate taxes) by giving $10,000 per person per year while you're still living.

➤ When you inherit money, use it to strengthen your finances by paying off "bad" debt and replenishing emergency funds.

---

# Part 5
# Investing Online

If you want to succeed you should strike out on new paths...rather than travel the worn paths of accepted success.

—*John D. Rockefeller*

*Computers rule when it comes to investing. They make it so incredibly easy and convenient! We've sorted out the basics for you just so you don't have to go out and buy another book on investing online. Yep, you can sit right there and apply everything you've learned in this book without ever leaving the comfort of your own home. Okay, you can go out for ice cream.*

*If you're not online and don't even know quite what it means, that's fine. We start from the ground up, baby. What kind of computer to buy, where to get software, the best online services to subscribe to for investing. We'll get you up and running.*

*Once you are, you need never bother with trying to reach a broker on the phone ever again. We'll show you how to bank online and how to research investments and manage your portfolio online. We'll direct you to the best discount brokerages and top investment-related web sites. You'll also learn how to spot fraudulent schemes.*

*Welcome to the future. It's fun!*

# Chapter 19

# Getting Started with Online Investing

---

**In This Chapter**

➤ How the Internet developed and what it can do for you

➤ What you need to invest online

➤ Choosing an Internet Service Provider

➤ Banking online

➤ Selecting an Internet broker

---

Several years ago, the Internet was considered a joke or a fad, depending upon your perspective. Today, it is universally viewed as the most dramatic and dynamic trend in the broad field of technology. In the next two chapters, we will show you how to bank, research investments, track your portfolio, and trade online. There is no substitute for poking around on your own, however, and we encourage you to do so.

A word of caution: Because websites are proliferating so rapidly and the information on each site is subject to change daily, we can't guarantee what we show and tell will be necessarily your experience when you go on the 'Net. With that caveat, let's buckle up and take a ride.

## Once Upon a Time There Was a Big Fat Computer

If we asked you how long the Internet has been around, you'd probably say that it came into being in the last five years or so. Well, believe it or not, the Internet has been around for some 30-odd years. (And you thought you were such a hotshot getting a modem in the '80s!) The Internet is a computer network that was developed in 1969 as a way for government scientists and military departments to communicate with each other via computer and have access to information stored on computers around the world. The first version of the Internet was the Department of Defense Advanced Research and Projects Agency (ARPA), which was a Cold War network designed to be less penetrable by "the enemy" (okay, the Russians) than the computer networks available at the time.

By the 1980s, university professors were hooked up, too, as were the Department of Energy and the National Institutes of Health. But the Internet was still primarily a geekfest until e-mail was developed in 1990, and both regular folks and commercial businesses got wise to the fun and the financial potential inherent on the 'Net. Fax machines were already transmitting data over phone lines, so hooking up computers to do the same was not a stretch for most businesses.

## The World Wide Web

The next step was the development of a computer language (HTML) that allowed graphics and sound to be combined in a document. These HTML documents were a lot more fun to look at than the complicated, code-strewn documents previously available online. When you look at a page on the World Wide Web, you are looking at HTML documents. The Web is a subset of the Internet and is coordinated by an organization called the World Wide Web Consortium. The Internet is not controlled by any one government or organization, but there is an Internet Society, the ISOC, that helps develop programming standards so computers can continue talking to each other. For your purposes, you will spend most, if not all, of your time online within the Web. Documents on the Web begin with "home pages" and are accessed by their Uniform Resource Locators (URLs), or addresses. The URL for the World Wide Web Consortium, for example, is **http://www.w3.org**. You will probably also explore newsgroups, which are special interest groups whose members "meet" online to exchange information and discuss topics by leaving each other messages. You can also meet new friends and business associates in chat rooms, which are online sites where people meet to talk "in real time." In a chat room, your message appears as you type it and anyone signed into the chat room can see it and type a response that you'll be able to see on your screen.

### Investor's Idiom

Chatting on the Web *in real time* simply means that you and whomever you are speaking with are having a discussion in the present time. The keyed messages you receive on-screen in a chat room occur in the same amount of time as if you were actually speaking.

Then, of course, there's e-mail, or electronic mail. Once you're online you can send and receive mail from over 30 million other users. That's a whole lot of mail.

## Take a Test Drive

The Internet has been likened to the old, early days of the Wild West: It's big, boisterous, growing, exciting, and loaded with open-ended opportunities, but it is also unregulated and unpoliced. So, caveat emptor (or, for those of you who missed that Latin lesson, let the buyer beware). Anyone can leave a message or create a website on the 'Net, and some get pretty weird. Also, on some websites you will be deluged with ads or may even be probed by a "cookie," a program that gathers marketing information from how you explore a given website without your being aware of it. Next thing you know, you are getting tons of unwanted junk e-mail. If computers give you hives, remember: You don't have to use the Internet. Probably 90 percent of what you want or need can be found in traditional forms: periodicals (newspapers, magazines), onsite visits (libraries, malls), and telephone contact.

Consider taking a test drive on the 'Net before signing up. Many metropolitan areas have Internet service sites where you can rent time for around $10 per hour and print any viewable page for a token fee. If you're in the Big Apple, for instance, try Cyberfelds Internet Cafe at 20 East 13th Street. A test drive is a much cheaper first step than bulking up with a new PC system just to get on the 'Net. Your public library may also offer free Internet access. There are thousands and thousands of sites on the Internet, and it is very easy to become overwhelmed and confused. We can help a little, but you'll have to do a lot of experimenting and eliminating on your own. And, remember, new sites emerge every day, and existing sites are constantly updated and revised.

### Investor's Idiom

The Internet is basically a world-wide network of computers talking to each other over phone lines via modems. Modems translate the data coming from the computer to a form that can be sent over the phone. E-mail, or electronic mail, is one type of document that can be sent via modem over the Internet; HTML documents are another. HTML, or hypertext markup language, is a computer language that allows sound and graphics to be included in a document and viewed on the Internet. HTML documents make up the colorful subset of the 'Net called the World Wide Web.

### Super Strategy

Worried that you won't be able to keep track of all those sites on the Web that you want to revisit? Never fear. When you get onto your Internet browser page, you'll notice on the menu at the top there will be an option called "Favorites." If you click on this, you will see an option called "add to favorites." Anytime you go to a Web page that you like and know you'll want to go back to, simply click on "Favorites" and then "add to favorites," and you will have saved the address of the page.

# Online Shopping

*Time* magazine reported a study by World Research that compared shopping online with more traditional methods and found no significant savings when consumers bought books, airline tickets, and other items online.

Of equal interest were the reasons people were not buying online:

Fear of hackers: 21 percent

Lack of products: 16 percent

Can't see the products: 15 percent

Must reveal personal information: 13 percent

*(Source: World Research)*

We think that there are savings, be they real or implied, because the Internet rips out an entire line of costs: the salesperson. Security trading on the Internet is surging for this reason, and we expect the same to hold true for clothing. But remember, shopping from the J. Crew catalog is very convenient, but not necessarily cheaper than buying at one of their retail stores.

**Fiscal Facts**

As of July 1998:

a. The median age of an online shopper was 33.

b. The estimated number of online shoppers in 1998 (16 million) is expected to spend $6 billion (which is less than 1 percent of total U.S. economic output). Those numbers are projected to grow to 61 million and $41 billion, respectively, in the year 2000.

*Source: The July 20, 1998, issue of Time magazine, pages 34–41.*

Last, but not least, not everything is free on the Internet. You can get some basic research on a company free, but if you want more in-depth investment info, it'll cost you money. You can download a company's prospectus for free, for example, but not an in-depth research report from a Wall Street analyst.

# Hey, How Do I Turn This Thing On?

Thus far, we've assumed you have a PC (personal computer). But maybe you're part of what we'll call the electronically challenged segment of the population. Don't worry, we're going to tell you exactly what you'll need to get up and running (or surfing, as the case may be) in no time.

Your first choice is used vs. new. If you don't have to have the newest and latest, think used. We checked several sources and confirmed that you could access the Internet for around $400. This buys a CPU, or central processing unit, a keyboard, and a monitor. If the CPU doesn't include a modem, you will need to buy a separate modem to attach to the computer. To further investigate buying a used machine, look in the Yellow Pages under "Computers-Dealers" or "Computers-Service & Repair." If you want to go new (and most people do), we've scoped out two all-inclusive possibilities.

1. Radio Shack's Compaq Presario 2510 sells for $1,407.99 as we're writing and includes:

   ➤ CPU with 300 megahertz processor, 56K fax/modem, Windows 98, etc.

   ➤ Keyboard that has Internet access keys on the upper right side for ease of entry

   ➤ Color monitor (color is not necessary for banking or investments, but what about shopping for clothes?)

   ➤ Printer

2. The Apple Macintosh IMAC, which is specifically designed for the Internet, sells for around $1,299.97 (printer not included). It includes a combination CPU and color monitor plus keyboard. Figure around $200 for an inkjet printer.

# Choosing an ISP

Next, you will need an Internet Service Provider (ISP).

Compare the telephone to a computer. If you have a telephone and a friend you are trying to reach also has a telephone, you two cannot communicate until your phones are "hooked up" via a telephone wire. Similarly, your computer can't talk to another computer hooked up to the Internet without that "wire."

The company that provides that wire is going to charge you a monthly fee (just like the telephone company). In fact, many phone companies, such as AT&T, Sprint, and MCI Worldcom, have gotten into the ISP business. If you want the comfort of dealing with them, go for it, but you may get better deals elsewhere. Be sure that your particular modem works best with the ISP you select; if it doesn't, replace it.

According to the November 1998 issue of *Money* magazine, there are over 5,000 ISPs! Of this total, 4,900 are regional, and 110 are national, providers. How do you decide? Do you go national (America Online, AT&T WorldNet, Microsoft Network, Prodigy Internet, Earthlink, IBM?) or regional, or even local (for the lowest cost)? Check out three issues: cost, reliability, and service.

1. **Cost.** If you are a "light" user of the Internet, e.g., under 10 hours a month, look for an ISP that offers a low-use fee (say $7–$9 per month). If you are a heavy user (e.g., three hours per day), get a plan with unlimited usage. Most plans charge $20–$22 per month for unlimited usage, but you can save with a one-year subscription. Also, ask about any start-up fees.

**Crash Alert**

Make sure the ISP of your choice has a local access number; otherwise, you could be paying phone charges of up to 10¢ per minute of online usage. You want your access to your ISP to be a local (read, free!) phone call. If you are in doubt, check the ISP access number with your local telephone company to make sure it's a free call for you.

2. **Reliability**. We think this is the most important factor to consider. If you get a lot of busy signals when you try to use the service, chances are there is a reliability problem. Check the Inverse Network Technologies call-failure ratings at www.inversenet.com. We feel very strongly that you should do this before making a final decision. According to *Money* magazine, one national ISP with an A+ rating from Inverse is Concentric Network (800-939-4262, or www.concentric.net).

3. **Service**. If you are having a problem, you don't want to be on hold for what seems like hours—you want to talk to a human being pronto. Check out the ISP's customer service and help lines before you sign up.

In addition to *Money* magazine and Inverse, we have two other sources of ISP info for you.

➤ **www.thelist.com**, which enables you to bring up those ISPs in your local area code. Just enter your area code and voilà! But don't be shocked to see a long list. Also, those won't help you if you travel a lot and use the Internet on your trips; if that's the case, you definitely need a national ISP.

➤ *Smart Money* magazine (jointly owned by Dow Jones & Co., which owns the *WSJ* and Hearst Corporation). Check out their website at **www.smartmoney.com**, and the Communications Best Buys pages. *Smart Money* currently recommends three ISP sources:

1. Concentric Network: Considered fast, reliable, and cost effective (see above for number and website)

2. MindSpring (888-MSPRING): Service, service, service!

3. IBM Internet Connection (800-821-4612): Reliability and speed at reasonable cost.

# You Need a Surfboard...We Mean, a Browser

Okay, you've got your PC, your modem, and your ISP. Now, you need a browser. This is software that enables your computer to surf (browse) the Web and read all those groovy HTML documents. Get either the Microsoft Internet Explorer Version 3.02 (or higher), or Netscape Navigator Version 3.02 (or higher). If you have Microsoft '95 or '98 (and who doesn't at this point?), you already have the Microsoft Explorer. If you want Netscape, go to its website and download Netscape Navigator. It's free. Here's a bonus factoid: Free software available on the Web is called "shareware."

## *Secret Agent Man*

If you want to trade and bank online, you will need a browser that meets bank and broker security standards. Specifically, you will need a qualified browser that supports 128-bit encryption. The browsers we recommended above do.

The strongest form of encryption available for commercial use over the Internet today is 128-bit encryption. There are billions of possible keys to de-encrypt information ("crack the code") that is passed over the Internet. Only one key can be used to allow access to your account information. And every time you initiate a new session by logging onto a site for trading or banking, a new key is randomly selected.

Browsers like the Microsoft Internet Explorer come with an ISP attached.

**Investor's Idiom**

En-what? *Encryption* is the scrambling of information as it is transmitted over the Internet to ensure your privacy and confidentiality. In other words, it's like sending messages in code.

# Banking Online

Now you're ready to bank online. This is a fairly simple financial task that is really a delight to do from home. It's a good warm-up to more advanced activities like trading stock online.

To illustrate Internet banking, we are going to describe the requirements, options, and services of Fleet Bank.

## *Sign Me Up!*

The first thing you need to do in order to bank online is register. Using America Online as the ISP in this example, you can access Fleet Web Banking in either of two ways:

1. By using your qualified browser (see above)

   ➤ Launch AOL and connect to the service.

   ➤ Minimize AOL after connecting.

   ➤ Launch your qualified Microsoft or Netscape browser.

   ➤ Go to **www.fleet.com** and select *Fleet Web Banking Logon*.

Note: If you are running Windows 95, you must upgrade to AOL Version 3.0 for Windows 95.

2. Use AOL Version 4.0

   ➤ Select the link in AOL Version 4.0 that will take you to the Internet.

   ➤ Go to **www.fleet.com**, then select *Fleet Web Banking Logon*.

You can follow a similar procedure with any other ISP. Fleet charges $4.50 per month for unlimited bill payments. Enrollment is by mail. Within 10 business days of applying at the website, you will receive your logon ID in the mail. Your password will be received under separate mailing.

## No More Waiting in Line When You're Online

Once you are registered, you can bank! Here's how you do it with Fleet.

1. Navigate to the Fleet home page at **www.fleet.com** and click on *Fleet Web Banking Logon*.

2. Type in your logon ID and password.

3. In the left-hand margin you will see five choices:

   ➤ Accounts

   ➤ Transfers

   ➤ Payments

   ➤ Mail

   ➤ Exit (to end your session)

Click on *Accounts* and you will see your account information illustrated as follows:

| Account Name/Number | Account Type | As of | Balance |
| --- | --- | --- | --- |
| Checking/12345678 | Checking | 09/25/98 | $2,456.19 |
| Savings/32145768 | Savings | 09/25/98 | $7,000.00 |
| Credit Card/87654321 | Credit Card | 09/25/98 | $934.78 |
| Money Market/35791357 | Money Market | 09/25/98 | $5,000.00 |

Once you're in your account, you can do pretty much everything you would if you were at a bank or at an ATM machine. You can:

➤ Click on *Transfer* to transfer funds between accounts.

➤ Click on *Payments* to pay down on one or more accounts or to pay bills to any business or individual in the United States.

➤ Click on *Mail* to send e-mail within the bank and *Exit* to end your session.

It's really that simple.

### Super Strategy

Banking online makes it easy to find the best rates for your deposits. BanxQuote, Inc., provides current rates for various savings instruments, such as money markets and CDs. At BanxQuote's website (**www.banx.com**), you can browse by term or location. You can also call BanxQuote at 212-643-8000.

Valuable info is also available via the Gomez Advisors, Inc., website at **www.gomez.com**, which profiles the top 20 Internet banks as ranked by users.

# The Best Financial Software

Once you get into banking online, it becomes a breeze to manage your finances online—but you'll need some specialized financial management software. Among the most popular are the following:

➤ Quicken (various versions, including Home & Business '98)

➤ Microsoft Money

➤ Managing Your Money

These each retail for around $90–$100, but if you're buying a new PC, your dealer may be willing to include your choice of the above for free (hey, it doesn't hurt to ask!).

# Now Can I Trade? Selecting an Internet Broker

Well, you're not quite ready to run with the bulls and bears just yet. You have to select an Internet broker! And that's not easy. Gomez Advisors, Inc., offers a list (and an evaluation) of all 71 brokers with transactional Internet sites. Gomez evaluated the Internet brokers on five criteria:

1. Ease of use

2. Customer confidence

3. Onsite resources

4. Relationship services

5. Overall cost

The scores in each category were then totaled for an overall score. The top five online brokers, according to Gomez, are the following:

1. E*TRADE
2. DLJDirect
3. Discover Brokerage Direct
4. Waterhouse Securities
5. Datek Online

Want another opinion? Go to *Smart Money* magazine's home page (**www.smartmoney.com**) and click on "Brokers: The Best and Worst Online Brokers." You will find 15 brokers evaluated by seven categories:

1. Commissions
2. Real-time quotes
3. Account information
4. Technical support
5. Fees
6. Online products
7. Research lines

Aren't online yet? Okay, we won't leave you in suspense. *Smart Money*'s top five are the following:

1. WebStreet
2. Datek Online
3. Discover Brokerage Direct
4. National Discount Brokers
5. Waterhouse Securities

Finally, the October 1998 issue of *Kiplinger's Personal Finance Magazine* had a very good evaluation of online brokers. If you can't find the magazine, try www.kiplinger.com or call 800-544-0155. *Kiplinger* didn't "crown" an overall winner, arguing (correctly, we think) that your choice depends on your particular needs. They did rank brokers by seven categories, with top picks in each:

1. Best for Commissions (equities only): (1) Brown, (2) SURETRADE.
2. Best for Other Fees: (1) Bull & Bear, (2) Waterhouse, (3) Datek (each charged only one of seven potential fees, e.g., wire transfer, inactive account, closing an account, stock certificate, etc.).
3. Best for Margin Rates: SURETRADE.

4. Best for Mutual Funds: Waterhouse.

5. Best for IRAs: SURETRADE.

6. Best for Products and Services (such as account information and quotes in real time, trading by touch-tone phone, free debit and credit cards, free check-writing privileges, free dividend reinvestment): (1) Waterhouse, (2) Fidelity and Schwab, (3) Quick & Reilly.

7. Best for Investor Tools (such as online research, ease of navigating websites, timely telephone and e-mail response): (1) Quick & Reilly, (2) DLJDirect, (3) E*TRADE.

Now, just to make things even that much easier for you, here is a list of the brokers we have mentioned thus far with their URLs and phone numbers:

| Broker | Website | Telephone |
| --- | --- | --- |
| E*TRADE | www.etrade.com | 800-387-2331 |
| DLJDirect | www.dljdirect.com | 888-456-4355 |
| Discover | www.discoverbrokerage.com | 800-347-2683 |
| Waterhouse | www.waterhouse.com | 800-934-4410 |
| Datek Online | www.datek.com | 888-463-2835 |
| WebStreet | www.webstreet.com | 800-932-8723 |
| National Discount Brokers | www.ndb.com | 800-888-3999 |
| Brown | www.brownco.com | 800-822-2021 |
| SURETRADE | www.suretrade.com | 401-642-6900 |
| Bull & Bear | www.bullbear.com | 800-285-5232 |
| Fidelity | www.fidelity.com | 800-544-7272 |
| Schwab | www.schwab.com | 800-435-4000 |
| Quick & Reilly | www.quick-reilly.com | 800-837-7220 |

We believe Gomez, *Smart Money*, and *Kiplinger* are the three best resources for evaluating online brokers. We strongly urge you to visit their websites and use all the evaluation pages to help you select an Internet broker. Hey, it's free advice! What's better than that?

# Evaluating Your Online Trading Needs

No matter what Gomez et al., recommend, however, the final decision regarding an Internet broker must be yours, and this means critically evaluating your online trading needs. For example: Do you really need to trade online? If you are an infrequent trader and a long-term investor happy with your present broker, why bother?

If you're definitely going to the 'Net, then carefully consider the following:

➤ The type of accounts you want to open online: Will you open just an IRA account, just a taxable account, or one or more of each? If an IRA account is involved, you will want to flag those brokers that:

1. charge either no or minimal fees for opening, closing, transferring, etc.

2. provide good legal updates, reminders, and follow-ups.

3. have "stone walls" that prevent you from accidentally adding to your IRA account or taking a withdrawal prematurely. Simple mistakes here can cost you taxes and/or penalties, which a "warning flag" can avert.

For a taxable account, check the Web pages for the manner in which the broker records gains and losses. Also, does the broker allow you to designate specific lots of a given security for realizing gains and losses?

If you bought shares of the same stock at different times and three different prices, you have three different "lots," e.g.:

100 shares purchased at 20 on 4/11/92
100 shares purchased at 40 on 5/13/95
100 shares purchased at 60 on 7/7/97

Total: 300 shares          Average price: $40

Your statement may just show "300 shares at 40"—but what if you want to sell the first lot you purchased to realize the gain now that the price of the stock has moved up to 60? You need a statement that allows you to designate specific lots so you can make buying and selling decisions and have them properly reflected in your records.

➤ Types of assets in which you plan to invest:

Do you plan to invest in equities, treasuries, other fixed income, or mutual funds? Some brokers won't trade fixed-income securities or only Treasuries, and discourage such transactions with high fees or charges.

If you want to invest in mutual funds online, find out if the broker offers funds you presently own or like. Check the fees and compare to your offline broker. If you use mutual funds in an IRA, dividend and capital gains reinvestment is important; will your prospective broker accommodate?

If you are interested in purchasing stocks on margin or playing the options and futures markets (see Chapters 21 and 22), the rates the broker offers on margin loans are a very significant factor for you to consider.

➤ Activity: How frequently do you intend to trade online? The greater the number of trades, the more important the following should be to you:

1. Cost of trading

2. Real-time quotations

3. Quick and consistent entry to website

4. Good, prompt execution

# The Online Commission Picture

All 'Net brokers advertise low commission rates of around $5–$25 per trade. But some also charge 1¢–3¢ per share for trades over 5,000 shares. This is still much cheaper than full-service brokerage and discount brokerage, but the differential is narrowed. Let's say a broker charges $14.95 per trade plus 1¢ per share for trades over 5,000 shares:

4,999 shares = $14.95

5,000 shares = $50 + 14.95 = $64.95

Wow, that 1¢ per share adds up!

Not all 'Net brokers charge for larger orders like this, but some do. So ask before you enroll!

# If You Are a Frequent Trader...

If you are an infrequent trader with a long-term perspective, whether you are looking at a current quotation or one with a 20-minute lag may be immaterial. But if you are a frequent trader, and certainly if you are a day trader, you are looking to ring up many small gains. These three things are essential to your success:

1. You must have current quotations, especially during periods of high market volatility.

2. You must be able to reach and log on to your broker's website quickly.

3. Your broker must provide a touch-tone telephone order system as a back-up. You don't want to miss making a critical trade because your broker's website was down.

Finally, good and prompt execution is critical for frequent/day traders. How long does it take to execute your order once it's placed? Note your order time and check the time of order execution (if the time is not shown, request it). Remember, most orders are not going directly to the Exchange, they are being executed via a market maker, so time is of the essence. Ask friends and associates for recommendations for brokers who can handle frequent trades efficiently. And stick to market orders, which usually confirm the price of the trade before you go offline. (This might be a good time to revisit our discussion of market and limit orders from Chapter 10.)

None of these issues regarding activity is critical if you are an infrequent trader. However, you should still follow our recommendations regarding market vs. limit orders.

# Investment Research

Is research critical to your investment decision-making process? Then focus on those 'Net brokers that offer the widest array of research. You're looking for Securities & Exchange Commission filings, consensus earnings estimates, Standard & Poor's reports, etc.

There are some amazing research sites on the Web that you can access yourself, such as:

➤ www.briefing.com (analysts' upgrades and downgrades)

➤ www.hoovers.com (company profiles and financial data)

➤ www.marketguide.com (earnings estimates from First Call, insider trading from Vickers, and stock screening from Stock Quest)

➤ www.personalwealth.com (Standard & Poor's info, including Wall Street analysts' recommendations and consensus earnings estimates)

➤ www.sec.gov (essentially all Securities & Exchange Commission filings by companies)

➤ www.zacks.com (consensus earnings estimates, broker recommendations and insider trading)

We especially like www.marketguide.com. Be careful of leaning on a given broker's in-house research. Just like a baseball team, a broker's research team includes a mix of superior, average, and inferior analysts.

There tends to be at least an indirect correlation between low commission rates and minimal additional services (including research). So, if research is important to you, plan on paying higher commissions for quantity and quality.

# The Comfort Factor

Some people are uncomfortable turning their money over to a "stranger," i.e., a broker they've never heard of, no matter how strongly recommended the broker may be. If you are that type of person, you may wish to simply tap into the online equivalent of your present brokerage. Many brokerages now have an online presence—DLJDirect (Donaldson, Lufkin) and Discover (Morgan Stanley Dean Witter) are just two examples.

Similarly, you may be most comfortable dealing with bank-related brokerage firms, especially if the bank is one you presently use. Examples include Fleet Bank, which has Quick & Reilly and SURETRADE; Citibank; Mellon (Dreyfus); Fifth Third Bank; NationsBank; Norwest; and Wachovia. You may even find that your existing bank relationship enables you to receive "freebies" on the Internet brokerage site not offered to nonbanking customers. Check it out.

## Ancillary Services

Is there something else you want from your online broker? Free checking, for example, or perhaps free credit/debit cards? One appealing feature is the ability to transfer funds back and forth electronically between a bank checking account and a brokerage account—at no or minimal cost, ideally. Make out your wish list, then see which broker comes closest to matching it.

**Crash Alert**

Beware of "teaser" research: barebones research offered at no charge to entice you to purchase "in-depth" research at an additional charge. The in-depth reports may be worth the money, but just be conscious of when a carrot is being dangled in front of you.

**Super Strategy**

Choose an online broker by:

1. drawing up your wish list
2. prioritizing it
3. checking out the three references we recommended (Gomez, Smart Money, Kiplinger's)
4. talking to friends/business associates about their own experiences, good and bad

One service that should not be compromised in any way is a same-day "sweep" of any of your uninvested cash into a money market fund with a competitive interest rate. And make sure you are given a choice between taxable money market funds (where you can stash IRA cash) and tax-free money markets (for protecting uninvested cash from taxable accounts).

Now you're ready to trade!

## The Least You Need to Know

➤ The Internet is basically a worldwide network of computers talking to each other over phone lines. The World Wide Web is a subset of the Internet made up of websites that can include text, graphics, and sound.

➤ Make sure you choose an Internet Service Provider (ISP) that you can access with a local (free!) call.

➤ If you want to trade and bank online, you will need a browser that meets bank and broker security standards; specifically, you will need a qualified browser that supports 128-bit encryption.

➤ If you intend to trade frequently online, carefully research your choice of an online broker—look into fees and execution lags and make sure your broker offers a telephone back-up trading system.

# Chapter 20

# Online Trading and Tracking

---

**In This Chapter**

➤ Avoiding online fraud

➤ How to use an online broker

➤ The best search engines for investors and how to use them

➤ Lots of great financial web sites

---

In this chapter we will explore the basics of how to trade and manage your portfolio online. This chapter is also loaded with the URLs for some of our favorite financially friendly web sites. So plug in and hang on!

## Speed and System Backups

Okay, you've narrowed your choice of Internet brokers to just a few, based on our criteria. Before you make that final choice, please, we beg of you, run your top choices past a few experienced friends. The surveys we've recommended in the previous chapter are terrific starting points but do tend to overlook one important factor: speed. Speed of order entry and reporting, that is. Many brokers' sites are so heavily secured that the basic order entry process moves at a crawl. If speed matters to you, ask fellow investors if a particular broker is quick or slow.

Another issue is system failure backups; what happens if the site crashes or is unavailable? Can your order be phoned in? Many online brokers have had system failures without any back-up systems in place for their customers to use to continue trading. This situation can cost you plenty and wipe out any savings from trading online.

## Crash Alert

Online investing is ripe with fraud. Here are some tips for avoiding fraudulent brokers:

➤ Stick with brokerages that appear in national magazine surveys.

➤ All legitimate brokers are SIPC insured. If you're thinking about using a lesser-known broker, ask for proof of SIPC insurance. "SIPC" stands for Securities Investor Protection Corporation. It currently insures securities and cash in a brokerage account for up to $500,000, no more than $100,000 of which may be in cash.

➤ Avoid penny stockbrokers, online or otherwise.

➤ Chat room and newsgroup advice should be treated with great caution.

Many participants are there to promote their interests, couching their sales pitches as hot tips. Remember, free advice is unregulated by the SEC!

Finally, try to get a feel for your broker's telephone responsiveness before you sign up. Some brokers will keep you on hold for a half hour—not fun when you're trying to execute a trade or get some help.

# How to Use an Online Broker

Once you have selected your online broker, you need to complete the "paperwork." Nearly all brokers offer a form that you can fill out from your PC keyboard, print out, sign, and mail in. You can e-mail the form, but the broker still needs your signature on file, so you will have to use the good old U.S. Postal Service (also affectionately known as "snailmail"). By return mail, you should receive a log-on ID and password.

When you receive your ID and password, you may be able to "save" them to avoid having to reenter (and remember!) them each time you trade. SURETRADE and Dreyfus are two brokers that offer this feature.

## *The Typical Broker's Home Page*

Once logged on, you will find yourself at the broker's "home page," which is like a book's table of contents. Typically, the home page is subdivided into three sections:

1. About the Broker. This is for prospective customers and typically includes the firm's history, information on how to open an account, and sample screens and portfolios. Look over this section for every broker you are considering before making your final decision.

2. Your Account Information. Included here will be trading-related pages, including a verification page you can use to look over a trade order you've placed. In other words, this is your last chance to "chicken out" of a trade! Next, you'll see a series of pages relating to the status of your account, including the individual assets in your portfolio, the current market value of your portfolio, gains and losses year-to-date, and a trading history page showing all transactions going back three months to a year (depending on the broker). You should also expect to receive monthly statements and daily confirmations of your trades, via mail or your PC.

3. Investor-Related Information. Just as Section 2 was customer specific (you), Section 3 tends to provide information for all the broker's customers. Examples would include individual stock quotes, current stock and bond market statistics and information, general news items, and links to other Websites. Many of these Websites are merely online versions of printed material (e.g., *Wall Street Journal*, *Fortune*, *USA Today*). At this point, most brokers will remind you to use a browser (Netscape or Microsoft) to expedite your visit to other Websites. Check out each site initially to see which, if any, you will want to return to on a more or less daily basis, and keep a list of these handy. As we mentioned in the last chapter, your browser probably includes a feature that allows you to keep a "hot list" of the Websites you'd like to note and return to under the item on your toolbar entitled "Favorites."

# How an Online Broker Works

As of September 24, 1998, the number one online broker in the U.S. was E*TRADE Securities, Inc. Let's take a look at how E*TRADE works.

E*TRADE commission rates are $14.95 for "listed" (New York Stock and American Stock Exchange) securities and $19.95 for NASDAQ securities, up to 5,000 shares. Add 1¢ per share once you go over 5,000 shares—and that's for all the shares, not just those over 5,000. This policy discourages investors from purchasing large blocks of "penny" stocks (remember those? Penny stocks sell for a few dollars or less).

E*TRADE requires a $1,000 minimum to open an account. Not all online brokers require a minimum (SURETRADE does not, for example). At E*TRADE, you can talk to a "live" broker, if necessary, for a $15 fee.

When opening an account with any Web dealer, you first print out an account form from the website, fill it out, sign it, and mail it to the brokerage. Once you've been informed that your account has been opened and given a password, you can log on.

When you log onto E*TRADE you will see a page with the following subheadings:

HOME / PORTFOLIO & MARKETS / STOCKS & OPTIONS / FUNDS / TRADING / MY ACCOUNTS / COMMUNITY / MARKETPLACE

Click on PORTFOLIO & MARKETS and you will see the day's price charts on the Dow Jones Industrial Average as well as the NASDAQ composite. Down below you will see your portfolio holdings prices plus market headlines. E*TRADE offers price quotes in "real" time; if any quotes are delayed, they are noted as such on the screen.

Click on MY ACCOUNTS and you will see the value of the account as of the current date, broken down between cash (held in money market funds) and equities. Again, you will notice a number of account records options in the left-hand margin. You've just looked at "Account Balances," so click on "Account Positions." This will show you each of your equity holdings by symbol, name, number of shares, and current price.

If you click on "Account Activity" in the left margin, you will see listed all the transactions in your account for the last three months. This includes principal transactions (B for buys, S for sells) as well as income transactions (interest and dividends received).

Again in the left margin, you can click on "Unrealized Gains & Losses" to see individual holdings broken down between cost and current market value, with the net gain (or loss) in the far right margin. You can also click on "Tax Records" in the left margin to see realized gains or losses year-to-date.

If you wanted to make a trade, you would click on TRADING in the top margin. A stock order page would appear allowing you to enter an order, with options in the left-hand margin. You would indicate the type of transaction (buy, sell, etc.), number of shares, stock symbol, and type of order (market, limit, etc.). Next you can click either "Place Order" to execute or "Cancel Order."

If you wanted to check out the broker's mutual funds offerings or look at your mutual fund holdings, you would click on FUNDS. E*TRADE provides ratings and performance data for each fund showing the fund's performance (up to 10 years if available), fees, and composition. If you wished to purchase the fund, you would click on TRADING in the upper margin, then "Funds," and then "Enter Order" from the left margin.

An online broker like E*TRADE will also supply business and company news, as well as its analysts' stock reports.

### Super Strategy

Develop an alternative plan for those frustrating moments (and they will occur) when you can't get online or can't get your online broker account to work. Backups might include telephone contact, a full-service or discount broker, or patience (what's your hurry, anyway; aren't you a long-term investor?). E*TRADE, for example, allows you to talk to a broker directly (1-800-STOCKS-5), or you can use their automated telephone system (Telemaster).

# Researching Investments Online

There's a lot of hype about how the Web is "empowering" individual investors. But it may sometimes seem as if the Web is overwhelming infoseekers rather than providing them with useful tools to manage and make more money.

## *Avoiding Investment Research Overload*

To avoid investment research overload, try to prune. Most of the better stuff is still disseminated the old-fashioned way: books, newspapers, and magazines. The quality of some of the magazines, such as *Smart Money*, *Fortune*, *Worth*, and *Forbes*, is constantly improving. Many offer online versions—we list some URLs at the end of this chapter.

But don't go nuts and sign up for pricey subscriptions for a bunch of online magazines. You can receive most online subscriptions on a trial basis. Go that route first and see whether a subscription adds true value to your investment life. If you have a subscription to *The Wall Street Journal*, however, you may want to subscribe to its interactive edition for a small additional fee. The *WSJ* is still the paper of record for financial news.

Many online brokers are offering research at their web sites for their customers. This research is generally from highly regarded outside parties such as Standard and Poor's, Zacks, or Reuters. If you have some extra cash to burn and find yourself deeply into investing after reading this book, you may wish to sign up for a Bloomberg terminal for about $1,200 a month. Bloomberg is the Tiffany's of investment information systems, providing up-to-the-second price quotes and tons of exclusive info.

## *Search Engine Fun*

Okay, you can snap out of your Bloomberg fantasy now! The average investor will do just fine without a Bloomberg terminal, especially if he or she becomes familiar with search engines. Search engines are businesses that collect and index Web pages. Search engines (or portals, as they are sometimes called) are like electronic libraries. And, obviously, the largest libraries with the most "books," or Web pages, are the most convenient. Your browser or online service will include a link called "Net Search" or "Search Engines" that will hook you up with an array of search engines.

Currently more than 200 search engines exist. By far, the number-one search engine is Yahoo!, which offers 115 million Web-page views. It is definitely the largest electronic library and is usually rated number one by investors for the following reasons:

1. Yahoo! provides both comprehensive and dynamic financial information, 24 hours a day.

2. Yahoo! provides rudimentary data that most investors can use.

3. It's easy to use.

4. The investment information on Yahoo! tends to be quite timely.

### Fiscal Facts

The great majority of search engines are free, because the site developer sells advertising space. Eventually, you will either adapt to the advertising or develop an acute case of nausea and swear off the portals. When you think about it, though, the ads are no different from what you face in your local newspaper, so please don't get too annoyed.

Other excellent search engines include Excite, Lycos, and Infoseek. Excite is probably Yahoo!'s closest competitor. Excite may be more appropriate for the beginner investor, because it provides broader information (on home mortgage rates, for example).

## Using a Search Engine

When you visit a search engine's web site, you will see a flashing cursor inside a small box. You type in that box a word or phrase that best describes what kind of information you are looking for, then you click "Search" and within minutes the search engine will provide you with a bunch of URLs for sites with information on your topic. The search engine will also provide tips to help you narrow your search.

### Investor's Idiom

A *search engine* is a business that collects and indexes the zillions of proliferating web sites (so you don't have to!). Think of it as a big electronic library with a super-fast librarian who can find you any book in the world in a matter of minutes. Search engines are also referred to as "portals."

Use a search engine the same way you would look up an author's books in the library or a service in the Yellow Pages. If you want to research EE bonds for example, type in "EE bonds" using quotation marks so the search engine knows to provide only sites about EE bonds and not every bond site out there! Some search engines recommend that you type +EE+bonds to communicate that you want only sites that include both "EE" and "bonds."

Finally, use that ancient implement known as the telephone to call a company you are researching. Where do you find the telephone number? On the company's website. Or use Yahoo!'s phone directory.

## Portals Just for Investors

The portals listed below are those we find particularly useful for investors. Be careful, though, as some research, such as company profiles, is provided for free, while more in-depth research may be pricey.

1. **www.justquotes.com**. This portal provides data on individual stocks from Standard & Poor's and other sources.

2. **www.bloomberg.com**. A very good source for general business news and both broad-market and security-specific information. Anyone who has ever used a Bloomberg machine appreciates its many attributes. Really a must. (The site, not that expensive terminal!)

3. **www.ceoexpress.com**. A portal that bills itself as "for the busy CEO," it provides a very broad variety of business-related Website links, alphabetically listed.

4. **www.kiplinger.com**. Kiplinger Online provides stock quotes, lists of great Internet sites for investors, lists of top mutual funds, business news and forecasts, and even online calculators to help you track your portfolio.

# Tracking Your Portfolio

Most brokers keep a log of your portfolio that will show its value on a daily basis. You will also receive a confirmation for each trade, either in the mail or via your PC. Monthly statements are mailed if the account was active; these statements include dividends, margin activity, and trading.

Brokers also provide year-end summaries that will help you file Schedule D on your tax returns. These summaries include dividends, margin interest, and a 'Net proceeds summary that is also furnished to the IRS. The latter is referred to as a 1099. Active traders ought to consider buying a commercial software program such as Quicken to tabulate their "buys and sells." This will come in especially handy when it's time to fill out that Schedule D.

## *Portfolio Management Programs*

Your online broker automatically updates your portfolio, but what if you have several different accounts with different brokers? How do you keep track of it all?

Programs are available online that can help you keep excellent records of every security you own. These programs will automatically apply daily price changes to your holdings, calculate your portfolio's value, and compare your current return to your financial goals. Most portfolio management programs will also help you with asset allocation and even alert you when securities hit prices at which you may want to buy or sell.

There are two kinds of portfolio management programs available online:

1. Web-based portfolio management programs. These are programs you can access by registering at Websites that offer them. Yahoo!, for example, offers a portfolio management program at **www.edit.my.yahoo.com/config** that provides charts and data you can use to create your own spreadsheet. Other popular Web-based programs include:

   ➤ Thomson MarketEdge Portfolio Tracker, **www.thomsoninvest.net**

   ➤ Stockpoint Portfolio Management, **www.stockpoint.com**

   ➤ The *Wall Street Journal*'s portfolio tracker, **www.wsj.com**

2. PC-based portfolio management programs. These are software programs you download from the Internet to your computer. These programs can offer more functions than Web-based programs, but, on the other hand, they don't provide the daily stock quote and other financial information that the Web-based programs can. Some popular PC-based portfolio management programs are:

   ➤ Wall St. Access, **www.stockcenter.com**

   ➤ PointCast, **www.pointcast.com**

   ➤ Inside Track Lite, **www.quote.com/info/microquest/liteinst.html**

**251**

# Three Isn't Necessarily a Crowd

Finally, we'd like to briefly discuss a technical matter generally overlooked by most articles and books about investing online, yet should be understood by all: third-market execution.

How can an online broker offer to trade thousands of shares for average commissions of only about $15? The answer is that your broker may well be selling your order to a third-market dealer or broker that pays your broker a fee for that order. In Wall Street jargon, this arrangement is known as "payment for order flow." It is perfectly legal and has the blessing of the regulators. Your purchase of a New York Stock Exchange stock through an online broker is not actually executed on the NYSE but through a third-market dealer.

Do you receive an inferior trade execution as a result? We don't think so. In fact, you are benefiting from tapping into the world of specialized traders who move huge amounts of capital in the blink of an eye. It is our view that if you can get NYSE executions at cheap Internet rates, go for it!

Now, to send you merrily surfing across the 'Net, here's our final offering—a list of our favorite financial Websites!

## Financial Markets

http://biz.yahoo.com/reports/stocks.html (U.S. markets)

http://www.amex.com (American Exchange)

http://beta.nasdaq.com (Nasdaq)

http://www.nikkei.co.jp/enews/home.html (Nikkei)

http://www.nyse.com (NYSE)

http://dir.yahoo.com/Business_and_Economy/Finance_and_Investment/Bonds (Bonds)

http://dir.yahoo.com/Business_and_Economy/Finance_and_Investment/Futures_and_Options (Futures and Options)

## Quotes

http://quote.yahoo.com

http://www.bigcharts.com (BigCharts)

http://www.dbc.com (DBC Online)

http://biz.yahoo.com/zacks/extreme.html (Earnings Surprises)

http://www.justquotes.com (Just Quotes)

http://fast.quote.com/fq/quotecom/quote

http://www.thomsonrtq.com/index.sht (Real Time Quotes)

http://www.stockmaster.com (Stockmaster)

http://www.stocksite.com (StockSite)

http://www.investorama.com/screening.html (Stock Screening Sites)

# Financial News

http://fnews.yahoo.com/street (Wall Street news)

http://fnews.yahoo.com/oli (general financial news)

http://dailynews.yahoo.com/headlines/business

http://biz.yahoo.com/industry (financial news and info by industry)

http://biz.yahoo.com/reports/world.html (international business news)

http://biz.yahoo.com/bw (BizWire)

http://headlines.yahoo.com/Full_Coverage/Business

http://dir.yahoo.com/Business_and_Economy/Finance_and_Investment/
News_and_Media (Financial News)

http://dir.yahoo.com/News_and_Media/Business (Business News)

http://dir.yahoo.com/Business_and_Economy/Finance_and_Investment/
News_and_Media/Quotes/International_Markets

# Investment Research

http://biz.yahoo.com/research/earncal/today.html

http://biz.yahoo.com/reports/ipo.html (reports on initial public offerings)

http://www.ipocentral.com (IPO Central)

http://dir.yahoo.com/Business_and_Economy/Companies/Financial_Services/
Investment_Services/Brokerages/Online_Trading

(Online Trading)

http://biz.yahoo.com/snp (Standard &Poor's)

http://dir.yahoo.com/Business_and_Economy/Finance_and_Investment/
Reference_and_Guides (Reference Guides)

http://midam.com/ecb/mdmpag.htm

(Commodities Charts)

http://www.bbb.org (Better Business Bureau)

http://www.annualreportservice.com (Annual Reports)

http://www.corporateinformation.com (Corporate Info)

http://www.disclosure.com (Disclosure)

http://businessdirectory.dowjones.com (Dow Jones Business Directory)

http://www.forbes.com/tool/toolbox/jan1 (Forbes Report on American Industry)

http://www.aaii.org (Assn.of Individual Investors)

http://www.investools.com (Investools Research)

## Investment Message Boards and Chat Rooms

http://messages.yahoo.com/yahoo/Business_and_Finance

http://chat.yahoo.com/?room=investments@news (Stock Chat)

http://events.yahoo.com/Business_and_Economy/Finance_and_Investment

http://features.yahoo.com/finance/survey (Marketplace Poll)

## Investment Clubs

http://clubs.yahoo.com/Business_Finance

http://fnews.yahoo.com/fool (home of The Motley Fool)

## Mutual Funds

http://www.morningstar.net (Morningstar)

http://www.fool.com (Motley Fool)

http://www.brill.com (Mutual Funds Interactive)

http://www.thestreet.com (The Street)

http://www.moneypages.com/syndicate/index.html

http://dir.yahoo.com/Business_and_Economy/Companies/Financial_Services/Investment_Services/Mutual_Funds (Mutual Funds)

## Financial Magazines

http://www.businessweek.com

http://www.cfonet.com

http://www.economist.com

http://www.feer.com (Far East Economic Review)

http://www.fastcompany.com/home.html (Fast Company)

http://www.ft.com (Financial Times)

http://www.forbes.com

http://www.fortune.com

http://www.hbsp.harvard.edu (Harvard Business School Publishing)

http://www.industryweek.com

http://www.investors.com (Investor's Business Daily)

http://www.joc.com (Journal of Commerce)

http://www.kiplinger.com (Kiplinger)

http://business-times.asia1.com.sg (Singapore Business Times)

http://www.smartmoney.com/si/brokers/online

http://www.strategy-business.com (Strategy & Business)

http://www.worth.com

## Technology Magazines

http://www.byte.com (BYTE)

http://www.computerworld.com (Computerworld)

http://www.eb-mag.com (Electronic Business)

http://www.electronicmarkets.org/electronicmarkets/electronicmarkets.nsf/pages/index.html (Electronic Markets)

http://www.techweb.com (TechWeb)

http://www.Webfinance.net (Web Finance)

http://www.hotwired.com/frontdoor (Wired)

## Insurance Sites

http://insurance.yahoo.com

http://insurance.yahoo.com/auto.html (auto insurance)

http://insurance.yahoo.com/life.html (life and health insurance)

http://insurance.yahoo.com/home.html (home and renters insurance)

## Government Agencies

http://www.nttc.edu/gov/independents/frs.html (Federal Reserve )

http://www.law.vill.edu/fed-agency/fedWebloc.html (Federal Web Locator)

http://www.business.gov (U.S. Business Advisor)

http://www.sec.gov/news/newsindx.htm (SEC Digest)

http://www.sec.gov/edaux/searches.htm (SEC Database)

## Investor Services

http://www.ameritrade.com

http://www.datek.com

http://www.discoverbrokerage.com

http://www.dljdirect.com

http://www.etrade.com (E*TRADE)

http://www.fid-inv.com (Fidelity Investments)

http://www.schwab.com (Schwab Online)

http://www.waterhouse.com (Waterhouse)

http://www.ddsi.com/banking (Internet Banking Index)

http://www.jpmorgan.com (JP Morgan)

http://www.lehman.com (Lehman Brothers)

http://www.ml.com (Merrill Lynch)

http://www.ms.com (Morgan Stanley)

http://www.smithbarney.com (Salomon Smith Barney)

http://www.vfinance.com (Venture Capital Resources)

http://www.wellsfargo.com (Wells Fargo)

# Media and Other Resources Available Online

Online Television News: ABC I BBC I CBS I CNN I CNNfn I Fox I MSNBC I PBS

Business Magazines: Business Week I CFO I Economist I Electronic Business I

Far East Economic Review I Fast CompanyI Forbes DigitalTool I Fortune I

Harvard B. School Publishing I Inc. I Industry Week I IW-Growing Co. I

Money I NewsweekI Red Herring I Sloan Mgmt Review I Smart Money I The Standard I
Strategy & Business I Time I Upside Online I US News I Web Finance I Worth

Technology Magazines: BYTE I CIO I cInet I CNET Radio I Computerworld I Electronic
Markets I Emmerce I First Monday I Intranet Journal I MIT TechReview I TechWeb I
Wired I ZDNet

Custom News: CNN I Excite I Infobeat I Inquisit I My Yahoo I Netscape Business I
Newspage Newsfeeds: AP Wire I Bloomberg I Bloomberg Audio I Broadcast.com I
Business Wire I Canada Newswire I Drudge Report I Industry.net I NewsLink I NewsReal
I PR Newswire I Reuters

Internet Search Engines: Alta Vista I Deja News I Dogpile I Domain Name Search I
Excite I HotBot I Infoseek I LibrarySpot I Magellan I Metacrawler I Mining Co I Northern
Light I Snap I Wall Street Search I WebCrawler I YahooI Search Tips I

Financial Markets: AMEX I Averages & Composites I Nasdaq I Nikkei Net I NYSE I
Commodities Charts (T-bills, etc.) I Futures/Options Markets I Other Stock Exchanges

Analysis: Deutsche Bank I Dismal Scientist

SEC: Edgar Online People I FreeEdgar I SEC Digest I SEC DatabaseI SIC Codes

Government Agencies: Federal Reserve System I Federal Web Locator I Foreign Gov't
Resources I Gov't Printing Office I Int'l Trade Administration I IRS I OSHA I U.S. Business Advisor I US Patents & Trademarks I All Government Agencies

Statistics: Bureau of Labor Stats I Cyber Atlas I Fedstats I Population Lookup I Economic
Research Data I U.S. Statistical Abstract I Statistics USA I UMich Documents Center I US
Census Datamaps

Legislature: C-Span | Congressional VoteWatch | Federal Register | Legislator Search Engine | State Legislatures | Thomas Legislative Search | U.S. House (e-mail) | U.S. Senate (Email)

Business Links: CorpFinet | Financial Data Finder | FinWeb | Invest-o-rama | IOMA Business Directory | Research Links

Real Estate: HomeAdvisor | HomeScout | IRED | Move Central | Nat'l Real Estate Investor | Net Properties | Real Estate News | Shopping Center Database

Quotes and Market News: BigCharts | DBC Online | Earnings Surprises | Just Quotes | Quicken on fn | Quote | Real Time Quotes (free) | Stockmaster | StockSite | Stock Screening Sites | Upgrades & Downgrades | Yahoo Finance

Online Investor Services: Ameritrade | Datek | Discover Brokerage | DLJ Direct | E*TRADE | Fidelity Investments | Schwab Online | Waterhouse Securities

Banking & Finance: Bank Rate Monitor | Cowen & Co | Finance Student's Web World | Hambrecht & Quist | Internet Banking Index | JP Morgan | Lehman Research | Merrill Lynch | Morgan Stanley | Salomon Smith Barney M&A: Venture Capital Resources

Small/Family Business: Better Business Bureau | Business Forms | Business Toolkit | Chambers of Commerce | Government Resources | Idea Cafe | Institute for Family Business | MoneyHunter | Sample Business Plans | SCORE| SBA | SmallbizNet | Small Business State Profiles | Smartbiz | Taxes | Yahoo Small Business

Investing & IPO Research: 1998 Fortune Investor's Guide | Alert IPO | Assn. of Individual Investors | CDA Insider Watch| Final Bell | First Call | Investools Research | IPO Central | Microsoft Investor | MoneyNet | Money Talks | Morningstar | Motley Fool | Mutual Funds Interactive | The Street | Syndicate | Tech Investor | Zacks

Bankruptcy: American Bankruptcy Institute | Bankruptcy Stats | Internet Bankruptcy Library

References: Dictionary | Encyclopedia.com | Hypertext Dictionary | Internet Public Library | Learn2 | Library of Congress | Virtual Reference Desk | National Archives | NetLingo | One Look Dictionary | Technical Support Search | Thesaurus | World Holiday Calendar | Beginner's Central

Directories: AnyWho (AT&T) | Area Code Finder | Four11 | Switchboard | 800 Directory | Yellow Pages | Zip Code Finder

Computers/Software: Buy Direct | CDW | Cyberian Outpost | Egghead | Insight | NECX | Shopper.com

**The Least You Need to Know**

➤ If speed matters to you, ask fellow investors if a particular online broker is quick or slow.

➤ Treat chat room and newsgroup advice with great caution. Many participants are there to promote their interests, couching their sales pitches as hot tips.

➤ Have an alternative trading method for those frustrating moments when you can't get online or can't get your online broker account to work.

➤ Search engines are businesses that collect and index Web pages.

➤ Portfolio management programs are available online that can help you keep excellent records of every security you own.

# Part 6
# Advanced Investment Plays

Money is better than poverty, if only for financial reasons.

—Woody Allen

*By now you've developed your own investment I.Q. And it's pretty darn high. You're now capable of understanding some fairly complex investments and can decide whether or not to include them in your portfolio.*

*Most of us will never trade pork bellies or gold, but we can use the same tools that commodities traders use—such as options and futures contracts—to strengthen our own portfolios and protect them from volatile market swings. This section builds on everything you've learned so far and shows you how to apply advanced plays to your investments.*

*Take a look at the offerings in this section—even if you never intend to exercise an option or put a put. It'll feel good to have a clue when you hear about hedge funds, or real estate investment trusts, or private equity funds at a party or on the news. You may even find that not only do you understand these investments, but they may also help you meet your goals. And that's what this book is all about.*

# Chapter 21

# Hedging Your Options

---

### In This Chapter

➤ All about options

➤ Protecting your portfolio with puts and calls

➤ Selling short vs. trading options

➤ Protecting stock positions

➤ Advanced hedging strategies

---

Well, we promised that at the end of this book we would get into some advanced investment plays, and here we are—about to tackle options. Can you believe you even know enough to get into this topic? But if you've been with us so far, you definitely do! Options are contracts that give you the option, but not the obligation, to buy or sell a specified quantity of stocks or bonds. Options have two purposes:

1. To protect you against a sickening drop in stock prices
2. To enable you to profit from an exciting rise in stock prices

Both options and futures contracts, which we'll discuss in the next chapter, are called *hedges*. You've no doubt heard the phrase, "He's hedging his bets." Options and futures contracts can be used to hedge your bets on the stock market. A caveat: The strategies we'll be discussing in this and the next few chapters are quite sophisticated and should not be undertaken without careful research and the support of a trusted pro.

Our goal is simply to give you enough background so you can ask that trusted pro intelligent questions. Toward that end, we've gone a bit deep on some topics; if you can get through it, great, but if you can't, don't sweat it now. Just keep us around as your personal reference. Should you find yourself considering any of these investments in the near future, we'll still be here. Right on your shelf.

### Investor's Idiom

An *option* is a contract that is listed on an exchange just like a stock. The contract states what is to be delivered for what price and what time period. At the end of the designated time period, the option loses all its value. The option is a right, but not an obligation, to exercise the rights stated in the contract.

### Investor's Idiom

The *strike price*, also called the *exercise price*, is the price at which the holder of an option contract can buy ("call") or sell ("put") the underlying security. For example, a ComputerNerd, Inc., 50-call option means you can buy 100 shares of ComputerNerd, Inc. at $50 per share. A ComputerNerd, Inc., 50-put option means you can sell 100 shares of ComputerNerd, Inc., at $50 per share.

# Puts and Calls

There are two kinds of option contracts: *puts* and *calls*. When you buy a call option, you are buying the right to purchase a stock at a set price, called the *strike price*, for a specified period of time—usually a few months.

Here's a very simple example of how an call option contract works. Let's say you're thinking about buying 100 shares of ComputerNerd, Inc., stock, which is currently selling for $40 a share. You've heard that the company's coming out with an awesome new spreadsheet software and the stock price could rise sharply as a result. Hmmm…what to do?

You could lay out the $4,000 now for the 100 shares and hold them, praying nightly that you were right about that software and looking forward to selling your stock for $6,000 when the share price rises to $60 for a tidy $2,000 profit. But what if there's a glitch in the software and ComputerNerd doesn't release it on schedule and the stock price sinks to $20? Oy! This could make for some very restless nights.

## *Hedge Your Bet with a Call*

This is where an option comes in very handy. Instead of laying out $4,000 for 100 shares of ComputerNerd, Inc., contact your broker and buy a three-month call option on 100 shares of Computer Nerd stock at a strike price of $40. The option will only cost you, say, $400. Now, if the stock does rise to $60 before your three months are up, you have a contract entitling you to buy the stock for only $40. You'd pay only $4,000 for $6,000 worth of stock. You could turn around and sell the stock right away for a $2,000 profit. Pretty nifty!

If the stock price falls below $40, simply don't exercise the call option. Sure, you're out the $400 you spent on the option contract, but that's a lot easier to swallow than having spent $4,000 on the stock and watching its value shrink to $3,000 or $2,000 or less. With the call option, you've hedged your bet.

A put option is the opposite of a call option. A put is a contract that gives you the option to sell a security at a specified price until the contract's expiration date. With a call, you are hoping for the price of the security to rise, but with a put, you are praying for the price to fall.

## Prevent Portfolio Wipeout with a Put

Let's say you're bearish on ComputerNerd, Inc. You're convinced the company's spreadsheet software, which everyone else thinks is going to turn the industry on its ear, is a stinker. Unfortunately, your spouse thinks differently and insisted on buying 100 shares of ComputerNerd at $40 a share. How do you protect yourself from disaster?

Call your broker and buy a three-month put option with a strike price of $36. This contract guarantees that for three months you can dump those 100 shares of ComputerNerd for at least $36 per share. If the stock tanks within the next three months, you can get out at $36, even if the share price drops to, say, $18. Instead of watching helplessly as your $4,000 stake in ComputerNerd drops to $1,800, you can exercise your option when the stock price hits $36 and get out with $3,600 intact. Because you've hedged your spouse's bet, you lose only $400, plus whatever you spent on the put option contract.

### Investor's Idiom

An option *expires*—becomes worthless—on its expiration date. Options expire on the Saturday following the third Friday of the month in which they can be exercised. For example, ComputerNerd, Inc., December 50 options expire on December 19, 1998. Nine months is typically the maximum expiration date on an option.

# How Did This Get Started?

Options trading has been around about as long as securities trading, but until the 1970s, options traded in an informal, unregulated manner. Brokerage houses specializing in "puts and calls" would advertise their specials of the day in publications like *The Wall Street Journal*. There was no regulated market.

After the 1973–74 bear market for stocks took prices of popular indices like the Dow Jones and the S&P 500 down some 40 percent, it became clear that options could play an important role in stabilizing the market and protecting investors from severe drops. The government got involved in standardizing options trading. This led to the creation of the Chicago Board Options Exchange (CBOE). With the creation of the CBOE and its sister institution, the Options Clearing Corporation (OCC), trading in options grew phenomenally.

# Risk-Loving Speculator Seeks Cautious Hedgehog

Options can be viewed in two ways: as rank speculation ("I bet you $200 that ComputerNerd, Inc., stock will go up 20 points in 90 days") or as a hedge ("I can protect myself against my ComputerNerd stock going down by buying put options with a $40 strike price for three months"). When you think about it, it takes both a speculator and a hedger to complete a contract.

An option's price is called a *premium*. The premium is the price the options buyer pays and the options writer receives for the option. The premium is like a commission, except that the premium diminishes in value steadily until the contract expires. A three-month contract offered June 1, 1998, to buy a ComputerNerd, Inc., 50-call option might sell for $3, for example, when it's first offered. The price will decline, however, over the course of the three months. Why? Because as time passes, the option is protecting the buyer for less and less time.

The option's price, or premium, is the maximum loss that the buyer of the contract can experience. An option for 200 shares at $3 costs $600. That's the premium. If the price of the stock doesn't go your way and you never exercise the option, you lose the $600. But that's all.

## In the Money

Options are referred to as either:

➤ "In the money"
➤ "Out of the money"
➤ "At the money"

This swinging lingo simply defines the difference between the option strike price and the current price of the underlying stock.

If the strike price is less than the current market price, for example, a call option would be described as "in the money." You are already ahead by the difference (or spread) between the strike price and market price.

This same situation would be described as "out of the money" for a put option, however. Why? Because, you are behind by the same amount for the put. You are betting the stock will go down, but, darn, it's going the other way.

"At the money" means the stock price and strike price are equal.

# Reading an Option Table

Let's take a look at several examples from Section C of the September 4, 1998, *Wall Street Journal*, using AT&T.

| | | | Call | | Put | |
|---|---|---|---|---|---|---|
| Option/Strike | | Exp. | Vol. | Last | Vol. | Last |
| *AT&T* | *50* | *Oct* | *212* | *$3^3/_8$* | *435* | *$2^1/_4$* |
| $51^{13}/_{16}$ | 50 | Jan | 84 | $5^3/_8$ | 283 | $3^1/_2$ |
| $51^{13}/_{16}$ | 55 | Sep | 169 | $5/_8$ | 45 | $3^1/_2$ |
| $51^{13}/_{16}$ | 55 | Oct | 1056 | $1^9/_{16}$ | 41 | $4^3/_4$ |
| $51^{13}/_{16}$ | 55 | Jan | 248 | $3^1/_8$ | 21 | $5^5/_8$ |
| $51^{13}/_{16}$ | 60 | Oct | 265 | $1/_2$ | 61 | $9^1/_8$ |
| $51^{13}/_{16}$ | 60 | Jan | 335 | $1^7/_{16}$ | 13174 | $9^3/_4$ |

Let's look at the first contract, on the first line. This is the AT&T October 50-call option. The buyer of the contract has the right to purchase 100 shares of ATT at $50 per share, which is $1^{13}/_{16}$ less than where the stock closed on September 3, 1998. This is an example of a call option that is "in the money," because the buyer has the right to purchase the stock for a lower price than it is selling for on the open market.

The contract runs out on October 17, 1998. How do we know? Because *Oct* stands for October, and all contracts expire on the Saturday following the third Friday in the month. The volume on September 3 was 212, or 212 contracts. Since each contract equals 100 shares, the AT&T Oct 50-call options traded an equivalent of 21,200 common shares.

The last (or closing premium) of $3^3/_8$ means that it would cost you $3 $^3/_8$ times 100 (everything being expressed in 100 share terms), or $337.50, to purchase this call option contract. And notice that your break-even point (strike price + premium – closing price) is 50 + $3^3/_8$ – $51^{13}/_{16}$, or $1^9/_{16}$. If the stock price goes up more than $1^9/_{16}$ the next trading day, you are ahead of the game. Of course, each day, the stock price and the premium are subject to change (but that's the exciting part, right?).

Now, check out the put. Notice that there is a put option for the same contract. Here, the purchaser is wagering that the share price will decline. Since the strike price is less than the closing price, the put option contract is presently "out of the market." The stock would have to decline by more than the difference, or more than $1^{13}/_{16}$ to be "in the market." Notice that the break-even point is different: first, you have to get back to "at the money," which is the 1 $^{13}/_{16}$ strike price; then, you have to recover your premium, or $2^1/_4$, for a total stock price decline of $4^1/_{16}$.

## Options Galore

The second contract listed on the table, with the same strike price ($50), has a January 1999 expiration. Each stock has options with four different months: the two closest months (in this case September and October, plus two other months). However, newspapers can't justify showing data on all the months. See how the October 50 premium is less than the January 50 premium? The closer an option is to expiring, the smaller its premium.

## Most Active Contracts

Finally, take a look at the very heavy volume for the final listed put contract: the January 60. In fact, this contract made the "most active contracts" list in the *Journal* for September 3, 1998. Under the most active contract list for that day, you would have found the following information for AT&T:

| Option/Strike | Vol. | Exch | Last | Net Chg | Close |
|---|---|---|---|---|---|
| AT&T Jan 60 P | 13,174 | CB | $9^3/_4$ | $+1^1/_4$ | $51^{13}/_{16}$ |

The P stands for Put; since September 3 was a "down" day in the market, the contracts with the biggest gains were put contracts. CB stands for the CBOE. The net change of $+1^1/_4$ means that the premium rose $1^1/_4$ to $9^3/_4$ from the September close of $8^1/_2$. In other words, had you purchased the put option (AT&T Jan 60) at the close on September 2 and sold it at the close on September 3, you would have made 14.7 percent for the day! ($1^1/_4 \div 8^1/_2 = +14.7$ percent.) In dollar terms, if you spent $850, you made $975, for a profit of $125.

# Selling Short vs. Trading Options

Before the options market developed, speculators who wanted to bet that a stock's price was going to fall had only one play—to "short" the stock. When you short a stock, you don't actually buy the shares—you borrow them from a broker. You take the stock you've borrowed and sell it. Then you pray (a lot!) that the price of the stock will fall before you have to give the shares back to the broker.

Because what are you going to use to buy the shares to give back to the broker? That's right, the money you made selling the borrowed stock. What if you don't make any money selling the borrowed stock? You're in big trouble.

Let's say you borrowed 100 shares of ComputerNerd, Inc., agreeing to return them the next day. You go out and sell the 100 shares for $40/share and make $4,000. If the stock price falls to $32, you'll only need to use $3,200 to buy the 100 shares to return to the broker. You can pocket $800 profit. Pretty swift.

But what if the stock price shoots up to $50/share. Uh oh, you're gonna need $5,000 to purchase those 100 shares. Well, you've got $4,000 from selling short. That other $1,000 is going to have to come out of your pocket. Big bummer.

Using the AT&T example, if you had "shorted" the stock at the close of September 2 ($52 $^5/_{16}$) you would have sold the borrowed stock for $5,231.25, and purchased it the next day for $5,181.25. Your profit would have been $^1/_2$ point (51 $^{13}/_{16}$ – 52 $^5/_{16}$ = $^1/_2$), or $50. This is a return of less than 1 percent! Compare this to the 14.7 percent that you could have made by trading the put option.

Now you understand why the vast majority of option contracts are not exercised: the buyer of the put or call option is interested in trading the contract, not the underlying stock. The potential for profit is so much greater with option contracts.

## Risky Business

Throughout this book, we've harped on the relationship between risk and return—and options are no exception. The very fact that you can reap such high returns with options should tip you off that they are very risky.

The day someone made 14.7 percent on AT&T January 60-put contracts, for example, someone else could have lost a bundle on Dell Computer September 105-call contracts. The contract closed at 9, off 1$^1/_4$, for a day decline of 12.2 percent (–1$^1/_4$ ÷ 10$^1/_4$)! The underlying common stock of Dell lost only 2.0 percent that day. The option took a much heavier hit.

**Crash Alert**

If you are a buyer of an option contract (put or call), you stand to make *or* lose a lot in percentage terms. And don't forget that any gains are going to be short-term, which means they are subject to income tax, at rates up to 39.6 percent.

Sellers of option contracts take on even more risk. As we said before, the buyer's maximum loss per contract is the amount of the premium. If you sold a call option on the ATT January 50, for example, you would receive the $537.50 premium. But if the stock rose to $60 in November, you would have to spend $6,000 to be in a position to deliver if, by some chance, your contract was exercised. So, worst-case scenario, you could suffer an out-of-pocket cost of $5,462.50 ($6,000 – $537.50). Oh, the pain.

## Option Strategies That Protect Your Stock Positions

In the previous example, we assumed that you, as the option writer, did not actually own the stock and would have to go buy it if the option you sold was exercised.

But suppose you did own the stock. You could write (sell) an option contract on the stock. This is called "covered call writing." When you own the underlying stock, writing a call is a conservative course of action. When you do so, you earn additional income minus the premium the option buyer pays you—which can help offset any minor price weakness in your stock. If the stock moves up in price and, for some reason the option is exercised, you already own the stock, so you won't take a hit on the price. Pretty much a win-win deal.

### Super Strategy

A variation of the covered call strategy is called a "buy-write" program, where you simultaneously buy, let's say, 100 shares of AT&T and write a call option on them. This can be an especially effective tool in tax-deferred accounts, such as IRAs, and defined benefit accounts, but using it is not a part-time job. Some professional firms hire individuals specifically for their buy-write expertise to add value to the retirement accounts under their management.

## Using Puts for Downside Protection

An even more conservative step is to purchase a put option for a stock you already own. This gives you unlimited downside protection for simply the cost of the put. And, of course, you would fully benefit if the price of the stock went up.

You get unlimited upside, as well as protection on the downside, because the value of the put increases as the price of the stock decreases. This works especially well if the strike price is at or close to the market price, and you purchase the longest put contract, which has the lowest premium and provides more time for the strategy to pay off. This strategy works best if you are concerned about a significant correction in the stock market or your particular stock.

Again, remember that all these strategies involving put and call options trigger income tax events for taxable accounts. Repeat after us: "I will visit my trusted professional should I become intrigued with these strategies."

## Stock Index Options

Unlike individual stock options, stock index options give you a chance to hedge your entire equity portfolio—assuming it is diversified as we have advised.

Stock index options dominate the options scene now due to the broad acceptance of the product by money managers. *The Wall Street Journal* lists 37 different indices upon which options can be written/purchased. These include well-known broad indices, such as the Dow Jones Industrials, S&P 500, S&P 100, NASDAQ 100, Russell 2000, sector or industry indices, and indices for foreign stock markets.

## S&P Index Options

The contracts are listed under Index Options Trading in *The Wall Street Journal*. Let's take a look at the options contracts for two indices: the S&P 100 and the S&P 500.

If we look under S&P 100 Index (OEX) and scan down to Sep 480c and Sep 480p (c standing for call and p for put), we can see the volume, last price, and net change for each:

| Strike | Vol. | Last | Net Change |
|--------|------|------|------------|
| Sep 480c | 7,273 | $16^1/_2$ | $-^1/_{12}$ |
| Sep 480p | 1,224 | 14 | $+1^3/_4$ |

We selected these two contracts because they are closest to the current price ($481.33). How do we know that? Because there is a table set into the Index Options Trading page called Ranges for Underlying Indexes. And the fourth index down is the S&P 100. The value of the contract, the total exercise price, and the premium are each derived by multiplying each by 100:

$100 \times \$481.33 = \$48,133 =$ contract value

$100 \times 480c = \$48,000 =$ total exercise price

$100 \times 16^1/_2 = \$1,650 =$ cost to purchase option

You can exercise the contract on any day, just like with individual stock options; however, the contract is settled with cash, not with the security.

The S&P 500 follows the same format and procedure as the S&P 100, with one important difference: the S&P 500 option can be exercised only on the expiration date. This is referred to as a European-style option. American-style options can be exercised on any given day.

## Hedge Strategies for Index Options

Hedge strategies for index options are similar to those for individual stock options. Suppose you wanted to hedge your diversified stock portfolio by purchasing the correct number of put contracts. By "correct number" we mean that you would buy put contracts with values that approximate the decline in your equity portfolio that you are worried about experiencing.

Similar to purchasing insurance—which, in effect, this is—your premium is your maximum cost. Let's assume your equity portfolio is presently worth $1 million and is invested similarly to the S&P 100. Multiply $100 times the current value of the S&P 100 ($481.33) and you'll get $48,133. Divide this into $1 million and you'll get $20,775 (round up to 21). To hedge your portfolio, you'll need to buy 21 put contracts.

Pick the put contract closest to the current index price, or 480p, for the month you want. The premium for 21 December 480-put options is $35^1/_4$. What's the maximum cost to you? $35^1/_4$ times $100 is the cost per contract, and you need 21 contracts. Your cost is $74,025, or 7.4 percent of your equity portfolio. As you can see, this is not cheap insurance. Equity index hedging is not for your everyday amateur.

# The Braveheart of Wall Street

Still with us? Good! If you're still hankering for more, we've got two more aggressive strategies for you:

1. Straddles. These are the simultaneous purchase of a put and call for the same stock or index at the same strike price and expiration date. The straddle buyer makes money if the price of the stock moves significantly up or down. The straddle writer makes money even if there is little or no stock price movement by capturing two premiums. This is a very hot strategy among professionals.

2. The spread. This is the purchase and sale of options on the same stock, only the options have either a different strike price with same expiration date or the same strike price and different expiration dates.

   ➤ A bull spread involves purchasing an option with a lower strike price (i.e., "in the money") and the sale of an option at a higher strike price (i.e., "out of the money").

   ➤ With a bear spread, you sell the option at a lower strike price and purchase the option at a higher strike price.

These strategies can get quite esoteric and should not be tried in the comfort of your own home. And remember, again, that any success translates into short-term gains, which means you'll be paying income tax on them. So don't even consider using these strategies for any portfolio except your tax-sheltered IRA account.

# LEAPS

Finally, we have LEAPs, which stands for Long-Term Equity Anticipation Security. These are long-term option contracts that are very popular with individual investors. There are two main differences between LEAPs and regular options:

1. LEAPS can be written for up to a three-year expiration date vs. a maximum of nine months for traditional options. If you are really convinced that the market is

going to move strongly in a certain direction, a LEAP gives you more time than a traditional option to wait for that move to happen. All LEAPs expire in December on the Saturday following the third Friday.

2. The price of a LEAP is one-tenth the price and size of a traditional option. This is much more manageable for individual investors than having to buy 100 round lots every time you want to buy a regular option.

The combination of a longer-term and lower contract size (one-tenth the size of standard contracts) make LEAPs attractive to individual investors. Just be sure you look before you leap—all the strategies in this chapter are from a very volatile and sophisticated game best left to experts.

---

### The Least You Need to Know

➤ Options are contracts that give you the option, but not the obligation, to buy or sell a specified quantity of stocks or bonds.

➤ Options and futures contracts are called "hedges."

➤ A "put" is an option to sell; a "call" is an option to buy.

➤ You can conservatively use options to protect your portfolio from stock market moves.

➤ Enlist the aid of an experienced broker if you want to get involved with options.

---

# Chapter 22

# Fancy Futures

---

**In This Chapter**

➤ How a future differs from an option

➤ Butter to zinc—the seven main types of commodities

➤ Buying on margin

➤ Using futures to offset uncertainty

---

Looking for a bright future? Well then, you've come to the right chapter. A futures contract is a legal agreement between two parties. One agrees to purchase from the other a specified asset at a specified price at a specified time in the future. Futures contracts are made on everything from commodities, like pork bellies or sugar, to stocks and indexes.

There are also options on futures. Now, don't let this confuse you. Just remember that the purpose of these "advanced play" chapters is simply to give you some background in these complicated investments.

Both options and futures are called *derivatives* because they "derive" their value from the underlying security, index, or commodity they represent. Derivatives tend to be short-term "plays" dominated by large institutions. You participate at your own peril. If you do decide to participate, be sure you work with a very experienced full-service broker specializing in options/futures.

## What Is a Commodity?

A *commodity* is a basic food or raw material. If you turn once again to our old friend, *The Wall Street Journal*, you will see toward the back of Section C a subheading entitled

### Investor's Idiom

A *commodity* is a basic food or raw material, such as cotton, gold, or pork bellies. There are seven main categories of commodities that trade on specialized exchanges.

### Fiscal Facts

Futures trading is regulated by a federal agency: The Commodity Futures Trading Commission (CFTC). The CFTC, in turn, oversees the National Futures Association (NFA), which is the industry's self-regulating body.

Cash Prices. Listed here are cash prices for seven broad commodity categories, plus the London Metal Exchange Prices. The seven categories are:

1. Grains and Feeds (barley, bran, corn, cottonseed meal, hominy, bonemeal, oats, sorghum, soybean meal, and wheat)

2. Foods (beef carcass, broilers, butter, cheddar cheese, cocoa, coffee, eggs, flour, hams, pork bellies and loins, steers, and sugar)

3. Fats and Oils (coconut oil, corn oil, grease, lard, palm oil, soybean oil, and tallow)

4. Fibers and Textiles (burlap, cotton, and wool)

5. Metals (aluminum, copper, lead, mercury, steel scrap, tin, and zinc)

6. Miscellaneous (rubber and steer hides)

7. Precious Metals (gold, platinum, and silver)

For each of these items, the *Journal* reports the previous day's closing price. On September 3, 1998, the *Journal* reported that Top Quality Minneapolis Barley was priced at $2.10 per bushel (Note: "Minneapolis" here refers to the exchange on which the barley is traded, not a type of barley). The London Metal Exchange reports prices per metric ton for aluminum, tin, copper, lead, nickel, and zinc.

# It All Began with Farmers

The first commodity exchange in the United States, and currently the largest futures exchange, is the Chicago Board of Trade (CBOT). The CBOT was formed some 150 years ago to serve as a medium of exchange for farmers' cash crops—wheat and corn. Futures trading began shortly after the end of the Civil War. Today, futures contracts are made not only for commodities but also for:

➤ Interest rates on all kinds of notes and bonds, including Treasury bills, notes, and bonds

➤ Indices like the Dow Jones Industrials, the S&P 500, and the NASDAQ 100

➤ Currency, from the Japanese yen to the South African kruggerand

# How a Future Differs from an Option

An *option* is a right, but not an obligation, to buy or sell something at a specified price within a specified time. A *futures contract*, in contrast, is an obligation accepted by both the buyer and seller to make a specific trade at a specified time and price. Where an option buyer pays a premium, both parties in a futures contract put down a deposit, which is called *margin*.

The buyer of a future is "long" or has a "long position." A seller is "short" or has a "short position." Futures orders are entered with a broker just like stock orders.

Buying or selling futures is like trading stocks. "Long" means you own "it" (a stock, a bushel of wheat, whatever) and are betting that "it" will rise in price. "Short" means you do not intend to buy it and are betting that it will decline in price (and if it declines enough, you'll buy it then).

➤ "Market" means at the market price

➤ "Limit" means at or below the limit price to buy, at or above the limit price to sell

➤ "Stop loss" means execute the order if the contract declines (or rises) to a predetermined price, at which point the order is executed on a "best price" basis

In the old days, a futures contract could literally result in 5,000 bushels of wheat being dumped on your front lawn! Today, few contracts go to the delivery date, and when they do, delivery is acknowledged by warehouse receipts. The reason delivery rarely takes place is because the buyer doesn't really want the commodity; he or she simply wants to make money by trading it! So, at some point before delivery date, the buyer will sell, and the seller will buy, canceling the contract.

It's like a stock trade: If you buy 100 shares of General Electric at 10 a.m. and sell those 100 GE shares at noon, you no longer have a position in the stock. You probably bought the stock because you thought the price was going to go up and you could sell it for more than you paid for it. Once you've sold the stock you have what we in the biz call "no position."

**Investor's Idiom**

A *future*, or *futures contract*, is an agreement between a buyer and seller to make a specific trade at a specified future date and price. Both parties put down a deposit, called a *margin*.

# How Margins Work

When you buy a futures asset, you need to put down that deposit, called a margin. Before you can buy a future, your broker needs to be sure that you have sufficient money in your account to cover the margin.

Margin takes two forms:

➤ Initial or original—what you have to have in your account to initiate the purchase of the futures contract

➤ Maintenance—what you have to have in your account to maintain (keep) the futures contract

The initial margin is set by the exchange that trades the futures contract you are interested in purchasing. This amount will vary, depending on market conditions, but is usually around 10 percent. Your brokerage firm, however, may require a higher margin. Its decision is binding (unless you choose to take your business elsewhere).

The maintenance margin is also determined by the exchange. Typically, the maintenance margin is 75 percent of the initial margin.

**Crash Alert**

If your maintenance margin falls below the level required by your brokerage, you will receive a "margin call" warning you to put up sufficient cash to return your balance to the original margin level. If you fail to respond, your broker will liquidate your position by selling securities in your account. Maybe even the ones Grandma gave you. Yes, it's a cold, cruel world.

Here's an example: Let's say you buy a $10,000 futures contract with an initial margin of $1,000. If the contract value declines to $9,750, your margin will drop, as a result, to the maintenance level, which is $750 (75 percent of $1,000).

Why? Well, your initial margin was $1,000, but the contract's value has since declined by $250 ($10,000 – $9,750 = $250). That decline comes out of your margin, reducing it from $1,000 to $750 ($1,000 – $250 = $750). At this point, you're still okay, because your margin hasn't fallen below the maintenance level. If the contract drops further, though—to $9,500, for example—your margin is cut to $500. You will be informed that you must deposit an additional $500 to bring your account back up to the initial margin of $1,000.

This simple example shows just how risky futures contracts can be. A small move in the price of the underlying commodity translates to a large dollar gain or loss for the contract holder.

## Using Futures to Offset Uncertainty

Why do people mess with these risky investments? Because, just as with options, there are hedgers and there are speculators. Speculators are in the market to "make a killing" (or get killed). Hedgers are trying to offset a future unknown. Let's look at a couple of examples of how ordinary people use futures contracts as hedges against risk and uncertainty.

Suppose you're a cotton farmer. The current price of 74¢ per pound would provide you with a decent profit, but your crop won't be ready to go on the market for another six months. What if the price of cotton declines to 60¢ per pound by then? You could be wiped out. So, you sell (go short) March '99 cotton futures. If cotton does drop to 60¢, you make money on your short—the premium for which you sold it. This money offsets the loss on your "cash" crop. If cotton stays at 74¢, you can cover your short position by purchasing a contract at 74¢. Now you have a loss, but you can offset it with the profitable sale of your cash crop.

Here's another example: Suppose you are a home builder about to open up a new development. You accept contracts for completion of new homes six to nine months from now. You've agreed to sell each house at a fixed price—but what if lumber prices go through the roof in the next six months and eat up all your profit?

Well, you could buy lumber futures at $288.70 per 1,000 board feet. If the price of lumber goes up, you have two choices:

1. You could pay the higher price for the lumber and offset it by selling your lumber futures contract for a profit. Remember, if the price of lumber has gone up past $288.70 per 1,000 board feet, somebody out there will be happy to buy your contract.

2. You could accept delivery of the lumber from your futures contract.

What if the price of lumber goes down? Well, the loss on the contract is offset with the lower price you actually pay for your lumber. Either way, you've hedged very nicely. This is a form of insurance, and that's what a hedger is looking for.

# Financial Futures

Financial futures currently dominate the futures market. How would an investor use financial futures to hedge? Suppose you are the proud owner of a $1 million equity portfolio (taxable). You have a feeling that stock prices are going to start falling, but you're not absolutely sure, and if you sell some or all of your stocks and prices rise, you've lost an opportunity. And incurred taxable capital gains. You look in *The Wall Street Journal* on September 4, 1998, and under the Future Prices heading you see the following:

## DJ Industrial Average (CBOT) – $10 Times Average

|        | Open | High | Low  | Settle | Chg | High | Low  | Open Interest |
|--------|------|------|------|--------|-----|------|------|---------------|
| Sept   | 7780 | 7785 | 7580 | 7723   | –52 | 9418 | 7150 | 16,747        |
| Dec    | 7860 | 7830 | 7650 | 7792   | –52 | 9515 | 7415 | 2554          |
| Mar 99 | 7780 | 7870 | 7730 | 7856   | –53 | 9586 | 7550 | 992           |

These are futures contracts on the Dow Jones Industrial Average. *Open, high, low,* and *settle* are the prices for the previous day, September 3, 1998. *Chg* is the change in price for that day's trading. Here, it's –52 points. High and low are the lifetime high and low prices for the contracts, and open interest is the number of outstanding contracts.

If your portfolio is fairly similar to the Dow Jones Industrials, you could use these futures contracts to neutralize the negative effect a market decline would have on the value of your portfolio.

The March contract, for example, is valued at 7856 × $10 = $78,560. Your $1 million equity portfolio divided by $78,560 per contract would require 12.7 contracts ($1,000,000 ÷ $78,560) to neutralize a market decline. You could buy 12 or 13 contracts and plan to sell them for March 1999 delivery. If the market declines, your profit on the sale of the contract offsets your "paper" (unrealized loss) on your equity portfolio. If the market goes up, your equity portfolio appreciation offsets the loss on your contract.

Note, however, that if the market declines, and you close out your contracts at a profit, that profit will be taxed at ordinary income tax rates (you have to hold an investment for at least a year to get the better capital gains tax rate). Hence, this hedging works much better for tax-deferred accounts. The taxable investor fearing a market decline has three options:

1. Use futures contracts, accepting the margin costs and tax consequences

2. Sell stocks, incurring capital gains and commission dollar consequences

3. Do nothing and ride out the potential storm

As we've noted throughout this book, over time the stock market has consistently recovered from even the most wrenching declines. Individual investors do best when they choose option 3, and just ride it out. But we thought you should know a little about financial futures anyway, if only to impress somebody.

# Options on Futures. Oy!

Options on futures contracts are about as risky as you can get. Like regular options, options on futures are a right, not an obligation, to buy or sell. As with regular options, you can either buy calls or sell puts. Interest rate options on futures, especially on Treasury bonds, are extra hot right now.

In *The Wall Street Journal*, under "Futures Options Prices," you will find "Interest Rate," and under that subheading the following:

T-Bonds (CBT)

$100,000; points and 64ths of 100%

If you wanted to purchase March 1999 call options with a strike price of 126, your premium would be 3–18. Since the option is quoted in 64ths, 3–18 means 3 $^{18}/_{64}$, or 3.28125. Each premium point amounts to $1,000, so the premium would cost you 3.28125 times $1,000, or $3,281.25. You can also buy puts/calls on stock index futures.

The contracts are for specific months and can extend out to two years.

# Spread Strategies for Speculators

Speculators toy with all these different futures contracts. Spreads are one of the more famous commodity futures strategies used by speculators. Typically, the speculator is looking for the price differential to widen or narrow between two different crops, like wheat and oats. He buys a futures contract on the commodity he expects to go up more in price, and sells a contract on the other. What happens to the spread in price between the two commodities is critical, not whether one or both go up or down in price.

If you expect oats to increase in price versus wheat, for example, you would buy an oats contract and sell a wheat contract. If you're right, you can make a lot of money. If you're wrong, you can lose a bundle. That's why it's called speculation.

## Program Trading

"Program trading" is an expression you've probably heard on the news to describe why the stock market went up or down sharply in the last hour or so of a trading day. Program traders work for large institutions and set up automated hedges that are triggered when the market hits certain key prices. In effect, they establish a spread—between the S&P 500 Index and a future contract on the index, for example.

When the spread widens because the future price rises, program traders automatically sell futures and buy the index. If the spread narrows via a lower futures price, they sell the index and buy the futures contract. Because the process tends to be highly automated, several institutions buying or selling large sums at any given time can have a dramatic impact on the stock market.

# Gold Nuggets

Earlier in this chapter, just for fun, we showed you where to find prices for all kinds of commodities in *The Wall Street Journal*. Unless you're a farmer or building bridges, these markets should not concern you, with one possible exception: precious metals.

For centuries, the civilized (and sometimes not-so-civilized) world measured wealth in gold. Paper currencies were backed by it, dreams were spun from it, and wars were fought for it. It was, without exception, the one insurance policy against the ravages of inflation. In this country, some 25 years ago, President Richard Nixon severed the last direct tie between our currency and gold, freeing the dollar to seek its ultimate value. With the quadrupling of

**Fiscal Facts**

Whether gold will ever regain even a vestige of its former allure is open to question. "Gold bugs" argue vociferously that the only long-term financial discipline for individual nations in a global economy is direct linkage of local currencies to gold. Fortunately or unfortunately (depending on your views), national leaders don't want to have their economic policies limited by a fixed amount of currency in circulation.

oil prices and double-digit inflation during Nixon's term, gold had soared from around $30 per ounce to over $800 per ounce. It currently trades for less than $300 per ounce.

As a result of the severance of gold's link with the dollar, investors no longer view gold as a monetary asset, but rather as a commodity. If this view is correct, gold will trade in the same wide cyclical ranges as other commodities, and will attract more speculators than investors. Will gold wrench back its rightful role of inflation hedge from the current holder: the U.S. dollar? We think it's possible, having seen the dollar's value fluctuate over the years and the varying degree of respect shown to it by other nations. Right now the dollar is king, but we don't subscribe to those who think its reign will last forever.

The question for you, the investor, is whether you should own some or no gold. The answer depends entirely on how you feel about inflation and the dollar. If you decide to own some gold, we suggest that it compose no more than 5–10 percent of your total portfolio.

**Super Strategy**

How to hold gold (and other precious metals): You can buy and store gold bars or coins, but these provide no income return, and storage—even in a safe deposit box—costs money. A better strategy is to hold shares of precious metals companies or precious metals mutual funds.

## Precious Metal Companies and Funds

Because we're your pals, here's a list in alphabetical order of 10 precious metal companies, along with phone numbers and exchange list/ticker symbols:

1. Barrick Gold Corp. NYSE ABX 416-861-9911

2. Battle Mountain GoldCo. NYSE BMG 713-650-6400

3. Coeur D'Alene Mines Corp. NYSE CDE 208-667-3511

4. DeBeers Consolidated Mines NASDAQ DBRSY (Diamonds) 36 Stockdale Street, Kimberly 8300, South Africa

5. Echo Bay Mines Ltd. ASE ECO 303-714-8600

6. Franco-Nevada Mining TSE (Toronto Stock Exchange) FN 416-480-6480

7. Hecla Mining Co. NYSE HL 208-769-4100

8. Homestake Mining NYSE HM 415-981-8150

9. Newmont Mining Corp. NYSE NEM 303-863-7414

10. Placer Dome Inc. NYSE PDG 604-682-7082

If you prefer the diversification of mutual funds (and, as you well know by now, we do), the five largest no-load precious metal funds, listed alphabetically, are:

1. American Century Global Gold 800-345-2021

2. Invesco Strategic Gold 800-525-8085

3. Midas Funds 800-400-6432

4. Scudder Gold Fund 800-225-2470

5. Vanguard Special Gold and Precious Metals 800-662-7447

---

### The Least You Need to Know

➤ A futures contract is a binding agreement between two parties. One agrees to purchase from the other a specified asset at a specified price at a specified time in the future.

➤ A commodity is a basic food or raw material.

➤ When you buy a futures asset, you need to put down a 10 percent deposit, called a margin.

➤ Futures are used to hedge against anticipated changes in prices.

➤ If you want some precious metal in your portfolio, consider shares in mining companies or in precious metal mutual funds.

# Chapter 23

# Realizing Real Estate Dreams

---

## In This Chapter

➤ Bad reasons to invest in real estate

➤ REITs—great "hands-off" real estate investments

➤ How rental income hits your tax return

➤ What to look for in a location

---

Everybody needs a place to live, and in Chapter 15 we talked about how to put a roof over your head and finance it, too. In this chapter we take a look at real estate as investment, not just shelter.

## Why Own Real Estate?

Investors are attracted to real estate for many of the same reasons they own common stocks and bonds. Most of the reasons investors cite for wanting to include real estate in their portfolios, however, are not all that strong. Let's take a look:

1. Income. Real estate can generate income (rent!). With real estate, the income you earn from the investment is the difference between the rental income you receive and your operating expenses. Bonds and most stocks also generate income, however, and it's typically more reliable and secure than the income coming from a rental property. This is especially true of U.S. Government securities and high quality, above-average-growth common stocks.

2. Appreciation. Real estate's value can increase over time. But, again, so can stocks and, to a limited degree, bonds.

3. Leverage. Real estate can be bought on leverage. You might, for example, put $20,000 down to buy a $100,000 property. If the property's value increases 10 percent in two years, or $10,000, you've made a 50 percent return on your $20,000 investment. Of course, if the property's value declines 10 percent, you lose 50 percent! If the leverage game appeals to you (it doesn't to us), you can satisfy it with less hassle using options or futures.

# The REIT Stuff

We hate to break it to you if you had visions of becoming the next Donald Trump, but there's another reason real estate may not be a great investment for taxable accounts—gains on real estate are taxed as ordinary income! You don't get that nice capital gains tax break you get when you hold stocks or bonds for over one year.

There is one way you can rake in some of the benefits of investing in real estate while avoiding the potential tax hit. Real Estate Investment Trusts (REITs), which were created in 1960, are exempt from taxes as long as they distribute at least 95 percent of their operating income to the shareholders and as long as they invest primarily in real estate. All the larger REITs are listed on either the New York or American stock exchanges.

Because operating income typically exceeds net or reported income, a portion of the income received by the shareholder and reported on Form 1099 is considered a tax-deferred return of capital. This means, among other things, that that portion may be converted to capital gains income and taxed at capital gains rates.

## Types of REITs

There are three categories of REITs:

1. Equity REITs invest primarily in real estate properties.

2. Mortgage REITs invest primarily in real estate mortgages.

3. Hybrid REITs invest in a combination of properties and mortgages.

### Super Strategy

We recommend that you exclude mortgage REITs and concentrate on equity and hybrid REITs. Mortgage REITs fill basically the same purpose in your portfolio as fixed-income securities, and, as we've discussed throughout this book, Treasuries are your best bet there. If you insist on a mortgage-based product, focus on three U.S. Government-created agencies discussed previously: Federal National Mortgage Association, Federal Home Loan Mortgage Corporation, and the Government National Mortgage Association. Their short names are: Fannie Mae, Freddie Mac, and Ginnie Mae, respectively.

REITs respond to two different investment stimuli: the bond market and the real estate market. They are considered conservative investments and tend to mimic the bond market. On the other hand, they are sensitive to trends in their particular real estate market (apartments, commercial or shopping centers, and industrial structures/parks). They are especially sensitive to trends in property values and rental rates. As a result, prices of REITs often run counter to the general stock market.

## Emphasize Quality and Safety

If you want to pursue REITs for 5–10 percent of your equity portfolio, we strongly suggest that you emphasize quality and safety. To get you started, we have taken the REITs followed by Value Line and isolated those with at least a 2 safety rank (1 being highest), and a B++ financial strength rating. And the winners are...

| Name | Symbol | Type of Investments |
|------|--------|---------------------|
| Archstone Communities | ASN | Mixed/Apartments |
| BRE Properties | BRE | Apartments |
| Federal Realty | FTT | Shopping Centers |
| New Plan Realty | NPR | Shopping Malls/Apartments |
| Weingarten Realty | WRI | Shopping Centers |

Please note that these ratings are as of July 31, 1998; you should check current ratings before buying any of these REITs.

# Types of Real Estate Ownership

A REIT is as far removed from the day-to-day management as you can get and still retain the basic benefits of real estate investing. More hands-on types of investment in real estate include:

1. Single ownership: you and you alone.

2. Partnership: a way to finance the purchase of larger, more expensive buildings. Partnerships don't always go smoothly, so be sure you have the right or option to buy a controlling interest.

3. Corporation: not a good move for the individual investor because you will end up paying taxes at both corporate and individual levels. Also, you lose the tax shelter benefit of deducting any depreciation on your property from your personal income.

4. Limited Partnership: We delve into this type of ownership in greater detail in Chapter 24. But, basically, a limited partnership comprises a general partner and a number of limited partners (including you). This form was popular in the previous decade but has dropped in popularity because investors have realized how hard it can be to sell your share in the partnership and get your money back. Liquidity and marketability are drawbacks of limited partnerships. Limited partnerships are also used for energy (oil and gas) investments.

# So, You Want to Own Real Estate

If we haven't talked you out of investing in real estate yet, here are the eight basic forms of real estate you can explore:

1. Duplex. Typically, you live in one half and rent out the other half.

2. Apartment Building. Here again, you could live "on site," or retain a resident manager to live on site and perform necessary odd jobs. Depending on the size and age of the building, you might need a property manager. The property manager would be responsible for collecting rents, paying bills, maintaining the grounds, contracting for repairs, etc. This could run you up to 10 percent of your gross rental income from the building.

3. Hotels/Motels. Years ago, "Ma and Pa" motels were fairly common, but the chains have turned this into a tough business. The "bed and breakfast" business, though a charming fantasy for many beleaguered urban couples, is even tougher. Sure, that cozy inn in Vermont looked good on Bob Newhart's show, but bear in mind that to run a bed and breakfast you've got to be on call 24 hours a day as chef, handyman, and concierge.

4. Office Buildings. Unlike singles, duplexes, and apartment buildings, office buildings rent on a per-square-foot basis. Leases are usually longer for offices—five years with additional option years, for example, compared to one/two year rentals for residential property.

5. Shopping Centers. Mini-malls, medium-size malls (with one major or anchor tenant plus local tenants), larger malls (two anchors, one on each end plus local stores in between), and super regional malls, like the Mall of America—this country loves malls. But unless you're very wealthy, you probably wouldn't be invited to invest in the partnerships and corporations that own most malls. If you invest in REITs, though, you'll end up with a piece of the action, as most REITs eventually own the best shopping centers.

6. Warehouses and Industrial Buildings.

7. Mobile Home Parks.

8. Land.

Land is the most speculative real estate investment because there is no depreciation to help cut your taxes and no rental income. You could sell cutting rights to a logger or grazing/planting rights to ranchers/farmers, but that's about it. You could get lucky and sell out for big bucks to a developer. But while you're waiting, you'll be paying taxes and loan payments (if you borrowed to purchase the land). We maintain that the only really good reason to buy land is if you intend to build a home for yourself on it. Then again, there is only a fixed amount of land. In the spirit of Will Rogers: "Buy land, they ain't makin' any more of it."

# Purchase and Rental of Homes and Apartment Buildings

In Chapter 15 we discussed the purchase vs. rental decision, pointing out that owning a home at the first opportune moment is not necessarily the best move. Let's review these thoughts, as they also apply to buying real estate as an investment.

## *Financially Prepared and Market-Wise*

First and foremost, be financially prepared and market-wise. "Financially prepared" means, ideally, to have your down payment set aside. Having to hustle up the down payment by selling assets for cash or borrowing (mortgaging your future) is not smart. Also, you should already have spoken to a mortgage banker to ensure that you will qualify for the mortgage. In fact, if you can be preapproved, it adds to your attraction as a prospective buyer. Check with a realtor or mortgage banker about what you need to do to be preapproved.

"Market-wise" means you know what's available in the area where you would like to own and have researched the prices of the types of properties you want to own. Market-wise also means you've regularly taken the market's pulse for at least a year. You can tell when it's rising sharply, flat, or declining—and you can spot a buying opportunity.

Many newspapers include information on recent home/condo sales to assist you. Brokers will also give you data on recent sales and trends. The Sunday *New York Times*, for example, listed a home in New Jersey on September 20, 1998, that sold for several thousand dollars more than the asking price, in less than a week. What does that indicate about that market? Several other homes in the area also sold within one/two weeks of listing, very close to the asking price. This is a sign of a hot—if not over-heated—residential real estate market.

# How Rental Income Hits Your Tax Return

Let's say you're about to make your first foray into real estate investment by renting out a home that you own. How does the rental income hit your income tax statement? See the following page for an example of what Schedule E (Supplemental Income and Loss) of Form 1040 would look like, assuming that the rental contract begins July 1.

Because it's a July 1 rental, you are going to record 5/12 of your annual income and expenses. And in this case, the tenant is paying (or reimbursing) you for telephone, heat, and electricity, but not cable TV (which is the $137 next to Line 18). Now, let's go over this form blow by blow:

➤ Under Line 1 you would put "residential property" and the specific address.

➤ Line 2 is primarily for people who rent out a second or vacation home. You are entitled to up to 14 days for your personal use. If you use the home for more than 14 days, your tax situation gets more complicated, and you should work with an accountant.

➤ Line 3 is actual rents received. $10,000 is equivalent to a monthly rent of $2,000 (times 5 months).

➤ Line 8 is the broker's commission of 10 percent.

➤ Line 9 is homeowner's insurance, again apportioned.

➤ Line 12 is mortgage interest (but not any portion allocable to principal paydown).

➤ Line 16 is real estate taxes.

➤ Line 18 is the aforementioned cable bills.

➤ Line 19 is the subtotal of expenses.

➤ Line 20 is depreciation.

➤ Line 21 is total expenses after depreciation.

➤ Line 22 is a loss, but one that we cannot use unless we have a gain in other "passive"(e.g., real estate) income.

| SCHEDULE E | Supplemental Income and Loss | OMB No. 1545-0074 |
|---|---|---|

**SCHEDULE E**
**(Form 1040)**

Department of the Treasury
Internal Revenue Service    (99)

## Supplemental Income and Loss
**(From rental real estate, royalties, partnerships,**
**S corporations, estates, trusts, REMICs, etc.)**
➤ **Attach to Form 1040 or Form 1041.**    ➤ **See Instructions for Schedule E (Form 1040).**

OMB No. 1545-0074
**1998**
Attachment
Sequence No. **13**

Name(s) shown on return

Your social security number

**Part I**   Income or Loss From Rental Real Estate and Royalties   Note: *Report income and expenses from your business of renting personal property on Schedule C or C-EZ (see page E-1). Report farm rental income or loss from Form 4835 on page 2, line 39.*

| 1 | Show the kind and location of each **rental real estate property:** | 2 For each rental real estate property listed on line 1, did you or your family use it during the tax year for personal purposes for more than the greater of: | Yes | No |
|---|---|---|---|---|
| A | **Residential Property** | • 14 days, **or** | A | XX |
| B | | • 10% of the total days rented at fair rental value? | B | |
| C | | (See page E-1.) | C | |

| Income: | | | Properties | | | Totals (Add columns A, B, and C) | |
|---|---|---|---|---|---|---|---|
| | | | A | B | C | | |
| 3 | Rents received . . . . . . | 3 | 10,000 | | | 3 | 10,000 |
| 4 | Royalties received . . . . . | 4 | | | | 4 | |
| **Expenses:** | | | | | | | |
| 5 | Advertising . . . . . . . | 5 | | | | | |
| 6 | Auto and travel (see page E-2) . | 6 | | | | | |
| 7 | Cleaning and maintenance . . . | 7 | | | | | |
| 8 | Commissions . . . . . . . | 8 | 1,000 | | | | |
| 9 | Insurance . . . . . . . | 9 | 195 | | | | |
| 10 | Legal and other professional fees | 10 | | | | | |
| 11 | Management fees . . . . . . | 11 | | | | | |
| 12 | Mortgage interest paid to banks, etc. (see page E-2) . . . . . | 12 | 5,546 | | | 12 | 5,546 |
| 13 | Other interest . . . . . . | 13 | | | | | |
| 14 | Repairs . . . . . . . . | 14 | | | | | |
| 15 | Supplies . . . . . . . . | 15 | | | | | |
| 16 | Taxes . . . . . . . . . | 16 | 1,700 | | | | |
| 17 | Utilities . . . . . . . . | 17 | | | | | |
| 18 | Other (list) ➤ .................. .................. .................. .................. | 18 | 137 | | | | |
| 19 | Add lines 5 through 18 . . . . | 19 | 8,578 | | | 19 | 8,576 |
| 20 | Depreciation expense or depletion (see page E-2) . . . . . . | 20 | 5,388 | | | 20 | 5,388 |
| 21 | Total expenses. Add lines 19 and 20 | 21 | 13,966 | | | | |
| 22 | Income or (loss) from rental real estate or royalty properties. Subtract line 21 from line 3 (rents) or line 4 (royalties). If the result is a (loss), see page E-3 to find out if you must file **Form 6198** . . . | 22 | 3,966 | | | | |
| 23 | Deductible rental real estate loss. **Caution:** *Your rental real estate loss on line 22 may be limited. See page E-3 to find out if you must file* **Form 8582**. *Real estate professionals must complete line 42 on page 2* . . . . . . | 23 | ( 0 )( )( ) | | ) | | |
| 24 | **Income.** Add positive amounts shown on line 22. **Do not** include any losses . . . . . . . | | | | | 24 | |
| 25 | **Losses.** Add royalty losses from line 22 and rental real estate losses from line 23. Enter total losses here | | | | | 25 ( | ) |
| 26 | Total rental real estate and royalty income or (loss). Combine lines 24 and 25. Enter the result here. If Parts II, III, IV, and line 39 on page 2 do not apply to you, also enter this amount on Form 1040, line 17. Otherwise, include this amount in the total on line 40 on page 2 . . . . . . . . . . | | | | | 26 | |

**For Paperwork Reduction Act Notice, see Form 1040 instructions.**          Cat. No. 11344L          **Schedule E (Form 1040) 1998**

Note that even though we can't use the tax loss, we still have a "profit" of $1,422 (Line 3 less Line 19) on which we have no tax due. Pretty snazzy.

# Location, Location, Location

Location, location, location: the three rules of real estate investing! But what's "location?" Let's define it this way (you want as many of the following as possible):

1. Good Schools. Good schools act like a magnet (who doesn't want their kids to go to a good school?). They are the first thing many potential buyers or renters look for when planning a move into the area.

2. Low Taxes. You can avoid high property taxes, in part, by avoiding smaller municipalities where the school, police, and fire costs are spread over a smaller taxable populace. But high taxes are only one issue; the other is the rate of increase in taxes. Rapidly growing townships often mean rapidly increasing costs and, for you, higher tax bills. So, look for areas that are already largely built up.

3. Convenience. Buy property with easy access to main roads or arteries as well as convenient public transportation to shops, entertainment, and places of worship.

These are the three issues that will be important to whoever rents or buys your property.

# Financing Real Estate Investments

A mortgage is a generic product, and there is no advantage to shopping around with local banks, except that they may be familiar with the property you want to buy. Remember, the mortgage amount is driven by the appraised value of the property, and banks tend to use the same limited list of appraisers.

You want a mortgage at the lowest rate (excluding points that you do not want to pay) per term (15 years,

20 years, 30 years, or adjustable). The term depends on your ability to pay—a 15-year will cost you about 30 percent more per month than a 30-year, but will enable you to reduce the mortgage principal much more rapidly. An adjustable rate is initially quite low but can rise beyond a 30-year mortgage's rate quickly, especially when interest rates are rising.

The first thing you should do when seeking a mortgage on a property is check the yield curve. The *yield curve* is the difference in yield between one interest rate and another, as it would appear on a graph. If the line between the two yield points is steep, there's obviously a big difference between the yields. If it's flat, there's very little difference.

If the yield curve is flat, there is no incentive to opt for an adjustable-rate mortgage (ARM), and the "spread" (yield difference) between 15-year and 30-year mortgages may not lead you to a 15-year mortgage. Check with your broker, check all the local mortgage companies locally yourself, and check further on the Internet.

Best of luck making your real estate dreams come true!

**Fiscal Facts**

Want to use the Internet for online quotes? Here are three websites:

1. E-loan at **http://www. eloan.com**

2. Quicken Home and Mortgage at **http://www. quicken.com/mortgage**

3. HomeShark at **http://www. homeshark.com**

## The Least You Need to Know

➤ Most of the goals investors cite for wanting to include real estate in their portfolios would be better met by investments in stocks and bonds.

➤ The 1986 Tax Reform Act rules that real estate losses can be used only to offset real estate income, thus ending one of the best reasons for individual investors to own real estate—the tax break.

➤ Gains on real estate are taxed at income tax rates, not at capital gains rates.

➤ Real Estate Investment Trusts (REITs) are an opportunity to rake in some of the benefits of investing in real estate while avoiding the potential tax hit.

➤ Don't buy mortgage REITs; concentrate on equity and hybrid REITs.

# Chapter 24

# Alternative Investments

**In This Chapter**

➤ Investments once available only to the rich

➤ Exploring hedge, venture capital, and LBO funds

➤ Investing in business dealings via private equity funds and limited partnerships

➤ Pros and cons of UITs and SPDRs

"We're so glad we've had this time together...." Sorry, got caught up in a Carol Burnett moment. But seriously, we hope you've enjoyed this book. If you've read all (okay, most) of the chapters, you now have a solid grounding in investment basics that will help you sail through your financial life. You've also explored some fun stuff, like options, futures, and precious metals. In this, our final chapter, we'll zip through a few of the "alternative investments" that used to be discussed only in exclusive country clubs among millionaires but have, in the last decade, become available to the average investor (that's you!).

## How Regular Folk Discovered Alternative Investments

"Alternative investments" are equity products like hedge funds or venture capital funds that used to strictly be the province of very wealthy investors, large public and private retirement plans, or universities with huge endowments like Harvard or Yale. These funds used to require $10–$20 million minimum investments, so they were only reasonable investments for people or institutions who had at least 10 times that much in their portfolios—because you wouldn't want to invest more than 5–10 percent of your portfolio in these investments.

A few years back, however, two events occurred that introduced alternative investments to the rest of us. One was a made-for-TV movie on HBO called "Barbarians at the Gate," which depicted, in an entertaining way, the efforts of firms like Kohlberg Kravis Roberts (KKR) to take over R.J. Reynolds via a "leveraged buyout."

In a *leveraged buyout* (LBO), one firm will offer to buy up any and all stock of another company at a price significantly higher than the current trading price of the stock. The idea is that the stockholders will be so excited by this higher price that they will sell all their stock to the takeover company. Once KKR owns all of R.J. Reynolds stock, for example, it owns R.J. Reynolds and can do with it what it will. And what it will do is send in a team to pare down debt and cut costs (meaning fire lots of people), making the revamped R.J. Reynolds lean and mean and very attractive to new potential stockholders. Then it will take the firm public again, selling its stock and making a fortune on the sale.

The second event was the media spotlight turned on investors like George Soros, whose hedge funds were blamed by several national leaders for adversely affecting and artificially manipulating currency values around the world.

# Hedge Funds

Hedge funds historically had limited the number of investors to fewer than 100 participants, which meant that they didn't have to register under the Investment Company Act of 1940 ("The '40 Act"). Because they are unregistered, hedge funds can invest in currencies, commodities, public stocks and bonds, or whatever they like, and can do so by going long (buying), going short (selling borrowed shares), or using options and futures, etc.

### Investor's Idiom

A *hedge fund* is an unregistered investment fund whose managers can pretty much do whatever they want—invest in currencies or commodities, go short or long, use options and futures, etc. Some funds are very conservative. Others are quite aggressive and make all kinds of risky currency and interest rate plays.

# Venture Capital and LBO Funds

While hedge funds move in and out of markets quickly, basically speculating with options and futures and the like, other funds invest for the long haul in new or recently created businesses. These "private equity" funds are more like partnerships than traditional mutual funds. With a straightforward mutual fund, you own shares in whatever publicly traded stocks the mutual fund managers buy. Private equity funds invest in privately owned businesses that do not have stock trading in a public market.

Venture capital funds, for instance, provide the capital for start-up businesses. Investors in a venture capital fund are limited partners. The manager of the fund is the general partner.

Leveraged buyout funds are also proliferating. LBOs use primarily, if not entirely, borrowed money to purchase the outstanding stock of a publicly traded company by offering to purchase it from stockholders at a premium. This turns that company from a public to a private company, owned by the LBO's investors. Then the LBO team rigorously reduces the company's costs, pays down its debt, and takes it public once again—kind of like taking a race car with a blown engine off the track, rebuilding the engine, and putting it back on the track.

The rewards? Industry data is hard to come by since there are no reporting requirements for these funds, but they seek to do at least 150 percent better than the Standard & Poor's 500 Index.

# The Private Equity Fund of Funds

Historically, as we said, investment in hedge funds and private equity funds was limited to large institutional investors and wealthy individuals. In effect, Wall Street was servicing Park Avenue. In part, because of the voracious appetite for new capital, Wall Street, along with some major trust banks, have introduced a new concept: the private equity fund of funds. This doesn't mean Wall Street is serving Main Street U.S.A., but it is a step in that direction.

A private equity fund of funds also has a general partner (GP) and investors who are limited partners (LPs). The GP receives typically a 1–2 percent annual fee, and a 5 percent share of the profits. What does the GP do? The GP selects other private equity funds (typically 10–15) in which to invest.

If you are a limited partner in a private equity fund of funds, you become, essentially, a limited partner in whatever funds your GP chooses to buy.

## What You Need to Qualify for a Fund of Funds

How do you get to be an LP in a private equity fund of funds? Let's start with financial requirements. A limited partnership interest typically requires a

**Fiscal Facts**

Unlike publicly traded funds, which are corporate entities owned by shareholders, private equity funds are partnerships. More specifically, there is a general partner, who creates the fund, and limited partners who provide the capital. Typically, the general partner (GP) receives a 1–2 percent annual fee for managing the fund, and 20 percent of the profits realized. The limited partners (LP) receive the remaining 80 percent of the profits (after the return of their capital).

**Investor's Idiom**

A *venture capital fund* invests in new businesses by providing start-up capital. The investors in a venture capital fund are limited partners in the businesses in which the fund invests and are entitled to a share of its profits. A leveraged buyout fund, on the other hand, borrows money to buy a company, revamp it, and take it public. Investors profit from what the LBO fund makes when it resells the company's stock.

minimum commitment of $500,000. This doesn't mean you write out a check for $500,000 and sit back to wait for the profits to roll in. (For one, who has an extra $500,000 just lying around?) It means that over the next three to six years you will receive "calls" to kick in as much as $500,000, typically in 5 percent pieces ($25,000), with the first 5 percent due when you sign the partnership papers. Obviously, this is a much easier check to write out!

Because the partnership interests are not registered as securities under the Securities Act of 1933, you also have to qualify as an "accredited investor." This is defined as someone with more than $1 million of net worth or more than $200,000 ($300,000 if filed/ filing joint return) of adjusted gross income (remember what that is?) for the previous two years and expected for the current year.

On top of that, you are required to affirm that you are acquiring your LP interest as an investment and not for resale or distribution, and that you will not assign or transfer your interest without the consent of the GP. Got that? Now you can dazzle your cocktail crowd!

But wait, there's more! Congress also stated in a follow-up bill passed in 1940 that to participate in a limited partnership you must also be a "qualified purchaser." Today that's typically defined as meaning that you must have more than $5 million in investments (stocks, bonds, real estate held for investment purposes, commodities, and cash all qualify). How did Congress know back in 1933 and 1940 what current dollar worth would qualify someone as an "accredited investor" and a "qualified purchaser"? They didn't. What they did do was entrust the Securities and Exchange Commission (SEC) to establish and revise, from time to time, the definitions of an "accredited investor" and a "qualified purchaser." The General Partner (GP) of a limited partnership knows that if any of his limited partners is not qualified, the GP could lose his or her exclusion from the '33 Act and '40 Act. Therefore, the GP takes on the responsibility and ultimate authority to approve your application to be a limited partner.

## How Limited Partnership Works

Assuming you are approved to invest as a limited partner in a fund of funds, what is the sequence of events?

1. You will honor the first capital call, which is 5 percent of your total commitment at the closing. So, if you have agreed to a total commitment of $500,000, you will write out a check for $25,000 at the closing.

2. You will receive additional capital calls of, say, 5 percent over the first six years or so.

3. You may begin to receive distributions (moolah!) from the fund as early as the third year.

4. As a limited partner, you are entitled to a return of your "invested" capital, plus a pre-determined return (called the "preferred return").

5. After the LPs receive back their invested capital and the preferred return, the GP is entitled to a "carried interest amount" equal to 5 percent of the "carried interest account." The carried interest account is the difference between the aggregate portfolio distributions and the invested capital—in other words, 5 percent of the gain. This is called a "catch-up distribution."

6. After #4 and #5 have been honored, subsequent distributions are split (e.g., 5 percent GP, 95 percent LPs).

7. The fund will last for the number of years in the contract or until all assets are distributed, whichever occurs last.

**Crash Alert**

If you fail to honor a capital call from a limited partnership within 20 days you could, at the least, face interest charges, and at the worst, run the risk of having your interest sold for as little as 50 percent of book value. You definitely don't want to miss a call!

# Pros and Cons of LP Investments

There are several points to consider before getting involved with a fund of funds:

1. You will receive an IRS Form K-1 to use to report partnership income each year. These are not usually available to meet the April 15 tax deadline, however. You can choose to either file an amended return or pay 110 percent of the previous year's taxes. We recommend that you choose the latter option.

2. Because your fund has multiple fund holdings and multiple investment holdings in each fund, you will probably face state tax returns in at least several states other than your own.

So, if you are able to invest and decide that investing in an LP is for you, keep in mind the following advantages:

1. Potentially (and historically) superior returns to the public equity market

2. A diversified portfolio of private equity investments

3. An opportunity to participate in an equity class traditionally reserved for very wealthy individuals

...and disadvantages:

1. These are risky and illiquid investments.

2. You have to make a very long-term commitment to the fund.

3. The tax filing requirements are a pain in the neck.

# Unit Investment Trusts

Another alternative investment product that might be dangled in front of you at some point is Unit Investment Trusts, or UITs. This is a hybrid product within the mutual fund category. UITs have two distinguishing characteristics: front-end loads (remember them?) and a fixed maturity or termination. Originally, UITs were fixed-income products that provided investors with a predetermined sum at a fixed rate.

More recently, equity UITs have been developed, the most notable being the "Dogs of the Dow." The concept is simple: the UIT invests in the 10 highest-yielding or the 10 worst-performing stocks in the Dow Jones Industrial Average. The trust matures after one year, and you "rollover" (if you wish to continue the game) into another new UIT, repeating the process every year. The original "load" may be $2^3/_4$–3 percent, and the rollover load may run $1^3/_4$–2 percent.

Although the management fees are low (approaching those of index funds), we think the loads make the product, which is sold by brokers, pricey compared to mutual funds or individually investing. There is one possible exception: SPDRs.

# Along Came a SPDR

Standard & Poor's Depository Receipts (SPDRs) are American Stock Exchange–traded securities that represent ownership in the SPDR Trust. The Trust, in turn, is a UIT that holds securities intended to track the performance of the Standard & Poor's 500 Stock Index.

**Super Strategy**

SPDRs are very marketable, and, almost without exception, they are the most actively traded stock on the American Stock Exchange each trading day. And, as with any listed stock, you can sell short as well as go long.

Specifically, the shares attempt to represent one-tenth of the value of the S&P 500. So, if the S&P 500 closes on any given day at 1,000, the SPDRs would close at an approximate price of $100. They are listed on the American Stock Exchange with the symbol SPX, and if you purchase them, you pay only a commission, not a load. Like other stocks, SPDRs trade in round lots of 100, and can also be purchased in odd-lot numbers. Total expenses are 18.45/100 of one percent (0.1845 percent), which is competitive with most, if not all, S&P 500 Index mutual funds. More recently, MidCap SPDRs (symbol MDX) have been introduced. These trade on the American Stock Exchange and track the S&P MidCap 400 Index.

The SPDR Trust has an interesting termination date: January 22, 2118, or (according to the Standard & Poor's Depository Receipts SPDR Trust, Series 1 Prospectus) "the date 20 years after the death of the last survivor of 11 people named in the trust agreement, the oldest of whom was born in 1990 and the youngest of whom was born in 1993," whichever occurs first!

It's an interesting product! And no doubt the investment world will continue developing new products for you, the savvy individual investor. Be smart, and have fun!

### Investor's Idiom

Standard & Poor's Depository Receipts (SPDRs) are a subset of Unit Investment Trusts, or UITs. Both are mutual fund hybrids that trade for a fixed period of time.

---

### The Least You Need to Know

➤ "Alternative investments" are equity products like hedge funds or venture capital funds that used to be strictly the province of very wealthy investors.

➤ A hedge fund is an unregistered investment fund whose managers can pretty much do whatever they want—invest in currencies or commodities, go short or long, use options and futures, etc.

➤ Private equity funds invest in privately owned businesses that do not have stock trading on the stock market.

➤ Venture capital funds provide the capital for start-up businesses.

# Useful Investing Info

## Government and Regulatory Contacts

Federal Reserve Board's World Wide web site: www.bog.frb.fed.us/PBS/Leasing/Guide.htm

Federal Trade Commission, Consumer Response Center:
For information on credit reporting agencies, call (202) 326-3761. The FTC web site is: http://www.ftc.gov.

Internal Revenue Service:
Call 1-800-424-1040 for free help with filing the 1040 income tax return. Order all tax forms from the IRS by calling 1-800-829-3676.

Securities and Exchange Commission (SEC):
The Office of Consumer Affairs
Securities and Exchange Commission
450 5th Street N.W.
Washington, D.C. 20549

Social Security Administration:
Call 1-800-772-1213 or visit http://www.ssa.gov. If you want information on Medicare, call Social Security at 1-800-772-1213 and request Publication No. 05-10043 (Medicare), which explains Medicare hospital and medical insurance.

We also recommend an excellent article in the September 1998 issue of *Consumer Reports* entitled "Medicare: New Choices, New Worries." Reprints of this special report are available for $3 per copy. Call 1-800-766-9988 or visit *Consumer Reports'* web site: www.ConsumerReports.org.

U.S. Treasury:
You may purchase T-bills directly from the U.S. Government via the Treasury Direct Program or via banks or brokers, usually for a service fee. If you buy direct from the Treasury, you can do so in person, by mail, by phone (1-800-943-6834), or via the Internet at www.publicdebt.treas.gov. To utilize the latter two alternatives, you will need to provide a signature to open your account.

## Financial Exchanges

Most exchanges will let you come in and check out their pits full of screaming traders. It's a sight (and sound) worth experiencing at least once in your life!

New York Stock Exchange (NYSE)
11 Wall Street
New York, NY 10005
(212) 656-3000

American Stock Exchange (AMEX)
86 Trinity Place
New York, NY 10006
(212) 306-1000

Other exchanges include the Chicago Mercantile Exchange, Boston Stock Exchange, Montreal Stock Exchange, and the Philadelphia Stock Exchange.

# Credit Reporting Agencies

For personal credit histories, contact:

Trans Union National
1-800-916-8800

TRW
1-800-422-4879

Equifax
1-800-685-111

If you own a business, you'll want to run a credit check on it periodically, too. The three top credit reporting agencies in this field are the following:

Dun & Bradstreet
1-800-234-3867

NCR Corp
1-800-262-7782

TRW Business Credit Services
1-800-526-0677

# Consumer Info

*Consumer Reports:*
1-800-205-2445 or visit the web site at www.ConsumerReports.org.

*Edmund's Automobile Buyer's Guide:*
www.edmund.com

*Kelley Blue Book* (indispensable when selling or trading cars):
www.kbb.com

# Investment Research

Value Line:
1-800-833-0046. A one-year subscription costs $570.

*Standard & Poor's Stock Guides*:
1-800-221-5277 or visit the web site at http://www.stockinfo.standardpoor.com.

*The Wall Street Journal:*
To order a subscription to the *Journal*, call 1-800-521-2170, ext. 247. The Internet address is http://wsj.com.

# Amazing Online Research Sites

There are some amazing research sites on the Web that you can access yourself, such as the following:

➤ www.briefing.com (analysts' upgrades and downgrades)

➤ www.hoovers.com (company profiles and financial data)

➤ www.marketguide.com (earnings estimates from First Call, insider trading from Vickers, and stock screening from Stock Quest)

➤ www.personalwealth.com (Standard & Poor's in. including Wall Street analysts' recommendations and consensus earnings estimates)

➤ www.sec.gov (essentially all Securities & Exchange Commission filings by companies)

➤ www.zacks.com (consensus earnings estimates, broker recommendations, and insider trading)

# Mutual Funds

**Large Cap Growth:**

Columbia Growth  800-547-1707
Harbor Capital Appreciation  800-422-1050
Vanguard Index Growth  800-662-7447

**Large Value:**

Clipper  800-776-5033
Kemper Value S  800-621-1048
Preferred Value  800-662-4769
Vanguard Growth & Income  800-662-7447
Vanguard Index Value  800-662-7447

**Large Cap Blend (Value and Growth):**

BT Investment Equity 500 Index  800-730-1313
T. Rowe Price Blue Chip Growth  800-638-5660
T. Rowe Price Equity Index  800-638-5660
Torray  800-443-3036
Vanguard/Morgan Growth  800-662-7447

**Mid-Cap Growth:**

T. Rowe Price Mid-Cap Growth  800-638-5660
T. Rowe Price New America Growth  800-638-5660
William Blair Growth  800-742-7272

**Mid-Cap Value:**

Homestead Value 800-258-3030

**Mid-Cap Blend (Value and Growth):**

Excelsior Value & Restruct 800-446-1012
Nicholas II 800-227-5987
Strong Opportunity 800-368-1030
Vanguard Index Extended Market 800-662-7447

**Small Growth:**

Janus Enterprise 800-525-8983
Warburg Pincus Emerging Growth 800-927-2874

**Small Value:**

FAM Value 800-932-3271

**Small Blend (Value and Growth):**

Acorn 800-922-6769
Nicholas Limited Edition 800-227-5987
Safeco Growth No Load 800-426-6730
T. Rowe Price Small Cap Stock 800-638-5660

**Foreign Stock:**

Acorn International 800-922-6769
Fidelity Diversified International 800-544-8888
Preferred International 800-662-4769
Scudder International 800-225-2470

**Long Government:**

American Cent-Ben Tar Mat 2020 800-345-2021 (Treasuries)
Vanguard F/I L/T US Treasury 800-662-7447

**Intermediate Government:**

T. Rowe Price GNMA (Mortgage) 800-638-5660
Vanguard F/I Inter-Term U.S. (Treasury) 800-662-7447

**Long-Term Bonds:**

USAA Income 800-382-8722

**Intermediate-Term Bonds:**

Dodge & Cox Income 800-621-3979

**Muni National Long:**

USAA Tax-Exempt Long-Term 800-382-8722
Vanguard Muni High Yield 800-662-7447
Vanguard Muni Long-Term 800-662-7447

**Muni National Intermediate:**
USAA Tax-Exempt Interim-Term  800-382-8722

# Money Market Funds

| Assets ($millions) | Fund Name |
|---|---|
| **U.S. Treasury Funds** | |
| 3,101.6 | Benham/Capital Presv. Fund I |
| 1,905.6 | Fidelity Spartan U.S. Treas. MMF |
| 4,107.8 | Vanguard Admiral/U.S. Treas. MMF |
| 3,494.7 | Vanguard Treasury Fund/Treas. MMP |
| **U.S. Government & Agencies Funds** | |
| 772.8 | Fidelity Spartan U.S. Govt. MMF |
| 1,275.5 | Fidelity U.S. Govt. Reserves |
| | SSgA U.S. Govt. MMF/Cl A |
| 3,722.5 | Vanguard MMR/Federal Port |
| 671.9 | Zurich Government Money Fund |
| **General Money Market Funds** | |
| 10,521.2 | Dean Witter/Active Assets MT |
| 3,698.0 | IDS Cash Management Fund |
| 2.662.5 | J. P. Morgan Prime MMF |
| 5,548.8 | SSgA Money Market Fund/Cl A |
| 1,467.3 | T. Rowe Price Summit Cash Reserves |
| 2,397.9 | USAA Money Market Fund |
| 29,257.1 | Vanguard MR/Prime Port/Retail |
| 4,516.5 | Zurich Money Market Fund |
| **Tax-Free Money Funds** | |
| 4,774.9 | Fidelity Municipal MMF |
| 1,197.5 | J. P. Morgan Tax-Exempt MMF |
| 1,595.4 | USAA Tax Exempt MMF |
| 5,721.3 | Vanguard Muni Bond/MMF |
| 806.6 | Zurich Tax-Free Money Fund |

*(Source: IBC Financial Data, Inc./290 Eliot St., PO Box 9104, Ashland, MA 01721-9104; 508/881-2800; http://www.ibc.data.com.)*

# College Contacts

Involve your child in the decision about where to go to college by getting him or her a copy of a great reference guide: *The College Handbook,* published by the College Entrance Examination Board. The handbook profiles 3,215 colleges.

Unique College Investing Plan, sponsored by the State of New Hampshire and managed by Strategic Advisors, Inc., a part of Fidelity Investments. 1-800-544-1722.

# Internet Connections

*Smart Money* currently recommends three:

➤ Concentric: Considered fast, reliable, and cost effective.

➤ MindSpring (888-MSPRING): Service, service, service!

➤ IBM Internet Connection (800-821-4612): Reliability and speed at reasonable cost.

# Internet Brokers

| Broker | Web site | Telephone |
|---|---|---|
| E*TRADE | etrade.com | 800-387-2331 |
| DLJDirect | dljdirect.com | 888-456-4355 |
| Discover | discoverbrokerage.com | 800-347-2683 |
| Waterhouse | waterhouse.come | 800-934-4410 |
| Datek Online | datek.com | 888-463-2835 |
| Web Street | webstreet.com | 800-932-8723 |
| National Discount Brokers | ndb.com | 800-888-3999 |
| Brown | brownco.com | 800-822-2021 |
| SURETRADE | suretrade.com | 401-642-6900 |
| Bull & Bear | bullbear.com | 800-285-5232 |
| Fidelity | fidelity.com | 800-544-7272 |
| Schwab | schwab.com | 800-435-4000 |
| Quick & Reilly | quick-reilly.com | 800-837-7220 |

# Mortgages

Want to use the Internet for online mortgage quotes? Here are three web sites:

1. E-loan at http://www.eloan.com
2. Quicken Home and Mortgage at http://www.quicken.com/mortgage/
3. HomeShark at http://www.homeshark.com

# Glossary

**Adjustable-rate mortgage (ARM)** A mortgage with an interest rate priced off the yield for the 10-year Treasury note. Since the yield on the note changes every six months, so will the interest rate on the ARM.

**Adjusted gross income** AGI is gross income from your W-2 form, plus interest income, rents, royalties, etc., minus medical account deductions, alimony payments, and other adjustments.

**Alternative investment** An equity-based investment, such as a hedge fund or venture capital fund. Alternative investments used to be available only to very wealthy investors.

**Amortize** To write off a debt or fee over time.

**Annual report** Report, prepared by a corporation, that includes full disclosure of its financial statements.

**Annuity** An investment that yields fixed payments during the investment holder's lifetime or for a stated number of years.

**Asked price** The price that an owner of stock is asking for it in the market.

**Assets** Any item of value—from baseball cards to stocks—that you own.

**Back-end load** Fee charged when you redeem (sell) your shares in a mutual fund. Also referred to as "back-end," "back-door" load, or "deferred sales charges."

**Balance sheet** A financial statement that shows what you own (your assets) and what you owe (your liabilities) at a given point in time.

**Bid price** The price a buyer is willing to pay for a stock.

**Bill** An IOU that a corporation or government agency issues when it wants to borrow money for less than a year. The issuer agrees to pay back the lender at a specified maturity date, with interest.

**Bond** An IOU that a corporation or government agency issues when it wants to borrow money for more than ten years. The issuer agrees to pay back the lender at a specified maturity date, with interest.

**Broker** A generic name for middlemen who facilitate trades between buyers and sellers.

**Browser** Software that enables your computer to surf the Web and read all those groovy HTML documents. Popular browsers include Netscape and Microsoft's Internet Explorer.

**Business plan** Document prepared by entrepreneur to show exactly how a new business will be operated; includes projections for sales and profits.

**Call option** Contract giving the contract holder the right to purchase a stock at a set price, called the strike price, for a specified period of time, usually a few months.

**Capital** A fancy word for money that is used for business purposes. Corporations issue stock to raise capital, for example.

**Capital gain** Any money you make from an investment—from selling a stock for a profit, for example. If you've held the investment longer than one year, the capital gain is not subject to income tax; instead, it's subject to capital gains tax, which is typically lower.

**Cash equivalent** Investment that can be turned into cash within 24 hours. Treasury bills, CDs, savings accounts, and money market funds are examples of highly liquid cash equivalents.

**Certificates of deposit** Money market instruments typically sold by banks in three-month, six-month, or one-year maturities. CDs are very safe investments because they are fully insured by the Federal government, up to $100,000.

**Charge card** An account that allows you to carry debt for a specified time, after which you incur fees and penalties.

**Collateral** Something you own that can be pledged against a loan.

**Combined income** Adjusted gross income plus nontaxable interest (interest on municipal bonds, for example) plus half of your Social Security benefits.

**Commission** A percentage fee paid to a broker for executing a trade.

**Commodity** Any product sold in the financial markets that can actually be weighed, such as gold, silver, pork bellies, sugar, or grain.

**Compound interest** The money you earn on interest (or dividends or capital gains) that you earned in a previous period. Compound interest enables your money to grow exponentially.

**Corporation** A business structure composed of stockholders who all share in its ownership. Because no one person "owns" a corporation, the people who work for it are protected if the corporation is sued.

**Credit card** An account that enables you to carry a debt indefinitely, as long as you pay interest.

**Credit report** Report created by private credit reporting agency (CRA) that is based on what creditors have said about you.

**Debit card** Card that enables you to make purchases with a direct deduction from your checking account.

**Deductible** The amount of expense you agree to cover before your insurance kicks in.

**Defined benefit plan** An employer-financed retirement plan that pays you an annual sum upon retirement.

**Depreciation** The loss in value of an item over time, due to wear and tear.

**Discount** The amount a bond is trading below par (100).

**Discount broker** Broker who simply executes trades, for a lower commission and without the additional services provided by a full-service broker.

**Diversification** A method of decreasing risk by increasing the variety of assets in a portfolio. If you own lots of different stocks, for example, your whole portfolio won't tank if one company goes bankrupt.

**Dividend** A payment to the owner of a share of corporation's stock; represents the owner's portion of the corporation's profits.

**Dow Jones Average (DJIA)** An average of thirty well-known companies, such as AT&T or McDonald's, chosen by the editors of *The Wall Street Journal* to represent trends in the stock market.

**Education IRA** Introduced in 1998, this is an IRA to which you can make tax-deferred contributions of up to $500 per year, per beneficiary, until your kids are 18. Withdrawals for qualified educational purposes are tax-free.

**E-mail** Electronic mail, sent via modem over the Internet.

**Encryption** The scrambling of information as it is transmitted over the Internet to ensure your privacy and confidentiality.

**Equity** Ownership of property, such as stock or a house.

**Executor** Person who makes sure that the provisions of a will are carried out.

**Expiration date** Date by which an option contract must be exercised or lose its value.

**Fixed-income** Investment that provides income that remains constant and doesn't fluctuate (like stock prices do, for example). Bonds are fixed-income investments because when you buy a bond you are promised regular, steady interest payments.

**Fiduciary** A person or entity responsible for investing money on behalf of another person or entity and expected to earn a reasonable rate of return on the investments made.

**Fixed annuity** An annuity that promises to provide a fixed (predetermined) sum in an annual or other regular (e.g., monthly) interval.

**401(k)** Retirement savings plan that allows employees who are eligible to choose how much of their pay is to be deducted for investment purposes and how the dollars are to be invested.

**403(b)** A version of the 401(k) used by public employers, such as schools, hospitals, and governmental bodies.

**Front-end load** Sales charge deducted from the principal invested in a mutual fund.

**Future** or **Futures contract** An agreement between a buyer and seller to make a specific trade at a specified future date and price.

**General obligation bond** A bond backed by the tax-raising ability of the issuing state or municipality.

**Hedge fund** An unregistered investment fund whose managers can pretty much do whatever they want—invest in currencies or commodities, go short or long, use options and futures, etc.

**HTML (Hypertext Markup Language)** A computer language that enables programmers to include graphics and sound in documents.

**Income statement** A financial statement that compares income and expenses.

**Index fund** A mutual fund designed to mimic the performance of a given set of securities.

**Inflation** A general rise in prices.

**Initial public offering (IPO)** A corporation's first stock sale.

**Institutional investor** As opposed to an individual investor, an institutional investor is an institution, such as a corporation, hospital, city government, or other large entity that has a portfolio.

**Interest** Payment you receive for lending someone your money. Interest is also the fee you pay when you borrow money.

**Internet (the Net)** A computer network developed in 1969 as a way for government scientists and military departments to communicate with each other via computer and access information stored on computers around the world. Today over 30 million people use the Internet.

**Internet Service Provider (ISP)** A company, such as America Online or CompuServe, that provides you with access to the Internet for a fee.

**IRA** An Individual Retirement Account, which is bascially a shell that protects money you put in it from taxation until you start to take money out.

**Keogh** Pension plan that allows business owners to shelter more income than SEPs or SIMPLEs do and to create vesting schedules for employees.

**Layaway** Plan that allows you to make a down payment and monthly payments toward the purchase of an item.

**Leverage** A way to finance the purchase of something with debt.

**Leveraged buyout fund** Fund that borrows money to buy a company, revamp it, and take it public. Investors profit from what the LBO fund makes when it resells the company's stock.

**Liability** A debt you owe. The opposite of an asset, which is something you own.

**Lien** A legal right to take someone's property and hold it until the owner pays a debt.

**Liquidity** The ease with which an investment can be converted to cash.

**Living trust** Legal document that names someone to manage your assets if you die or are incapacitated.

**Load** Sales fees and commissions charged to investors in a mutual fund.

**Long bond** The 30-year Treasury bond.

**Long-Term Equity Anticipation Security (LEAPS)** Long-term option contracts that are very popular with individual investors.

**Lump sum** The entire value of an investment taken in cash at once.

**Margin** Deposit put down by both parties in a futures contract.

**Marginal tax rate** The tax rate you pay on the last few dollars you earn.

**Medicare** A national health program that pays certain medical and hospital expenses for elderly and disabled people.

**Modem** Device used to connect a computer to a phone line.

**Money market** Instruments highly liquid investments with rates that vary from day to day, week to week, or month to month.

**Municipal bond** A bond issued by a "municipality," like your city, town, or county. The interest paid by municipal bonds is, with a few exceptions, not taxed by the federal government.

**Mutual fund** A company that collects money from investors and invests on their behalf, usually in diversified securities.

**Net asset value (NAV)** The dollar value of all the marketable securities (stocks, for example) owned by a mutual fund, less expenses and divided by the number of the fund's shares outstanding.

**Net earnings from self-employment** The amount of income on which you pay self-employment tax, minus the tax itself.

**Note** An IOU that a corporation or government agency issues when it wants to borrow money for between one and five years. The issuer agrees to pay back the lender at a specified maturity date, with interest.

**Option** A contract that states what is to be delivered for what price and what time period. The option is a right, but not an obligation, to exercise the rights stated in the options contract. At the end of the designated time period, the option loses all its value.

**Options buyer** or **"holder"** Pays an options writer a premium for the right to exercise the option contract created by the options writer.

**Options writer** or **"seller"** or **"issuer"** Creates an options contract, and must stand ready to honor the terms of the contract.

**Par** The original price of a bond, note, or bill. It is also the amount that the security will pay back at maturity and is referred to as "100."

**Penny stock** Stock sold for under a dollar.

**Pension** A regular payment made to you (or your family, if you pass away) by your employer that reflects how much you earned and how many years you worked at your job.

**Portfolio** The mix of assets in which you've invested. A portfolio contains investment instruments that you've selected to achieve your financial goals.

**Premium** The amount that a bond is trading above par (over 100).

**Pre-nuptial agreement** A legally binding document signed by two people before they get married. Most pre-nuptial agreements simply spell out who owns what and who will get what in a divorce.

**Pre-tax** Describes dollars that are deducted from your pay before taxes are applied. Pre-tax contributions to a 401(k) or 403(b), for example, are deducted from your pay before it is taxed.

**Principal** The original dollar amount of a fixed-income investment; the amount received upon maturity.

**Probate** State court that decides how an estate will be distributed when the deceased person's will is nonexistent or unclear.

**Prospectus** A legal document prepared by a mutual fund and sent out to potential investors that describes the fund and its operations.

**Put option** A contract that gives you the option to sell a security at a specified price until the contract's expiration date.

**Return on investment (ROI)** The amount you expect to earn from an investment over a given period of time. ROI is also called rate of return (ROR) and is expressed as a percentage of your original investment.

**Revenue bond** A bond issued by an agency of a city, county, or state for a specific purpose. Revenues from that agency pay the interest on bonds that are outstanding.

**Revolving line of credit** Credit that puts an upper limit on what you can borrow. You can borrow up to that amount, and you pay interest only on what you actually draw down.

**Rollover IRA** Used to shelter money that's in a 401(k) if you change jobs and can't put the money in your new job's retirement plan.

**Roth IRA** A new type of IRA that is more flexible than the traditional IRA but is only available to families earning under $100,000 a year. As long as your Roth IRA has been open for at least five years, you can withdraw up to $10,000 to buy a first home.

**Round lot** 100 shares of stock.

**Savings Incentive Match Plan for Employees (SIMPLE) IRA** A new option for self-employed people, growing in popularity because it's very easy to use.

**Search engine** Also called a portal; a business that collects and indexes Web pages. You can access search engines on-line and use them for free to look for Web pages on topics that you specify.

**Securities and Exchange Commission (SEC)** Regulatory agency started in 1933 by Congress to protect investors.

**Self-employment tax** A tax self-employed people have to pay into Social Security because they don't have an employer contributing on their behalf.

**Simplified Employee Pension (SEP) IRA** Essentially an IRA for someone who is self-employed. A SEP is like a 401(k), but contributions are limited to 15% or $30,000, whichever is less. A good retirement plan for a sole proprietor who doesn't have employees.

**Social Security** A system managed by the federal government, which provides money to people who are retired or are not able to work because of disability.

**Sole proprietor** Someone who owns a business alone, without partners.

**Spread** The difference between the asked and the bid price of a security or between interest rates.

**Standard & Poor's Depository Receipts (SPDRs)** A subset of Unit Investment Trusts, or UITS. Both are mutual fund hybrids that trade for a fixed period of time.

**Stock market** The stock market doesn't exist as a physical place—stocks are traded at various stock exchanges, such as the New York Stock Exchange or The American Stock Exchange. All the exchanges together are considered the stock market.

**Stock option** The right, but not the obligation, to buy a stock at a fixed price after a fixed period of time (usually twelve months) for a fixed period of time (ten years).

**Stock split** A division of stock that increases the number of shares outstanding and decreases share price of the stock.

**Strike price** Also called the exercise price; the price at which the holder of an option contract can buy (call) or sell (put) the underlying security.

**Trade** To buy or sell securities on the financial markets.

**Treasury bill securities** Securities issued by the U.S. Treasury that mature in under a year. Treasury securities are fully guaranteed by the government and can be sold within 24 hours.

**Treasury bonds** Long-term securities issued by the U.S. Treasury with maturities over ten years. Historically, the Treasury has issued twenty- or thirty-year bonds.

**Treasury notes** Securities issued by the U.S. Treasury that offer maturities from one year to ten years.

**Treasury strip** A piece of a Treasury security, such as a coupon or principal payment, that has been stripped from the original security.

**12b-1** Shareholding servicing fee charged on mutual fund.

**Unit Investment Trust (UITS)** Hybrid mutual funds that invest like mutual funds but, unlike them, have a fixed termination date.

**URL (Uniform Resource Locator)** Address for a document on the Internet.

**Variable annuity** An annuity that provides an undetermined amount that depends upon the return of the annuity's underlying mutual fund; basically a mutual fund wrapped around an insurance contract.

**Venture capital fund** Fund that invests in new businesses by providing start-up capital. The investors in a venture capital fund are limited partners in the businesses in which the fund invests and are entitled to a share of its profits.

**Vested** Eligible to receive a pension. An employee is typically considered vested after five years at a company.

**Will** A legal document, signed by you and witnessed, that gives explicit directions as to who or what is to get whatever specific assets of yours you choose to list.

**World Wide Web (the Web)** A subset of the Internet organized by an organization called the World Wide Web Consortium. Documents on the Web, called home pages, include graphics and sound.

**Yield** The return on an investment expressed as a percentage.

# Index

## Symbols

8-K reports, 132-133
10-K reports, 132-133
10-percent habit, 8
10-percent rule (emergency funds), 30
12b-1 fees (mutual funds), 156
15-year mortgages, advantages of, 191-192
128-bit encryption (Internet browsers), 235
401(k) plans, 46-47, 60
    after-tax contributions, 65
    borrowing from, 66
    changing employers, 67
    company stock, 67-68
    matching employer contributions, 65-66
    pre-tax contributions, 64-65
    taxes on contributions, 102
    transferring, 171
403(b) plans, 46-47, 60
    after-tax contributions, 65
    pre-tax contributions, 64-65
*1998 Retirement Confidence Survey*, 37

## A

*A History of Interest Rates*, 96
*AARP Bulletin*, 39-40, 59
account executive (AE), 135
adjustable-rate mortgages (ARM), 189-190, 291
adjusted gross income (AGI), 70
    AGI limits (educational funds), 203-204
    determining, 100

itemized deductions, 100-101
standard deductions, 100-101
alternative investments, 293-294
    hedge funds, 294
    leveraged buyout (LBO) funds, 294-295
    private equity fund of funds, 295-297
        pros and cons, 297
    Standard & Poor's Depository Receipts (SPDRs), 298-299
    Unit Investment Trusts (UITs), 298-299
    venture capital funds, 294-295
American Stock Exchange (Amex), 114
    address/phone number, 302
    Web site, 252
Ameritrade Web site, 255
amortization, 81
Annual Report Service Web site, 253
annual reports, 132-135
    8-K reports, 132-133
    10-K reports, 132-133
    balance sheets, analyzing, 134-135
    Income Statements, analyzing, 133-134
annual return, 27
Annual Savings Required Table (retirement), 44-45
annuities, 63, 211-212
    defined benefit plans, 63-64
apartment buildings (real estate), 286
Apple Macintosh IMAC, 233

applying for Social Security benefits, 175
ARM (adjustable-rate mortgages), 189-190, 291
ARPA (Department of Defense Advanced Research and Projects Agency), 230
asked price (stocks), 114
asset allocation (portfolios), 123-125
    rebalancing assets, 123-124
assets, 18, 49
Association of Individual Investors Web site, 253
"at the money" (option contracts), 264-265
auctions, 31

## B

back-end loads (mutual funds), 156
balance sheet, 49-50
    married couple example, 52-53
    single male example, 54-55
balance sheets (annual reports), analyzing, 134-135
bank accounts, joint accounts, 181
bank rates, 11
banking online, 235-237
banks, choosing, 84-85
BanxQuote Web site, 237
Barchoff, Herbert, 19
basis points, 158
bears (stock market), 115
being vested, 41
beneficiary-designated accounts, 218
benefits packages, questions to ask personnel, 169-171

Better Business Bureau Web sites, 253
bid price (stocks), 114
BigCharts Web site, 252
bills, 64, 142
    par, 147
Bloomberg Information TV, 132
Bloomberg Web site, 250
blue chip, 23
bond funds, disadvantages, 161-162
bonds, 12, 21, 64, 142, 144-147
    bond tables, reading, 147-149
    comparing to stocks, 145
    corporate debt, 147-149
    discount, 147
    EE savings bonds, setting up college funds, 199-200
    effects of inflation, 145
    Federal Home Loan Mortgage Corp., 151
    Federal National Mortgage Association, 151
    Government National Mortgage Association, 151
    inflation-indexed bonds, 75
    junk bonds, 144
    municipal bonds, 106-108
        general obligation (GO) bonds, 106
        revenue bonds, 107
        tax-equivalent yields, calculating, 107-108
    par, 147
    portfolios
        asset allocation, 124-125
        rebalancing assets, 123-124
    premium, 147
    reasons to own bonds, 146
    Resolution Funding Corporation (RFC), 151
    Student Loan Marketing Association, 151
    transactions
        offsetting gains with losses, 105-106
        tax deductions, 104-106
        wash sale rule, 105-106
    Treasury STRIPs, 73-74

borrowing from 401(k) plans, 66
Briefing.com Web site, 242
broad investment classes, 20-21
broker compensation (stocks), 115
brokers, 135-137
    buyer's broker (real estate), 192-193
    commission, 128
    discount brokers, 135, 137
    full-service brokers, 135
    online brokers, 245-246
        ancillary services, 243
        comfort, 242-243
        commission rates, 241
        E*TRADE Securities, 247-248
        evaluating your needs, 239-241
        fraudulent brokers, avoiding, 246
        frequent trader issues, 241-242
        home page contents, 246-247
        information sources, 306
        log-on IDs/passwords, 246
        research capabilities, 242
        selecting, 237-239
        speed factor, 245-246
        system failure back-ups, 245-246
        third-market execution, 252
        Web sites, 239
    placing orders with, 136-137
Brown Web site, 239
browsers, 234-235
    128-bit encryption, 235
bulk purchases, 80-81
Bull & Bear Web site, 239
bulls (stock market), 115
*Business Week* Web site, 254
businesses, starting, 36-37
"buy-write" program (option contracts), 268
buying a home
    buyer's brokers, 192-193
    closing costs, 190-191
    down payments, 36, 185-186

mortgages
    fixed-rate vs. adjustable-rate, 189-190
    mortgage rates, 187
    *see also* mortgages
    real estate market, 186-187
    recommended percentage of income, 189
    renting vs. owning, 187-189
    renting your old home, 193
buying in bulk, 80-81
buying on leverage, 284
*BYTE* magazine Web site, 255

## C

call feature (fixed-income securities), 142-143
call option contracts, 262-263
capital, 9
capital calls (limited partnerships), 296
capital gains, 68, 100
capital gains rates, 105
cars
    buying, 83
    insurance, 207-208
        purchasing, 84
    leasing, 81-83
        advantages, 81-82
        disadvantages, 82
cash equivalents, 31
CBOE (Chicago Board Options Exchange), 263
CBOT (Chicago Board of Trade), 274
CDs (certificates of deposit), 32, 152
    pros/cons, 34
CEO Express Web site, 250
*CFO* magazine Web site, 254
CFTC (Commodity Futures Trading Commission), 274
changing jobs
    401(k) plans, transferring, 171
    benefits, questions to ask personnel, 169-171
charge cards, 86, 92
Charitable Lead Trusts (CLTs), 221

Charitable Remainder Trusts (CRTs), 221
charitable trusts, 221
charts, Future Value Chart, 6-7
chat rooms, 230
checking accounts
    debit cards, 95
    joint bank accounts, 181
Chicago Board of Trade (CBOT), 274
Chicago Board Options Exchange (CBOE), 263
children
    college fund, 35-36
        AGI limits, 203-204
        scholarships, 203
        setting up, 196-201
        student loans, 202
        tax credits, 202
        taxes, 203-204
        vs. retirement funds, 196
    life insurance, 212
closed-end mutual funds, 154-155
closing costs (home buying), 190-191
CLTs (Charitable Lead Trusts), 221
CNBC, 132
collateral, 108
college contacts (information resources), 306
college education funds, 35-36
    AGI limits, 203-204
    scholarships, 203
    setting up, 196-200
        Education IRA, 198-199
        EE savings bonds, 199-200
        Roth IRA, 198
        traditional IRAs, 197-198
        Unique College Investing Plan, 200-201
    student loans, 202
    tax credits, 202
    taxes, 203-204
    vs. retirement funds, 196
*College Handbook, The*, 196
college loans, 48-49
combined income, 174
commercial paper, 33
commission
    stock brokers, 128
    online brokers, 241

commodities, 273-274
    Chicago Board of Trade (CBOT), 274
    precious metals, 279-281
        companies, 280-281
        no-load precious metal funds, 281
    spreads, 279
Commodity Futures Trading Commission (CFTC), 274
common stock, 20
companies
    annual reports, 132-135
        8-K reports, 132-133
        10-K reports, 132-133
        balance sheets, analyzing, 134-135
        Income Statements, analyzing, 133-134
    annual return, 27
    normalized earnings, 118
    pre-strike earnings, 118
    precious metal companies, 280-281
    quality companies (stock investments), 129-130
    quarterly rate of return, 27
    stock
        purchasing, 67-68
        stock options, 68-69
Compaq Presario 2510, 233
compound interest, 4-5
    calculating, 5-7
        Future Value Chart, 6-7
    time factor, 7-8
*Computerworld* Web site, 255
Concentric Network Web site, 234
consumer information, 302
Consumer Price Index (CPI), 189
*Consumer Reports*, 301-302
    auto insurance price comparison line, 84
    Web site, 83, 177, 301-302
convertible debenture, 148
cookies (Internet), 231
corporate debt, 147-149
Corporate Information Web site, 253
corporate ownership (real estate), 286
cost (securities), 104

covered call writing (option contracts), 267-268
CPI (Consumer Price Index), 189
credit cards, 86, 92-95
    as a reporting device, 94-95
credit reporting agencies (CRAs), 90-92, 302
    checking credit reports, 91
    Federal Fair Credit Reporting Act (FCRA), 91-92
    top CRAs, 91
credit reports, 90-92
    checking, 91
    establishing good credit, 92-93
    Federal Fair Credit Reporting Act (FCRA), 91-92
credit shelter trust (CST), 220-221
CRTs (Charitable Remainder Trusts), 221
Crummy Powers trust, 223
current market value (securities), 104
cutting expenses, 79-80
    banks, choosing, 84-85
    buying in bulk, 80-81
    car insurance, 84
    credit cards, 86
    leasing cars, 81-83
        advantages, 81-82
        disadvantages, 82
    life insurance, 85
    real estate taxes, 85-86
    saving tips, 87
    spending, gathering information on, 77-78
    tax withholdings, 79

## D

Datek Web site, 239, 255
DB (defined benefit plan), determining benefits, 41-42
DBC Online Web site, 252
debit cards, 95
debts, 48-49
    college loans, 48-49
    debt-to-equity ratio, 284
    emergency funds, 96-97
    financing, 141

good debt vs. bad debt, 96
lien, 90
mortgages, 48-49
reducing, 95-96
deductions (taxes)
health insurance deductions
(self-employment), 104
home equity loans, 108-109
itemized deductions (ad-
justed gross income),
100-101
medical savings account
deductions, 103-104
non-reimbursed health/
dependent care expenses,
103
securities transactions
gains and losses, 104-106
offsetting gains with
losses, 105-106
wash sale rule, 105-106
standard deductions
(adjusted gross income),
100-101
deep discount brokers,
135, 137
deferred sales charge (mutual
funds), 156
defined benefit plans (DBs),
41-42, 60-64
annuities, 63-64
characteristics, 61
determining benefits, 41-42
lump sum option, 63-64
monthly pensions, deter-
mining, 61-63
Pension Benefit Guaranty
Corp. (PBGC), 64
defined contribution plans,
42, 46-47, 60, 64-68
401(k) plans, 46-47, 60
after-tax contributions, 65
borrowing from, 66
changing employers, 67
company stock, 67-68
matching employer
contributions, 65-66
pre-tax contributions,
64-65
transferring, 171
403(b) plans, 46-47, 60
after-tax contributions, 65
pre-tax contributions,
64-65

delaying retirement, effects on
Social Security, 175
Department of Defense
Advanced Research and
Projects Agency (ARPA), 230
depreciation, 81
real estate, 290
derivatives, 273
disability insurance, 212
Disclosure Web site, 253
discount (bonds), 147
discount brokers, 135, 137
discount rate, 11
Discover Brokerage Web site,
239, 255
diversification, 21-22
stock portfolios, 138-139
dividends, 9, 20
divorce, 182-184
dividing assets, 183
negotiation, 183-184
no-fault divorces, 184
pre-nuptial agreements,
179-180
DLJ Direct Web site, 239, 255
dollar cost averaging (stock
portfolios), 123-124
doubling investments (Rule of
72), 8
Dow Jones, 9
Dow Jones Industrial Average
(DJIA), 10
Dow Jones Business Directory
Web site, 253
down payments (home
buying), 36, 185-186
Dun & Bradstreet, 91, 302
duplex (real estate), 286

**E**

E*TRADE Securities, 247-248
E*TRADE Web site, 239, 255
E-loan Web site, 291, 306
early retirement, 173
Social Security, effects on,
173-175
Economist Web site, 254
*Edmund's Automobile Buyer's
Guide*, 302
Web site, 83, 302
Education IRA, 198-199

Education-Loan Interest
Deduction, 202
educational funds
AGI limits, 203-204
scholarships, 203
setting up, 196-200
Education IRA, 198-199
EE savings bonds,
199-200
Roth IRA, 198
traditional IRAs, 197-198
Unique College Investing
Plan, 200-201
student loans, 202
tax credits, 202
taxes, 203-204
vs. retirement funds, 196
EE savings bonds, 150
*Electronic Business* Web site, 255
*Electronic Markets* Web site, 255
emergency funds, 30-35, 96-97
10-percent rule, 30
cash equivalents, 30-31
Certificates of Deposit
(CDs), 32
evaluating investment
options, 34-35
money market funds
(MMFs), 33-34
repos, 33
savings accounts, 33
Treasury bills (T-bills), 31-32
yields, 32
Employee Benefit Research
Institute, 37
Employee Retirement Income
Security Act of 1974
(ERISA), 64
employer group health plans
non-reimbursed health/
dependent care expenses,
103
taxes, 102
employer-sponsored retirement
plans, 60-61
defined benefit plans, 41-42,
60-64
annuities, 63-64
characteristics, 61
lump sum option, 63-64
monthly pensions,
determining, 61-63

Pension Benefit Guaranty Corp. (PBGC), 64
defined contribution plans, 42, 46-47, 60, 64-68
   401(k) plans, 46-47, 60, 64-68
   403(b) plans, 46-47, 60, 64-65
employers
   benefits, questions to ask personnel, 169-171
   changing, 67
   company stock, 67-68
   relocation packages, 192-193
   retiree health insurance, 176
   stock options, 68-69
encryption (Internet browsers), 235
Equifax, 91, 302
equity, 9, 20
equity financing, 141
equity mutual funds, rebalancing, 164-165
equity REITs, 284-285
ERISA (Employee Retirement Income Security Act of 1974), 64
establishing good credit, 92-93
estate planning
   estate taxes, 218-220
      Estate Tax Return Form 706, 219
      Generation Skipping Transfer Tax (GST), 220
      inheritances, 223-225
      tax-saving strategies, 220-223
      unified credit, 218
      unlimited marital deduction, 220
   executors, 216
   probate, avoiding, 217-218
      beneficiary-designated accounts, 218
      joint ownership, 217-218
      living trusts, 217
   wills, 216
estates, 215
   inheritances, 223-225
   list of items included in definition, 219
event risk, 21
exchanges, 301-302

Excite Web site, 250
executors (estate planning), 216
exercise price (option contracts), 262
Experian, 91
expiration dates (option contracts), 263

## F

Fannie Mae (Federal National Mortgage Association), 151
Far East Economic Review Web site, 254
*Fast Company* Web site, 254
Federal Deposit Insurance Corporation (FDIC), 33
Federal Estate Tax Return Form 706, 219
Federal Fair Credit Reporting Act (FRCA), 91-92
federal funds rate, 11
Federal Home Loan Mortgage Corp. (Freddie Mac), 151
Federal Insurance Contributions Act (FICA), 40
Federal Reserve, 10-11
   interest rates, 11-12
Federal Reserve Board Web site, 83, 301
Federal Reserve Web site, 255
Federal Trade Commission (FTC), 301
   Web site, 91, 301
Federal Web Locator Web site, 255
FICA (Federal Insurance Contributions Act), 40
Fidelity Investments Web site, 239, 255
financial futures, 277-278
financial magazine Web sites, 254-255
financial management software, 237
financial market Web sites, 252
financial news Web sites, 253
*Financial Times* Web site, 254
financing real estate investments, 290-291
first level standard deviation, 19

fixed income funds, disadvantages, 161-162
fixed percent of salary, 47
fixed-income investments, 74
fixed-income securities, 141-147
   bonds, 144-147
      bond tables, reading, 147
      corporate debt, 147-149
      discount, 147
      effects of inflation, 145
      Federal Home Loan Mortgage Corp., 151
      Federal National Mortgage Association, 151
      Government National Mortgage Association, 151
      par, 147
      premium, 147
      reasons to own bonds, 146
      Resolution Funding Corporation (RFC), 151
      Student Loan Marketing Association, 151
   debt financing, 141
   equity financing, 141
   interest, 142-144
      call feature, 142-143
      sinking fund payments, 143-144
   Treasuries, 149-151
      buying, 150
      savings bonds, 150-151
fixed-rate mortgages, 189-190
Fleet Bank, 235-237
   Web site, 235-236
Forbes Web site, 253-254
Form 1040 (Schedule E), 288-290
Form SSA-1099, 175
Form SSA-7004 (Request for Personal Earnings and Benefit Estimate Statement), 41
*Fortune* Web site, 254
fraudulent online brokers, avoiding, 246
FRCA (Federal Fair Credit Reporting Act), 91-92
Freddie Mac (Federal Home Loan Mortgage Corp.), 151
front-end loads (mutual funds), 155-156

FTC (Federal Trade Commission), 301
  Web site, 91, 301
Full Employment Act
  of 1946, 10
full retirement age (Social
  Security), 173-174
full-service brokers, 135
funds rate, 11
Future Value Chart, 6-7
futures contracts, 274
  Commodity Futures Trading
    Commission (CFTC), 274
  comparing to options, 275
  financial futures, 277-278
  hedges against risk and
    uncertainty, 276-277
  limit, 275
  long, 275
  margins, 275-276
  market, 275
  National Futures Association
    (NFA), 274
  options on futures contracts,
    278
  program trading, 279
  short, 275
  spreads, 279
  stop loss, 275

## G

general obligation (GO) bonds,
  106
general partner (GP), 295-297
Generation Skipping Transfer
  Tax (GST), 220
gifting, 222
Ginnie Mae (Government
  National Mortgage Association), 151
gold, 279-280
Gomez Advisors
  evaluation of online brokers,
    237-238
  Web site, 237
good credit, establishing, 92-93
good 'til canceled (GTC), 136
government agency Web sites,
  255
government contacts (investment information), 301

gross income, 70
  determining, 100

## H

Harvard Business School
  Publishing Web site, 254
health insurance, 84
  deductions (self-
    employment), 104
  Medicare, 40, 176-177
  retiree health insurance, 176
health plans
  non-reimbursed health/
    dependent care expenses,
    103
  taxes, 102
hedge funds, 294
hedges, 261
  futures contracts, 276-277
  index options, 269-270
HH savings bonds, 150-151
*A History of Interest Rates*, 96
history of the Internet, 229-230
home businesses, *see* self-
  employment
home buying
  buyer's brokers, 192-193
  closing costs, 190-191
  down payments,
    36, 185-186
  mortgages
    fixed-rate vs. adjustable-
      rate, 189-190
    mortgage rates, 187
    *see also* mortgages
  real estate market, 186-187
  recommended percentage of
    income, 189
  renting vs. owning, 187-189
  renting your old home, 193
home equity loans, 108-109
  tax deductions, 108-109
  vs. second mortgages, 109
homeowner's insurance,
  212-213
homes
  real estate taxes, 85-86
  selling, 194
HomeShark Web site, 291, 306
Hoover's Online Web site, 242

Hope Scholarship Credit, 202
hotels (real estate), 286
HTML documents, 230-231
Humphrey-Hawkins Act, 10
hybrid REITs, 284-285

## I

IBC Financial Data Web site,
  163, 305
IBM Internet Connection, 234
IMAC computer (Apple), 233
"in the money" (option
  contracts), 264-265
income
  adjusted gross income
    (AGI), 70
  combined income, 174
  gross income, 70
  recommended percentage
    for housing, 189
  rental income, taxes,
    288-290
income statement, 49-52
Income Statements (annual
  reports), analyzing, 133-134
index funds, 120, 154, 156-158
  large-cap stocks, 120-122
  managing, 123
index options, 268-270
  hedge strategies, 269-270
  S&P index options, 269
Individual Retirement Account
  (IRA), 66, 69-74
  Education IRA, 198-199
  Keogh, 43, 74-76
    self-employment, 172
  money purchase pension
    trust, 75-76
  profit sharing plans, 75-76
  Rollover IRA, 66-67, 69
  Roth IRA, 69-71
    advantages, 70-71
    setting up college funds,
      198
  SEP-IRA, 69, 74-75
    self-employment,
      172-173
  SIMPLE-IRA, 69, 74-75
    self-employment,
      172-173

stock mutual funds, 72-73
traditional IRA, 69
  converting to Roth IRA,
    71-72
  setting up college funds,
    197-198
Treasury STRIPs, 73-74
*Industry Week* Web site, 254
inflation, 10-12
  bonds, effects on, 12, 145
  stocks, effects on, 12
inflation-indexed bonds, 75
information resources
  college contacts, 306
  consumer information, 302
  credit reporting agencies, 302
  financial exchanges, 301-302
  government and regulatory
    contacts, 301
  Internet connections, 306
  investment research, 302-303
    online research sites, 303
  money market funds, 305
  mortgages, 306
  mutual funds, 303-305
inheritances, 223-225
initial margin (futures contracts), 276
Inside Track Lite Web site, 251
insurance
  annuities, 211-212
  car insurance, 207-208
    purchasing, 84
  disability insurance, 212
  health insurance, 84
    deductions (self-
      employment), 104
    Medicare, 40, 176-177
    retiree health insurance,
      176
  homeowner's insurance,
    212-213
  liability insurance, 84, 213
  life insurance, 84, 208
    comparison data, 210-211
    determining amount
      needed, 208-209
    estate taxes, paying, 222
    for children, 212
    joint life insurance
      policies, 210
    purchasing, 85

survivorship policies, 210
term life insurance
  policies, 209
universal life insurance
  policies, 210
variable life insurance
  policies, 210
whole life insurance
  policies, 209
Medicare, 176-177
Web sites, 255
interest, 4
compound interest, 4-5
  calculating, 5-7
  Future Value Chart, 6-7
  time factor, 7-8
fixed-income securities,
  142-144
  call feature, 142-143
  sinking fund payments,
    143-144
income, municipal bonds,
  106
rates, 10-12
  bonds, effects on, 12
  stocks, effects on, 12
Internal Revenue Service (IRS),
  301
Internet, 229-231
  browsers, 234-235
    128-bit encryption, 235
  connections, 306
  cookies, 231
  history of, 229-230
  investment research,
    248-250
    Bloomberg terminal, 249
    search engines, 249-250
  modems, 231
  online shopping, 232
  World Wide Web, 230
Internet banking, 235-237
Internet Banking Index Web
  site, 256
Internet brokers, 245-246
  ancillary services, 243
  comfort, 242-243
  commission rates, 241
  E*TRADE Securities, 247-248
  evaluating your needs,
    239-241
  fraudulent brokers, avoid-
    ing, 246

frequent trader issues,
  241-242
home page contents,
  246-247
information sources, 306
log-on ID/password, 246
research capabilities, 242
selecting, 237-239
speed factor, 245-246
system factor back-ups,
  245-246
third-market execution, 252
Web sites, 239
Internet Explorer (Microsoft),
  234
Internet Service Providers
  (ISPs), selecting, 233-234
Inverse Network Technologies
  Web site, 234
Invest-o-rama Web site, 253
investing
  10-percent habit, 8
  long-term perspective, 9
  risk factor
    returns over time (stock
      market), 13-14
    stock market example,
      9-10
  Rule of 72, 8
  time factor, 7-8
    returns over time (stock
      market), 13-14
    stock market example,
      9-10
Investment Advisors Act of
  1940, 154
investment chat room Web
  sites, 254
investment classes, 20-21
investment club Web sites, 254
Investment Company Act of
  1940, 294
investment message board Web
  sites, 254
investment research Web sites,
  253
investment theory, standard
  deviation, 18-20
Investools Research Web site,
  253
Investor Communications
  Business Inc. Web site, 132

investor services Web sites, 255-256
*Investors Business Daily*, 132
 Web site, 254
IPO Central Web site, 253
IRA (Individual Retirement Account), 66, 69-74
 Education IRA, 198-199
 Keogh, 43, 74-76
  self-employment, 172
 money purchase pension trust, 75-76
 profit-sharing plans, 75-76
 Rollover IRA, 66-67, 69
 Roth IRA, 69-71
  advantages, 70-71
  setting up college funds, 198
 SEP-IRA, 69, 74-75
  self-employment, 172-173
 SIMPLE-IRA, 69, 74-75
  self-employment, 172-173
 stock mutual funds, 72-73
 traditional IRA, 69
  converting to Roth IRA, 71-72
  setting up college funds, 197-198
 Treasury STRIPs, 73-74
IRS (Internal Revenue Service), 301
ISPs (Internet Service Providers), selecting, 233-234
itemized deductions (adjusted gross income), 100-101

**J-K**

jobs, changing
 401(k) plans, transferring, 171
 benefits, questions to ask personnel, 169-171
joint bank accounts, 181
joint life insurance policies, 210
joint ownership, 217-218
joint portfolios, 181-182
Journal of Commerce Web site, 254
JP Morgan Web site, 256
junk bonds, 144

Just Quotes Web site, 250, 252
*Kelley Blue Book*, 302
 Web site, 83, 302
Keogh plans, 43, 74-76
 self-employment, 172
*Kiplinger Personal Finance Magazine*
 online broker evaluation, 238-239
 Web site, 238
Kiplinger Web site, 250, 254

**L**

land (real estate), 287
large-cap stocks, 120-122
LBO (leveraged buyout) funds, 294-295
LEAPS (Long-term Equity Anticipation Security), 270-271
LeaseSource Web site, 83
leasing cars, 81-83
 advantages, 81-82
 disadvantages, 82
Lehman Brothers Web site, 256
lending, 12
leverage, 284
leveraged buyout (LBO) funds, 294-295
liabilities, 18, 49
liability insurance, 84, 213
lien, 90
life insurance, 84, 208
 comparison data, 210-211
 determining amount needed, 208-209
 estate taxes, paying, 222
 for children, 212
 joint life insurance policies, 210
 purchasing, 85
 survivorship policies, 210
 term life insurance policies, 209
 universal life insurance policies, 210
 variable life insurance policies, 210
 whole life insurance policies, 209

lifestyle funds, 164
Lifetime Learning Credits, 202
limit (futures contracts), 275
limit orders (stocks), 136
limited partners (LPs), 295-297
 capital calls, 296
 real estate ownership, 286
liquid investments, 31
liquidity, 21
living trusts, 217
load funds, 155-156
loans
 collateral, 108
 college loans, 48-49
location issues (real estate), 290
long (futures contracts), 275
Long-term Equity Anticipation Security (LEAPS), 270-271
long-term gains (securities), 105
long-term investment perspective, 9
LPs (limited partners), 295-297
 capital calls, 296
 real estate ownership, 286
lump sums, 63
 defined benefit plans, 63-64
 lump-sum retirement benefits, 177

**M**

maintenance margin (futures contracts), 276
marginal tax rate, 78, 101-102
 calculating, 79
margins (futures contracts), 275-276
market (futures contracts), 275
market capitalization, 120-122
Market Guide Web site, 242
market orders (stocks), 136
marriage
 divorce, 182-184
  dividing assets, 183-184
  no-fault divorces, 184
 joint bank accounts, 181
 joint portfolios, 181-182
 marriage tax break, 180-181
 pre-nuptial agreements, 179-180

maturity, 12
MBS (mortgage-backed securities), 151
media resources online, 256-257
medical savings account deduction, 103-104
Medicare, 40, 176-177
Merrill Lynch Web site, 256
Microsoft Internet Explorer, 234
MidAmerica Commodity Exchange Web site, 253
MindSpring (ISP), 234
modems, 231
money market accounts, writing checks against, 94-95
money market funds (MMFs), 33-34, 162-163
    information resources, 305
    pros/cons, 34
    repos, 33
money market instruments, 21
Money Pages Web site, 254
money purchase pension trust, 75-76
Morgan Stanley Web site, 256
Morningstar Principia software, 160
Morningstar Web site, 254
mortgage payments, 96
mortgage rates (home buying), 187
mortgage-backed securities (MBS), 151
mortgage REITs, 284-285
mortgages, 48-49
    15-year vs. 30-year, 191-192
    adjustable-rate mortgages (ARM), 190
    fixed-rate vs. adjustable-rate, 189-190
    information sources, 306
    paying off, 191
    points, 101
    real estate investments, 290-291
    second mortgages, 191
motels (real estate), 286
Motley Fool Web site, 254
municipal bonds, 106-108
    general obligation (GO) bonds, 106

revenue bonds, 107
tax-equivalent yields, calculating, 107-108
mutual fund Web sites, 254
mutual funds, 73, 119-120, 153-165
    12b-1 fees, 156
    advantages, 157-159
    back-end loads, 156
    choosing, 159
    closed-end funds, 154-155
    equity mutual funds, rebalancing, 164-165
    front-end loads, 155-156
    index funds, 120, 154, 156-158
        large-cap stocks, 120-122
        managing, 123
    information resources, 303-305
    lifestyle funds, 164
    list of attractive funds, 160-162
    load funds, 155-156
    money market funds (MMFs), 33-34, 162-163
    net asset value (NAV), 154
    no load funds, 155-156
    no-load precious metal funds, 281
    open-end funds, 154-155, 157
    popularity of, 153
    prospectus, 156
    rebalancing mutual fund holdings, 164-165
    tax-advantaged funds, 156-157
    tax-efficient funds, 164
    variable annuities, 163-164
Mutual Funds Interactive Web site, 254

**N**

NASD (National Association of Securities Dealers), 157
NASDAQ (National Association of Securities Dealers Automated Quotations), 114-115
    top 10 stocks, 129
    Web site, 252

National Association of Securities Dealers (NASD), 157
National Discount Brokers Web site, 239
National Futures Association (NFA), 274
NAV (net asset value), 154
Navigator (Netscape), 234
NCR Corporation, 91, 302
net earnings, 172
net worth, 49
Netscape Navigator, 234
New York Stock Exchange (NYSE), 114-115
    address/phone number, 301
    Web site, 252
*New York Times, The*, 116
    mutual fund supplement, 162
Nightly Business Report (PBS), 132
Nikkei Web site, 252
Nilson Report, 93
no-fault divorces, 184
no load funds, 155-156
no-load precious metal funds, 281
non-reimbursed health/ dependent care expenses, taxes, 103
normalized earnings (companies), 118
notes, 64, 142
    par, 147

**O**

OCC (Options Clearing Corporation), 263
office buildings (real estate), 287
online banking, 235-237
online brokers, 245-246
    ancillary services, 243
    comfort, 242-243
    commission rates, 241
    E*TRADE Securities, 247-248
    evaluating your needs, 239-241
    fraudulent brokers, avoiding, 246

frequent trader issues, 241-242
home page contents, 246-247
information sources, 306
log-on ID/password, 246
research capabilities, 242
selecting, 237-239
speed factor, 245-246
system factor back-ups, 245-246
third-market execution, 252
Web sites, 239
online research, 242, 248-250
Bloomberg terminal, 249
search engines, 249-250
teaser research, 243
Web sites, 303
online resources, 256-257
online shopping, 232
open-end mutual funds, 154-155, 157
option contracts, 261-263
"at the money," 264-265
"buy-write" program, 268
call option contracts, 262-263
Chicago Board Options Exchange (CBOE), 263
comparing to futures contracts, 275
covered call writing, 267-268
expiration, 263
"in the money," 264-265
index options, 268-270
hedge strategies, 269-270
S&P index options, 269
LEAPS (Long-term Equity Anticipation Security), 270-271
option tables, reading, 265-266
Options Clearing Corporation (OCC), 263
"out of the money," 264-265
premiums, 264
put option contracts, 263
downside protection, 268
risk factor, 267
selling short, 266-267
spreads, 270
straddles, 270
strike price, 262
trading, 266-267

options buyer, 264
Options Clearing Corporation (OCC), 263
options on futures contracts, 278
options writer, 264
"out of the money" (option contracts), 264-265
ownership (real estate), 286
owning a home
advantages, 188
comparing to renting, 187-189

**P**

P/E (price/earnings) ratio, 117
relative P/E, 118-119
par, 147
Part A (Medicare), 176
Part B (Medicare), 176
partnerships (real estate ownership), 286
paying off mortgages, 191
payment for order flow, 252
PCs (personal computers), buying, 232-233
penny stocks, 128
Pension Benefit Guaranty Corp. (PBGC), 64
pensions (defined benefit plans), 42, 61
annuities, 63-64
lump sum option, 63-64
monthly pensions, determining, 61-63
*see also* retirement plans
percentages, 5
personal balance sheet, 49-50
married couple example, 52-53
single male example, 54-55
personal computers, buying, 232-233
Personal Earnings and Benefit Estimate Statement, 41
personal income statement, 50-52
personal residence trust, 223
Personal Wealth Web site, 242
Philadelphia Stock Exchange, 114

planning for retirement, 37-38
employer-sponsored plans, 60-61
defined benefit plans, 60-64
defined contribution plans, 60, 64-65
PointCast Web site, 251
points (mortgages), 101
portals, 249-250
portfolio management programs, 251
portfolios, 18
asset allocation, 124-125
bonds, reasons to own, 146
diversification, 21-22, 138-139
event risk, 21
joint portfolios, 181-182
rebalancing, 123-124, 138
mutual fund holdings, 164-165
three broad classes of investments, 20-21
tracking, 251
pre-nuptial agreements, 179-180
pre-strike earnings (companies), 118
pre-tax dollars, 65
precious metals, 279-281
companies, 280-281
no-load precious metal funds, 281
preferred stock, 20
premiums
bonds, 147
option contracts, 264
price/earnings (P/E) ratio, 117
relative P/E, 118-119
private equity fund of funds, 295-297
capital calls, 296
pros and cons, 297
probate, avoiding, 217-218
beneficiary-designated accounts, 218
joint ownership, 217-218
living trusts, 217
profit-sharing plans, 75-76
program trading (futures contracts), 279
progressive tax, 79
prospectus, 156

Publication No. 05-10043 (Medicare), 176-177
put option contracts, 263
    downside protection, 268

# Q

Qualified Terminable Interest Property Trust (QTIP), 221
quality companies (stock investments), 129-130
quarterly rate of return, 27
quarters, 27
Quick & Reilly Web site, 239
Quicken Home and Mortgage Web site, 291, 306
quizzes
    Risk Tolerance quiz, 22-25
    Time Horizon quiz, 25-27
Quote.com Web site, 252
quotes, Web sites, 252-253, 291

# R

*Random Reminiscences*, 3
rate of return, 16
real estate, 283-291
    depreciation, 290
    financial preparation, 287-288
    financing, 290-291
    gifting, 222
    location issues, 290
    market-wise, 287-288
    ownership, types of, 286
    REITs (Real Estate Investment Trusts), 284-285
        quality and safety, 285
        types, 284-285
    taxes, 85-86
        on rental income, 288-290
    types, 286-287
real estate agents, 194
real estate market (home buying), 186-187
Real Time Quotes Web site, 252
realized gains (securities), 104
realized losses (securities), 104
rebalancing mutual fund holdings, 164-165

rebalancing stock portfolios, 123-124, 138
reducing debt, 95-96
registered representative (RR), 135
regulatory contacts (investment information), 301
REITs (Real Estate Investment Trusts), 284-285
    quality and safety, 285
    types, 284-285
relative P/E, 118-119
Relief Act of 1997, 218
relocation packages, 192-193
rental income, taxes, 288-290
renting homes
    advantages, 189
    comparing to owning, 187-189
renting your home, 193
repos, 33
Request for Personal Earnings and Benefit Estimate Statement (Form SSA-7004), 41
researching
    financial magazine Web sites, 254-255
    government agency Web sites, 255
    information resources, 302-303
        online research sites, 303
    insurance Web sites, 255
    investment club Web sites, 254
    investment decisions, 242
    investment message boards/chat rooms Web sites, 254
    investment research Web sites, 253
    investor services Web sites, 255-256
    media resources online, 256-257
    mutual fund Web sites, 254
    online research, 248-250
        Bloomberg terminal, 249
        search engines, 249-250
    online resources, 256-257
    stocks, 131-132
        annual reports, 132-135
        *Investors Business Daily*, 132

*Standard & Poor's Stock Guides*, 132
*Value Line Investment Survey*, 131-132
*Wall Street Journal, The*, 132
    teaser research, 243
    technology magazine Web sites, 255
Resolution Funding Corporation (RFC), 151
retail funds, 162-163
retiree health insurance, 176
retirement benefits
    delaying retirement, effects on Social Security, 175
    lump-sum payments, 177
    retiring early, 173
        Social Security, effects on, 173-175
*Retirement Confidence Survey*, 37
retirement funds vs. educational funds, 196
retirement investing (portfolio asset allocation), 124-125
retirement plans, 37-38
    401(k) plans, 46-47, 60
        after-tax contributions, 65
        borrowing from, 66
        changing employers, 67
        company stock, 67-68
        matching employer contributions, 65-66
        pre-tax contributions, 64-65
        transferring, 171
    403(b) plans, 46-47, 60
        after-tax contributions, 65
        pre-tax contributions, 64-65
    average annual benefit (AARP figures), 42
    defined benefit plan (DB), 41-42, 60-64
    defined contribution plans, 42, 46-47, 60, 64-68
    employer-sponsored plans, 60-61
    IRA (Individual Retirement Account), 66, 69-74
        converting traditional IRA to Roth IRA, 71-72
    Keogh, 43, 74-76

money purchase pension
trust, 75-76
profit sharing plans, 75-76
Rollover IRA, 66-67, 69
Roth IRA, 69, 70-71
SEP-IRA, 69, 74-75
SIMPLE-IRA, 69, 74-75
stock mutual funds, 72-73
traditional IRA, 69
Treasury STRIPs, 73-74
Medicare, 176-177
Savings Incentive Match
Plan for Employees
(SIMPLE), 43
self-employment, 42-43,
171-173
Simplified Employee
Pension (SEP), 43
Social Security, *see* Social
Security
*see also* pensions
retirement savings worksheet,
43-48
Annual Savings Required
Table, 44-45
return, 16
calculating, 16
standard deviation, 19-20
return on investment (ROI), 16
annual return, 27
calculating, 16
quarterly rate of return, 27
risk factor, 17-18
returns over time (stock
market), 13-14
revenue bonds, 107
RFC (Resolution Funding
Corporation), 151
risk, 16
diversification, 21-22
event risk, 21
return on investment (ROI),
16-18
calculating, 16
risk tolerance level, determining, 22-25
standard deviation, 18-20
first level standard
deviation, 19
stock market, 9-10
returns over time, 13-14
Risk Tolerance quiz, 22-25

Rockefeller, John D., 3
Rollover IRA, 66-67, 69
Roth IRA, 69-72
advantages, 70-71
converting traditional IRA
to Roth IRA, 71-72
setting up college funds, 198
Rule of 72, 8

# S

S & P 90, 13
S & P 500, 10
S & P 500 index, 119
large-cap stocks, 121-122
S & P Barra Growth Index,
large-cap stocks, 121-122
S & P index options, 269
Sallie Mae (Student Loan
Marketing Association), 151
Salomon Smith Barney Web
site, 256
saving for children's college
fund, 35-36
saving money, 79-80
banks, choosing, 84-85
buying in bulk, 80-81
car insurance, 84
credit cards, 86
for emergencies, 30-35
10 percent rule, 30
cash equivalents, 30-31
certificates of deposit
(CDs), 32
evaluating investment
options, 34-35
money market funds
(MMFs), 33-34
savings accounts, 33
Treasury bills (T-bills),
31-32
for retirement (worksheet),
43-48
Annual Savings Required
Table, 44-45
leasing cars, 81-83
advantages, 81-82
disadvantages, 82
life insurance, 85
real estate taxes, 85-86
saving tips, 87
tax withholdings, 79

savings accounts, 33-34
savings bonds, 150-151
EE savings bonds, setting up
college funds, 199-200
Savings Incentive Match Plan
for Employees (SIMPLE), 43
SIMPLE-IRA, 69, 74-75
Schedule E (Form 1040),
288-290
scholarships, 203
Schwab Web site, 239, 255
search engines, 249-250
SEC Database Web site, 255
SEC Digest Web site, 255
second mortgages, 191
vs. home equity loans, 109
sectors (stocks), 138-139
securities
fixed-income securities,
141-147
bonds, 144-147
call feature, 142-143
interest, 142-144
sinking fund payments,
143-144
Treasuries, 149-151
buying, 150
savings bonds, 150-151
Securities and Exchange
Commission (SEC), 301
8-K reports, 132
10-K reports, 132
Web site, 242, 303
securities transactions (gains
and losses)
offsetting gains with losses,
105-106
tax deductions, 104-106
wash sale rule, 105-106
self-employment, 36-37
health insurance deduc-
tions, 104
retirement plans, 42-43,
171-173
Social Security, 42
taxes, net earnings, 172
selling homes, 194
selling short (option contracts),
266-267
SEP (Simplified Employee
Pension), 43
SEP-IRA, 69, 74-75
self-employment, 172-173

Separate Trading of Registered Interest and Principal (STRIPs), 74
Series EE savings bonds, 150
Series HH savings bonds, 150-151
Series I savings bonds, 150
shareware, 234
shopping centers (real estate), 287
shopping online, 232
short (futures contracts), 275
short-term gains (securities), 104-105
SIMPLE (Savings Incentive Match Plan for Employees), 43
SIMPLE-IRA (Savings Incentive Match Plan for Employees), 69, 74-75
    self-employment, 172-173
*Singapore Business Times* Web site, 254
single ownership (real estate), 286
sinking fund payments (sinkers), 143-144
small businesses
    health insurance deductions, 104
    retirement plans, 42-43
        Keogh plans, 74-76
        money purchase pension trust, 75-76
        profit-sharing plans, 75-76
        SEP-IRA, 74-75
        SIMPLE-IRA, 74-75
    Social Security, 42
    starting, 36-37
*Smart Money* magazine
    Best and Worst Online Brokers list, 238
    Web site, 234, 254
Social Security, 40-41, 173
    applying for benefits, 175
    collecting benefits while working, 175
    delaying retirement, 175
    FICA, 40
    full retirement age, 173-174
    maximum benefit, 42
    Medicare, 40, 176-177
        Part A, 176
        Part B, 176

Publication No. 05-10043, 176-177
    Personal Earnings and Benefit Estimate Statement, 41
    self-employment, 42
    taxes on benefits, 174-175
Social Security Administration, 301
    Web site, 41, 301
Social Security Benefit Statement (Form SSA-1099), 175
software
    financial management software, 237
    portfolio management programs, 251
sole proprietors, 76
SPDRs (Standard & Poor's Depository Receipts), 298-299
speculative securities, 128
speculators, 279
spending habits, gathering information on, 77-78
splits (stocks), 116
spread (stocks), 114
spreads
    futures contracts, 279
    option contracts, 270
Standard & Poor's, 10
*Standard & Poor's Stock Guides*, 132, 302
    Web site, 302
standard deductions (adjusted gross income), 100-101
standard deviation, 18-20
    first level standard deviation, 19
Stock Center Web site, 251
stock market, 9-10, 114-115
    bears, 115
    bulls, 115
    estimated value of American stocks, 19
    exchanges, 114-115
    market drops, 126
    NASDAQ, 114-115
    returns over time, 13-14
stock mutual funds (IRAs), 72-73
stock options, 68-69
stock tables, 116-117
    price/earnings (P/E) ratio, 117

relative P/E, 118-119
    reading, 116-117
Stockmaster Web site, 252
Stockpoint Portfolio Management Web site, 251
stocks, 9-10, 20-21
    asked price, 114
    bid price, 114
    broker compensation, 115
    brokers, 135-137
        commission, 128
        discount brokers, 137
        full-service brokers, 135
        placing orders with, 136-137
    buying, 137
    common stock, 20
    comparing to bonds, 145
    dividends, 20
    index funds, 120
        large-cap stocks, 120-122
        managing, 123
    investing in quality companies, 129-130
    large-cap stocks, 120-122
    mutual funds, 119-120
    options, *see* option contracts
    penny stocks, 128
    portfolios
        asset allocation, 124-125
        diversifying, 138-139
        rebalancing, 138
        rebalancing assets, 123-124
    preferred stock, 20
    price/earnings (P/E) ratio, 117-118
        relative P/E, 118-119
    researching, 131-132
        annual reports, 132-135
        *Investors Business Daily*, 132
        *Standard & Poor's Stock Guides*, 132
        *Value Line Investment Survey*, 131-132
        *Wall Street Journal, The*, 132
    S & P 500, 10
    sectors, 138-139
    speculative stocks, 128
    splits, 116

spread, 114
stock tables, reading, 116-117
taxes on profits, 128-129
tips for trading like a pro, 128
transactions
    offsetting gains with losses, 105-106
    tax deductions, 104-106
StockSite Web site, 253
stop loss
    futures contracts, 275
    stocks, 136
straddles (option contracts), 270
*Strategy & Business* Web site, 255
Street Web site, 254
strike price, 262
STRIPs (Separate Trading of Registered Interest and Principal), 74
Student Loan Marketing Association (Sallie Mae), 151
student loans, 202
SURETRADE Web site, 239
survivorship insurance policies, 210

# T

T-bills (Treasury bills), 31-32, 64
    pros/cons, 34
    yields, 32
Tax Rate Schedules, marginal income tax rates, 101-102
tax-advantaged funds, 156-157
tax-deferred plans, 60
tax-efficient funds, 164
tax-equivalent yields, calculating, 107-108
taxable accounts, rebalancing, 165
taxable income, calculating, 99-101
taxes
    401(k) plan contributions, 102
    adjusted gross income
        determining, 100
        itemized deductions, 100-101

standard deductions, 100-101
capital gains rates, 105
deductions
    health insurance (self-employment), 104
    home equity loans, 108-109
    itemized deductions (adjusted gross income), 100-101
    medical savings accounts, 103-104
    non-reimbursed health/dependent care expenses, 103
    securities transactions, 104-106
    self-employment retirement plans, 172-173
    standard deductions (adjusted gross income), 100-101
educational funds, 202-204
    AGI limits, 203-204
    tax credits, 202
estate taxes, 218-220
    Generation Skipping Transfer Tax (GST), 220
    inheritances, 223-224
    tax-saving strategies, 220-223
    unified credit, 218
    unlimited marital deduction, 220
Federal Estate Tax Return Form 706, 219
Form 1040, Schedule E, 288-290
gross income, determining, 100
group health plans, 102
marginal tax rate, 78-79, 101-102
    calculating, 79
marriage tax break, 180-181
municipal bonds, 106-108
    tax-equivalent yields, calculating, 107-108
non-reimbursed health/dependent care expenses, 103

progressive tax, 79
real estate taxes, 85-86
Relief Act of 1997, 218
rental income, 288-290
securities transactions, 105-106
self-employment, net earnings, 172
Social Security Benefit Statement (Form SSA-1099), 175
Social Security benefits, 174-175
stock profits, 128-129
taxable income, calculating, 99-101
withholdings, 79
Taxpayer Relief Act of 1997, 104, 197-199
teaser research, 243
technology magazine Web sites, 255
*TechWeb* Web site, 255
term insurance, 85
term life insurance policies, 209
The List Web site, 234
The Street Web site, 254
third-market execution (online brokers), 252
Thomson MarketEdge Portfolio Tracker Web site, 251
time as money-making asset, 7-8
    Rule of 72, 8
    stock market, 9-10
        returns over time, 13-14
Time Horizon quiz, 25-27
*Time* magazine, 232
tracking portfolios, 251
trading online, *see* online brokers
trading options, 266-267
traditional IRA, 69
    converting to Roth IRA, 71-72
    setting up college funds, 197-198
Trans Union National, 91, 302
transferring 401(k) plans, 171
Treasuries, 149-151
    buying, 150
    savings bonds, 150-151
Treasury bills (T-bills), 31-32, 64

pros/cons, 34
yields, 32
Treasury bonds, 64
Treasury notes, 64
interest, 142
Treasury STRIPS, 73-74
Treasury Web site, 32, 301
trusts, 222-223
TRW, 302

# U

U. S. Treasury notes, 64
interest, 142
U.S. Business Advisor Web site,
255
U.S. Securities & Exchange
Commission Web site, 242
U.S. Treasury Web site, 32, 301
UITs (Unit Investment Trusts),
298-299
unified credit, 218
Unique College Investing Plan,
200-201
universal life insurance
policies, 210
unlimited marital deduction,
220
credit shelter trust (CST),
220-221
Qualified Terminable
Interest Property Trust
(QTIP), 221
unrealized gain (securities), 104
unrealized losses (securities), 104
URLs (Uniform Resource
Locators), 230

# V

Value Line, 302
*Value Line Investment Survey*,
131-132
Vanguard, 164
variable annuities, 163-164
variable life insurance policies,
210
variable universal life insurance
policies, 210
venture capital funds, 294

Venture Capital Resources Web
site, 256
vesting, 41

# W-X

Wall Street Journal portfolio
tracker Web site, 251
*Wall Street Journal, The*, 10,
132, 157, 164, 303
Annual Reports Club, 132
Cash Prices, 273-274
Money & Investing Section,
33-34
mutual fund supplement,
162
Web site, 132, 303
wash sale rule (securities),
105-106
Waterhouse Web site, 239, 255
*Web Finance* Web site, 255
Web sites
American Exchange (Amex),
252
Ameritrade, 255
Annual Report Service, 253
Association of Individual
Investors, 253
BanxQuote, 237
Better Business Bureau, 253
BigCharts, 252
Bloomberg, 250
Briefing.com, 242
Brown, 239
Bull & Bear, 239
*Business Week*, 254
*BYTE* magazine, 255
CEO Express, 250
*CFO* magazine, 254
*Computerworld*, 255
Concentric Network, 234
*Consumer Reports*, 83, 177,
301-302
Corporate Information, 253
Datek, 239, 255
DBC Online, 252
Disclosure, 253
Discover Brokerage, 239, 255
DLJ Direct, 239, 255
Dow Jones Business Direc-
tory, 253

E*TRADE, 239, 255
E-loan, 291, 306
Economist, 254
*Edmund's Automobile Buyer's
Guide*, 83, 302
*Electronic Business*, 255
*Electronic Markets*, 255
Excite, 250
*Far East Economic Review*,
254
*Fast Company*, 254
Federal Reserve, 83, 255, 301
Federal Trade Commission
(FTC), 91, 301
Federal Web Locator, 255
Fidelity, 239, 255
financial magazines, 254-255
financial markets, 252
financial news, 253
*Financial Times*, 254
Fleet Bank, 235-236
*Forbes*, 253-254
*Fortune*, 254
Gomez Advisors, 237
government agencies, 255
Harvard Business School
Publishing, 254
HomeShark, 291, 306
Hoover's Online, 242
IBC Financial Data, 163, 305
*Industry Week*, 254
Inside Track Lite, 251
insurance, 255
Internet Banking Index, 256
Inverse Network Technolo-
gies, 234
Invest-o-rama, 253
investment clubs, 254
investment message boards/
chat rooms, 254
investment research, 253
Investools Research, 253
Investor Communications
Business Inc., 132
investor services, 255-256
*Investor's Business Daily*, 254
IPO Central, 253
*Journal of Commerce*, 254
JP Morgan, 256
Just Quotes, 250, 252
*Kelley Blue Book*, 83, 302
Kiplinger, 250, 254

LeaseSource, 83
Lehman Brothers, 256
Market Guide, 242
Merrill Lynch, 256
MidAmerica Commodity
  Exchange, 253
Money Pages, 254
Morgan Stanley, 256
Morningstar, 254
Motley Fool, 254
mutual funds, 254
Mutual Funds Interactive,
  254
NASDAQ, 252
National Discount Brokers,
  239
New York Stock Exchange
  (NYSE), 252
Nikkei, 252
online brokers, *see* online
  brokers
online research sites, 303
Personal Wealth, 242
PointCast, 251
Quick & Reilly, 239
Quicken Home and Mort-
  gage, 291, 306
Quote.com, 252
quotes, 252-253, 291
Real Time Quotes, 252
Salomon Smith Barney, 256
Schwab, 239, 255
SEC Database, 255
SEC Digest, 255
Securities & Exchange
  Commission, 303
*Singapore Business Times*, 254
*Smart Money*, 234, 254
Social Security Administra-
  tion, 41, 301
Standard & Poor's Stock
  Guides, 132, 302
Stock Center, 251
Stockmaster, 252
Stockpoint Portfolio Man-
  agement, 251
StockSite, 253
*Strategy & Business*, 255
SURETRADE, 239
technology magazines, 255
*TechWeb*, 255

The List, 234
The Street, 254
Thomson MarketEdge
  Portfolio Tracker, 251
U.S. Business Advisor, 255
U.S. Securities & Exchange
  Commission, 242
U.S. Treasury, 32, 301
Venture Capital Resources,
  256
Wall Street Journal portfolio
  tracker, 251
*Wall Street Journal*, The, 132,
  303
Waterhouse, 239, 255
*Web Finance*, 255
Web Street, 239
Wells Fargo, 256
*Wired* magazine, 255
World Wide Web Consor-
  tium, 230
Worth, 255
Yahoo!, 249-250
Zacks Investment Research,
  242
whole life insurance policies,
  209
wills, 216-218
  executors, 216
  probate, avoiding, 217-218
*Wired* magazine Web site, 255
worksheets
  personal balance sheet, 49-50
    married couple example,
      52-53
    single male example,
      54-55
  personal income statement,
    50-52
  retirement savings, 43-48
    Annual Savings Required
      Table, 44-45
World Wide Web, 230
World Wide Web Consortium,
  230
Worth Web site, 255

## Y-Z

Yahoo! Web site, 249-250
yields (Treasury bills), 32

Zacks Investment Research
  Web site, 242